Not Without Our Consent

YOU ARE HAVING A GREAT
IMPACT ON YOUR PEOPLE &
NATIVE STUDIES. VINE
WOULD BE HONORED — A
STUDENT GONE DOCTOR ACTUALLY
HELPING THE PEOPLE.

YOU ARE AN INTELLECTUAL WARRIOR!

your Brother
Edward
11/11

Not Without Our Consent

Lakota Resistance to Termination, 1950–59

EDWARD CHARLES VALANDRA

Foreword by Vine Deloria Jr.

UNIVERSITY OF ILLINOIS PRESS
Urbana and Chicago

Library of Congress Cataloguing-in-Publication Data
Valandra, Edward Charles, 1955–
Not without our consent : Lakota resistance to termination, 1950–59
Edward Charles Valandra ; foreword by Vine Deloria, Jr.
p.   cm.
Includes bibliographical references and index.
ISBN 0-252-02944-5 (Cloth : alk. paper)
1. Rosebud Sioux Tribe—Legal status, laws, etc.
2. Teton Indians—Legal status, laws, etc.
3. Indians of North America—Legal status, laws, etc.—South Dakota.
4. Indian termination policy—South Dakota—History—20th century.
I. Title.
KF8228.R67A3   2006
342.7308'72—dc22   2003028179

What is now needed on this reservation are dedicated
men and women on the council who have the general welfare
of the people at heart. We need council members who will study
their constitution and by-laws and the history of the tribe and use
this knowledge for the betterment of the people and not against
them. Most important, we need leaders who will work towards
the restoration of the original right the tribe had as a
sovereign nation.

—Frank D. Ducheneaux (1903–1976)
  Cheyenne River Sioux Tribe
  Lakota Journal

Contents

Tables

Foreword

VINE DELORIA JR.

World War Two brought frightening times for American Indians. Wartime budgets drastically reduced domestic spending to support war expenditures and the Bureau of Indian Affairs suffered proportionately. A stirring of the civil rights conscience was felt when it was observed that the German prisoners of war were treated better than were African Americans in the South. German concentration camps became the embarrassment of the civilized world, and South African apartheid and American Indian reservations were considered less extreme instances of negative racial policies. Two waves of reform originated in the immediate postwar world: a desire to reduce the size of government and a determination to resolve racial problems in the United States.

The Hoover Commission studied the size of the federal government and recommended a laundry list of suggestions for reform and reduction. But the commission went far beyond its mandate by offering gratuitous advice regarding Indians. Failing to understand the centuries-old relationship between Indians and the national government, the commission suggested that the states could provide many of the services that flowed from the federal relationship. Such a move would place rural Indian communities in great jeopardy because the social programs that the Indians needed were virtually nonexistent in the various states. The fast-escalating movement toward African Americans receiving full citizenship rights threatened to swallow Indians in a society determined to assimilate them. Indians appeared to be old fashioned and reactionary when they expressed a desire to live apart from the rest of American society in their rural communities.

The authorization of the Indian Claims Commission in 1946 gave tribes permission to sue the United States for loss of lands and for unfair compensation for lands lost in treaties and agreements. That tribes could receive multimillion dollar settlements as a result of their claims litigation irritated some congressional representatives, and they sought to be rid of the Indian issue as quickly as possible. Some Indians, returning from war and having seen the world outside the reservations, chafed at the idea of keeping themselves and their property in the hands of ignorant or callous federal bureaucrats.

In 1950 a massive study was done of the state of Indian affairs and pressure began to build for the government to get out of the Indian business. Dillon Myer, the Indian commissioner and former superintendent of Japanese internment camps, sent out a letter requiring Indian agents on the reservation to prepare the tribes for a termination of their federal benefits and protections. In 1953 a congressional resolution declared that Indians would be "freed" from the federal government as quickly as possible. With a Republican majority in control of Congress, it was not long before hearings were held to determine which tribes could be separated from their federal relationship and how quickly.

With little forethought, bills to terminate the Klamath, Menominee, Ute, Grand Ronde, Siletz, and Texas tribes were presented to the joint committee, which promptly approved the bills and sent them to the floor of Congress for passage. The National Congress of American Indians held emergency meetings to slow the movement for termination, and tribes pressured their congressional representatives to protect them from the actions of the committee. The Osage of Oklahoma, certain to be placed on the list of most capable tribes, chartered an airplane and hastened to Washington to ensure that their delegation exempted them from the tidal wave of terminal legislation then coming from the committee.

A number of bills did become law, and by the late 1950s the government was cutting loose tribes that had been nearly self-supporting with minimal government aid. Even more radical schemes were proposed when the movement began to lag under protests from the Indians. Glen Emmons, the commissioner of Indian affairs, suggested that all the Indian land be appraised and purchased by the United States and the funds distributed on a per-capita basis to all federally enrolled Indians. Everyone ridiculed the idea. Graham Holmes, the superintendent of the Rosebud Sioux Reservation in South Dakota, was driving into Washington, D.C., with an old councilman and suggested that the councilman propose the plan to the commissioner. The councilman looked at Graham for a minute and then said: "Why, he'd think I was crazy to suggest something like that!!!"

For the most part, the Sioux tribes of North and South Dakota escaped the immediate threat against their rights, but it was not simply the formal severing of ties that worried them. A program, which was called "Relocation," to move Indians from reservations to cities siphoned off some of the best and most substantial families who tried to enter the American economic mainstream. Local institutions and traditional customs were severely damaged by this program, which sought to terminate the tribe family by family. For most people, relocation did not work, and it was not until a decade later, with the development of the poverty programs, that progress was made in stabilizing and educating rural families and enrolling younger people in colleges or vocational schools. Finally, with the development of tribal colleges, reservations began to become the homelands that they were intended to be. This book is the story of one People—the Lakota Nation—during those perilous times.

Abbreviations

AAIA	Association on American Indian Affairs
ADC	Aid to Dependent Children
ALR	Arizona Law Review
BIA	Bureau of Indian Affairs (U.S.)
BIAM	Bureau of Indian Affairs Manual
CCST	Crow Creek Sioux Tribe
CCSTC	Crow Creek Sioux Tribal Council
CRST	Cheyenne River Sioux Tribe
CRSTC	Cheyenne River Sioux Tribal Council
EHWC	Education, Health, and Welfare Committee (S.D.)
FST	Flandreau Sioux Tribe
FSTC	Flandreau Sioux Tribal Council
HB	House Bill (S.D. Legislature)
HCIA	House Committee on Indian Affairs (S.D.)
HCR No.	House Concurrent Resolution Number (U.S. Congress)
H.R.	House of Representatives bill (U.S. Congress)
H. Rpt.	House Report (U.S. Congress)
HUAC	House on Un-American Activities Committee (U.S.)
ICRA	Indian Civil Rights Act (U.S., 1968)
ITF	Indian Task Force (U.S., Hoover Commission's)
IRA	Indian Reorganization Act (U.S., 1934)
KLLA	Kyle Livestock and Landowners Association
LBST	Lower Brule Sioux Tribe
LBSTC	Lower Brule Sioux Tribal Council
LJC	Lakota Jurisdiction Collection
LRC	Legislative Research Council (S.D.)

MSGAPRR	Merchants & Stock Growers Association of the Pine Ridge Reservation
OAA	Old Age Assistance
OST	Oglala Sioux Tribe
OSTC	Oglala Sioux Tribal Council
RST	Rosebud Sioux Tribe
RSTC	Rosebud Sioux Tribal Council
S.	Senate bill (U.S. Congress)
SB	Senate Bill (S.D. Legislature)
S.D.	South Dakota
SDBA	South Dakota Bar Association
S. Rpt.	Senate Report (U.S. Congress)
SDSGA	South Dakota Stockgrowers Association
SRST	Standing Rock Sioux Tribe
SRSTC	Standing Rock Sioux Tribal Council
SWST	Sisseton-Wahpeton Sioux Tribe
SWSTC	Sisseton-Wahpeton Sioux Tribal Council
TLE	Tribal Land Enterprise (RST)
U.S.	United States
USD	University of South Dakota
YST	Yankton Sioux Tribe
YSTC	Yankton Sioux Tribal Council

Chronology

1830	Indian Removal Act ordered the forced removal of all Native Peoples living east of the Mississippi River to the west of the river
1831	*Cherokee Nation v. Georgia:* U.S. Supreme Court (Marshall) described the sovereign Cherokee Nation as a "domestic, dependent nation" and introduced "ward" status as an analogy
1832, Feb. 28	*Worcester v. Georgia* elaborated "dependent nation" status, essentially as colonization
1863, Jan. 1	Homestead Act of 1862 became law, stealing vast Native lands and giving them to white settlers
1868	Fort Laramie Treaty between the Great Sioux Nation and the United States
1878	Episcopal missions established on Lakota reservations
1882	*United States v. McBratney:* U.S. Supreme Court ruled that a state's criminal jurisdiction applied only to non-Indians on a reservation
1885	Major Crimes Act subjected Native Peoples to U.S. criminal jurisprudence
1886	Catholic missions established on Lakota reservations
1887	General Allotment Act (Dawes) broke up reservations into individual allotments; Atkins, commissioner of Indian affairs, required that only English be used in government-run Indian schools
1889	Great Sioux Nation was rearranged into six separate reservations; the remaining portion was declared surplus land, opened for white settlement, and is now considered "former" Indian Country

1889, Feb.	U.S. Congress passed Enabling Act requiring states to disclaim all right and title to Indian lands as a condition for joining the Union
1889, Nov. 2	South Dakota became a state and was accepted into the Union on the condition that its constitution included the "Compact with the United States," whereby its citizens forever abandoned any intention to claim Lakota lands
1890, Dec. 29	Wounded Knee massacre
1896	*Plessy v. Ferguson:* U.S. Supreme Court's "separate but equal" decision
1898	S.D. citizens approved a constitutional amendment giving them the powers of the initiative and the referendum
1901	Chapter 106: South Dakota ceded jurisdiction on reservations to the United States
1903	United States accepted the jurisdiction that South Dakota relinquished
1904–19	Unallotted reservation lands were declared to be "surplus" and "opened" to white homesteaders
1906	Burke Act amended the 1887 allotment law by giving the Interior Department free rein in determining a Native's competence for receiving a patent-in-fee; *Peano v. Brennan:* S.D. Supreme Court amplified the state's constitutional disclaimer
1910	Congress gave the Interior Department wide discretionary authority to lease Native allotments
1917	Sells's policy to link white blood quantum to decisions on Native land-tenure, forcing fee-patents on Natives
1924	Indian Citizenship Act imposed U.S. citizenship on Natives without their consent
1929	S.D. amended Chapter 106 to reserve concurrent criminal jurisdiction on reservations (Chapter 158)
1934	Wheeler-Howard (Indian Reorganization) Act (IRA) imposed American model of government on Native Nations
1935, Dec. 14	Oglala Lakota electorate adopted a constitution, which the Interior Secretary approved 15 Jan. 1936
1938, Apr. 15	Administration of submarginal lands transferred to Interior Department to be of benefit to Indians
1939–45	World War II
1943	Tribal Land Enterprise (TLE) incorporated to stop the increasing loss of the RST's land base
1944	Interior Department's ten-year development program report documented severe poverty on reservations throughout the U.S.

1944, Dec. 22	Flood Control Act enacted; Pick-Sloan Missouri Basin Program directed the Army Corps of Engineers to build multiple dams on the Missouri River
1947, Feb.	Senate Committee on the Post Office and Civil Service held hearing on cutting costs by reducing the number of federal employees; William Zimmerman, Jr. testified and outlined reservation Groups I-III
1948–63	Oahe Dam built on the Missouri River, flooding Dakota/Lakota reservations; CRST's Rehabilitation Program developed to help displaced Lakota families
1948	1903 statute accepting the jurisdiction that South Dakota relinquished (1901) removed from U.S. federal code
1948, June 4	S. Rpt. No. 1489 recommended the transfer of criminal jurisdiction over Haudenosaunee territory to New York State
1948, Oct.	ITF report to the Hoover Commission: "law and order on reservations is unsatisfactory"
1948, Oct. 15	Interior Department–sponsored report on the Standing Rock Reservation documented how whites had acquired large tracts of Lakota land for ranching
1949, Mar.	Hoover Commission's report on reorganizing the executive branch of the U.S. government; ITF proposed a Native policy of pre-termination
1949, Apr. 22	OST "Grazing" Resolution 34-49 (amended in Apr. 1950) levied a nominal tax on nonmembers' use of reservation land
1950	PL 80-881, an early termination law affecting Native populations in New York, was enacted
1950, Nov. 1– 1953, 31 Oct.	Three-year period covered by OST grazing resolution for leases and grazing privileges
1950, Dec. 1	MSGAPRR proposed to S.D. governor that state assume jurisdiction over reservations
1951, Feb. 10	SB No. 278, a confused and confusing jumble of termination options, was introduced in the S.D. state senate
1951, Feb. 24	Having passed the senate, SB No. 278 passed the all-white house unanimously and was signed by the governor three days later
1952, Jan.	Chamberlain's city officials unanimously adopted a resolution opposing the relocation of the BIA agency to Chamberlain due to flooding from Fort Randall Dam, which was dislocating Dakota families on the Crow Creek Reservation
1952, Nov.	*Iron Crow v. Ogallala Sioux Tribe:* Farrar filed a complaint with the U.S. District Court of South Dakota on behalf of Iron Crow (and white stock growers) against the OST land-use tax

1952, Dec.	H. Rpt. No. 2503 released: a voluminous investigation of the Bureau of Indian Affairs that recommended gradual termination of federal services to Native Peoples
1953, Jan. 6	H.R. 1063 (termination bill that became PL 83-280) introduced in U.S. House of Representatives
1953, Jan. 7	Berry introduced H.R. 1220 to amend the Navajo and Hopi Rehabilitation Act seeking to gain federal funds for South Dakota
1953, Jan. 8	OST passed a revised grazing resolution 1-53 to cover the next five-year period
1953, May 27	Sixty-second SDSGA annual convention
1953, June 9	HCR No. 108 introduced to U.S. House of Representatives stating termination policy; first meeting of the Oglala Lakota, the BIA, and members of the SDSGA in Pierre, S.D., to discuss the OST's grazing resolution
1953, June 12	OST's closing date for sale of grazing privileges
1953, Aug. 1	Having passed the house, HCR No. 108 passed the senate unanimously
1953, Aug. 12	Interior Department news release outlined BIA's position on grazing resolution controversy
1953, Aug. 15	H.R. 1063 signed into law as PL 83-280
1953, Nov. 1	Beginning of new five-year grazing period under OST's 1953 grazing resolution
1955	O. A. Hodson case of range unit trespassing
1955, Feb. 18	*State of North Dakota v. Lohnes:* N.D. Supreme Court required the state as a section 6 state to modify the disclaimer language in its constitution before seeking jurisdiction over Native lands
1955, Feb. 24	*Iron Crow* ruling: Judge Mickelson upheld Oglala Lakota's authority to levy taxes
1955, May 16	LRC established committees and assigned the "Indian Problem" to the EHWC
1955, June 7	Institute of Indian Studies, University of South Dakota, began a series of conferences on Indian affairs
1956	Fort Randall Dam (Missouri River) completed
1956	The AAIA released a study, "The American Indian Relocation Program," that documented pervasive poverty on reservations
1956, Feb. 20	Lakota and state officials attended a highly charged "fact-finding" meeting of LRC's EHWC
1956, Mar. 6	*Iron Crow:* U.S. Eighth Circuit Court of Appeals affirmed Mickelson's ruling supporting OST's sovereign authority to tax
1956, July	SDBA's Committee on Criminal Law issued a report recommending state jurisdiction

1956, Sept. 7	SDBA's membership approved recommendation of S.D. state jurisdiction over reservations at their twenty-fourth annual meeting
1956, Sept. 19	LRC's EHWC issued a report recommending state jurisdiction on racist grounds
1956, Nov. 8	*Oglala Sioux Tribe v. Barta:* Mickelson ruled again in the OST's favor; the OST had the legal authority to assess taxes and could use the federal courts to sue for delinquent taxes
1957, Jan. 14	The "four-states bill" (S. 574) proposed race-related federal subsidies to Midwestern states
1957, Feb. 6	LBSTC passed Resolution No. 56-109 requesting that South Dakota enact a law to assume criminal jurisdiction over the Lower Brule Reservation; this resolution became the basis for HB No. 892
1957, Feb. 12	HB No. 721 and HB No. 892 were both introduced
1957, Feb. 18, 20	HCIA hearings on HB No. 721 only; no hearings set for HB No. 892
1957, Feb. 26–28	Amendments added to HB No. 892, one of which was a referendum clause requiring Lakota consent
1957, Mar. 9	Having passed the house, HB No. 892 passed the senate, but after the legislative session had officially ended (coat over the clock)
1957, Mar. 18	HB No. 892 signed by Governor Foss (but not effective for ninety days)
1957, Spring	Clinton Richards's *South Dakota Law Review* article, "Federal Jurisdiction over Criminal Matters Involving Indians"
1957, Apr. 23	High Pine and Woman Dress arrested
1957, Apr. 26	In S.D. Circuit Court, Judge Lampert granted writ of habeas corpus to High Pine and Woman Dress
1957, May	RST President Burnette suggested to Berry that the RST purchase submarginal lands; Berry complied by drafting two bills: for the RST, H.R. 7626; for the OST, H.R. 7631
1957, June	KLLA, a group of Native ranchers, organized
1957, June	At SDSGA's sixty-sixth annual convention, the membership denounced both sale of submarginal lands to the Lakota and CRST's Rehabilitation Program
1957, June	Farber's study on the law-and-order "Indian Problem" concluded for the Government Research Bureau of the University of South Dakota
1957, June 6	HB No. 892 went into effect contingent on the fulfillment of conditions, notably "Lakota consent"
1957, June 14	LBST's "town hall" meeting voted to accept state jurisdiction

1957, June 16–17   Institute of Indian Studies' third annual conference on Indian affairs (USD)

1957, Oct. 1–
1958, Oct. 1   Legally prescribed timeframe for Lakota's reservation-wide referenda

1957, Nov. 21   *Petition of Matthew High Pine et al:* Lampert issued a court order releasing High Pine and Woman Dress from their initial sentence of incarceration

1957, Nov. 28   The state appealed *High Pine* to the S.D. Supreme Court

1957, Dec. 15   Ducheneaux's rebuttal to white ranchers' attacks on CRST's Rehabilitation Program

1958, Jan. 7   RST referendum rejected state jurisdiction

1958, Sept. 2   CRST referendum rejected state jurisdiction

1958, Sept. 6   SRST referendum rejected state jurisdiction

1958, Sept. 10   OST referendum rejected state jurisdiction

1958, Sept. 18   On a radio program, Interior Secretary Seaton publicly supported Native consent as a prerequisite for state jurisdiction

1958, Mar.–
Sept.   SRST, CCST, Lake Traverse Reservation, and FST held referenda rejecting state jurisdiction

1958, Oct. 15   *Barta:* Eighth Circuit Court upheld Mickelson's decision affirming the OST's sovereignty

1958, Nov.   Senator Watkins (rabid terminationist and Berry's cohort) defeated in his reelection bid

1959, Jan. 12   *Williams v. Lee:* U.S. Supreme Court decision upheld Native self-governance

1959, Jan. 15   Hanley, the counsel for High Pine and Woman Dress, countered the state's appeal

1959, Jan. 30   SB No. 210 was introduced (later passed), claiming for the state concurrent jurisdiction over reservation highways

1959, Feb.   Robert Burnette of RST testified in Washington, D.C., before House Interior and Insular Affairs' subcommittee on Indian affairs about pervasive racism in South Dakota

1959, May   SDSGA president Louis Beckwith advocated state jurisdiction

1959, Nov. 2   *High Pine:* S.D. Supreme Court rejected the state's appeal and ruled against state jurisdiction over Lakota lands

1961, Jan. 19   HB No. 659 introduced to extend state jurisdiction, to cover some costs, but to require a federal subsidy for most costs

1961, Mar. 9   Governor Gubbrud signed HB No. 659 into law

1961, Mar. 23   Interior Department news release stated that the U.S. would not finance a would-be state responsibility

1961, Mar. 27   Gubbrud notified commissioner of Indian affairs that, lacking federal funding, HB No. 659 would not go into effect

1962, Aug.	Interim Investigating Committee report released that recommended state civil and criminal jurisdiction over Lakota lands based on racial profiling of welfare recipients
1962, Aug. 4	Julia Hankins arrested and released
1962, Oct. 22	LRC report, *Jurisdiction over Indian Country in South Dakota,* released
1962, Nov. 15	Conference by state commission on Indian affairs
1962, Dec. 7	Judge Lampert upheld Hankins's writ of habeas corpus
1963, Feb. 8	HB No. 791 introduced: the ultimate, all-out state termination bill; no requirement of federal subsidy and no Lakota consent provision
1963, Mar. 2	The state appealed Lampert's writ of habeas corpus ruling
1963, Mar. 3	HB No. 791 adopted
1963, Mar. 15	Governor Gubbrud signed HB No. 791 into law
1963, June 4	Lakota gathered 20,231 signatures to petition for statewide referendum on HB No. 791
1964, Jan. 30	*South Dakota v. Hankins:* S.D. Supreme Court upheld Lampert's ruling, declared HB No. 659 invalid, and named South Dakota as a section 6 state
1964, Nov. 3	Statewide referendum rejected HB No. 791 by an overwhelming margin
1966	U.S. Supreme Court *Miranda* ruling, affirming legal rights for those arrested
1966	Brophy's lengthy report, *The Indian, America's Unfinished Business,* issued, giving Native justice systems a positive verdict
1968, Apr.	Indian Civil Rights Act (ICRA) amended PL 83-280 to require Native consent

Not Without Our Consent

Introduction

In October 1985, as a newly elected tribal council representative from Rosebud Reservation's St. Francis community,[1] I recall that modern Sicangu Lakota governance had just undergone substantive and exciting political changes in constitutional reform. One experimental reform included amending the long-standing two-year term to a four-year term of service on the tribal council.[2] It was during this four-year period of my term, from November 1985 to November 1989, that I became interested in documenting how the Lakota in the 1950s resisted PL 83-280 (appendix A), the infamous federal law that in many states terminated tribal governance and replaced it with state jurisdiction. From the beginning to the end of my term, the Rosebud Sioux Tribal Council (RSTC) as well as eight other Lakota/Dakota tribal councils experienced how the state of South Dakota tried unilaterally to compromise the political reality of self-governance throughout Lakota Country.[3]

On 10 December 1985 Newton Cummings, the president of the Oglala Sioux Tribe (OST), received a letter from Mark Meierhenry, South Dakota's attorney general, which stated that South Dakota would "not recognize nor authorize the Oglala Sioux Tribe to license vehicles of its tribal members."[4] In concluding his letter to Cummings, Meierhenry noted in passing that, according to a 1959 state law,[5] South Dakota had assumed jurisdiction over all reservation highways. In other words, any Lakota licensing of vehicles owned by Lakota individuals would be—within and without the boundaries of any Lakota homeland—legally "ineffective." Evidently, South Dakota's late-twentieth-century Native policy construed any acts of Lakota self-determination as a hostile threat to the state's political integrity and would respond to such threats, perceived or otherwise, accordingly.

As a member of the Rosebud Sioux Tribal Council who participated in the protracted political fight that followed, I remember that the tribal council's first response to Meierhenry's state-instigated challenge of Lakota governance was to enact a January 1986 resolution supporting the Oglala Lakota's political efforts to resolve the licensing matter with South Dakota.[6] Notwithstanding the Oglala Lakota's earlier efforts to resolve this contentious jurisdictional matter, state officials remained adamant in asserting jurisdiction. As a result, the Rosebud Sioux Tribe (RST) witnessed with growing apprehension an alarming trend toward state-initiated jurisdiction that involved South Dakota's juridical community. From January 1986 through May 1987,[7] South Dakota's fifth and sixth circuit courts were inching unequivocally toward the position Meierhenry took in his 10 December 1985 letter to OST President Cummings: a unilateral assumption of state criminal and civil jurisdiction over portions of Lakota Country.

Of course, the crux of this particular political fight was not about who could or could not issue license plates but about who had jurisdiction over Lakota territory: the Oglala Sioux Tribe and any of the other eight Lakota governments or the state of South Dakota. This debate finally culminated in the U.S. Eighth Circuit Court of Appeals' 1990 decision, which rejected South Dakota's claims to jurisdiction over Lakota territory. According to the federal court, South Dakota could not brazenly assert criminal or civil jurisdiction in our homelands without ever securing our political consent for them to do so.[8]

Indeed, several months prior to the circuit court of appeals' decision, numerous events were forcing the Lakota toward an eventual political confrontation with South Dakota. First, on 14 May 1986 the Rosebud Sioux Tribe's legal counsel of Finch, Viken, Viken, and Pechota filed an injunction in the federal district court of South Dakota to restrain South Dakota "from exercising jurisdiction over Indians on highways within the Rosebud Sioux Reservation."[9] On 31 March 1989, almost three years from the date of filing the suit, federal judge Donald J. Porter issued a thirty-four-page memorandum declaring that the parties shared a concurrent rather than an exclusive, separate jurisdiction over reservation highways.[10] As I remember, Porter's decision of concurrent jurisdiction not only stunned tribal councils throughout Lakota Country but also apparently gave South Dakota's white community the official legal encouragement it desperately wanted either to leverage its way into the internal affairs of the Lakota community or to resist

Lakota governance altogether.[11] While Porter's presumably Solomon-like opinion encouraged the state to alter its behavior toward the Lakota community, it immediately ignited political resistance throughout the Cheyenne River, Crow Creek, Flandreau, Lower Brule, Pine Ridge, Rosebud, Sisseton, Standing Rock, and Yankton reservations.

Second, the most memorable and perhaps galvanizing moment of Lakota political resistance to South Dakota's aggressive encroachment came on 17 April 1989. Despite Porter's ruling, the RST president, the late Alex Lunderman Sr., issued Executive Order 89-01, which banned S.D. Highway Patrol, the state's primary law enforcement agency, from the Rosebud Sioux Reservation.[12] Since Porter's decision extended to all Lakota homelands, the next immediate step was to nationalize the RST's ban throughout Lakota Country. In nationalizing the ban, each of the eight other tribal councils would have to enact legislation "to take any and all action necessary to prevent South Dakota from exercising civil and criminal jurisdiction on all highways."[13] By 9 June 1989, eight of nine tribal councils supported the RST's efforts, and six passed legislation against South Dakota's highway jurisdiction.[14] Instead of having to contend with the thirty-nine-member Rosebud Sioux Tribal Council,[15] South Dakota found itself facing a Lakota-unified political front forged among the more than one hundred tribal council members, who together represented a substantial portion of the Lakota Nation.

As a counterresponse, South Dakota engaged in politico-economic extortion against the Lakota People by halting a major highway construction project on the Rosebud Sioux Reservation, opposing the RST's business licensure of white enterprises that conducted trade and commerce on the reservation, and objecting to the RST's law that provided employment and contract preferences for the Lakota labor force. As the late Lakota Elder Marvin Thin Elk's spring 1989 appeal to the Sicangu Lakota shows, the whites and the Lakota were spiraling toward a confrontation that included the specter of political violence:

> This appeal goes out to all Lakota [P]eople of this Nation. Our Tribal Sovereignty is being threatened by the State of South Dakota. Now is the time to make a stand as Lakota [P]eople. There is no tomorrow. We must stand as one on this issue [of Lakota sovereignty]. . . . A great majority of us, have volunteered to fight for our Country [the United States] and all that it stands for. Now, we must fight again; against the same Country we fought for—to enjoy our right to be Indian and live in peace amongst ourselves. . . . In closing, once again as Lakota [P]eople, let's fight the good fight as one people. Lay everything aside and let's stand together as our Forefathers [the Lakota of Little Big Horn fame] did and we will win.[16]

Undeniably, our highly charged act of Lakota national solidarity in banning South Dakota's primary law enforcement agency entailed personal and political risks. At worst, the personal risks included the possibility that the tribal council officials would be cited for being in contempt of a federal court order, which would have resulted in incarceration or fines or both. Political risks included the possible negative reactions of the federal judges at the Eighth Circuit Court of Appeals to the Lakota's increasing acts of political unrest.[17]

South Dakota indeed fanned a public perception of the Lakota leadership's political behavior as subversive. In the State of South Dakota's 1989 reply brief to the circuit court, the state charged that Lakota institutions had little regard for the federal court rulings: "Given the lack of respect for the rulings of the federal courts by the tribal courts and tribal councils, the conclusion follows quite easily that the protections to be afforded by those institutions will be 'erratic.'"[18] If South Dakota had been successful in promoting its spin on Lakota political behavior as being acutely subversive to the Euroamerican legal process, the consequence might have been an extremely adverse ruling by the appeals court.

Fortunately, that did not happen. Regardless of the real or imagined confrontational politics involved, the circuit court of appeals reversed Porter's ruling, affirming the Lakota argument that, without any evidence of Lakota consent, South Dakota had no criminal or civil jurisdiction over any portion of Lakota Country. When South Dakota officials chose to ignore this all-important and long-established principle of political consent, the Lakota community and the state's white community found themselves locked in a heated emotional struggle that brought out the bitter feelings and ill-will that the whites bore toward the Indians.

At this point, one might ask: What does this 1980s story that I lived through as a tribal council member have to do with the earlier story of the 1950s and 1960s—the story that concerns this book? During the controversial time I experienced, I came across various Lakota political and legal documents, such as tribal council resolutions and court briefs, that often cited a November 1964 statewide referendum. In that referendum, both peoples—the Lakota and the whites—rejected a law that granted South Dakota criminal and civil jurisdiction over Lakota territory. Indeed, the referendum's vote against state jurisdiction is impressive: 201,389 voters rejected any state assumption, while only 58,289 voters voted for it.

If the 1964 referendum's outcome was as definitive as it was impressive, why, then, did it have little, if any, post-1964 political impact or legal bearing on Lakota–South Dakota relations? Why did the mid-1980s Lakota–South

Dakota jurisdiction conflict happen at all? Moreover, if this referendum vote is acknowledged by both the politico-legal community and the Lakota as an authoritative foundation for contemporary Lakota-white relations, why is so little known about this historic, relations-altering event? Asking such questions, of course, led me to discover another seminal event that has been largely unknown and was quite startling: a referendum on the same issue was held six years before the one held in 1964.

My discovery of a previous referendum opened many more questions. Naturally, I wanted to know about the 1958 and 1964 referenda themselves. But in a larger sense, I also wondered what it was about the state jurisdiction question that made it possible to hold two referenda on the same issue with virtually the same outcome six years apart? Who were the players, and what were the forces—the motives, strategies, factors, and goals—shaping the processes? Moreover, while the 1958 and 1964 outcomes were the same, the processes leading to them were vastly different. In 1958, for example, only the Lakota were allowed to vote on the question of state jurisdiction; the white community was excluded. In 1964, both communities voted.

Of course, allowing only the Lakota to vote in one referendum and then allowing both communities to participate in another raised my interest considerably about what happened in the first referendum. With so many questions and with only a superficial knowledge of the 1964 referendum, I was embarrassed to admit that I had known absolutely nothing about the 1958 referenda.[19] Granted, because I knew so little of these two previous and much more intensely fought political battles over jurisdiction during the late 1950s and early 1960s, it did not occur to me until much later when I began this project that the late 1980s highway jurisdiction fight with South Dakota was a direct descendent of those earlier battles.

Vine Deloria Jr., perhaps more than most people, understands the need to know Native history during the twentieth century in order to frame current events within historical patterns. As I witnessed on the tribal council, a long-familiar pattern of political struggle between the Lakota and South Dakota was repeating itself, but at the time, I lacked the full appreciation of the Lakota–South Dakota jurisdiction history. Deloria's 1974 comment on the importance of Native history also pointed to the cause of the recurring patterns of conflict, namely, the longstanding problem that whites have with Native Peoples:

> It is imperative that Indian history move immediately into this century [the twentieth], . . . We are fast approaching the final decades of this century, and

we have been without any discernible Indian policy since 1958, when termination was practically abandoned by the Interior Department. Since that time, both Congress and the executive branch have operated on an ad-hoc, let's-put-out-the-fire, basis which has served neither the federal government nor the Indians but has only postponed the solution of longstanding problems. When one gets a good perspective on the twentieth century, then the nature of these problems is illuminated so that the problems which plague Indians are seen as indications of a long process of change of cultural and economic forms which repeat basic patterns over and over again.[20]

My lack of knowledge about this specific period of Lakota political history can, therefore, be explained in part by the simple fact that, while much has been written about Native Peoples, most of what has been written has focused on pre-twentieth-century Native North America. Though a generation of scholars has since matured under Deloria's 1974 disconcerting exposé and redirected considerable energies toward the study of twentieth-century Native North America, my inability to answer the many questions I had surrounding both the 1958 and 1964 referenda stemmed from a deficiency in contemporary Native North American literature. The scholarship suffers not from any lack of detail but from where the scholarship has focused.

Today, there are several hundred books, studies, and articles written about the Termination Era; they are informative, but I still find them wanting. For one thing, the Termination Era literature includes very few written materials on the Lakota response to Public Law 83-280. But more than that, Steven Schulte's article about congressman E. Y. Berry's role throughout the Termination Era identifies more precisely why the literature on termination remains inadequate: "Unfortunately, scholars have tended to overlook the importance of termination politicians' backgrounds and possible economic motivations by concentrating on the actual formulation of the policy. While this approach is important and fruitful, it is time to move beyond discussions of when or why the termination issue evolved to an analysis of its proponents' motivations."[21]

Not knowing at the state level who the leading proponents and opponents of termination were or their motivations leaves tremendous gaps in understanding the Lakota's 1958 and 1964 responses to Public Law 83-280. Not surprisingly, many people suffer from this socially constructed but entirely curable form of historical amnesia, which, as of the time of this writing, often derails any meaningful solutions to the long-standing Lakota–South Dakota jurisdiction debate.

Given all that was at stake for the Lakota, both in 1958 and 1964, none of the post-1964 political conflicts between the greater Lakota community and South Dakota's white community substantively compare to these two referenda.[22] Having made such a sweeping statement about these referenda's significance, I see my task in writing this book as one of conveying the larger human story of the 1958 referendum. I hope that readers, much as I did, will come to appreciate this story as an incredible, profound, Lakota drama.[23]

Telling the Lakota's Story

As the 1964 South Dakota state and federal elections were approaching, the more populous white community of South Dakota was preparing to vote on the significant, relationship-altering question of whether the state should accept a political transfer of federal responsibilities pursuant to Public Law 83-280. This question of transferring the political administration of Native affairs from the federal to the state level was on a 1964 statewide referendum ballot; yet as of this writing, no such political transfer from the United States to South Dakota has ever materialized. Arguably, why this has never happened is due entirely to the Lakota's successful political battle against the forces that strongly advocated such a transfer in 1957–58. Despite the serious political and legal ramifications of this pivotal, defining moment in Lakota–South Dakota relations, the compelling account of the Lakota's 1958 response and its implications has never been adequately told.

Because this Lakota story has not yet been articulated or rigorously examined, we find ourselves entering the twenty-first century without the direction that such a defining and powerful moment—a capstone really—could provide both the Lakota People and South Dakota's white community. In 1990, for example, S.D. officials initiated an effort to reconcile what is often described as an acrimonious relationship between South Dakota and the Lakota, yet the movement failed miserably within eight months. Such a failure strongly suggests that the state's effort, though laudable, misread what history says compellingly about Lakota–South Dakota political relations. The Lakota did not automatically jump on the bandwagon of the superficial, "feel-good," political whims of the white community—fads which historically have either marginalized or excluded Native participation whenever whites both defined the problems and designed the solutions for Natives. Instead, the Lakota maintained in 1990 as they did in 1958 and 1964 that any meaningful relationship between the two culturally and politically distinct communities had to begin with Lakota consent.

This current discourse investigates the Lakota People's political response to Public Law 83-280 and critically assesses what that response entailed for those engaged in the struggle at that time. Undoubtedly, telling this story will contribute to the ongoing and, at times, volatile debate surrounding the still-evolving relations between the Lakota and non-Lakota communities of South Dakota. Yet the Lakota's story bears significance in the broader picture as well. It illustrates through one people's drama how, since the 1960s, communities of color throughout North America have been restructuring or renegotiating their relationships with the white community.

To explore the Lakota's response to Public Law 83-280 from the moment it was enacted in the 1950s, I will lay out an analytical framework that consists of three chapters. Chapter 1 provides a historical investigation of the Termination Era and the social and political context from which Public Law 83-280 emerged. This chapter traces not only some of the prevailing sentiments toward Native Peoples in U.S. society but also how these sentiments invariably found expression as U.S. policy and law despite Native Peoples' vehement opposition.

Two leading U.S. measures in particular, House Concurrent Resolution No. 108 and Public Law 83-280, expressed white intentions toward Native Peoples and ignited conflicts that continue to this day. When read together, these documents state the long-term philosophical agenda of white society: by whatever means necessary, to totally incorporate Native Peoples into the U.S. mainstream.

Of course, the obvious defect of these two U.S. legislative measures was a glaring absence of Native political consent. In the formation of these laws, Native Peoples were not asked whether they desired such incorporation, neither were their voices included in the decision-making process. Only in 1968—after fifteen years of national protest by Native Peoples—was Public Law 83-280 finally amended to incorporate a Native consent provision.

For the Lakota, though, perhaps the most disconcerting aspect of South Dakota's involvement was how hard the state would strain in its interpretation of PL 83-280 to assume unilateral jurisdiction over Lakota Country. Terminationists intentionally equivocated over sections 6 and 7 of the law and how they applied to South Dakota, creating confusions that would—if they got away with it—allow the state to arbitrarily determine whether and when it would impose its brand of criminal and civil jurisdiction over Lakota homelands.

Ironically, as both federal and state legislative histories disclose, South Dakota was neither economically prepared nor politically willing to assume total criminal and civil jurisdiction over Lakota territory without the guarantee of a U.S. subsidy. Nor were the Lakota willing—U.S. subsidy or not—to submit to state jurisdiction. Nonetheless, between 1955 and 1965, South Dakota's legislators enacted several jurisdictional measures to the contrary.

Moreover, as the state's vigor in pursuing the 1959 *High Pine* case and others like it reveals, when the Lakota challenged state-inspired jurisdictional measures and won, South Dakota eagerly appealed these cases for the express political purpose of preempting Lakota authority. The obvious reason for the state's enthusiasm was that the white community had very little reason to believe that its own state court system might render an adverse ruling.

That South Dakota did attempt to exercise PL 83-280 on more than one occasion in highly suspect ways should raise serious doubts about the state's professed good intentions, claims to authority, or promises of benefits, were it to succeed in applying its criminal and civil jurisdiction over Lakota territory. Instead, the state's own comedy-of-errors pursuit of its terminationist policy exposed its willingness to act consistently in a manner that was clearly detrimental and nearly debilitating to the Lakota politically. Arguably, had Public Law 83-280 not existed, South Dakota most likely would have been less inclined to act upon its desire to assume criminal and civil jurisdiction over Lakota Country. But even if it had attempted such control, it would have had to negotiate any jurisdictional arrangements with the Lakota, knowing full well that Lakota consent would be required.

Chapter 2 outlines the Lakota's emerging political and economic activism throughout the 1950s and how such activism began undermining the Euroamerican community's colonial hegemony within Lakota territory. Over the course of the twentieth century, a distinguishing mark of this hegemony was the whites' use of Lakota land. Much of the land in question was either leased to white ranchers and farmers or their associations or, worse, sold to whites. Beginning in 1950, however, these non-Native individuals and their associations were sent a clear signal that Lakota governance had arrived, was proactive, and could not be dismissed.

Specifically, on 22 April 1949, the Oglala Sioux Tribe enacted Resolution 34-49—later amended by Resolution 147-50 (April 1950)—which levied a nominal assessment on whites leasing tribal land. Not until the early 1950s when the affected lessees sued the Oglala Lakota in federal district court (*Iron Crow v. the Ogallala Sioux Tribe of the Pine Ridge Reservation*) did the Lakota experience a vigorous jurisdictional challenge from South Dakota. *Iron Crow,* which the white lessees eventually appealed to the Eighth Circuit Court, recognized that the Oglala Lakota indeed had governmental taxing authority over any person or association that leased portions of their homeland. When the circuit court affirmed the lower court's decision, the ruling left the white community shell-shocked, serving notice that the colonial status quo it had previously enjoyed was no longer inviolable and was undergoing change.

Iron Crow and similar developments necessarily questioned and successfully challenged white hegemony within Lakota territory. As a result of these Lakota-initiated developments, South Dakota immediately launched in turn a decade-long effort that involved enacting several terminationist measures, the sole purpose of which was to stamp out the highly bothersome acts of Lakota self-governance.

Chapter 3 documents how and why South Dakota tried everything in its power to assume criminal and civil jurisdiction over Lakota Country in the mid-1950s. The chapter provides an in-depth sociopolitical analysis of South Dakota's true motives and the facile justifications the state employed for putting Public Law 83-280 into operation, culminating in two state bills: House Bill No. 721 and House Bill No. 892. The all-out terminationist effort used such institutions as the state's Legislative Research Council (LRC) and the S.D. Bar Association (SDBA), to name just two, to promote the state's assumption of jurisdiction.

But the all-out efforts of the state ultimately backfired. Lakota politico-economic activism gained a momentum that only increased the more South Dakota pushed to virtually overthrow Lakota governance. In addition, the unbridled deviousness and underhandedness of the whites' campaign against the Lakota exposed their moral turpitude—the extreme lengths that South Dakota's whites would go to hold on to their hegemony.

Of course, the classic Euroamerican pattern for maintaining its colonial hegemony is to define the "other" as the problem. Moreover, the way colonialists define that problem is notoriously designing and self-serving. South Dakota proved no exception to this pattern. Faced with issues that state jurisdiction hypothetically could have addressed, the Euroamerican community could have seriously examined the historical Lakota–South Dakota political relations to gain insights into resolving our respective community differences. Such a genuine discussion would have shown the necessity of gaining meaningful Lakota political consent before embarking on any plan of state criminal and civil jurisdiction. Instead, South Dakota's whites manipulated highly coded language around specific social projects, such as "law and order" or "welfare," to provoke their socially constructed, racist anxieties toward the "other"—the Lakota.

True to its colonialist role, the politically and economically stronger state of South Dakota began defining not only Lakota self-determination as its "Indian Problem" but also termination as its appropriate solution: the complete dismantling of Lakota politico-cultural structures that were giving rise to affirmative acts of self-determination. When South Dakota sought justification for its solution, it employed socially constructed racial and other "self-evident" truths about Native Peoples. Tapping into the white community's ingrained racism, terminationists could then cloak their real motives, which were to suppress the Lakota politically and thereby gain control of their land.

The *Iron Crow* decision shocked South Dakota's non-Lakota community into noticing that there was an Indian Problem after all, and chapter 3 examines in depth the whites' subsequent reactions as they scrambled to force through their solution. Given the legal opening that Public Law 83-280 provided, the colonialist's solution involved promoting several state measures: the 1951 Senate Bill No. 278 (appendix B), the 1957 House Bill Nos. 721 and 892 (appendices C, D, and E), and the 1959 Senate Bill No. 210 (appendix E). All these bills were introduced, some were enacted, and some were even adjudicated. Almost without exception, the driving goal of initiating each measure was to accept Public Law 83-280's offer to give the state full power to administer Native affairs.

These various state measures reveal South Dakota's increasing belligerency toward Lakota self-determination. To start, the 1951 Senate Bill No. 278 recognized the treaty-based criminal jurisdictional scheme between the Lakota and the United States and so upheld that South Dakota had no criminal jurisdiction within Lakota territory over Natives; the bill did, however, give the state the authority to prosecute non-Natives who committed a crime on a reservation. The 1957 House Bill No. 892 was the first and only state-enacted measure to actually provide for Lakota consent—albeit a highly conditional frame for obtaining that consent—in accepting the state's offer to extend its criminal or civil jurisdiction over Lakota Country.

The whites' increasing belligerence did not, however, reach its zenith in 1957 when South Dakota's legislators enacted House Bill No. 892. As the afterword discusses, the conflict over jurisdiction continued beyond the 1958 referenda through various seminal political and juridical events. In particular, the state jurisdiction advocates eventually succeeded in passing House Bill No. 791 in March 1963. Without question, House Bill No. 791 represented several years of extensive lobbying by the whites in South Dakota who wanted to completely undo all the Lakota-initiated political and economic gains—gains they viewed as threatening to their own political and economic interests. The Lakota had no choice but to respond to this specific measure, for had they not responded, in June 1963, South Dakota would have assumed complete criminal and civil jurisdiction over all Lakota territory.

In terms of political upsets, the Lakota response to House Bill No. 791 surpassed the extraordinary. Though none of the post-1957 South Dakota jurisdiction measures provided for Lakota consent, when the legislature passed this bill, the Lakota took an unprecedented but highly risky political move to challenge it through a referendum. The referendum allowed all qualified voters in South Dakota to settle the jurisdiction question through a 1964 statewide vote on it.[24]

To include the more populous Euroamericans in settling the criminal and civil jurisdiction question meant that the Lakota had to contend with a community whose socially constructed understanding of Native Peoples was invariably negative. Not surprisingly, the forces advocating state criminal and civil jurisdiction over Lakota territory did not hesitate to use disparaging, derogatory images of Native Peoples whenever such an image either served or furthered their cause. Given this anti-Native mood of the state, the prospect of a statewide referendum meant that the Lakota had to launch a major public relations campaign, which they did.

Engaging the state's referendum process as the Lakota's last-resort response to the bill underscored how critical both sides perceived it and grasped its implications. For the whites, by forcibly incorporating the greater Lakota community into the state-level polity, House Bill No. 791 promised a final Euroamerican solution to its Indian Problem. For the Lakota, neutralizing the bill would firmly establish the legitimacy of their self-determination and ensure that modern Lakota governance would continue to function as a potent shield against state hegemony.

Small wonder, then, that House Bill No. 791 and the ensuing 1964 referendum eventually became the Lakota's and South Dakota's definitive political response to Public Law 83-280. The referendum's outcome was all the more compelling considering that the necessity of the Lakota's political consent—and the lack of any measure in the bill for such consent—was why the Lakota opposed South Dakota's efforts to invoke Public Law 83-280 in the first place.

As a final note, Lakota participation in the 1964 referendum can be easily misunderstood and needs clarification—a clarification that applies to the 1958 referenda as well. Pundits use the 1964 referendum to support their well-worn contention: Native people vote in state-sponsored elections, because they want to effect change. On a cursory level, the pundits' argument seems valid enough, but a closer examination of the events surrounding HB No.

791 yields a far different interpretation of what the Lakota's intentions were in voting. One of the Lakota's long-held political positions on self-rule is to refuse to be drawn into state affairs. When they do get involved, they perceive their involvement quite differently from what the pundits describe. They participate only out of necessity—in this case, when their self-determination was at stake.

Because of the nonretrocessive nature of Public Law 83-280, had HB No. 791's enactment in 1963 gone unchallenged, South Dakota would have gained irrevocable control over the Lakota People and ultimately their homelands. Realizing that both the federal and state political processes had deliberately marginalized the Lakota by omitting Native consent, the Lakota leadership decided to invoke the only other option available to them: the state's referendum process.

Outnumbered and outresourced, the Lakota faced virtually impossible odds. Referring the bill to a statewide vote obviously favored the more populous Euroamericans. But more than that, the whites' fundamental cultural predisposition toward Native Peoples was indistinguishable from that of state representatives, who, between 1955 and 1965, overwhelmingly passed state laws to invoke Public Law 83-280. In other words, the Lakota made an exception and voted in the 1964 referendum only because Lakota sovereignty was seriously jeopardized.

In November 1964, South Dakota's Euroamerican community voted with the Lakota not to extinguish whatever sovereignty the Lakota community possessed. What politically profound implications can we draw from this lengthy jurisdictional controversy? Foremost, the Lakota's story drives home the necessity of seeking the consent of those most affected before formulating—much less pursuing—political action. Historically, the Euroamerican pattern is not to do this, not only with Natives but with people of color in general. The need to seek consent is perhaps the single most important lesson to be learned from this multi-decade drama over jurisdiction.

Specifically, House Concurrent Resolution No. 108 expressed the prevailing U.S. policy of the time, namely, to grant Native Peoples "all the rights and prerogatives pertaining to American citizenship." For Native Peoples, however, such a grant was not something they desired. It was formulated from specific U.S. termination measures or from Public Law 83-280, according to which the United States could, and did, confer on a state criminal or civil (or both) jurisdiction over the Native Peoples residing in that state.

In South Dakota, this process involved multiple obstacles. Certain legal barriers had to be removed before South Dakota could accept the U.S. offer.

But the far greater obstacle turned out to be the Lakota's unanticipated determination to have a voice, and their persistence in making their voice heard eventually forced South Dakota's non-Lakota voters to decide on the jurisdiction question. All of these factors involving South Dakota's attempt to invoke Public Law 83-280 and the Lakota resistance to those efforts suggest that the Lakota's participation in the 1964 referendum signified a great deal more than what Euroamericans and their Lakota supporters normally champion as the Lakota's newly found voting power.

Unquestionably, forced termination of Native self-governance was the Euroamerican agenda. U.S. and South Dakota jurisdiction legislation (including their legislative histories), the Lakota consent arguments, and correspondence between and among various Euroamerican and Lakota individuals all document the concerted effort to incorporate the Lakota wholly into the fabric of U.S. society at the state level. Based on their long experience with the United States, the Lakota realized without a doubt that incorporation was designed to be a forced affair; they themselves thought, sought, and fought otherwise. Between 1955 and 1965, using whatever means were available to them, the Lakota not once but twice successfully maneuvered the jurisdiction question into a plebiscite about their political status.

Although the term *plebiscite* has not been used around the jurisdiction conflicts, it applies. The many details surrounding those struggles—most notably, the direct vote of the qualified S.D. voters—suggest that the Lakota and the Euroamerican communities themselves irrevocably altered the course away from incorporation. By effectively changing the incorporation path, not only have the Lakota legitimately established consent as a foremost requisite, but, three decades after the last wholesale federal and state effort to completely dissolve Lakota governance, the Lakota are now in a far stronger position to redefine the sovereign nature of their political relationship with South Dakota.

Notes

1. St. Francis is one of twenty reservation communities with representation on the Rosebud Sioux Tribal Council; the other nineteen communities are Antelope, Black Pipe, Bull Creek, Butte Creek, Corn Creek, Grass Mountain, He Dog, Horse Creek, Ideal, Milk's Camp, Okreek, Parmelee, Ring Thunder, Rosebud, Soldier Creek, Spring Creek, Swift Bear, Two Strike, and Upper Cut Meat.

2. The four-year term was a short-lived experiment as the Sicangu membership approved a 1987 constitutional amendment that essentially reinstituted the two-year term.

3. The Lakota, Dakota, and Nakota are geo-linguistic dialects spoken by people who comprise the Oceti Sakowin Oyate, People of the Seven Fires. These seven fires or sociopolitical groups are Mdewakantun, Wahpetun, Wahpekute, Sisitun, Ihanktunwan, Ihanktunwani, and Titunwan. The first four speak Dakota, the next two speak Nakota, and the last speak Lakota.

4. In this first chapter, I rely on my personal papers that I acquired during my term (1985–1989) on the Rosebud Sioux Tribal Council. Herein such citations are noted as Edward Charles Valandra papers (ECV Papers).

5. Meierhenry quoted the wrong state statute, suggesting that South Dakota was not entirely clear of its unfolding strategy to assume criminal and civil jurisdiction over Lakota homelands.

6. See RST Resolution No. 86-34.

7. See *State v. Goodnick* (15 January 1986) and *State v. Medearis* (21 January 1986) in South Dakota's Fifth Circuit Court and *State v. Cloud* (24 March 1987) and *State v. Onihan* (27 May 1987) in the Sixth Circuit Court.

8. See *Rosebud Sioux Tribe v. State of South Dakota*, 1990, 900 F.2d 1164.

9. *Rosebud Sioux Tribe et al. v. State of South Dakota et al.*, Civil No. 86–3019, 2, ECV Papers.

10. Porter's decision relied on four significant cites: a 1988 South Dakota Supreme Court ruling (*State v. Onihan*); a 1979 U.S. Supreme Court case (*Washington v. Yakima Indian Nation*); a 1961 act—not 1959 as earlier indicated in Meierhenry's 10 December 1985 letter—(Chapter 464 of the Session of Laws of 1961); and a 1953 federal statute (Public Law 83-280), as amended by the Indian Civil Rights Act of 1968, which allows a state to assume and accept a political transfer of responsibilities from the United States to a state.

11. See, for example, Ann L. Davis, "BIA Blasts State's Contract Stand," *Rapid City Journal,* 26 May 1989; P. R. Gregg II, "Tribe Reinstates Decree Banning State Troopers," *Todd County Tribune,* 10 May 1989; Jerry Reynolds, "RST Bans State Patrol from Reservation Highways," *Lakota Times,* 9 May 1989; Jerry Reynolds, "RST Commercial Code Challenged," *Lakota Times,* 16 May 1989; Ivan Star Comes Out, "Tribes Unite Against State," *Lakota Times,* 23 May 1989; Ivan Star Comes Out, "State Capitol Could Be Next Target," *Lakota Times,* 20 June 1989; and Margret Figert, "License May Open Way for Legal, Political Relief," *Todd County Tribune,* 10 May 1989.

12. In response to Lunderman's subsequent Executive Order 89-02, which rescinded Executive Order 89-01, the Rosebud Sioux Tribal Council, by a 5 May 1989 motion, unanimously voted (24 Yes, 0 No, and 0 Not Voting) to rescind Executive Order 89-02 and reaffirm Executive Order 89-01.

13. Rosebud Sioux Tribe Ad Hoc Strategy Committee, ECV Papers.

14. See Crow Creek Sioux Tribal Resolution CC-89-06-06-11B, Standing Rock Sioux Tribal Resolution 97-89, Lower Brule Sioux Tribal Resolution 89-157, and the Oglala Sioux Tribal Resolution 89-55. Cheyenne River and Flandreau tribal councils passed resolutions of support: 128-89–CR and 89-25 respectively.

15. Prior to the reduction of the RSTC in 1989, the council membership included thirty-three council representatives elected from the twenty reservation communities (see note 1) and five officers: the president, vice president, secretary, treasurer, attorney general, and sergeant at arms.

16. ECV Papers.

17. Terry L. Pechota, 12 May 1989 letter to RST Secretary Sharon Burnette, ECV Papers.

18. *Rosebud Sioux Tribe et al v. State of South Dakota et al*, Reply Brief of Appellees/Cross-Appellants, p. 10, ECV Papers. South Dakota's primary evidence for its statement was based on a 14 February 1986 Oglala Sioux Tribal Court standing order issued by Judge Fast Horse that limited state criminal jurisdiction to a non-Indian offender and non-Indian victim and, of course, RST President Lunderman's 5 May 1989 Executive Order 89-03.

19. I employ the plural term *referenda* because each of the nine Lakota reservations had to hold a referendum between the dates of 1 October 1957 and 1 October 1958. Comparatively, in 1964 there was just one referendum held statewide.

20. Deloria, "The Twentieth Century," 166.

21. Schulte, "Removing the Yoke of Government," 50.

22. The exception to this statement is the 1973 Wounded Knee Conflict.

23. Personal narratives as story-based experiences provide the desperately needed context that is sadly neglected in the "refined" stories of formal, academic writing. As proof of the disparity that exists between stories based on social contexts and "refined" stories, I ask readers to compare both the Rosebud Sioux Tribe's and the State of South Dakota's Eighth Circuit Court of Appeals briefs with my narrative. I hope that readers will discern, and perhaps be appreciative of, a social text (i.e., the story) that is not conveyed otherwise.

24. Article 3, section 1 of South Dakota's Constitution provides for initiatives and referendums: "The legislative power of the state shall be vested in a legislature . . . except that the people expressly reserve to themselves the right to propose measures, which measures the legislature shall enact and submit to a vote of the electors of the state, and also the right to require that any laws which the legislature may have enacted shall be submitted to a vote of the electors before going into effect . . . Provided, that not more than five per centum of the qualified electors shall be required to invoke either the initiative or the referendum."

1

U.S. Termination Policy, 1945–53

Individuals who are familiar with or involved in Native affairs generally recognize the Eighty-third Congress's 1 August 1953 enactment of House Concurrent Resolution No. 108 (HCR No. 108) as the political document that officially crystallized U.S. termination policy regarding Native Peoples. The entire resolution is brief:

> Whereas it is the policy of Congress, as rapidly as possible, to make the Indians within the territorial limits of the United States subject to the same laws and entitled to the same privileges and responsibilities as are applicable to other citizens of the United States, to end their status as wards of the United States, and to grant them all of the rights and prerogatives pertaining to American citizenship; and
>
> Whereas the Indians within the territorial limits of the United States should assume their full responsibilities as American citizens: Now, therefore, be it
>
> Resolved by the House of Representatives (the Senate concurring), That it is declared to be the sense of Congress, *at the earliest possible time,* all of the Indian tribes and the individual members thereof located within the States of California, Florida, New York, and Texas, and all of the following named Indian tribes and individual members thereof, should be freed from Federal supervision and control and from all disabilities and limitations specially applicable to Indians: The Flathead Tribe of Montana, the Klamath Tribe of Oregon, the Menominee Tribe of Wisconsin, the Potowatamie Tribe of Kansas and Nebraska, and those members of the Chippewa Tribe who are on the Turtle Mountain Reservation, North Dakota.
>
> It is further declared to be the sense of Congress that, upon release of such tribes and individual members thereof from such disabilities and limitations,

all offices of the Bureau of Indian Affairs in the State of California, Florida, New York, and Texas and all other offices of the Bureau of Indian Affairs whose primary purpose was to serve any Indian tribe or individual Indian freed from Federal supervision should be abolished.

It is further declared to be the sense of Congress that the Secretary of the Interior should examine all existing legislation dealing with such Indians, and treaties between the Government of the United States and each such tribe, and report to Congress at the earliest practicable date, but not later than January 1, 1954, his recommendations for such legislation as, in his judgment, may be necessary to accomplish the purposes of this resolution. (Emphasis mine)

This resolution has had many consequences for Native affairs ever since its enactment.[1] The politico-cultural and legislative histories surrounding HCR No. 108 reveal at least four distinct elements, each intimately related to the others, that led to these consequences:

1. The cultural environment of the United States gave rise to a high degree of cultural homogeneity and political congeniality among the individuals who fostered, proposed, and implemented the termination program.

2. The pragmatic, bottom-line bent of Congress set the stage for the resolution's agenda to divest the federal government of its financial responsibilities to Native Nations. Congress took its cue from two sources about how to do this: William Zimmerman Jr.'s 1947 testimony before the Senate Committee on the Post Office and Civil Service about cutting costs by reducing or eliminating federal services to Natives Peoples, and the 1949 Hoover Commission's Indian Task Force Report "regarding the conduct of Indian Affairs by the Executive Branch of the Government."[2]

3. The history surrounding the "ward status" of Native Peoples and the resolution's aim to end that status played a major role in blurring treaty-defined commitments and justifying the United States' desire to abandon the government-to-government relationship it had with Native Nations, a relationship rooted in international law.

4. Finally, the committee-level conduct of the legislators, who used highly questionable maneuverings and manipulations, exposed the real motives behind termination policy. The disastrous result of their conduct was House Concurrent Resolution No. 108 and Public Law 83-280.

1. The Legislators: White, Male, Christian, Heterosexual, Racist, and Scared of Communism

During the five decades since the terminationist legislation passed, various explanations have developed to account for the rationale behind the Termination Era—its policies, its laws, and the people who made them. Certainly issues around race come to mind first. Since the formative years of the United States, an ideology of white supremacy has institutionally promoted the welfare of Euroamericans to the exclusion of all nonwhite communities.[3] Hence, a leading explanation for termination points to the extremely complex subject of race relations—a subject made all the more complex when appeals for racial equality were used to justify termination.

From a Native perspective, the notion of equality assumes different meanings and follows different paths depending on the community of color in question. For instance, the United States' long-established policy to racially segregate Blacks and whites—like slavery, Jim Crow, and now incarceration—developed institutional practices that, among other things, deliberately barred the Black Peoples from exercising their political will and advancing economically. As the Euroamerican Civil War amendments idealized and the short-lived experiment of Southern Reconstruction showed, a policy of equality requires that Black political expression and economic development be affirmed, yet this is precisely what whites and their strenuous racial discrimination would not allow.

Because of their deep-seated racial animus toward Black Peoples, whites have construed equality in the narrowest of terms, as the post–Civil War record shows. In spite of some obvious political and legal concessions that mistakenly mask for equality—such as the abolishment of white Southern primaries or the enactment of civil rights laws—strong racial prohibitions remain. Ingrained white aversion to assimilating the Black community unconditionally into mainstream society—culturally, politically, economically, and socially—has allowed acceptable degrees of segregation to continue.

By contrast, the Europeans' first experiences with Native North America tell a very different story about how the concept of equality has been used. Because Native communities were well-established thousands of years prior to European contact, imposing a policy of segregation on them in order to promote white supremacy would have had no effect on these already politically separate and economically autonomous Native Peoples. Yet guided by a white supremacist ideology, Europeans—and later Euroamericans—viewed Native Peoples as less than human and as incapable of comprehending the supposedly complex nuances of European civilization. This prevailing view of Native Peoples held by Europeans and their cultural heirs targets Native populations as prime candidates for extermination. Throughout five centuries, genocide was practiced by white governments and white populations as a culturally sanctioned program, since for whites, a policy to exterminate Natives was not perceived negatively.

Of course, the overwhelming Native resistance to their physical extermination made the social project too costly for whites to maintain. The fledgling United States was forced to reevaluate its extermination policy, slightly modifying it to pursue a subset of its extermination policy: the ethnicide—that is, the assimilation, integration, or acculturation—of Native Peoples. Whereas the United States' segregation policy narrowly circumscribed the integration of both Black Peoples and the white communities by the latter's long-held prejudice against fully assimilating the former, the United States' ethnicide policy promised Native Peoples full equality provided that they totally divested themselves of their cultural identity. In other words, Native Peoples were offered equality but at the price of the long-held values that distinguished them as distinct societies.[4]

Unquestionably, the most blatantly race-based tenet of the ethnicide policy placed a premium on attaining racially recognizable physical attributes of whiteness as a way to gain equality. The present day use of a blood-quantum standard to determine the degree of a person's non-Native blood perpetuates this ethnicide agenda and mindset.

As high-minded as it sounds, therefore, the term *equality* has been used historically to maintain white supremacy, but in ways skewed differently for Black and Native Peoples. The Euroamerican racial policies to segregate the Black community (separate but equal) and to eradicate Native Peoples (equal if no longer Native) twisted the meaning of equality to serve the single goal of maintaining white racial hegemony.

However transparent these calculated uses of the term have been to Natives, the history of termination policy reveals that non-Natives either have had difficulty understanding these differences or, if they did grasp the differences, have capitalized on them for political ends. Borrowing liberally from the Black-white context of the term's use, openly racist terminationists used righteous appeals to equality to promote the ethnicide of Native Peoples. For example, expounding on the termination policy, Arthur V. Watkins, a Utah senator and a major advocate of termination, described the proposed outcome of termination in terms that read more like a chapter from Black and white relations than from Native and white relations:

With the aim of "equality before the law" in mind our course should rightly be no other. Firm and constant consideration for those of Indian ancestry should lead us to work diligently and carefully for the full realization of their national citizenship with all other Americans. Following in the footsteps of the Emancipation Proclamation of ninety-four years ago, I see the following words emblazoned in letters of fire above the heads of the Indians—THESE PEOPLE SHALL BE FREE![5]

For the multitude of whites, their attitudes regarding race relations have been shaped largely by the Black Peoples' long-term civil rights struggles against fierce racism. Knowing this, Watkins employed rhetoric that evoked in whites powerful images of the extreme deprivations that the greater Black community has suffered at the hands of a white racist society and appealed to the corresponding emotions of guilt or shame that whites bear in order to build his case for termination. Native Peoples—and a few non-Native individuals versed in Native studies—knew what Watkins was doing. Lacking this background or knowledge, though, few non-Natives could see through the expedient uses of the term *equality*. As a result, whenever termination policy was packaged emotionally as a Native version of Black emancipation, whites found it hard to argue against it.[6]

A less conventional explanation for the Termination Era—one that has not been adequately addressed but that deserves mention—points to the cold war era and correlates its culturally oppressive atmosphere with the social and political move toward termination. After World War II, two western-based ideological spheres—the world of democracy and the world of Communism—emerged in sharp contrast. With each sphere viciously suspicious of the other, U.S. President Harry Truman declared a policy of Communist containment in the late 1940s, thus initiating the costly forty-year cold war between "democratic" and communist modern states.

After World War II, Europe was ravaged and exhausted, and non-European peoples seized the opportunity to gain independence from their European colonizers. As countries were forming and claiming their autonomy, cold war politics moved in. The competing first-world powers demarcated several regions as potential ideological hotspots, which essentially allowed them to use the emerging third world as an arena where they could compete for political and ideological hegemony.

However, U.S. involvement in the third world through economic aid and military assistance often smacked of designs beyond the simple aim to institute the "correct" political ideology. With U.S. advisers and technicians of all stripes influencing and supervising post–World War II development of the third world, U.S. assistance reinforced a virulent form of white supremacy that Frederick Jackson Turner had mapped out decades earlier.

After a 1893 celebratory white nationalist essay about how white Americans had closed the frontier in 1890, Turner's 1903 remarks alluded to a yet-to-be realized U.S. global imperialism. "This process being completed, it is not strange that we find the United States again involved in world-politics. The revolution [Spanish American War] that occurred four years ago, when the United States struck down that ancient nation [Spain] under whose auspices the New World was discovered, is hardly yet more than dimly understood."[7] In fact, Turner's observation about Euroamerican involvement in world affairs was not the least bit strange. Seven years later, in 1910, Turner framed the meaning of the Spanish American War so that its significance was no longer dimly but quite clearly understood:

> Having colonized the Far West [the "American" frontier], having mastered its internal resources, the nation turned at the conclusion of the nineteenth and the beginning of the twentieth century to deal with the Far East to engage in the world-politics of the Pacific Ocean. Having continued its historic expansion into the lands of the old Spanish empire by the successful outcome of the recent war, the United States became the mistress of the Philippines at the same time it came into possession of the Hawaiian Islands, and the controlling influence in the Gulf of Mexico. It provided early in the present decade for connecting its Atlantic and Pacific coasts by the Isthmian Canal, and became an imperial republic with dependencies and protectorates—admittedly a new world-power, with a potential voice in the problems of Europe, Asia, and Africa.[8]

Besides threatening the United States' historic agenda of expansion across the globe, Communism, though itself expansionist, threatened U.S. ideology on another count, and this time the threat operated within U.S. borders. Communism promoted an overall social project that most whites feared could influence their race- and class-based hegemony within the United States. Specifically, Communism's powerfully seductive call to restructure labor and management relations promised radical changes for the historically disempowered U.S. labor force. According to Communist philosophy, nonwhites and highly impoverished whites could have a voice on important economic decisions and thereby could work with management, sharing its power to shape the course of business. Yet such labor-inclusive collaborations with management have always been suspect in the United States—viewed as subversive to its capitalistic and "free-market" way of life.

Not surprisingly, then, in the highly charged atmosphere of the cold war, every person, movement, or culture that did not fit the "American norm" seemingly posed an internal threat to U.S. society. The 1945 elevation of the House Un-American Activities Committee (HUAC) to a standing committee showed how mainstream society's hysteria over Communism was also stirring up deep-seated prejudices, and these phobic, exclusionist currents were dominating U.S. domestic policy.

Because Congress is the largest political body in the United States and the one that was aggressively at the forefront of the anti-Communist campaign, a profile of that body's membership speaks volumes about the people behind the decisions. Between January 1947 and December 1953—the apex of both the cold war and termination—Congress could boast one senator of color and four female, albeit white, senators.[9] The House included three representatives of color and twenty female, again white, representatives.[10] From these figures, it is no exaggeration to say that Congress was virtually a white male institution.[11]

During the period of termination policy, then, the cultural meaning of the term *American* was quite narrowly defined. Those authorized to represent America—those who most exemplified what it was to be an American—were males of European descent (sex and race variables), upper middle income to wealthy (class variable), and heterosexual and Christian (sexual and religious orientation variables). People who fit this social profile reserved the term *American* for themselves. Others who, by virtue of the station of life they were born into, did not possess all or a substantial portion of the five significant variables were immediately placed in the highly vulnerable position of being viewed as un-American, as the Japanese "Americans" discovered during their World War II internment. Those whose identities were classed as un-American found that their activities—cultural or otherwise—became suspect as well.

These two factors—the expedient manipulation of the notion of racial equality and the cold war hysteria—converged to shape Congress's mid-twentieth-century Native policy. Not surprisingly, the result was chilling at best and devastating at worst for Native Peoples. A leading terminationist in Congress was E. Y. Berry, South Dakota's Congressional representative for the Second District (1951–1971). An ultraconservative and an ardent antagonist to all forms of Native self-determination, Berry summarized in a 1950s speech how issues of racial equality and the fear of Communism commingled to shape Native policy.

After expressing some impatience and outright contempt in general for people who supported equality for Black Peoples (Native-rights activists, liberals, Democrats, and other "do-gooders"), Berry went on to attack this group specifically as transparent hypocrites when they failed to support his termination policy and instead championed Native self-governance: "While they condemn segregation in the South, they themselves are demanding that the American Indian be segregated, that he be placed on a reservation [high on E. Y. Berry's list of grievances]. In other words to compel his [the American Indian's] constant segregation from the White people of this nation."[12]

Like Watkins, Berry was fully aware that Black-white race relations shaped the understanding of racial problems for an overwhelming majority of Americans. By comparing Native life on reservations with the south's segregation of Black communities, Berry astutely posed a persuasive contradiction that unnerved the critics of termination, intimating that they may, in fact, be closet racists.

After playing the race card—criticizing whoever presumably supported segregation in the guise of reservations and Native self-governance—Berry played the fear-of-Communism card. The Wheeler-Howard Act of 1934 ended one of the United States' most disastrous social-engineering programs, namely, the allotting of Native homelands, and ushered in the era of modern Native self-governance. But Berry condemned the Wheeler-Howard Act for being Communistic:

> The President and his social workers are demanding the colored man be given complete and wholly equal rights in the South. But what treatment is that same Administration giving to the Indian people? The President and his Socialist Democrats are making much ado about fighting Communists and Communism throughout the world, and yet, that same Administration passed the Wheeler-Howard Act which Communizes the Indian Reservations just as completely and just as fairly and just as unGodly as Communist Russia can hope to do.[13]

Shifting his critique of reservations from the charge that they impose racial segregation to the charge that they practice Communism, in Joseph McCarthy fashion, Berry elaborated the Communist charge by naming what he perceived as the three great providences of Communism that the Wheeler-Howard Act allegedly imposed and by implication prevailed on reservations:

> It provides the breaking up of family by compelling the family to send their children to communal schools. Second, it provides for communal ownership of all land, all land shall be broken up from individual ownership and all land and all property shall be the property of the tribe. Three, it provides for the

solemnizing of marriages by a member of the tribe, chosen by the tribe. It provides for the issuance of divorces upon application by a member of the tribe to the local tribal judge. Talk about fighting Communism? No, they are bringing it right to America and Communizing the Indian just as thoroughly as if they were citizens of Russia.[14]

Like his counterpart Senator McCarthy, who deliberately manipulated information and indulged in highly inflammatory, coded language in order to expose the supposed Communist influence within the United States, Berry chose these particular three providences (no local community control of education, no individual ownership of private property, and no marriages solemnized or divorces granted by a Christian-based or Christian-oriented institution)[15] precisely because they would fan the fears of people already afraid of Communists.

In sync with the mood of the 1950s, Berry had perfect timing. The xenophobic climate of mainstream society was primed for the kind of policy and legislation that has since defined the Termination Era. To justify and expedite the United States' longstanding policy of ethnicide, Congress was entirely willing to combine Black-white racial politics with the culturally repressive cold war politics and focus this propaganda weapon on Native affairs.

After all, who in Congress represented a voice different from mainstream white society? Again, the overall institutional profile of Congress showed it to be dominated by middle-class to wealthy males of European descent whose religious and sexual orientation were overwhelmingly Christian and heterosexual. With this one-flavor barrel of social candies to choose from, it is no wonder that the two major congressional committees responsible for Native policy (the Senate and House Interior and Insular Affairs Committees) mirrored this social profile as well.

But the profiles in conformity did not end there. From February 1947 when Zimmerman first presented his plan to reduce or eliminate federal services to Natives to November 1964 when the implementation of Public Law 83-280 was successfully defeated in South Dakota, a composite membership profile of both the House and Senate committees reveals two more factors that effectively excluded all but the dominant point of view. In addition to uniformity of gender, race, economic status, religion, and sexual orientation,[16] the committees' memberships intimately shared two other noteworthy factors: cultural homogeneity and political congeniality.

Of both the House and Senate Interior and Insular Affairs Committees, 165 members of Congress considered Native matters at some point in their political careers. A crucial but rarely mentioned cultural consideration is that

66 of these committee members were born prior to 1900, 39 others were born within the first decade of the twentieth century, and a significant number of these members came from various U.S. "territories" that, from 1889 through 1912, had relinquished territory status for that of statehood.[17] It was therefore far more than coincidence that, as the United States was actively engaged in "incorporating" an additional 598,350,000 acres (or about 31 percent of the pre-1959 U.S. land base) from these future states, these yet-to-be interior and insular committee members of both chambers were, throughout their formative years, reared on a steady cultural diet that included the following staples:

- extreme white nationalism, as Frederick Jackson Turner's seminal and much heralded 1893 cultural essay, "The Significance of the American Frontier," expressed;
- extreme white racial intolerance, if not hatred, toward communities of color—a position officially enunciated by the all-white U.S. Supreme Court's 1896 decision of Plessy v. Ferguson (the infamous "separate but equal" doctrine); and
- extreme white expansionism and imperialism, evidenced by the United States' 1898 military invasion of Cuba and Puerto Rico (a foreign policy that lost much of its luster during the Vietnam War).

These formidable cultural staples indoctrinated the post-1890 generations of white society with a staunch belief in the infallibility of their racial and cultural supremacy, so much so that by the mid-twentieth century, an ideological charge of being un-American could have devastating consequences for a person or group.

More important for Native Country, 122 of the 165 congresspeople involved in deciding on Native affairs represented twenty-three states west of the Mississippi River. The remaining members represented thirteen eastern states,[18] and 83 of the 165 congresspeople in question had served on either the House or Senate Subcommittee on Indian Affairs at least once. Another relevant termination-associated factor was that 76 of 83 congresspeople on the two subcommittees on Indian affairs represented states in which a substantial Native land base and population precariously coexisted with the non-Native community.

Constituency politics aside, the link between congresspeople and Native lands and populations may seem incidental until we take a broader historiocultural perspective. Indeed, it requires very little imagination to realize how approximately 54,556,000 (est. 1950) of unannexed or unceded acres of

Native land could be highly repugnant—and highly irresistible—to the cultural sensibilities of a powerful political organization that was so uniform in race and cultural outlook. Evidently, the individuals who went to Congress immediately after World War II had such a response. For them, the disconcerting existence of Native homelands blemished an otherwise self-congratulatory Euroamerican epic tale about the white man civilizing a "wild and untamed" continent. Given this cultural bent, the congresspeople serving on the Indian affairs subcommittees apparently adopted personal missions to rid the country of this Native-held blemish through a policy of termination.

Equally critical for the fate of Native Country during the Termination Era, however, was the close political congeniality—"the good old boys' club"—that was the way of doing business in Congress. This close congeniality operated between congresspeople of both the House and Senate Interior and Insular Affairs Committees and, in particular, among their respective subcommittees on Indian affairs.

Political pundits sometimes invoke the well-worn civics argument that bipartisanship was responsible for such congeniality—an argument that conveniently dismisses any motives concerning real estate, i.e., land grab. According to this explanation, when faced with any given political, legislative, or policy matter, the Democratic and Republican parties eventually reach an understanding or compromise in which, by splitting their supposed differences, neither political party fully receives or entirely loses what it wants. However, using bipartisanship to explain the insider congeniality that operated among the congresspeople involved with Native policy glosses over some glaring realities.

During the 1950s, vigorous adherence to party philosophy and staunch party loyalty were the rule and not the exception. Indeed, the two-party political system of the United States has always prided itself in supposedly providing at least two perspectives, so that one point of view does not dominate unchallenged. Yet these party behaviors were completely missing from the interactions of those involved in determining Native policy. When it came to charting a course as momentous as termination and its concomitant legislative agenda, the Democrats and Republicans in Congress engaged in none of the bitter and contentious political arguments that we would otherwise expect. Multi-perspective debates over termination never occurred.

Instead, congresspeople who were quite dissimilar with respect to their geopolitical sectionalism—that is, the racial segregation of the deep South; the natural resources exploitation of the far and arid West; the labor and management problems of the industrial northeast; and so forth—miraculously were able to forsake their partisanship and sectionalism whenever they considered Native matters.

For instance, between June 1940 and December 1947, the federal withdrawal of services from Native Country was on a limited reservation-by-reservation basis and not yet a full-fledged official policy.[19] However, not long after Zimmerman's 1947 testimony and just prior to the release of the 1949 Hoover Commission Report—both suggesting that federal services be cut—another strong protermination signal emerged. In 1947, Hugh Butler, a Republican senator from rural Nebraska's livestock region, closely collaborated with Leighton Wade of New York State's Joint Legislative Committee on Indian Affairs and with New York's House Representative Daniel Reed to promote S. 1683, a Senate bill calling for the withdrawal of federal services to Native Peoples in New York State.[20] Interestingly, Butler's 1947 measure did not affect the criminal jurisdictional scheme between his state and the Native community in Nebraska but only between New York and the Native communities there.[21]

True, bipartisanship cannot be entirely discounted as a plausible explanation for the political congeniality shown among the lead congresspeople promoting S. 1683. Yet their knee-jerk solidarity is suspicious, especially regarding legislation that transfers the political control of land from Natives to whites. When the Senate Interior and Insular Affairs Committee, dominated by western states, and the House Public Lands Committee, nearly dominated by western states, respectively close ranks as H. Rpt. No. 2355 reveals they did,[22] and when these committees subsequently request and almost routinely obtain a unanimous consent vote by Congress on such consequential legislation for an eastern state such as New York,[23] surely we have to consider explanations other than bipartisanship. Again, when it came to formulating Native policy and law, the usual partisanship and sectional rancor were notably absent from Congressional debates.

The historian Laurence M. Hauptman provides a revealing insight into how political congeniality formed among the termination-minded congresspeople who were intimately involved or familiar with Native affairs. Hauptman looks at Butler's and Reed's personal backgrounds to explain their collaboration on S. 192, a 1950 bill to transfer the civil jurisdiction of Native lands to New York. His social-context analysis speaks volumes about the inherent nature of political congeniality:

> Butler's background reveals insights into his motivation on Indian legislation. Born on the Iowa frontier in 1878, he moved with his family by covered

wagon to a homestead in Nebraska six years later. . . . After his graduation from Doane College in 1896, Hugh Butler worked for the Burlington Railroad, became a grain company manager, and eventually made a large fortune as head of the Butler-Welsh Company, one of the largest concerns on the Omaha Grain Exchange. Butler was elected to the United States Senate on a strong anti-New Deal platform in 1940 by cultivating his image as a self-made man, his pioneer background, his concern for farmers, and his philanthropic activities on behalf of Doane College. . . . Cast in the same mold as Congressman Daniel Reed of New York, Butler reflected the conservative's hostility toward big government and manifested distaste for much of the social experiments of the 1930s. It was in this context that he opposed treating the Indians as separate nations within the nation. Frequently using Lincolnesque metaphor, Butler insisted that Indiains [sic] be emancipated from BIA [Bureau of Indian Affairs] restraints, that the chains enslaving them to the federal bureaucracy be broken, and that they be allowed and encouraged to be just like other Americans.[24]

Butler and Reed both embraced a conservative agenda that, at least on political principle and philosophy, naturally opposed the Native initiatives conceived within the womb of the Democrats' liberal New Deal program, such as the Wheeler-Howard Act of 1934. According to Hauptman's observations, these men's backgrounds have a familiar-sounding ring of cultural homogeneity. Born in the 1870s, both Reed and Butler were undoubtedly influenced by late-nineteenth-century events that seemingly affirmed Euroamerica's hegemony. Moreover, like Butler, whose state had Native Peoples coexisting with the greater Nebraska community,[25] Reed represented a congressional district that included the Seneca homeland that he lived next to during childhood.[26]

Hence, Hauptman's brief biography of the Nebraska senator subtly unwraps a telling thread of the Reed-Butler connection. Notwithstanding conservative principles and party affiliation, these two individuals shared a common but virulent form of cultural ideology. This ideology automatically predisposed them to characterize Native Peoples' lifestyle unfavorably as "un-American." Indoctrinated with such an ideology, Butler and Reed—and other congresspeople like them—felt culturally motivated to promote legislation that amounted to the termination of the Six Nations and their political and cultural coexistence within New York.

2. Pre-Termination Pragmatics

The second distinct element shaping the 1953 enactment of HCR No. 108—the document officially launching U.S. termination policy—concerns how Native populations were first targeted for termination. The issue was money—ostensibly, cost-cutting—and it arose during a February 1947 hearing of the Senate Committee on the Post Office and Civil Service. This 1947 hearing on cost-cutting by reducing the number of federal employees set the stage for the legislation that followed in 1953.

Looking back, Senator Watkins gives ample credit to the then-acting Commissioner of Indian Affairs, William Zimmerman Jr., for putting the termination mindset in motion when he testified before the Senate committee about how to cut costs in the Bureau of Indian Affairs (BIA): "Statements made by the Acting Commissioner [Zimmerman] vividly recalled the Congressional attention to the fact that specific groups of Indians were then regarded as prepared for on-the-spot freedom from the wardship status. . . . This testimony [of Zimmerman's] at the 1947 hearings served as an effective stimulus toward renewed consideration of an end of wardship."[27] When Zimmerman later recalled his testimony, he confirmed (in the third person) that his 1947 plan had indeed influenced the terminationists in how they framed their policy, though perhaps not in the way he anticipated:

> The Committee's [the Senate Committee on the Post Office and Civil Service] announced purpose was to reduce the number of federal employees. The Indian Bureau was only one of many agencies to appear. Testifying under subpoena and replying to a demand from the Committee, the witness said that Bureau services could be curtailed or eliminated as to certain tribes and reservations, by groups. He specified certain criteria which the Congress should consider in such reduction in services, and he indicated that these criteria did not apply uniformly. In fact all four could not be applied to any one tribe.[28]

Zimmerman's four criteria for deciding which Native communities should have their services cut first present little more than a western-based model of Native Peoples' social evolutionary development. Zimmerman assigned Native populations to three separate groups (Group I, II, and III). Each group denoted a Native population's degree of readiness to have their federal services reduced or eliminated. The four criteria for evaluating the readiness of Native communities and placing them in these three groups were:

1. The degree of acculturation of the particular tribe, including such factors as the admixture of white blood, the percentage of illiteracy,

the business ability of the tribe, its acceptance of white institutions, and its acceptance by whites in the community;
2. The economic condition of the tribe, principally the availability of resources to enable either the tribe or the individuals, out of their tribal or individual assets, to make a reasonably decent living;
3. The willingness of the tribe and its members to dispense with federal aid; and
4. The willingness and ability of the State in which the tribe is located to assume the responsibilities.[29]

Having articulated these four criteria, the only remaining decision was to determine each Native group's relative degree of readiness. Those placed in Group I were presumably ready for immediate termination of federal services, suggesting that the Native Peoples in this particular group had attained a high level of acceptable assimilation. Ostensibly, Group II would attain Group I status within a decade. Group III may not be ready for termination for well beyond a decade to perhaps several decades. Simplifying the complexities of Native affairs in a budgetary—and blatantly Eurocentric—manner did not, however, lead terminationists to believe that their program would be as easy as categorizing Native Peoples into these three groups. Nonetheless, as Watkins noted, Zimmerman's plan eventually proved fundamental to the success of the forthcoming 1953 termination effort.

To a non-Native society largely unfamiliar with both the bureaucratic maze of the federal government and the stark realities of Native North America, Zimmerman's plan seemed reasonable enough. It promoted termination not only as cost-effective and as having the socially redeemable objective of assimilation, but also as having a clinical quality that completely masked termination's devastating scope and impact. Besides selling termination to mainstream America, the more pragmatic purpose of this propaganda tool becomes apparent when Zimmerman's administrative-speak is deconstructed to reflect its actual outcome: cutting BIA agencies and their services to Native Peoples. Zimmerman's list of Native Nations who were ready for the reduction or elimination of federal services was closely tied to BIA administrative or jurisdictional units. These agencies were sometimes but not always associated with a particular reservation (table 1).

Zimmerman's list, which involved sixty-one jurisdictional units, does not at first appear administratively unwieldy, especially when these jurisdictional units are further divided into three seemingly manageable groups. Yet a more knowledgeable look at what he was proposing tells a very different story.

Table 1. Zimmerman's 1947 Group List and Non-Zimmerman Group List by Jurisdictional Units and Reservations

Group	Number of Jurisdictional Units	Actual Number of Reservations	Estimated Population	Approximate Acres
I	10	129	55,963	3,014,687
II	19	44	69,026	12,859,171
III	32	89	342,646	38,322,064
Subtotals	61	262	467,635	54,195,922
IVª	30	93	34,790	3,118,442
Totals	91	355	502,425	57,314,364

Source: H. Rpt. No. 2503 (1953)
a. Group IV represents those jurisdictional units omitted by Zimmerman and not classified with either group. The Group IV designation is my own.

Of the ten Group I agencies listed, only the Flathead, Hoopa, Klamath, Menominee, Osage, and Prairie Band of Potawatomie BIA agencies corresponded one-on-one to these six reservations, while the Mission, New York, Sacramento, and Turtle Mountain agencies represented two or more reservations. In California, the Mission and Sacramento agencies had, respectively, thirty-two and eighty-three reservations/rancherias under their respective agency jurisdictions,[30] the New York agency had six reservations to administer,[31] while, in North Dakota, Turtle Mountain agency administered two reservations.[32]

This analysis of the jurisdictional units of each grouping yields a much clearer picture of Zimmerman's plan and its real impact. Instead of targeting only ten Group I jurisdictional units, according to Zimmerman's testimony and the corresponding numbers from the 1952 H. Rpt. No. 2503, his plan actually targeted for immediate termination of federal services 129 separate reservations comprising several different Native Nations and whose cumulative population was nearly fifty-six thousand. Under the Zimmerman plan, Group I represented about 49 percent of the reservations and approximately 12 percent of the Native population of all three groups combined.

Similarly, Group II's nineteen jurisdictional units fail to show the actual number of reservations and their populations that would have been affected by Zimmerman's plan. Of the nineteen agencies, fourteen had jurisdiction over a single corresponding reservation,[33] while the remaining agencies of Northern Idaho and Tomah each had four reservations under their jurisdiction;[34] the Great Lakes agency had twelve reservations;[35] the Consolidated Chippewa agency had seven;[36] and the Quapaw agency oversaw three reservations.[37] Thus, Group II's agencies represented about 17 percent of the reservations and 15 percent of the Native population soon to be targeted by Zimmerman.

Finally, of Group III's thirty-two agencies, twenty had jurisdiction over a single reservation.[38] Of the twelve remaining agencies, the United Pueblo agency oversaw twenty-two reservations;[39] the Western Shoshone agency administered thirteen reservations;[40] the Unitah and Ouray agency was responsible for seven reservations;[41] the Five Civilized Tribes and Truxton Canyon agencies each had five reservations under their respective jurisdictional units;[42] the Pima agency had four reservations;[43] the Colorado River, Sells, and Seminole agencies each had three reservations respectively;[44] and the Consolidated Ute agency had two.[45] In terms of the number of reservations and populations that would be affected, Group III covered eighty-nine reservations with a combined Native population of approximately 342,646.

Certainly, the plan was no small enterprise, even though Zimmerman's use of jurisdictional units made it seem otherwise. As a result, when the plan to withdraw federal supervision was broadly conveyed to mainstream society, the actual number of Natives that would be affected by withdrawal remained conveniently hidden.

For example, on 15 April 1947, two months following Zimmerman's congressional testimony, John Provinse, the assistant commissioner of Indian affairs, gave a speech about federal withdrawal to a national conference of social workers. He told them that Group I included only ten tribes or groups who would be affected, rather than giving the correct figure of 129 reservations with a combined land base of 3,014,687 acres.[46] Instead of mentioning that Group II's 44 reservations had a combined land base of almost 13,000,000 acres, Provinse simply noted that the second group comprised some 20 jurisdictions. Finally, although Provinse admitted that Group III comprised a majority of Native Peoples, he again failed to mention that the thirty-five Indian jurisdictions in this last group covered eighty-eight reservations.

In other words, the way Zimmerman framed his plan intentionally deceived the public about the magnitude of its impact on Native Peoples. For political expediency, he hid the fact that he was proposing that the U.S. government reduce or eliminate federal services to nearly 75 percent of all of Native Country's reservations and 93 percent of its population. Such a program, cloaked in such deception, reeked with an ideological agenda that, just a few years later, would inspire the advocates of termination.

Two years after Zimmerman's testimony, the Hoover Commission's March 1949 report on reorganizing the executive branch of the U.S. government revealed just how far the mantra of withdrawing federal services from Native communities had percolated throughout the federal government. An informal intragovernmental partnership between Congress and the executive branch was clearly forming that would set the direction of the just-around-the-corner termination policy. Here, the Hoover Commission's all-white Indian Task Force (ITF) proposed a Native policy that would soon become the heavy-handed, forced-assimilation, legislative movement known as termination:

> Our Task Force on Indian Affairs, supported by considerable body of thought both inside and outside the Government, advocates progressive measures to integrate the Indians into the rest of the population as the best solution of the "Indian Problem." In the opinion of the Commission this policy should be the keystone of the organization and of the activities of the Federal Government in the field of Indian Affairs.[47]

The ITF went on to detail how to accomplish this policy through five recommendations. These recommendations obviously included state but completely excluded Native governments as part of the ITF-proposed integration plan. In particular, the transfer of BIA programs to state-government administration dominated ITF's integration policy.[48] Among the twelve members of the Hoover Commission, Dean Acheson was one of three dissenters who expressed grave reservations about the commission's acceptance of the ITF's proposed policy:[49]

> The Commission recommends the transfer of the Bureau of Indian Affairs to the Federal Security Agency or its successor. It recommends also necessary improvement in the education and public health facilities provided for Indians. But the Commission goes beyond these recommendations for reorganization and improved efficiency and outlines objectives and purposes for an Indian policy. We are to integrate the Indian, remove "surplus" Indians from Indian lands, put the lands into private, individual, or corporate ownership, remove tax exemption, and, as soon as possible, merge the Indian, his life and lands with those of the people of the State where he resides, subject entirely to State jurisdiction.
>
> These recommendations seem to me beyond our jurisdiction. If they are said to fall within it because they abolish functions of the executive branch, it is equally true that they change substantive legislative policy established by the legislative branch. We have neither the right nor the duty to enter this field. On occasion common sense may tell us not to draw too fine a line.
>
> But, for me, this is not such an occasion. I have not the knowledge nor the time, in view of the vast amount of material before this Commission, to

acquire it, to pass judgment whether the policy recommended is wise, just, and understanding. Recollections of the painful history which surrounds the cases of *The Cherokee Nation v. The State of Georgia* (5 Peters I) and *Worcester v. Georgia* (6 Peters 534), make a novice in this field pause before endorsing a recommendation to assimilate the Indian and to turn him, his culture, and his means of livelihood over to State control.[50]

Such dissenting voices did not, however, carry the day. Instead, the termination machine was being systematically constructed. From June 1940 until September 1950, six termination-like laws passed that conferred limited criminal jurisdiction to a particular state over a particular reservation or reservations.[51] The 1947 Zimmerman testimony about federal withdrawal of services made termination seem cost-effective and clinically benign. And then the 1949 Hoover Commission Report calling for the integration of Native Peoples brought the executive branch on board.

With 1953 fast approaching, the clamor to "get out of the Indian business"—the terminationists' much broadcasted sound byte—continued unabated. The lumbering 1952 House report investigating the Bureau of Indian Affairs (H. Rpt. No. 2503), which collected a massive number of "facts" about Native Country, was being used by terminationists to make termination seem grounded on scientific research. In the hands of terminationists, the House report served to justify the whole concept of termination and to generate considerable support for the policy among congresspeople.

Following Zimmerman's plan, the 1952 report had suggested that termination proceed gradually according to the preparedness of each reservation to make up for the loss of federal services. But by 1953, the congressional momentum for termination was so strong that legislators abandoned the façade of being responsible and instead were busily finding ways to apply termination indiscriminately throughout all of Native Country. The costs to Native Peoples were quickly apparent. Several of the Native communities who had already become subject to HCR No. 108 (the much-called-for ITF policy) often found themselves extremely vulnerable to periodic assaults of racism. Acheson's deep concerns about handing Native affairs over to state control would prove prophetic.

3. Wardship: A Fictional, Socio-Legal Construction

Though Zimmerman's four conditions provided guideposts for determining whether federal services to Native Peoples would be terminated or reduced, they were never actually employed. Nonetheless, Zimmerman formulated them in response to the third element shaping termination policy, namely, the push to change wardship status. Historically, wardship was first posed as an analogy to describe the relationship between Native Peoples and white society. To the uninitiated, although the HCR No. 108 preamble did not explicitly use any language that outlined termination per se, it did suggest in its two opening paragraphs—veiled in a white-defined blueprint for making Natives conform to white ways—a promise of political equality for Native Peoples.

Therein lay the tension between termination and wardship: the core of termination was to get the government out of the Indian business; the core of wardship was for the government to have complete control over Indian Peoples. To achieve the first, termination, the federal government had to dispense with the second, wardship.

HCR No. 108 proposed to make Native Peoples ostensibly more American in various ways: by subjecting them to the same U.S. laws as non-Natives; by entitling them to the same privileges as Americans; by granting them all rights and prerogatives associated with U.S. citizenship; and by having them assume the responsibilities of that citizenship. In proposing this all-American makeover of Natives, HCR No. 108 uses language that is emotionally charged, value-laden, and highly coded. In this context, the statement about ending ward status appears rather odd and downright out of place. Yet like other terminology that Euroamericans use when they attempt to whitewash some skullduggery, *ward status* contains various hidden meanings. Indeed, without changing Native Peoples' ward status, termination would have lost virtually all its meaning and potency.

Historically, the wardship concept formally appeared in 1831 when the Cherokee community convincingly but unsuccessfully argued before an all-white male Supreme Court that it was a culturally and politically distinct society apart from Euroamerica. In other words, the Cherokee qualified as a foreign state pursuant to the U.S. Constitution and therefore could now sue "to restrain the state of Georgia from the execution of certain laws of that state, which . . . go directly to annihilate the Cherokees as a political society."[52] Taken by the Cherokee to the water's edge of envisioning a pluralistic society for North America, Chief Justice John Marshall retreated to the comfortable but culturally debilitating shores of a slave-owning society. In 1831, Marshall could not bring himself to wade into the full waters of cultural pluralism:

> This argument [Cherokee people as a distinct society] is imposing, but we
> must examine it more closely before we yield to it. The condition of the Indi-

ans in relation to the United States is perhaps unlike that of any other two
people in existence. In the general, nations not owing a common allegiance
are foreign to each other. The term foreign nation is . . . applicable by either
to the other. But the relation of the Indians to the United States is marked by
peculiar and cardinal distinctions which exist no where else.[53]

For Marshall, Native-U.S. relations bore "peculiar and cardinal distinctions" in that Native Country is part of U.S. territory; political and economic intercourse is only between Native Peoples and the United States; and
Native-U.S. treaty provisions in general acknowledge U.S. supremacy to the
exclusion of other foreign states. In a typically racist fashion, Marshall then
formulated what these distinctions really meant for Native Peoples: being a
domestic dependent nation "spontaneously" entailed existing in a state of
pupilage, too.

By describing Native societies as dependent domestic nations rather than
independent foreign states, the 1831 Marshall court could conveniently refuse
to assume federal jurisdiction. As a result, the Cherokee were deprived of
receiving any constitutional protection from the political violence directed
against them from the slave-holding state of Georgia.[54]

For the twentieth-century band of terminationists, however, the pupilage
status of Native Nations posed an obstacle. Terminationists found it thoroughly disagreeable for the U.S. government to honor any treaty-defined
responsibilities toward Native Nations. Accordingly, "wardship"—Marshall's
racist term for those responsibilities—represented a critical, institutional
barrier to termination's goal of "freeing the Indians."

Having described Native Peoples as domestic dependent nations, Marshall
tackled the next important question in the 1831 court case. This question
loomed even larger for the United States (represented by the Marshall court
and Georgia) and Native Country (represented by the Cherokee Nation),
because it concerned the territorial integrity of the so-called domestic dependent nations. Admitting the political existence of Native Country, the Marshall court then proceeded not only to qualify Native territories as being
highly temporal but also to define the exact nature of Native-U.S. territorial
relations:

> Though the Indians are acknowledged to have an unquestionable and, here-
> tofore, right to the lands they occupy, until that right shall be extinguished by
> a voluntary cession to our government; yet it may well be doubted whether
> those tribes which reside within the acknowledged boundaries of the United
> States can, with strict accuracy, be denominated foreign nations. They may,

more correctly, perhaps, be denominated domestic dependent nations. They occupy a territory to which we assert a title independent of their will, which must take effect in point of possession when their right of possession ceases. *Meanwhile they are in a state of pupilage.* Their relation to the United States *resembles* that of a ward to his guardian. . . . These considerations go far to support the opinion, that the framers . . . had not the Indian tribes in view, when they opened the courts of the union to controversies between a state of the citizens thereof, and foreign states.[55] (emphasis mine)

Marshall based his opinion on a wholly specious argument that whites use to assert blanket title to Native North America: the so-called doctrine of discovery.[56] From this patently absurd claim to land-ownership, Marshall then argued that Native Peoples had no absolute land title, only a right of perpetual occupancy and use. Woven into this right of occupancy and use was Marshall's bright idea of acknowledging that Natives have a right to live where they have always lived but now in a state of U.S. pupilage. Thus Marshall arrived at his infamous analogy: the pupilage appropriate to Natives in relation to the United States resembled the relationship of a ward to his guardian.

To appreciate both the impact of Marshall's wardship statement on Native North America and its profound significance to termination, two aspects of pupilage must be carefully examined: (1) the cultural context of the ward and guardian relationship, and (2) how this relationship infused Native land-tenure.

According to *Black's Law Dictionary,* the legal definition of a guardian is "A person [who in this instance would be the United States] lawfully invested with the power, and charged with the duty of taking care of . . . and managing the property and rights of another person [in this instance, the domestic dependent nations], who, for defect of age, understanding, or self-control, is considered incapable of administering his own affairs."[57]

Conceding the defect of age in which a person cannot manage his or her affairs because of a physical or mental limitation, Marshall's statement about pupilage broadly connoted something insidiously defective about the Native personality, especially considering the white supremacist cultural context in which he made this statement. He all but said outright that Native Peoples inherently lacked any understanding or self-control, which automatically rendered them incapable of managing and administering their own affairs. That being so, Marshall argued, they needed a guardian.

Moreover, *incapable* evolved to mean *incompetent,* which invariably came to imply that, by both social convention and legal reasoning, Native Peoples were considered *non compos mentis* (not of sound mind). Indeed, in his groundbreaking work on federal Indian law, Felix Cohen (1942) outlined ten common usages of federal wardship that strongly suggested an image of Native Peoples as being less than competent in handling their own affairs.[58] It is from this presumed initial condition of incompetence that Euroamericans expected Native Peoples to evolve away socially. Nearly twelve decades after Marshall's decision, Zimmerman's first condition reflected what Native Peoples were supposed to evolve into: white Americans.

As to how this notion of pupilage affected Native land-tenure, after proposing his novel but spurious concept of domestic dependent nations, Marshall shrewdly laid a path for Euroamerica to redeem Native Peoples from their unfortunate state of pupilage and, by extension, their incompetence: their state of pupilage, or the ward-guardian relationship, would come to an end when a Native Nation voluntarily ceded its limited land rights to the United States, the surrogate of white society. Indeed, Euroamerica's long-established policy of ethnicide of Native communities dovetailed fortuitously with the Marshall court's 1831 *Cherokee Nation v. Georgia* ruling. Thus, acculturation into white society and Native land cessions (through treaties initially and individual allotments later) became the two criteria for determining a Native Nation's or an individual's degree of competency. By the time termination became official policy, this view of Native competency had been widely discussed and was regarded as the unquestioned conventional wisdom about Native Peoples within mainstream society.

Ironically, Native Peoples witnessed plenty of laws applied to them that made no mention of their competence or purported lack of it—like the 1885 Major Crimes Act that subjected Native Peoples to U.S. criminal jurisprudence, the 1887 General Allotment Act that imposed individual ownership of private property on Native Country, the 1924 Indian Citizenship Act that declared Native people U.S. citizens, and so forth. These Congressional Acts were a matter of public record, and they clearly put to rest any charge by whites that Native people were either un-American or incompetent.

This record notwithstanding, by the 1950s, HCR No. 108 blatantly insinuated that Native people were either evading or only assuming halfheartedly their responsibilities as American citizens. To make such insinuations, HCR No. 108 had to intentionally overlook the well-known fact that Native males had served in World Wars I and II and the Korean War. These Native veterans and their families had obviously assumed the ultimate responsibility, which even the United States' premiere cultural standard-bearer, John Wayne, had successfully evaded. But whereas Wayne's evasion of military service did nothing to tarnish his reputation, Natives were being informed through HCR No. 108's language that their service record meant nothing to white society.

For Native Country, though, the veiled charge that they were evading their responsibilities as American citizens paled in comparison to the arrogant effrontery implicit in the December 1952 summary statement of a special five-member subcommittee (all white) empowered by the House-approved resolution H.R. 698 to investigate the Bureau of Indian Affairs.[59] On the cusp of termination being declared the United States' official policy, this special subcommittee concluded in H. Rpt. No. 2503 that the U.S.-created wardship status of Native Peoples was "not acceptable to our American way of life."[60]

4. Legislative Machinations and Maneuverings

The fourth element that shaped the consequences of termination for Native Peoples was the actual dynamics through which the two ideologically based termination measures, HCR No. 108 and PL 83-280, took form. The cultural environment and homogeneity prevalent in the United States combined with the political congeniality operating within Congress and the executive branch gave every sign of support for termination. Encouraged by such potent influences, the House Subcommittee on Indian Affairs—with the help of its counterpart in the Senate and other termination-minded people—finally initiated HCR No. 108 and PL 83-280 and placed them on a legislative fast-track.

These political dynamics were well known at the time. In 1956, the University of Chicago's anthropology department sponsored a workshop on American Indian affairs that not only documented HCR No. 108's legislative history but also illustrated how the cultural homogeneity and political congeniality among congresspeople paved a clear, speedy, and opposition-free path for the resolution's introduction and subsequent passage:

> House Concurrent Resolution 108 was introduced to the House of Representatives on June 9, 1953 by Mr. [William H.] Harrison, the [Republican] Representative from Wyoming. It was read in the House and then referred to the Committee on Interior and Insular Affairs. A report on this resolution was given on July 15, 1953 by Mr. [A. L.] Miller [Republican representative] from Nebraska. After this report the resolution was referred to the House Calendar. On July 20, the resolution came to the floor of the House. Mr. Harrison was absent, so Mr. [Wesley A.] D'Ewart [Republican representative from Montana] asked for the passage of the Resolution. On July 27, the Congressional Record

DELTA

EDWARD/VALANDRA
NOT VALID FOR
**TRANSPORTATION*

OMA DL DTW
PIECE 25.00
EBC   25.00

USD   25.00

USD25.00

PASSENGER RECEIPT   00   EXCESS BAGGAGE
03NOV11 0066   US   TICKET
         OMA FTO

DL/EP

PSGR TICKET 0062360910072   THIS IS YOUR RECEIPT

                HJPEL7 /DL

VIXXXXXXXXXXXXXXX8549/09021B

1

FOR CONDITIONS OF
CONTRACT - SEE
PASSENGER TICKET AND
BAGGAGE CHECK

NOT VALID FOR TRAVEL

0 006 8256655608 1   0 006 8256655608 1

0419-6000

read that there was no objection to the resolution, but the original draft was amended to strike out the State of Iowa and the Osage Tribe of Indians of Oklahoma. The amendment was offered by Mr. [Page H.] Belcher [Republican representative from Oklahoma]. The resolution was referred to the Senate Committee on Interior and Insular Affairs on July 28, 1953; then on July 30, it was introduced to the Senate. There was no objection to the resolution and the Senate passed it on August 1, 1953.[61]

The obvious lack of any substantive debate surrounding HCR No. 108 (no public hearings to provide for input, especially Native input), the rapidity surrounding its passage (fifty-four days from introduction on 9 June 1953 to its enactment on 1 August 1953), and the absence of any dissenting votes whatsoever (unanimity of Congress) are usually glossed over by non-Indian political pundits and other apologists in terms that trivialize the policy's genocidal flavor. By overlooking these clear deficiencies in a supposedly democratic process, they try to minimize the thrust of what was actually going on.

Specifically, these pundits and apologists often try to dismiss HCR No. 108's abbreviated legislative passage by saying that it was due to nothing more than technicalities. Pointing out that the resolution represented only a "sense of Congress," for example, they argue that it did not have the effect of law and so was not taken too seriously. They also defend the legislators' conduct by saying that the resolution was introduced late in the first session of the Eighty-third Congress, and, with few days remaining before adjourning on 3 August 1953, Congress was hurrying to address other outstanding legislative matters and so hastily enacted the resolution without fully appreciating its consequences.

However, others, like Gary Orfield,[62] Vine Deloria, Jr.,[63] and Donald Fixico,[64] suggest something more calculating. Both Orfield and Fixico have noted that the resolution, along with other bills of minor nature, was placed on the House's consent calendar and on its equivalent in the Senate. Deloria also calls attention to the close collusion concerning Native matters between E. Y. Berry, chair of the House Indian Affairs subcommittee, and Senator Watkins, chair of the Senate Indian Affairs subcommittee. Shortly after the introduction of their termination program (i.e., HCR No. 108), for example, both chairs decided to hold joint subcommittee "hearings on all Indian bills so that there would be no conflicts between the Senate and House versions of legislation."[65] Deloria wrote, "A decision by the Joint Subcommittee could pass both houses of Congress simultaneously, and opposition as well as public awareness could be held to a minimum."[66]

Avoiding public dialogue served the terminationists, preventing unwelcome opposition. Not only did the homogeneous political environment, the last-minute timing of the resolution's introduction, and the greased-skids procedural manipulation favor the resolution's quick passage, but also the prevailing international and domestic scene (e.g., Korea, third world decolonialization, emerging racial unrest, McCarthyism) likely "obscured the resolution, giving it minimal attention at best."[67]

Whatever the explanation for HCR No. 108's introduction and subsequent passage, clearly mainstream society's self-created paranoia over un-Americanism led a highly insecure country to vigorously resist, oppress, or suppress all social justice movements. Because Black civil rights and Native self-determination fundamentally challenged the "self-evident truths" of white nationalist or supremacist ideology, they were obviously regarded not only as highly suspect and unwelcome but also as threatening to Americanism. In view of this one-dimensional perspective of mainstream culture and its hegemony, it is not the least bit surprising that a document like HCR No. 108 would both emerge from and be automatically supported by the virtually all-white-male institution called Congress.[68]

Besides the inherent commonality of race and culture among both the House and Senate Interior and Insular Affairs committees, a further characteristic held in common by the two committees' memberships was, as mentioned before, the presence of a substantial Native land base and population within their respective states. Specifically, twenty of the twenty-one members of the 1953 House and Senate Subcommittees on Indian Affairs were from sixteen states that included about 88 percent (48,234,813 acres) of the Native land base and approximately 45 percent (225,869) of the reservation-based population.[69]

At a time when U.S. leaders were making rampant cold war charges of un-Americanism, they were glorifying a mindset that brought out society's long-held racial hostility, xenophobic fears, and social intolerance toward nonwhite populations—that is, whoever failed to fit the self-proclaimed white "norm." This social environment undoubtedly influenced how the subcommittee memberships perceived and understood the country's "Indian Problem" and the way to solve it, that is, to compel Indians to become "Americans."[70]

In other words, the apologists' arguments for what happened in Congress in the summer of 1953 fall far short of addressing the dynamics surrounding the termination legislation's passage. Indeed, if HCR No. 108 signified no more than a symbolic sense of Congress, how do the apologists account for PL 83-280 (appendix A), the U.S. law passed two weeks later that actualized HCR No. 108's "symbolic sense" as a full-blown, official policy of termination?

Public Law 83-280

Accounts of the passage of Public Law 83-280, then known as H.R. 1063, identify this particular law as the termination-conceived twin of HCR No. 108. Much like HCR No. 108's legislative history, H.R. 1063 sailed through the supposedly turbulent political waters of Congress and its committees unopposed. Although President Eisenhower expressed some "grave doubts as to the wisdom of certain provisions contained in H.R. 1063"[71] and voiced his objections to the bill because two particular sections (6 and 7) failed to include "a requirement of full consultation to ascertain the wishes and desires of the Indians and of final Federal approval,"[72] Eisenhower nonetheless signed the bill into law.

Yet his veto could have stopped its passage. Indeed, of the 181 bills that Eisenhower vetoed during his eight-year reign, Congress was successful only two times out of eleven in overriding his vetoes. Arguably, had Eisenhower vetoed H.R. 1063, the termination program would have been effectively curtailed long enough for Native Peoples to mobilize a preemptive campaign against further measures similar to H.R. 1063. At the very least, Native, state, and U.S. relations would have taken a much different course from what the Native population actually experienced.

For Natives, because termination increasingly resembled extermination, they opposed H.R. 1063—even more so when it was signed into law and became known as PL 83-280—with an emotional intensity far greater than non-Natives could have ever anticipated or appreciated. Natives had a highly charged response to PL 83-280 for three critically important reasons. First, the law radically altered a long-settled—albeit highly contentious—civil and criminal jurisdiction scheme between individual states and Native Nations. Second, though the recently approved HCR No. 108 sought to "Americanize" Native Peoples, the resolution—at least ostensibly—promised Natives a right to be intimately involved with matters directly affecting their lives. Yet in PL 83-280, any implied involvement by Natives was missing, and indeed the legislative process had included limited Native involvement. Instead, the highly suspect proceedings surrounding PL 83-280's enactment marginalized Native and amplified non-Native voices. Finally, once termination was exposed as having little to do with Americanizing Native Peoples, the real versus the purported motivations behind PL 83-280 became unmistakably clear.

As the bill worked its way through Congress, various termination-oriented congressional and state documents fraught with race-based demonizations of Native communities were used to justify the bill's passage.

The first reason Natives opposed PL 83-280 so vehemently was that the law would change the status of Native Nations relative to state and federal governments. Again, the history of these relationships goes back to Marshall's court. In *Cherokee Nation v. Georgia,* Chief Justice Marshall equivocated about the obvious fact that the Cherokee people are a nation in the full meaning of that term. Instead, Marshall decreed that Native Peoples are dependent domestic nations. Accordingly, he wrote, Native Peoples and Euroamericans have a peculiar relationship "unlike that of any two peoples in existence."[73] Given Marshall's analogy of ward and guardian, this peculiar relationship invariably became known over the years as ward status or wardship.

Yet the "domestic dependent nation" characterization brought with it various critically consequential meanings. One of these concerns the oppressive political space created by the status of so-called domestic, dependent nation. Marshall's second infamous decision about the Cherokee Nation, *Worcester v. Georgia,* established the parameters of a state's jurisdiction with respect to the politically independent Native Peoples, who had now become domestic dependent nations.

On 7 July 1831, Georgia's militia entered Cherokee territory and arrested several non-Cherokee people, including a man named Samuel Worcester. Tried, convicted, and imprisoned by Georgia, Worcester's legal counsel filed suit in federal court against his detainment by the then slave-sanctioning state of Georgia. On a successful appeal from the lower federal court to the U.S. Supreme Court, Marshall again delivered the majority opinion: on 28 February 1832, he ruled that Georgia "ought" to release Worcester. The Cherokee Nation's unique, federally recognized political status nullified Georgia's state power to arrest Worcester:

> The Cherokee Nation, then, is a distinct community, occupying its own territory, with boundaries accurately described, in which the laws of Georgia can have no force, and which the citizens of Georgia have no right to enter, but with the assent of the Cherokees themselves, or in conformity with treaties, and with acts of Congress. . . . It is the opinion of this court and that the judgment of the superior court for the county of Gwinnett, in the state of Georgia, condemning Samuel A. Worcester to hard labour, in the penitentiary of the state of Georgia, for four years, was pronounced by that court under colour of a law which is void, as being repugnant to the constitution, treaties, and laws of the United States, and ought, therefore, to be reversed and annulled.[74]

These two Supreme Court decisions involving the Cherokee Nation, *Cherokee Nation v. Georgia* and *Worcester v. Georgia*, quintessentially framed the relationship between federal and state governments and between the two separate levels of governance in the United States (national and state) and Native Nations. First, the federal, not state, governmental authority was determined to be controlling whenever matters regarding Native affairs arose.[75] Second, Native sovereignty, which preexisted the formation of the United States, automatically precluded any state from arbitrarily extending its authority over any Native homelands.

As a result of this jurisdictional scheme, Native Nations held a sovereign place above state jurisdiction. Native authority preempted a state's laws, which meant that state laws had no effect whatsoever within the boundaries of any Native homeland.[76] Therefore, when H.R. 1063 was enacted and signed into law by Eisenhower as PL 83-280, it clearly stood on its head a long-standing, long-negotiated corpus of Native-U.S. relations.

Radically altering twelve decades of established law, PL 83-280 now allowed a state—with federal acquiescence pursuant to sections 2, 4, 6, and 7—to assert its jurisdiction regardless of Native objections. When H.R. 1063 was first introduced on 6 January 1953 by Norris Poulson, a House Representative from California, it initially "would have extended the criminal laws of the State of California to all Indian country within that State."[77] The bill subsequently was referred to the House Committee on Interior and Insular Affairs—twenty-nine of whose thirty members were white. Since the bill involved a Native matter, the fifteen-member all-white House Subcommittee on Indian Affairs assumed the legislative lead for the bill.

Between the House subcommittee hearings on H.R. 1063 that began on 15 June 1953 to when it was finally signed into law on 15 August 1953,[78] the bill underwent two significant amendments. In addition to mandating a transfer of criminal jurisdiction to California (sections 2 and 4), a first amendment sought to mandate a similar transfer for six other states—a change that Orme Lewis, the assistant interior secretary, put in his 7 July 1953 letter to A. L. Miller, a House Representative from Nebraska:

> The [House] subcommittee [on Indian Affairs] also took action [on 29 June 1953] to amend H.R. 1063, a bill to confer civil and criminal jurisdiction on the State of California over Indians on their reservations in that State, to make it of general application rather than limit it to California and the subcommittee requested that representatives of this [the Interior] Department cooperate with the subcommittee in determining the States in which the amended bill should be made applicable. . . . The Bureau of Indian Affairs of this Depart-

ment has consulted with State and local authorities and with the Indian groups on the question of transfer of civil and criminal jurisdiction on the States . . . : California, Minnesota, Nebraska, Nevada, Oregon, Washington, and Wisconsin. Bills for each of the States except Nebraska and Washington are presently pending before Congress.[79]

Although Lewis's letter stated that the Interior Department had "consulted" with the Native communities in states where a mandated transfer of civil and criminal jurisdiction was being contemplated, Marvin J. Sonosky, an attorney for several Native governments, proved otherwise. Eight years after Native Country had been thoroughly subjected to the devastating effects of PL 83-280, Sonosky delivered an indictment of what ranks among the most shameful annals of congressional behavior—thus explaining why Native Peoples overwhelmingly and vehemently detested PL 83-280. In a 13 April 1961 letter lobbying Montana's two senators, Mike Mansfield and Lee Metcalf, to support amending PL 83-280 to incorporate the Native consent clause, Sonosky casts some heavy doubts about whether the Interior Department fully consulted its Native charges:

> As originally introduced, the bill [H.R. 1063] which became Public Law 280 was [pursuant to section 2 and 4] limited to extending state civil and criminal jurisdiction to the State of California. During the hearings, four states were added to the bill, Minnesota, Nebraska, Oregon, and Wisconsin. No general notice was issued to Indian tribes in the five states affected, or elsewhere. Some tribes became aware of the bill and made objections. For that reason, as finally enacted, P.L. 280 expressly excepts from its provisions, the Red Lake Reservation in Minnesota, the Warm Springs Reservation in Oregon, and the Menominee Reservation in Wisconsin.[80]

Hundreds of other Native Nations were not as fortunate as these three to have their concerns expressed and to be exempted from the federal mandate. As Sonosky stated unequivocally, the Native voice was extremely marginalized in the white-dominated decision-making process that turned H.R. 1063 into law.

Furthermore, just as Zimmerman used the BIA administrative unit to hide or at least minimize the impact of his 1947 plan for Native Country, so too the state as an administrative unit was now being used to hide or minimize the devastating impact on Native Country of H.R. 1063's application. Using the state as the administrative unit for Native affairs seemed to non-Natives less blatantly predatory and hence more emotionally palatable. In reality, the five mandated states would assume jurisdiction over 161 reservation-based

Native governments, whose combined land base was 6,364 mi.[2] or 4,072,960 acres. For comparison, the land involved was larger than three of the smallest forty-eight states. In other words, the law peremptorily expected Native governments to automatically and involuntarily relinquish their self-governance and quite possibly their land bases to the surrounding non-Native communities.

According to Sonosky's disturbing April letter to both Montana senators, a second amendment to H.R. 1063 added sections 6 and 7. These sections would soon have a huge impact on the Lakota, as well as on hundreds of other Native Nations that did not have an opportunity to appear before the House Subcommittee on Indian Affairs and directly voice their views on or opposition to H.R. 1063. Sonosky writes:

> On the morning of the final committee hearings [on 15 July 1953],[81] the bill [H.R. 1063] was limited to five states. In the afternoon, the committee reconvened, and at that time sections 6 and 7 were inserted [by Representative Hugh Butler (R-NE)] conferring the consent of the United States on any of the other 43 states "to assume jurisdiction at such time as the people of the state shall by affirmative legislative action obligate and bind the state to assumption thereof."[82] The [Interior] Department made no formal report on sections 6 and 7, but the views of its legislative representatives were well known and we understand those representatives were present with the committee when sections 6 and 7 were added.[83]
>
> Indian tribes of the 43 states . . . were not given any opportunity to be heard. On its face, this was a denial of the principle of self-determination that every American takes for granted. It seems ironic that an issue involving this very right should be taken from the Indians without a hearing or consent.[84]

H.R. 1063, particularly the two sections (6 and 7) inserted by Butler, eventually proved anything but noncontroversial. Sections 2 and 4 of PL 83-280 already mandated a transfer of complete jurisdiction (hence "mandated states") from the federal to the state government. To widen the net for termination beyond the originally mandated states, section 6 concerning option-disclaimer states and section 7 concerning option-nondisclaimer states allowed a state to assume jurisdiction at its leisure. In other words, all nonmandated states had the option to pursue termination whenever they so desired (hence "option states").

How an option state assumed jurisdiction over Native Country depended on the conditions under which a territory was originally admitted as a state. Several states, including South Dakota, had strict constitutional limitations concerning Native Peoples that posed legal obstacles to termination. Prior to Butler's solution of adding sections 6 and 7 to H.R. 1063, Lewis's 7 July 1953 letter to Miller raised these "legal impediments":

> It appears that there are legal impediments to the transfer of jurisdiction over Indians on their reservations in the case of a number of States. An examination of the Federal statutes and State constitutions indicates that enabling acts for the following states, and in consequence the constitutions of these States, contain express disclaimers of jurisdiction. These States are Arizona, Montana, New Mexico, North Dakota, Oklahoma, South Dakota, Utah, and Washington. In these cases the enabling acts required the people of the proposed States expressly to disclaim jurisdiction over Indian land and that, until the Indian title was extinguished, the lands were to remain under the absolute jurisdiction and control of Congress of the United States. In each instance the State constitution contains an appropriate disclaimer. It would appear in each case, therefore, that the Congress would be required to give its consent and the people of each State would be required to amend the State constitution before the State legally could assume jurisdiction.[85]

Fundamentally, PL 83-280 was federal consent legislation, that is, it gave states the federal government's consent to assume state jurisdiction over any Native homeland. To put it bluntly, it made legal the overthrow of Native governments, the stealing of their lands, and the extermination of Natives as Peoples and cultures.

Yet despite the considerable precedent for these white behaviors toward Native Nations over the last five centuries, as the Interior Department revealed to the subcommittee, there were actually some legal impediments in place that had to be overcome if the terminationists wanted to cloak this latest blend of extermination and heist in a shroud of legality. These legal impediments raised the question of whether the federal government and the disclaimer states could, respectively, transfer and assume immediate jurisdiction over Native Country without meeting additional requirements.

Specifically, four of the eight disclaimer states—Montana, North Dakota, South Dakota, and Washington—were subject to an 1889 federal law. This law, among other things, enabled the people of those territories to politically organize for eventual statehood, but they had to meet certain conditions before the state could be admitted to the union. One of them was for each state convention to constitutionally disclaim all right and title to Native Country:

That the people inhabiting said proposed states do agree and declare that they forever disclaim all right and title ... to all lands lying within said limits owned or held by any Indian or Indian tribes; and that until the title thereto shall have been extinguished by the United States, the same shall be and remain subject to the disposition of the United States and said Indian lands shall remain under the absolute jurisdiction and control of the Congress of the United States.[86]

In response to this federal condition, the territories in question adopted the appropriate language in their soon-to-be state constitutions. In this language, they agreed to disclaim all right and title to Native soil until such time as the United States extinguished Native title. By so doing, the people of a disclaimer state concomitantly acknowledged Congress's jurisdictional supremacy over Native affairs. Congress also stipulated that, short of its extinguishing Native title outright, such disclaimers were revocable only on the joint consent of the United States and the people of a disclaimer state. The statutory consent language of section 6 was added to H.R. 1063, therefore, to help remove what the federal government viewed as a legal impediment. In other words, the terminationists had to resolve the somewhat complicated issue of how to get around a state's constitutional disclaimer clause. Section 6 reads:

Notwithstanding the provisions of any Enabling Act for the admission of a State, the consent of the United States is hereby given to the people of any State to amend, where necessary, their State constitution or existing statutes, as the case may be, to remove any legal impediment to the assumption of civil and criminal jurisdiction in accordance with the provisions of this Act: *Provided,* That the provisions of this Act shall not become effective with respect to such assumption of jurisdiction by any such state until the people thereof have appropriately amended their State constitution or statutes as the case may be.[87]

By allowing the people of a disclaimer state to modify the offending language in their constitutions that prevented them from asserting state jurisdiction over their Native neighbors' lands, Congress formally gave the go-ahead for these particular states to act. Whereas the people of a disclaimer state had to adhere to both a state constitutional and a federal enabling standard, nondisclaimer states did not have to work so hard. They simply had to enact a law accepting jurisdiction over Native Country. According to PL 83-280's section 7:

> The consent of the United States is hereby given to any other State not having jurisdiction with respect to criminal offenses or civil causes of action, or with respect to both, as provided for in this Act, to assume jurisdiction at such time and in such manner as the people of the State shall, by affirmative legislative action, obligate and bind the State to assumption thereof.[88]

With twenty days remaining before the first session of the Eighty-third Congress adjourned, Butler used the deceitful and underhanded legislative tactic of inserting sections 6 and 7 at the last minute, guaranteeing that Native participation would be severely minimized. To cover their bases, the terminationists also arranged for H.R. 1063 to be placed on the noncontroversial bills calendars of both the House and the Senate. Hence, within a matter of hours of the final subcommittee hearing, the subcommittee's terminationists imperiously and unilaterally altered the entire course of Native-U.S. policy and history by adding the mandatory and option provisions.

With terms suggesting the singular, such as *state* or *Indian Country*, PL 83-280's statutory language evidently attempted to minimize the law's profound impact on Native populations. Yet anyone who examined the law's consequences in detail would have realized that the impact on Native Peoples would be enormous and devastating. Indeed, closer inspection of the documents surrounding termination and the bill's passage suggests that Congress was more than a little confused over its termination policy. To illustrate both PL 83-280's immense impact and Congress's general confusion about termination's impact on Native Country, Table 2 shows that 355 reservations—arranged according to Zimmerman's three groups and a fourth non-Zimmerman group—had suddenly and arbitrarily become subject to the various sections of PL 83-280.

While Zimmerman had outlined at least four conditions that were to be used to decide whether to reduce or eliminate federal services on a reservation-by-reservation basis, the terminationists now completely discarded these four conditions and turned the termination juggernaut on all Native Peoples indiscriminately. PL 83-280's mandatory and option sections authorized states to claim jurisdiction without ever investigating whether the Native communities located in the state were economically and socially ready for the elimination of federal services.

Apparently the terminationists, drunk with the brazenness of the crime they were plotting, no longer felt a need to even feign a concern for Native well-being, as Zimmerman's conditions might have done, and could instead elevate state interests over that of Native Peoples without compunction.

Table 2. Zimmerman's 1947 Grouping and Non-Zimmerman Grouping by Corresponding Number of Reservations and Acreage (in Millions) Associated with PL 83-280

Type[a]	Group I	Group II	Group III	Group IV	Total
M	117 (1.53)	19 (1.82)	—	24 (0.22)	160 (3.57)
OD	3 (1.06)	10 (8.09)	64 (35.52)	40 (1.93)	117 (46.58)
OND	9 (0.42)	15 (2.94)	21 (1.91)	26 (0.94)	71 (6.21)
OD/ND	—	—	3 (0.67)	1 (0.03)	4 (0.70)
OD/M	—	—	1 (0.24)	—	1 (0.24)
OND/M	—	—	—	2 (< 0.005)	2 (< 0.005)
	129 (3.01)	44 (12.85)	89 (38.32)	93 (3.12)	355 (57.30)

Source: H. Rpt. No. 2503 (1953)

a. Type is either section 2 and 4 or Mandatory (M), section 6 or Option-Disclaimer (OD), section 7 or Option-Non-Disclaimer (OND), or combinations thereof.

According to Zimmerman's 1947 list, an overwhelming number of Native Peoples would not be ready for reduction or elimination of federal services for at least two or more years (Groups II, III, and including Group IV), yet six years later, reservations were being abruptly terminated according to the mandatory sections of PL 83-280. The remaining reservations had no law protecting them from the terminationists' greedy ambitions. Depending on the volatile political and racial climate of a state, reservations could be terminated at a moment's notice.

Indeed, elevating states over Native Nations produced unanticipated logistical hardships for the latter. When, for instance, a particular Native Nation's boundary overlapped multiple states, that Nation found itself potentially subject to any combination of PL 83-280's sections as they applied to the different states. The Ute Mountain Reservation's boundaries, for example, extended into Colorado, a section 7 state, and into Utah, a section 6 state. The Ute people easily could have found themselves without jurisdiction over almost 90 percent of their lands if Colorado, by enacting a law, had decided to invoke PL 83-280.

Also, the Dine Nation's boundaries extended into three section 6 states: Arizona, New Mexico, and Utah. The Dine people had to face the constant concern about whether the three states would, either individually or collectively, invoke PL 83-280. If they did, the Dine government would be forced into an expensive lobbying effort to prevent each state from removing the disclaimer clause found in their respective state constitutions. If the states were successful in removing their disclaimer clauses, the Dine would then have to lobby against any state jurisdiction bill that may be introduced—all of which would demand considerable human and financial resources. While the Termination Era is in remission, Native Nations must still contend with PL 83-280 and the possibility of states invoking it, because it remains on the books as current federal law.

A second reason for Native Peoples' highly visible and vehement opposition to PL 83-280 concerned its greatest weakness: the law allowed a state—in an arbitrary and dictatorial fashion—to assume jurisdiction over Native Country without ever obtaining Native consent. At their discretion, non-mandatory states could merely enact a law or amend their constitutions and then assume complete jurisdiction over any number of reservations that lay within the state's boundaries. This state-level blackout on the critical matter of obtaining Native consent reaffirms how categorically the Native voice was marginalized in the entire termination process.

The only way Native Peoples could have been assured that their consent would be obtained before any state could claim jurisdiction was for Congress to incorporate a clause to that effect. However, the legislative history of H.R. 1063, much like that of HCR No. 108, shows that Native Peoples' participation was deliberately kept to a minimum. Native involvement in the bill or reaction to it appears largely after the bill passed and became law, precisely because Native Peoples were intentionally excluded from the legislative process at every step.

Perhaps equally egregious to the Native Peoples' marginalization was HCR No. 108's implied promise of political equality. Because integration or assimilation of Native Peoples into mainstream society was a goal that whites wanted and were trying to impose on Natives, according to the most basic, mainstream conceptions of democracy, Congress was particularly obliged to include, not exclude, Native Peoples from the decision-making process. HCR No. 108 even stated that it was U.S. policy to Americanize the un-American Native by granting Native individuals all the rights and prerogatives of U.S. citizenship. Yet by denying Native Peoples a forum in which to express their views on a law that politically attacked the cultural cohesion of tribes—the core of Native society—the termination policy immediately lost all claims to democratic legitimacy and exposed its deep-seated hypocrisy.

Because a Native consent provision was entirely missing from PL 83-280, Congress rendered all of Native Country totally dependent on the goodwill of whites. At the state level, if a state chose to honor the democratic ideal, it could naturally seek Native consent. Historically, though, goodwill by whites toward Indians was far from dependable. In a candid moment while consolidating the plenary power of Congress over that of the thirty-eight states, the 1886 U.S. Supreme Court left very little doubt about the unreliability of goodwill toward Native Peoples among white state populations. By describing the chronic pattern of ill will toward Native Peoples, the court cited the racist behavior that existed in states as grounds for prohibiting any state from pursuing expansionist designs over Native affairs:

> These Indian tribes *are* the wards of the nation. They are communities *dependent* on the United States. . . . They owe no allegiance to the States, and receive no protection. Because of the local ill feeling, the people of the States where they [the Native Peoples] are found are often their deadliest enemies.[89]

Arguably, the Court owed its 1886 comment about states' intolerance toward Native populations to the presidency of Andrew Jackson. As U.S. president, Jackson blatantly promoted states' interests over Native interests when he not only sided with Georgia against the Cherokee but also advocated the ethnic-cleansing policy of the 1830 Indian Removal Act. This infamous act was responsible for the forced removal of all Native Peoples living east of the Mississippi River to territories west of the river. Understandably, Native Peoples were not comfortable with having to depend on local goodwill, simply because there was so little of it displayed throughout the history of U.S.-Native relations. Indeed, nearly seven decades after the 1886 Supreme Court statement, Harold Fey of the *Christian Century* wryly cast termination policy in the larger frame of Native trust toward white Americans:

> Why don't the Indians trust us? We mean well toward them. We want them to succeed. Indeed, we would be glad if the Indians were just like ourselves, and what more could they desire than that? We are not like some nations we could mention—deceivers, slave-drivers, treaty-breakers. We are upright people, and it irritates us a little to have to say so. Some of us are in the habit of referring to the United States as a Christian nation. So if the Indian does not trust us, it must be because he has some unfortunate defect in his own character, such as innate suspicion. If so, that is something we should help overcome. . . . These things we say to ourselves to calm the uneasiness which clings to the fact that we are not trusted by the original Americans, who have known us longer than anybody else.[90]

HCR No. 108's rationale of Americanizing Native Peoples obviously had no real substantive meaning for members of either the House or the Senate Subcommittees on Indian Affairs, otherwise how could they move from applying criminal jurisdiction to one state (California) to applying *both* criminal and civil jurisdiction to *all* states without ever inviting Natives into the process?

If being an American citizen entitles a person to express his or her views, concerns, or opinions on legislation that materially affects that person to a congressional representative, the legislative history of H.R. 1063 shows that Native Peoples were wholly denied even this basic privilege or prerogative of U.S. citizenship. Whatever narrow legitimacy Congress bestowed on HCR No. 108 initially through "scientific" reports and political, "free the Indian" rhetoric disappeared in the whirlwind of Congress's thoroughly undemocratic, dictatorial conduct.

The third reason that Native Peoples intensely opposed termination policy and were extremely anxious about how Congress and the states were planning to put it into operation arose from how the terminationists characterized Native Peoples. Their words went beyond cultural blindness to outright race-based demonization. Arguably, charging Native Peoples with "un-Americanism" was one form of demonizing them. HCR No. 108 ostensibly corrected this un-Americanism by ending ward status and supposedly bestowing on Native individuals all the rights, privileges, prerogatives, and responsibilities of U.S. citizenship. However, demonizing Native Peoples went far deeper than simply labeling the hundreds of Native cultures as un-American; overt racism permeated the termination mindset.

E. Y. Berry and James Haley—much like the previously mentioned team of Butler and Reed who oversaw the termination program in New York—represented one of several formidable cultural bonds and political alliances among subcommittee members that affected the course of termination's legislative history. Berry was a northern Republican congressman from a rural state whose district's economy largely depended on the cattle industry. James Haley was a southern Democrat from Florida whose fame before being elected to Congress was that he had managed and then owned the Ringling Brothers Barnum and Bailey Circus. Despite their party and sectional differences, these two men shared a common cultural outlook that unquestionably shaped their image of Native Peoples and hence how they treated Native Nations.

At times, these committee friendships could lead to outbursts of rampant racism that exposed the inherent paradoxes of U.S. termination policy—open contempt and disregard for Native Peoples overlaid with appeals to respect, equality, and self-determination. For example, when the Missouri River was slated to be dammed and Lakota lands were soon to be flooded as a result, compensation for the loss of prime lands became a major concern for the Lakota/Dakota People of the Crow Creek, Lower Brule, Standing Rock, Yankton, and Cheyenne River reservations. In dealing with Congress, the leadership of the Cheyenne River Sioux Tribe quickly learned how to make "effective" presentations before congressional subcommittees on Indian affairs; they had to play and perform to the subcommittees' racist images of Indians:

> The other lesson was that the members of Congress want to talk to "real Indians," and that they were much happier when they were being addressed by stereotypic full-bloods in feathered headdress and beaded regalia than when they had to deal with less typical looking Indians, such as Frank Duch-eneaux, who wore business suits, smoked cigars, and talked like a lawyer. In order to satisfy this congressional whim, the tribal negotiators decided that John Little Cloud would speak in Sioux at the hearings and that Alex Chasing Hawk would then translate Little Cloud's remarks into broken English, *even though both men could speak perfectly good English.* The Congressmen were delighted. While the tribal negotiators succeeded in putting on a good show at the hearings, they were not as successful at getting the men in Washington to approve their requests for compensation.[91]

The Congressmen's racist fancies made a mockery of termination's purported goal to assimilate Natives into mainstream society. After all, if the people of the United States truly desired that Native Peoples become so-called Americans just like them, why perpetuate a Ringling-Brothers circus atmosphere that only reinforced the un-American image or lifestyle of Native Peoples that whites found so intolerable?

Moreover, this un-American image fed into one of the most overused and highly suspect rationales for transferring jurisdiction to the states: the claim that the Native personality was inherently lawless. This justification was increasingly used in the late 1940s when termination policy began taking shape. The 4 June 1948 S. Rpt. No. 1489 concerning the transfer of criminal jurisdiction to New York, for example, argued that reservation-administered law enforcement was ineffective. As evidence, the report included a 27 January 1948 letter to Butler from George Grobe, the U.S. attorney for the western district of New York. Grobe relied heavily on common white stereotypes about Natives as sufficient grounds for extending N.Y. state criminal jurisdiction throughout the Haudenosaunee Confederacy. Describing how the presence of just one law enforcement officer briefly but effectively preserved order on a reservation in western New York, Grobe noted what followed when the officer's position was eliminated due to budget cutbacks:

> Recently as a result of the economy drive the position of the special officer was abolished and we are now back where we were before; petty offenses are committed on the reservation and nothing much is being done about it. Recently

police officers of the local community attempted to arrest several Indians who were driving a car while intoxicated; the Indians got over the reservation line; one of them got out of the car and shot at the local officers; it was just fate the officer was not killed. Indians get drunk and beat their women and get into fights. Recently a white man was severely beaten by drunken Indians. Theoretically these petty offenses are within the jurisdiction of so-called Indian courts but there is no provision made for their punishment even if such were tried by said local Indian courts. It is a deplorable situation.[92]

This portrayal of Natives as fleeing arrest, shooting at officers, beating their women, getting into fights, and, on occasion, beating white men invoked an all-too-common image of drunken Indians with the not-so-subtle overtone of Indians as savages. Even more unsettling to whites than the specter of an unpredictable, drunken savage was the upshot of Grobe's field report: little to nothing was being done to punish these Native outrages, which were obviously spilling over into the nearby white communities. As the 1950 enactment of PL 80-881—an early termination law that affected Native populations in New York—shows, such a stereotype-laden report incites mainstream society's racist emotions and galvanizes them to do something about the purported lawlessness plaguing Native Country.

If the "wild" Indian stereotype were not enough to warrant imposing western standards of law and order on Indian Country, whites invoked charges of Native incompetence. The ITF law-and-order section of its October 1948 report to the Hoover Commission stated that the "system of law and order on Indian reservations today is unsatisfactory."[93] The report listed four problems as serious deficiencies that afflicted reservation systems of law and order: (1) the lack of extradition authority (when a resident Native offender leaves the reservation to another jurisdiction, he or she cannot be extradited); (2) the leniency of Native justice toward its offenders; (3) the susceptibility of Native justices to community pressure; and (4) the lack of adequate financing of Native justice systems.

None of these four deficiencies were insurmountable, and the failure to correct them exposed the fact that neither the state nor the federal governments were willing to work in concert with Native governments on matters of law and order. This unwillingness strongly suggests that the whites' charges were nothing more than culture-war criticisms of a Native community's traditional standards for administering justice.

The ITF's first-cited deficiency of Native systems of law and order—the extradition argument—stated that, "Now that reservations are not a place of confinement and Indians are coming and going freely, the culprit is likely to be gone before tribal policemen and tribal courts can do anything about his offense."[94] But there is nothing novel about this extradition problem, neither is it uniquely a problem for Native law enforcement systems.

As Article 4 of the U.S. Constitution shows, the problem invariably arises between different jurisdictions.[95] A politico-legal instrument between a Native and state governments regarding extradition could be negotiated. Historically, extradition problems arose between Native Country and states either when a state flatly refused, or even failed, to consider such an agreement with a Native government for the return of offenders fleeing from each other's jurisdictions or when state officials demanded one-sided conditions favoring greater state intrusion, rendering reciprocity a joke. Lack of easy extradition is an absurd argument for dispensing with Native self-governance.

The second and third deficiencies regarding lenient sentencing and susceptibility to community pressure are not novel arguments either. In fact, the white-run criminal justice system is vulnerable to these charges. American systems of law and order are notorious for their white-favoring patterns. A white person is often granted leniency not ordinarily given to a person of color, even though both might have committed the same offense.[96] Moreover, community pressure in the form of jury nullification has acquitted many a white of a crime. Because mainstream society has long engaged in the very practices that it charged Native Country with, such statements as "penalties are light and lightly applied by tribal judges;"[97] "Indians do not like to make enemies among their own people; [and] much of tribal attitudes and ethics still survives"[98] were wholly unfair criticisms of Native cultural norms.

From a Native perspective, these statements are offensive, revealing more about whites' unwillingness to appreciate or respect any culture but their own than about Native justice systems. Of the first statement, for example, unlike western justice, traditional Native justice is consistently more rehabilitative than punitive. Of the second and third statements, traditional kinship systems are integral to an offender's community rehabilitation.

These charges against Native justice systems were called into question by a later Congressional study. After conducting an extensive 1957 investigation designed to survey the status of Native judicial systems subsequent to HCR No. 108, William Brophy issued a lengthy 1966 report, *The Indian, America's Unfinished Business: Report of the Commission on the Rights, Liberties, and Responsibilities of the American Indian*. Brophy's report included an enlightening discussion of Native courts. Contrary to the ITF's previous criticisms about their deficiencies and unsatisfactory effectiveness, Brophy gave Native justice systems a positive verdict: "In view of the hundreds of statutes adopted and the thousands of trials conducted each year [in Native courts], remarkably few cases challenging the constitutionality of a tribal law or of the judicial proceedings have reached the outside courts."[99]

After giving the BIA its "due" for ensuring that Native laws were human rights–friendly and therefore accounting somewhat for the low incidence of Native cases reaching non-Native courts, the report went on to attribute this low incidence to the fact that in justice administration, "There is a substantial element of fairness in the tribal process."[100] Since Native traditions were far more concerned with fairness than with punishment, the report implicitly affirmed the effectiveness of Native traditions, which terminationists had self-servingly condemned as worthless.

Among the weaknesses in Indian law-and-order systems that the ITF report cited, only the lack of fiscal resources to adequately administer Native justice was of real consequence.[101] In terms of federal allocation, the Hoover Commission report noted that at least half the BIA's appropriation in the previous two decades was related to welfare.

Two years prior to the release of the Hoover Commission report, Zimmerman's testimony proposed ways to reduce both the number of employees and the expenses of the Indian service. Zimmerman impressed upon the committee his cost-saving argument that the BIA budget and its personnel increased or decreased in proportion to the number of Native Peoples receiving federal services. Zimmerman noted that if federal services were immediately withdrawn from Group I, 505 BIA employees could be eliminated from the federal payroll. With one move, the BIA could both reduce its bureaucracy and increase its savings.[102]

Accordingly, if the fiscal 1947 BIA budget of $44,376,898 were equivalent to a per-capita $88 per Native person, and if federal services for a Native population of 55,963 (Group I) were hypothetically eliminated as Zimmerman's plan proposed, the BIA would realize savings of $4,924,744. However, rather than reappropriate that surplus into reservation law-and-order programs, which already received less than half of the BIA's appropriation, the surplus would most likely be eliminated from next year's BIA budget. Clearly, downsizing the BIA became a politically expedient termination goal for which Native Peoples were being held responsible. Yet the terminationists' manufacture of this cost-cutting argument showed not only how irrationally divorced from real-life consequences the thinking was in Congress but also how this irrational mindset was guiding policy makers.

Interestingly, despite the lack of financial support for reservation law-and-order programs, the ITF had admitted in its October 1948 report that "Indian communities have 'gotten by' during the past years chiefly because there is little malicious or premeditated crime among Indian people."[103] In other words, the ITF had to grudgingly admit that Native traditions had enabled Indian communities to be less dependent on financial support because their traditions provided effective deterrents to crime, keeping the supposedly high Native crime rate that Euroamericans imagined in abeyance. Ironically, the ITF managed to twist even this fact of the lack of Native crime into providing further evidence of the incompetency of Native courts.

Congress was clearly in the mood to downsize the BIA by reducing or eliminating services. The question was, which services were to be reduced or eliminated? By making law-and-order appropriations compete with other BIA service areas, like education or realty, for less than half of the BIA's total budget, the ITF report actually made Congress show its hand, namely, that law and order was not as much of a congressional priority as terminationists would have everyone believe. Listing the lack of financial resources as a Native deficiency in order to promote state jurisdiction was a blatantly disingenuous argument, especially when it became obvious that the ITF willingly supported giving an adequate amount of federal aid to states that would assume criminal jurisdiction over reservations.

With the jurisdiction-to-the-states mold already cast a few years earlier when H.R. 1063 was being considered, terminationists, by reiterating ITF's primary but unconvincing law-and-order arguments in S. Rpt. No. 699, quickly stepped in to fill that mold:

> As a practical matter, the enforcement of law and order among the Indians in the Indian Country has been left largely to the Indian groups themselves. In many states, tribes are not adequately organized to perform that function; consequently, there has been created a hiatus in law-enforcement authority that could best be remedied by conferring criminal jurisdiction on States indicating an ability and willingness to accept such responsibility.[104]

As for the transfer of civil jurisdiction to the states, the report simply concluded that the "Indians of several States have reached a stage of acculturation and development that makes desirable extension of State civil jurisdiction to the Indian country within their borders."[105] Remarkably, of the 226 Native reservations that Zimmerman initially observed as requiring at least two or more years of acculturation—depending on their respective scale of social evolutionary development—somehow all progressed so rapidly and uniformly that, within six years, Congress deemed wholesale termination appropriate.

Because racist-inspired reasoning often justified termination and its spoils, the fact that a 57,314,364–acre Native Country remained to be exploited was not lost on termination advocates. Indeed, South Dakota's successive legislative attempts to invoke PL 83-280 in 1957, 1959, 1961, and 1963—in spite of the Lakota's repeated resistance to these attempts—reveals that white Americans were well aware of what was at stake. Not since 1887, when the General Allotment Act resulted in a five-decade loss of approximately two-thirds of 138 million acres of Native soil, had whites finagled such an unparalleled opportunity to seize control of Native Country's greatest tangible asset, its land.

In South Dakota, PL 83-280 unquestionably aided and abetted the all-white state legislature in trying to unilaterally assume criminal and civil jurisdiction over Lakota communities. Given South Dakota's multiple attempts to take over Lakota Country, PL 83-280 initiated a course that forced the Lakota into a struggle of historic political proportions. To provide the social context for appreciating their resistance to termination, the next chapter examines the Lakota's termination-ready status.

Notes

1. After nearly a generation, HCR No. 108 was finally repealed in the mid-1980s.

2. Hoover Commission, *Social Security*, 63. The Indian Task Force members were George Graham, a professor of political science at Cornell University; John R. Nichols, the president of the New Mexico College of Agriculture and Mechanic Arts (later the commissioner of Indian affairs, 1949–50); Charles J. Rhoads, former commissioner of Indian affairs, 1929–33; and Gilbert Darlington, the treasurer of the American Bible Society.

3. Slavery is but one example that remains sanctioned with legitimacy by the Constitution of the United States. See the Thirteenth Amendment, which carves out an exception, and compare that exception with the profile of those people who are incarcerated.

4. Not surprisingly the United States' Native policy reveals a path littered with schemes of genocidal social engineering and cultural modification, such as the application of non-Native concepts in determining justice (1885 Major Crimes Act), the application of private property ownership (1887 Allotment Act), and the fostering of non-Native civics among Native populations (1924 Indian Citizenship Act and 1934 Indian Reorganization Act), all of which promote western values at the expense of Native values.

5. Watkins, "Termination," 55.

6. In *Custer Died for Your Sins*, Vine Deloria Jr. provides an excellent analysis of how race relations between the Black and white communities have affected mainstream society's understanding of matters involving Native Peoples.

7. Faragher, *Rereading Frederick Jackson Turner,* 80.

8. Ibid., 122–23.

9. The male senator of color was Dennis Chavez (D-NM), and the four white females were Vera Bushfield (R-SD), Margaret Chase Smith (R-ME), Hazel Abel (R-NE), and Eva Bowring (R-NE).

10. The three male representatives of color were Antonio Fernandez (D-NM), William Dawson (D-IL), and Adam Clayton Powell Jr. (D-NY). The twenty-two white female representatives were Edith Rogers (R-MA), Jessie Sumner (R-IL), Frances Bolton (R-OH), Clare Luce (R-CT), Emily Douglas (D-IL), Helen Douglas (D-CA), Chase Woodhouse (D-CT), Helen Mankin (D-GA), Eliza Pratt (D-NC), Georgia Lusk (D-NM), Katherine St. George (R-NY), Reva Bosone (D-UT), Cecil Harden (R-IN), Edna Kelly (D-NY), Vera Buchanan (D-PA), Marguerite Church (R-IL), Maude Kee (D-WV), Ruth Thompson (R-MI), Gracie Pfost (D-ID), and Leonor Sullivan (D-MO).

11. From the first session of the Eightieth Congress (3 January 1947) to the second session of the Eighty-eighth Congress (3 October 1964), there were a total of ten congressmen of color (two senators and eight representatives), no congresswomen of color, and forty white congresswomen (five senators and thirty-five representatives).

12. Berry, "Indian Speech," 2, Box 168, E. Y. Berry Papers (herein EYB Papers).

13. Ibid., 3.

14. Ibid.

15. Contrary to Berry's three providences, a brief examination of the Wheeler-Howard Act shows that only section 11 concerns education: to appropriate funds for educational expenses incurred by Native people. Moreover, the history of Native education reveals that Christians established boarding schools to educate Native children and that much of that educational experience for Native communities was under extreme duress. In addition, federal boarding schools were established, but the ultraconservative Berry would not be opposed to a Christian education for Native people. Since the federal boarding schools were secular, Berry likely was referring to these schools. In either case, Native people were compelled to send their children to these schools regardless of the Wheeler-Howard Act.

Admittedly, by stopping the allotment of Native land, the Wheeler-Howard Act conflicted with an individual's ownership of private property. However, the Native experience with private property shows a devastating result. Much of the allotted land invariably ended up being owned by non-Natives. Consequently the act was an attempt to preserve what remained of Native land holdings.

Berry's alarm over domestic relations finds its source in section 16 of the act. This section establishes Native self-governance, which among other things recognizes Native and not non-Native authority to regulate all internal aspects of Native affairs, including the domestic relations of Native membership. Berry apparently had difficulty with this aspect of self-governance.

16. The exception to this social profile were the seven white females—Bosone (UT), Green (OR), Hansen (WA), Kee (WV), Pfost (ID), Reid (IL), and Simpson (IL)—and the five non-Euroamerican males were Diggs (MI), Fong (HI), Fernandez (NM), Powell (NY), and Fernos-Isern, a delegate from the U.S.-occupied Puerto Rico.

17. The ten states in question are North Dakota (2 November 1889), South Dakota (2 November 1889), Montana (8 November 1889), Washington (11 November 1889), Wyoming (10 July 1890), Idaho (21 August 1890), Utah (4 January 1896), Oklahoma (16 November 1907), New Mexico (6 January 1912), and Arizona (4 February 1912). The territories of Alaska and Hawaii became states on 3 January 1959 and 21 August 1959, respectively.

18. The western states are Alaska, Arizona, California, Colorado, Hawaii, Idaho, Iowa, Kansas, Louisiana, Minnesota, Montana, Missouri, Nebraska, Nevada, New Mexico, North Dakota, Oklahoma, Oregon, South Dakota, Texas, Utah, Washington, and Wyoming. The eastern states are Florida, Illinois, Kentucky, Maryland, Michigan, New York, North Carolina, Ohio, Pennsylvania, Virginia, West Virginia, Wisconsin, and Tennessee.

19. In addition to the two laws, PL 80-881 (S. 1863) and PL 81-785, (initially S. 1867, later S. 192) that affected the Native populations in New York, there were other such termination-like laws in existence prior to 1953: PL 76-565 (8 June 1940), an act to confer jurisdiction on the State of Kansas over offenses committed by or against Indians on Indian reservations; PL 79-394 (31 May 1946), an act to confer jurisdiction on the State of North Dakota over offenses committed by or against Indians on the Devils Lake Indian Reservation; PL 80-846 (30 June 1948), an act to confer jurisdiction on the State of Iowa over offenses committed by or against Indians on the Sac and Fox Indian Reservation; PL 81-322 (5 October 1949), an act to confer jurisdiction on the State of California over the lands and residents of the Agua Caliente Indian Reservation, and for other purposes.

20. S. 1683 was signed into law on 2 July 1948 as PL 80-881: an act to confer jurisdiction on the State of New York with respect to offenses committed on Indian reservations. Another bill, S. 1687, was later re-introduced as S. 192 on 5 January 1949 and signed into law on 13 September 1950 as PL 81-785: an act to confer jurisdiction on the courts of the State of New York with respect to civil actions between Indians or to which Indians are parties.

21. The targeted Native communities within New York are the Haudenosaunee (i.e., the Allegany, Cattaraugus, Oneida, Ononadaga, St. Regis, Tonawanda, and Tuscarora reservations).

22. The 1948 Senate Interior and Insular Affairs Committee members were Butler (R-NE), Cordon (R-OR), Downey (D-CA), Dworshak (R-ID), Ecton (R-MT), Hatch (D-NM), Malone (R-NV), McFarland (D-AZ), Millikin (R-CO), Murray (D-MT), O'Mahoney (D-WY), Robertson (R-WY), and Watkins (R-UT).

The 1948 House Public Lands Committee members were Barrett (R-WY), Bell (D-MO), Carroll (D-CO), Crawford (R-MI), Dawson (R-UT), D'Ewart (R-MT), Engle

(D-CA), Fernandez (D-NM), Hedrick (D-WV), Jennison (R-IL), LeCompte (R-IA), Lemke (R-ND), LeFevre (R-NY), A. L. Miller (R-NE), Morris (D-OK), Murdock (D-AZ), Peterson (D-FL), Poulson (R-CA), Redden (D-NC), Rockwell (R-CO), Russell (R-NV), Sanborn (R-ID), Sombers (D-NY), Taylor (R-NY), and Welch (R-CA). Members of the Public Lands Committee were Bartlett (D-AL), Farrington (R-HI), and Fernos-Isern (D-PR).

23. *Congressional Quarterly* (1950) notes that unanimous consent is used in lieu of a vote on noncontroversial motions, or bills, that may be passed in either chamber if no member voices an objection. Furthermore, the House consent calendar means that House members can place any noncontroversial measure on the Union or House calendar, but any objection by one member can block a measure's consideration by the House. If there are three objections, the measure is stricken from the consent calendar, yet remains on either the Union or House calendar. Measures that directly or indirectly appropriate money or raise revenue are placed on the Union calendar; otherwise all measures are placed on the House calendar. The Senate's calendar functions similarly to that of the House.

24. Hauptman, *Iroquois Struggle,* 47–48.

25. These Native Peoples are the Ponca, Omaha, Sac and Fox, and Winnebago.

26. Reed represented the Forty-third District, which included the southwestern New York counties of Chautauqua, Cattaraugus, Allegany, and Livingston. According to Hauptman, Reed was reared in Silver Springs, New York, a non-Native border community next to the Cattaraugus Reservation.

27. Watkins, "Termination," 47.

28. Zimmerman, "Role of the Bureau of Indian Affairs," 36.

29. U.S. Congress, *Report,* 163 (herein cited as H. Rpt. 2503).

30. The thirty-two reservations or *rancherias* of the Mission agency are Agua Caliente, Augustine, Barono Rancheria, Cabazon, Cahuilla, Campo, Capitan Grande, Cuyapaipe, Inaja-Cosmit, La Jolla, LaPosta, Laguna, Los Coyotes, Manzanita, Mesa Grande, Mission Creek, Morongo, Pala, Pauma and Yuima, Pechanga, Ramona, Rincon, San Manuel, San Pasqual, Santa Rose, Santa Ynez, Santa Ysabel, Sobaba, Sycuan, Torres-Martinez, Twenty-nine Palms, and Viejas.

The eighty-three reservations or *rancherias* of the Sacramento agency are Alexander Valley, Alturas Indian Rancheria, Auburn, Berry Creek, Big Bend, Big Lagoon, Big Sandy, Big Pine, Big Valley Rancheria, Bishop Colony, Blue Lake Rancheria, Buena Vista Rancheria, Cache Creek, Cedarville Rancheria, Chemehuevi, Chicken Ranch, Chico, Cloverdale, Cold Springs, Colfax, Colusa Rancheria, Cortina, Coyote Valley, Dry Creek, Elk Valley, Enterprise, Fort Bidwell, Fort Independence, Fort Yuma, Greenville, Grindstone Creek, Guideville, Hopland, Indian Ranch, Jackson Rancheria, Klamath Strip, Laytonville, Likely, Lone Pine, Lower Lake, Lytton, Manchester-Point Arena, Mark West, Middle Town, Montgomery Creek, Mooretown, Nevada City, North Fork, Paskenta, Picayune, Pinoleville, Potter Valley, Quartz Valley, Redwood Valley, Redding, Resingnini Rancheria, Roaring Creek, Rohnerville, Robinson, Round

Valley, Ruffeys, Rumsey Indian Rancheria, Santa Rosa, Sebastopol, Scotts Valley, Sheep Ranch, Sherwood, Shingle Springs, Smith River, Stewarts Point, Strathmore, Strawberry Valley, Susanville, Table Bluff, Table Mountain Rancheria, Taylorville, Trinidad Rancheria, Tule River, Tuolume, Upper Lake, Wilton, and XL Ranch.

31. The New York agency comprises the six reservations of the Haudenosaunee people: Cattaraugus, Oneida, Onondaga, St. Regis, Tonawanda, and Tuscarora.

32. The Turtle Mountain agency in North Dakota has two reservations, Turtle Mountain Chippewa and Fort Totten, under its jurisdiction. However, the former reservation is in Group I and the latter in Group II.

33. These agency reservations are Blackfeet, Cherokee, Cheyenne River, Colville, Crow, Fort Belknap, Fort Peck, Fort Totten, Grand Ronde, Taholah, Umatilla, Warm Springs, Wind River, and Winnebago.

34. The Coeur d'Alene, Kalispel, Kootenai, and Nez Percé reservations are under the Northern Idaho agency, while the Sac and Fox, Oneida, Stockbridge, and Winnebago reservations are administered by the Tomah agency.

35. The Great Lakes agency comprises the following reservations: Forest City Potwatamie, Hannahville Indian Community, Scattered Ottawa, Bay Mills, Keweenaw Bay, Saginaw, Sakagoon, Bad River, Lac Courte Oreilles, Lac du Flambeau, Red Cliff, and St. Croix.

36. The Consolidated Chippewa agency reservations are Cass Lake, Fond du Lac, Grand Portage, Leech Lake, Mille Lac, Nett Lake, and White Earth.

37. The three Quapaw agency reservations are Quapaw, Seneca-Cayuga, and Wyandotte.

38. These agency reservations are Cheyenne-Arapaho, Crow Creek, Fort Hall, Hopi, Jicarilla, Kiowa, Mescalero, Navajo, Northern Cheyenne, Pawnee, Pine Ridge, Red Lake, Rocky Boy, Rosebud, San Carlos, Sissiton, Shawnee, Standing Rock, Yakima, and Wind River.

39. The United Pueblos comprise the Acoma, Cochiti, Laguna, San Felipe, Santa Ana, Santa Domingo, Zia, Canyoncito, Alamo, Ramah, Jemez, Nambe, Pojoague, San Ildefonso, San Juan, Santa Clara, Tesuque, Isleta, Picuris, Sandia, Taos, and Zuni.

40. The Western Shoshone agency reservations are Duck Valley, South Fork, Goshute, Skull Valley, Austin Colony, Battle Mountain Colony, Beowawe Colony, Carlin Colony, Elko Colony, Ely Colony, Eureka Colony, Ruby Valley Colony, and Wells Colony.

41. The Unitah and Ouray agency reservations are Kaibab, Cedar City, Kanosh, Koosharem, Indian Peak, Shivwits, Uintah, and Ouray.

42. The Five Civilized Tribes agency reservations are Choctaw, Chickasaw, Cherokee, Creek, and Seminole. The Truxton Canyon agency reservations are Camp Verde, Havasupai, Hualapai, Moapa River, and Yavapai.

43. The Pima agency reservations are Fort McDowell, Gila River, Salt River, and Maricopa.

44. The Colorado River agency reservations are Cocopah, Colorado River, and Fort Mohave. The Sells agency reservations are Gila Bend, Sells, and San Xavier. The Seminole agency reservations are Big Cypress, Brighton, and Dania.

45. The Consolidated Ute agency reservations are Southern Ute and Ute Mountain Ute.

46. For the content of Provinse's speech, "The Withdrawal of Federal Supervision of the American Indian," see H. Rpt. 2503, 179–89.

47. Hoover Commission, 63.

48. The five recommendations of this task force were the following: (1) the federal "administration of social programs for Native People should be progressively transferred to State governments"; (2) all agencies, federal and state but not Native, "involved with Indian affairs should take part in a comprehensive planning-of-programs to carry out this policy"; (3) adequate education for Indians, an adequate standard of living, progressive reduction of mortality and morbidity rates in the Indian population, transfer of the responsibility of medical services to non-Native governments or quasi-, non-Native public bodies, transfer of commonly held Native property from Native governments to Indian-owned corporations, participation of Indian people in political and civic life of non-Native states, and termination of Native lands' tax exemption; (4) a program of assistance for economic stability that has two components, that "young employable Indians and the better cultured families should be encouraged and assisted to leave the reservations and set themselves up on the land or in business," and that "Tribal and Indian enterprises should be put on a corporate or cooperative basis as far as possible"; and (5) each important enterprise should have its own charter and board of directors, policies and objectives should be incorporated into the charter, board of directors should be preponderantly drawn from the Indian community and held financially accountable, other board members should be appointed because of their business or technical competence, and creation of these corporations should be a part of the comprehensive program for each area.

49. The other two dissenting commissioners were James H. Rowe Jr. and James Forrestal.

50. Hoover Commission, 77–78.

51. See note 19.

52. Getches and Wilkinson, *Federal Indian Law,* 46. For a full reading of this important case, see also *Cherokee Nation v. Georgia,* 30 U.S. (5 Pet.) 1, 8 L.Ed. 25.

53. Ibid., 47. Interestingly, Getches and Wilkinson also note that the Cherokee Nation decision was in no way unanimous among the seven white justices. Two of the justices, Marshall and McLean, embraced Native Peoples as having domestic nation status rather than foreign nation status. Two other justices, Johnson and Baldwin, viewed Native Peoples outside the pale of either domestic or foreign nation status. Finally, Thompson and Story believed that Native Peoples had the full status

of foreign nations. Duvall was absent and did not participate. From the 2-2-2 split, there was no conclusive opinion about Native Peoples' political status—although the events and relations between Europeans and Native Peoples prior to the 1831 decision overwhelmingly supported the Thompson-Story opinion.

54. Critics will point to *Worcester v. Georgia,* an 1832 case that immediately followed *Cherokee Nation v. Georgia.* Not surprisingly, an interesting difference between the two cases seems racially motivated. On the one hand, Cherokee political integrity was recognized only when Samuel A. Worcester, a white man, successfully challenged his imprisonment pursuant to the illegal application of Georgia laws in Cherokee territory. On the other hand, Corn Tassel, a Cherokee who was condemned to death and later executed by Georgia for the killing of another Cherokee, could not prevent the same. Dale Van Every notes:

> An obscure murder trial in Georgia offered [William] Wirt [a former Attorney General in Monroe and Adams' administrations and President Jefferson's special prosecutor at former Vice-President Aaron Burr's 1807 treason trial] his immediate opportunity to bring the Cherokee case to the attention of the Supreme Court. . . . Upon Wirt's plea, the Supreme Court December 12, 1830 cited the State of Georgia to appear to show cause of a writ of error should not issue. Georgia was infuriated by this attempted intervention by a federal court which could so clearly lead to a questioning of the validity of the state's new anti-Indian laws. The Supreme Court's order was ignored. . . . Georgia's scorn of the court's citation in the Tassel case appeared to Wirt to have opened the way to urging the main Cherokee case upon the court's consideration. As the legal representative of the Cherokee nation he moved in March, 1831, for an injunction against Georgia arguing that the state's recent anti-Cherokee legislation was in violation of treaties of the United States, of laws of the United States and of the Constitution. The court's position on the motion turned on the constitutional status of the Cherokee community. Was it constitutionally eligible to sue a state in the Supreme Court of the United States? (*Disinherited,* 141–42)

The answer in *Cherokee Nation* of course was no.

55. Getches and Wilkinson, *Federal Indian Law,* 47 (emphasis mine). For an exhaustive treatise on the use of ward or wardship in regard to Native Nations, see Felix S. Cohen's 1942 *Handbook of Federal Indian Law.* An unabridged, limited, reprint of the original 1942 edition was published in 1986 by Five Rings Press of Five Rings Corporation.

56. See *Johnson v. McIntosh,* 21 U.S. (8 Wheat) 543, 5 L.Ed. 681 [1823]. In 1823, the U.S. Supreme Court held that the land titles obtained by individuals directly from Native Nations were invalid. To obtain a valid title for Native land, an individual needed to be granted a title from the United States. The Court invoked a spurious

argument, the doctrine of discovery, to divest Native Peoples from their absolute title to their respective homelands.

57. Black, *Black's Law*, 635.

58. Cohen's ten usages of wardship or wards are (1) domestic dependent nations; (2) tribes subject to congressional power; (3) individual subject to congressional power; (4) subjects of federal court jurisdiction; (5) subjects of administrative power; (6) beneficiaries of a trust; (7) noncitizens; (8) wardship and restraints on alienation; (9) wardship and inequality of bargaining power; and (10) subject of federal bounty.

59. H.R. 698 was approved by the House on 1 July 1952. The special investigative committee members were Wayne Aspinall, Reva Bosone, Wesley D'Ewart, Toby Morris, and Frank Bow.

60. H. Rpt. 2503, 124.

61. University of Chicago, "Federal Indian Legislation." According to Fixico, Henry Jackson, a Democratic senator from Washington, sponsored HCR No. 108 by introducing the resolution in the Senate (1986, 93).

62. See Gary Orfield's "A Study of the Termination Policy," in *The Education of American Indians: The Organization Question*, Senate Subcommittee on Indian Education of the Committee on Labor and Public Welfare, 91st Cong., 1st sess., November 1969, 4: 673–816.

63. For an understanding of a Native point of view concerning contemporary Native-U.S. relations, see Deloria, *Custer Died for Your Sins*. This particular text is especially instructive since much of it was written when termination policy was waning in the late 1960s.

64. For a political and policy understanding of the Termination Era, see Donald Fixico's *Termination*.

65. Deloria, *Custer*, 68.

66. Ibid.

67. Fixico, *Termination*, 94.

68. The executive editor Harold E. Fey of the *Christian Century* raises the question, "What considerations caused Congress to adopt [HCR No.] 108?" Fey went to the BIA, inquired about HCR No. 108, and admitted that he "was not able to learn who wrote 108" except that "it was not written in the Indian Bureau." After a brief summary of legislative history surrounding HCR No. 108, Fey concluded that "there can be no doubt that the termination drive came mainly from Congress." "Our National Indian Policy," *Christian Century* 72 (13): 395–97.

69. The 1953 members of both the Senate and House Subcommittees on Indian Affairs were Senators Watkins (UT), Dworshak (ID), Kuchel (CA), C. Anderson (NM), and Smathers (FL) and Representatives A. L. Miller (NE), D'Ewart (MT), Saylor (PA), Harrison (WY), Wharton (NY), Berry (SD), Westland (WA), Young (NV), Rhodes (AZ), Engle (CA), Aspinall (CO), Donovan (NY), McCarthy (MN),

Haley (FL), Shuford (NC), and Bartlett (AL territory). Since Alaska was not yet a state, Alaska's Native population or land base was omitted in the combined totals.

70. Exactly how the ending of the Indian Problem (i.e., ward status) would proceed is found in HCR No. 108. Its model presents the ending of ward status as a three-tiered process. Native populations are to be immediately freed from federal supervision and control first; then from all disabilities and limitations specifically applicable to Native Peoples; and, finally, all BIA offices serving Native populations are to be abolished.

71. 15 August 1953 Presidential Press Release, Box 183, EYB Papers.

72. Ibid. Of course, Native Nations did not want consultation but rather consent.

73. *Cherokee Nation v. Georgia,* 30 U.S. (5 Pet.) 1, 8 L. Ed. 25. Much of this decision can be found in Getches and Wilkinson, *Federal Indian Law.* This text appears on page 46 of their book.

74. Getches and Wilkinson, *Federal Indian Law,* 58.

75. Almost without exception, Native scholars agree that Article 1, sec. 1 and sec. 8 (the House representation clause and the commerce clause, respectively) and Article 2, sec. 2 (the treaty clause) of the U.S. Constitution expressly provides not only for federal preeminence over states but also, as the Tenth Circuit Court ruled in *Native American Church v. Navajo Tribal Council* (17 November 1959), for Native Nations having a political status higher than that of states.

76. Although this preemption is not absolute, in 1882, the Supreme Court, in *United States v. McBratney,* ruled that reservation-based crimes involving a non-Native offender and a non-Native victim are state, not federal or Native, matters.

77. *U.S. Code Congressional and Administrative News,* (herein *USCCAN*), 2411. The legislative history of H.R. 1063, S. Rpt. No. 699, and H. Rpt. No. 848 are in the *USCCAN.* According to the *USCCAN,* the former report "repeats in substance" the latter report.

78. The first session of the Eighty-third Congress convened on 3 January 1953 and adjourned on 3 August 1953; in other words, it was in session for 213 days, not including recesses.

79. *USCCAN,* 2413–14.

80. Lakota Jurisdiction Collection (herein LJC).

81. There were two House Subcommittee on Indian Affairs Hearings, 29 June 1953 and 15 July 1953. The latter was the final committee hearing prior to the subcommittee releasing its H. Rpt. No. 848 on 16 July 1953. See Carole E. Goldberg's "Public Law 280: The Limits of State Jurisdiction over Reservation Indians," *UCLA Law Review* 22 (1975): 535–94.

82. The brackets in the passage are based upon the evidence presented in PL 83-280's legislative history, Marvin Sonosky's 13 April 1961 memorandum to Senators Mansfield and Metcalf about section 6 and 7, and Larry W. Burt's 1982 work, *Tribalism in Crisis,* in which Burt discloses that Butler in a "controversial move . . . added sections which allowed any other state to assume jurisdiction" (25).

83. In the 1969 Labor and Public Welfare Committee print, a 17 October 1969 Department of Interior position paper regarding the termination policy lends strong support to Sonosky's view about the Bureau of Indian Affairs' hand-in-glove collusion with the chairs of the House and Senate subcommittees. For example, three months before HCR No. 108 was introduced in Congress, the Interior Department's paper admits as much:

> On March 13, 1953, as a result of conferences between Assistant Secretary [Orme] Lewis of the Department of the Interior and the chairmen of the House and Senate Indian Affairs Subcommittees, with a subsequent conference between Assistant Secretary Lewis and [Interior] Secretary [Douglas] McKay, the Assistant Secretary advised the House and Senate subcommittees by letter [that]:
>
> Federal responsibility for administering the affairs of individual Indian tribes should be terminated as rapidly as the circumstances of each tribe will permit. This should be accomplished by arrangement with the proper public bodies of the political subdivisions to assume responsibility for the services customarily enjoyed by non-Indian residents of such political subdivisions and by distribution of tribal assets to the tribes as a unit or division of tribal assets among the individual members, whichever may appear to be the better plan in each case. In addition, responsibility for the trust properties should be transferred to the Indians themselves, either as groups or individuals, as soon as possible (652).

84. Since Alaska and Hawaii were territories until 1959, the total number of states is forty-eight. Alaska was added to the original five states in 1958.

85. *USCCAN*, 2409.

86. U.S. Statutes at Large 25 (1889): 676. *Enabling Act of 1889.*

87. Public Law 280, 83rd Congr., 1st sess. (15 August 1953).

88. Ibid.

89. Getches and Wilkinson, *Federal Indian Law,* 197.

90. Fey, "Our National Indian Policy," 395.

91. Lawson, "Reservoir and Reservation," 182 (emphasis mine).

92. *U.S. Code Congressional Service,* 2286. Both Senate and House Report Nos. 1489 and 2355, respectively, provide the legislative history of S. 1683, a bill conferring on the state of New York jurisdiction over the Haudenosaunee Confederacy.

93. Indian Task Force (herein ITF), "October 1948 Report of the Committee on Indian Affairs to the Commission on Organization of the Executive Branch of the Government," 1, Box 168, EYB Papers.

94. Ibid., 2.

95. Article 4's second section declares that "A person charged in any state with treason, felony, or other crime, who shall flee from justice, and be found in another state, shall, on demand of the executive authority of the state from which he fled, be delivered up, to be removed to the state having jurisdiction of the crime."

96. For a treatment of the disparities (or causes thereof) in the U.S. criminal justice system concerning communities of color, see Ward Churchill and J. J. Vander Wall's *Agents of Repression: The FBI's Secret Wars against the Black Panther Party and the American Indian Movement* (Boston: South End Press, 1988) and *Cages of Steel: The Politics of Imprisonment in the United States* (Washington, DC: Maisonneuve Press, 1992); Manning Marble's *The Crisis of Color and Democracy: Essays on Race, Class, and Power* (Monroe, ME: Common Courage Press, 1992) and *Black Liberation in Conservative America* (Boston: South End Press, 1997); and Nathan McCall's *Makes Me Wanna Holler: A Young Black Man in America* (New York: Vintage Books, 1994).

97. ITF, "October 1948 Report of the Committee on Indian Affairs," 2, Box 168, EYB Papers.

98. Ibid.

99. Brophy, *The Indian, America's Unfinished Business*, 43.

100. Ibid., 44.

101. The BIA's formal involvement with reservation law and order can be traced to 1883 when the Interior Department established a Court of Indian Offenses. Today these courts are commonly called "25 CFR courts" in reference to Title 25—Indians, Part 11, Code of Federal Regulations (CFR).

102. H. Rpt. 2503, 164. The numbers of BIA employees, in parentheses, associated with each BIA agency in Group I are Flathead (43), Hoopa (69), Klamath (121), Menominee (58), Mission (81), New York (8), Osage (71), Potawatomi (19), Sacramento (27), and Turtle Mountain (118).

103. ITF, "October 1948 Report," 3, Box 168, EYB Papers.

104. *USCCAN*, 2411–12.

105. Ibid., 2412.

2

Lakota Termination-Ready Status:
Zimmerman Applied

From Zimmerman's four criteria, one could safely conclude that the Lakota's overall readiness or desire for termination lay somewhere in the far-distant future. None of the Lakota reservations and communities were in Group I or even mentioned in HCR No. 108. Only the Cheyenne River (S.D.), Fort Peck (M.T.), and Fort Totten (N.D.) reservations were in Group II, while Crow Creek (S.D.), Pine Ridge (S.D.), Rosebud (S.D.), and Sisseton (S.D.) reservations received Group III status. Notably missing from all three groups were Flandreau community (S.D.), Lower Brule (S.D.), Standing Rock (S.D.), Yankton (S.D.), and Santee (N.E.) reservations, as well as the four Lakota communities in Minnesota (Prairie Island, Lower Sioux, Upper Sioux, and Prior Lake).

However, the moment Congress passed H.R. 1063 and it became Public Law 83-280, all the timelines changed, and termination for the Lakota suddenly became imminent. H.R. 1063 catapulted the Lakota People from the bottom of the social-evolutionary scale to the top—a remarkable feat considering that Zimmerman's initial listing implied that ten or more years of intensive Euroamerican social engineering of Lakota society would be necessary. Until then, the notion of reducing or eliminating federal services to the Lakota was considered out of the question. But with PL 83-280 enacted, Zimmerman's graduated time scheme was forgotten. The Lakota realized that, contrary to the apologists' suggestion that HCR No. 108 lacked the force and effect of law, the United States was fully determined to terminate every single Native Nation.

Since Congress's 1953 termination policy implied that Native Peoples had made unprecedented advances since Zimmerman's report, what degree of Americanization had the Lakota achieved in 1947 when he first proposed his four conditions? Zimmerman's first criterion was clearly based on a social evolutionary development scale sprinkled liberally with ethnic-cleansing features. Cast in the language of biological hybridization, his report used the quantity of white blood—and not other nonwhite blood—to determine a Native Nation's readiness for termination. This first criterion—biological and race-based as it was—made plain how the United States intended to measure Native readiness for the withdrawal of federal services.

Three assimilation factors—race, literacy, and fee-patent lands—had influenced Graham D. Taylor's pre-1953 appraisal of the early years of implementing the 1934 Indian Reorganization Act. Whereas Zimmerman later used similar factors in his graduated plan to eliminate or reduce federal services to Native communities, Taylor applied them to gauge a Native Nation's degree of assimilation (high, medium, or low) into mainstream society. Tellingly, Taylor's racial variable figured the extent only of "white intermarriage with the Indian group,"[1] suggesting that nonwhite intermarriage with Native Peoples did not produce the appropriate mix for assimilative purposes. Zimmerman thought the same.

Consequently, whenever a significant percentage of a Native Nation's population possessed a sufficient proportion of white blood, whites used that mixed-blood racial component to make some arbitrary assumptions about a Native community's degree of assimilation. According to Taylor's pre-1953 data, a high degree of assimilation meant any Native community whose population was at least 50 percent mixed-blood, as was the case on the Yankton, Cheyenne River, and Rosebud reservations. Medium assimilation referred to a mixed-blood population between 25 percent and 50 percent of a Native community, as existed on the Crow Creek, Fort Peck, Fort Totten, Pine Ridge, and Standing Rock reservations. Low assimilation denoted a Native community with a 25 percent mixed-blood population.

The results of Zimmerman's grouping scheme contrasted sharply with Taylor's, indicating that increasing levels of assimilation did not in fact correspond to increasing degrees of white blood. Basing readiness to assimilate into mainstream society on the amount of white blood an individual possessed turned out to be a highly questionable enterprise, far less objective and far more subjective than it appeared. Nonetheless, this use of white blood as the yardstick for being accepted as an American shows unmistakably that being considered an American (or not) was defined in terms of race. For most whites, any Native person with a significant quantity of white blood was seen as being farther away from the inferior position of ward status and closer to the superior position of white American.

Although possessing white blood was considered important, it was not a significant indicator that a Native Nation or individual was advancing. According to Zimmerman's program, English literacy, not literacy in a Native tongue, figured heavily in the acculturation equation. Indeed, the Cherokee Nation's highly successful 1820s experiment with—and mainstream society's vehement opposition to—biculturalism foreshadowed what lay in store for Native-based literacy efforts in North America.

As part of an earlier Christian effort to convert Native Peoples, white missionaries had laboriously learned and then arduously transcribed several Native languages into difficult-to-read written forms. While these early literacy-type efforts on the part of Christians were crude, they showed the potential of adapting spoken Native languages, such as Cherokee, to written forms. Yet these linguistic efforts proved a formidable challenge to Europeans and later to Euroamericans: "The Moravian with world-wide and century-old experience in dealing with strange languages, had been unable after years of effort to hit upon any pattern that might lead toward a transposition of spoken Cherokee into an intelligible written form. The early New England missionaries, armed by their linguistic training in Latin and Greek, were likewise baffled."[2]

In contrast to the very limited non-Native success at developing a written form of Cherokee, Sequoyah, after a twelve-year study of his language, produced the Cherokee alphabet that revolutionized his society. At an 1821 public demonstration, Sequoyah and his six-year-old daughter astonished Cherokee spectators when his young daughter "proved able to stand at a distance and read with ease any message given to her father by the observers for written transmission to her."[3] Astonished but not readily convinced by the father-daughter demonstration, the Cherokee leadership organized a more stringent test in which a "group of youths unacquainted with Sequoyah was recruited." "After a few hours of his instruction they proved as able as had been his daughter to understand his written messages. . . . What immediately ensued was no less a miracle than had been Sequoyah's achievement. Within a matter of months Cherokee by the hundreds and then by the thousands had learned to practice the new knowledge."[4]

In a century in which non-English-based literacy was achieved within a few short years among the people of the Cherokee Nation, rather than advancing Sequoyah's unprecedented accomplishment as the model for Native North America to achieve levels of literacy comparable to that of the surrounding white community, the Cherokee experience made it entirely clear to Natives that any developed and highly successful written Native language held no literacy value in an English-only society. Indeed, learning to read and write in English alone would remain the prevailing assimilation standard for Native Peoples. In an 1887 report, J. D. C. Atkins, the Commissioner of Indian Affairs, stated:

> To teach Indian school children their native tongue is practically to exclude English, and to prevent them from acquiring it. This language, which is good enough for a white man and black man, ought to be good enough for the red man. It is also believed that teaching an Indian youth in his own barbarous dialect is a positive detriment to him. The first step to be taken toward civilization, toward teaching the Indians the mischief and folly of continuing their barbarous practices, is to teach them the English language.[5]

To whites, the post-1900 proliferation of various white institutions in Native Country (schools; churches; and political, fraternal or other social organizations) suggested both a Native acceptance of these institutions and a white acceptance of Native Peoples. Whites thought that an increase in fee-patented Native land meant the same. To be sure, fee-patented Native land was a surefire way to increase the white presence on a reservation. For Natives, though, this increased presence was highly unwelcome. Yet given the whites' considerably self-serving assumption that more white presence was good, it is no surprise that Taylor's study linked the amount of fee-patent land within a reservation to a degree of Native assimilation into mainstream society. Zimmerman followed Taylor's thinking. In his assessment of Native readiness for termination, Zimmerman likely viewed the consequences of the allotment policy (e.g., fee patents) as indicative of Native acceptance of whites and their institutions.

However, increasing the white presence in Lakota territory resulted only in a corresponding increase of Lakota *interaction* with, not necessarily acceptance of, white institutions. Such social interaction might have superficially lulled whites into believing that the Lakota accepted their institutions. In reality, the Lakota had the opposite reaction. Their increased contact with whites and their institutions merely entailed higher levels of *unwanted* white encroachment into the greater Lakota community.

For example, the excessive number of Christian churches now found within the boundaries of Lakota reservations is a function of history and policy first and an increase in the white population second. Other than the Interior Department, churches—the Episcopal (est. 1878) and the Catholic (est. 1886), both having U.S. sanction to monopolize the several Lakota reservations—were the prevailing white institutions among the Lakota for quite some time. Despite their presence, Lakota acceptance of these particular white institutions was considerably reserved. In the late 1950s and early 1960s, Ernest Schusky observed that even after several decades of missionary work among the Lakota at Lower Brule, the Lakota on that reservation always understood the inherent colonialism of white Christianity:

> Although the Christian denominations do not have a relationship with Indian communities that is highly structured by legislation, their position is strikingly similar to that of the Bureau of Indian Affairs. The denominations which have a policy of centering power in local congregations or regional organizations are also faced with the dilemma of providing money without retaining control over its expenditure. In no case on Dakota reservations were mission boards able to separate financing from authority. . . .
> Furthermore, [Lakota] behavior and attitudes toward national mission boards correspond with those toward the Bureau. A national office is conceived as a far-off and somewhat hostile force. . . . Plans or even suggestions coming from either of the distant offices are regarded with suspicion, apathy, or outright hostility, simply because they are associated with an outside social system in which Indians lack any significant voice.[6]

Schusky's observation should send a clear warning to any white, terminationist or otherwise, that colonialism and the corresponding adjustments that the Lakota People have had to make to colonialism do not in any way signify acceptance. With much of the political and economic power of the reservations concentrated in white hands, Lakota People have had no choice but to interact with these invasive white institutions.

Furthermore, because the allotment program at the turn of the twentieth century declared unallotted Lakota land "surplus" and then sold it to whites for homestead purposes, the number of whites rapidly increased on or near Lakota reservations, as did the number of white institutions. The proliferation of churches on Lakota reservations reflected a variety of Protestant denominations only among the white population; as Schusky observed, it had little to do with the Lakota's acceptance of these denominations.

Ironically, the degree to which Lakota people were actually accepted by whites can be seen in the behavior of various reservation-based churches. The strong religious rivalries among the various Christian denominations prevented any ecumenical effort that might inspire individuals to convert to a rival denomination. Combined with the jealously guarded missionary monopoly by the Catholic-Episcopal axis, these rivalries ensured that the Protestant churches that came onto the reservations later would remain exclusively Euroamerican. The result was de facto racial segregation. More tellingly, when the churches had a chance to make a profound social statement about integration—that is, white acceptance of Lakota people—the greater Christian community chose to perpetuate segregation. They established separate but same-denominational Native and white churches in communities where the number of same-denomination members would not warrant a second church.[7]

White racism was clearly an impediment to the assimilation goals that any white group or institution wanted to impose on Natives. Zimmerman, for example, believed that white acceptance of Native Peoples was important, if not critical, both to the withdrawal of federal services to Native communities and to Native integration as "full American citizens." Yet he fell short of addressing the white racism and white supremacist attitudes that stood in the way of what he and other terminationists wanted. For all the misleading statements about the impact of termination on Native Peoples, Provinse's 1947 speech at the National Conference of Social Work in San Francisco did at least identify white hostility toward Natives as a factor:

> Just as citizenship is a two-way affair so far as the Indian is concerned, so also must it be a two-way occupation so far as relations between Indians and non-Indians are concerned. Many Indians who now are able and willing to participate as citizens are precluded from so doing by the attitudes and behavior of their non-Indian neighbors. Many Indians prefer to remain on their reservations, even with inadequate opportunity, because the attitudes and behavior of the white outside world are such as to make that outside world completely uninviting them. The apathy and ignorance of the American people generally about Indians and Indian problems can be explained but it cannot be excused.[8]

Citing the racist treatment that the Native population received at the hands of New Mexico's white community, like being "denied access to all but the most unsanitary and undesirable eating, lodging, and restroom facilities,"[9] Provinse further noted that the racism in New Mexico was not unique among western states with significant Native populations. A few years after Provinse's remarks in San Francisco, and despite HCR No. 108's much-heralded Americanization of Native Peoples project, whites remained largely indifferent toward their Native neighbors except when termination directly affected their community or individual interests. Then the racist stench of white supremacy to which Provinse alluded and against which he cautioned would let loose, seriously undermining the racial tolerance that the termination policy theoretically required for its success.

Indeed, when the Missouri River in South Dakota was dammed during the 1950s, several Lakota communities were forcibly displaced when thousands of acres of soon-to-be-flooded lands were sacrificed to this massive development project. The utter inhumanity and cruelty with which whites responded to this white-caused crisis underscored both Zimmerman's and Provinse's very real concerns about white attitudes and behaviors that as a rule excluded rather than included Native Peoples.

On 25 July 1951, in an all-too-rare voice of moral indignation among South Dakota's whites, R. C. Bakewell, a judge on South Dakota's Fourth Circuit Court, wrote E. Y. Berry about the severely adverse effects that damming the Missouri River would have on the Dakota people living on the Crow Creek Reservation. After addressing the enormous disruption to community life on the Crow Creek reservation, Bakewell outlined the problem of relocating the BIA agency headquarters to Chamberlain, South Dakota, a white community bordering both the Lower Brule and the Crow Creek Sioux reservations:

> I cannot say they [the Dakota of the Crow Creek Reservation] are reconciled to this [the dislocation of the community due to the flooding caused by damming], any more than you or I would be were we to be suddenly evicted from the occupation of the only fertile, livable part of our holdings, but on top of that the government now proposes to move the agency entirely off the reservation, and this the Indians naturally cannot understand. They have no horses or roads upon which to drive them; they have few cars or other means of transportation. They must necessarily be in close communication with the Superintendent's office, for it is there they get their supplies, their allotment checks, and the other supposed gratuities which the "Great White Father" gives them as some small recompense for the appropriation of their vast domain.
>
> Our treatment of the Indian has been bad enough, but this, I think, is the crowning achievement of cruelty and indifference to the needs and rights of these people. I have no idea how far this plan has progressed, but I assume that unless something is done very soon to prevent it, we will have the spectacle of a reservation operated by remote control from a distance of 25 or 30 miles and to which the Indians can't get.[10]

Bakewell's letter initiated an ongoing discussion between himself, Berry, and BIA officials about relocating the agency. In his 31 August 1951 letter to E. Y. Berry, Dillon S. Myer, who was the commissioner of Indian affairs and the former director of the Japanese American internment program during World War II, advanced his termination-riddled propaganda for such a move:

> We have tried to explore the problem from all feasible angles, and of all the possibilities that have come to light we favor removal of the agency to Chamberlain over the others. The main, overall reason we favor this is because we think the time is drawing near when Indian agencies, as such, located out on the reservations, should become unnecessary and should cease to exist. The Indians of South Dakota, I am sure you will agree, are at a point where they should be mingling more and more with the neighboring non-Indian population instead of living as a tight, close-knit group within the mental and physical confines of a reservation. One of the most logical ways to bring this about would be to enroll the school-age Indian children in public schools. If the agency were moved to Chamberlain, we believe that most of the Indian students could be transported by bus . . . to attend the public schools there.[11]

Only after Myer gave his social commentary about the virtues of mingling the Dakota and white populations as a direct result of the agency's relocation did he answer Bakewell's concern about the enormous inconveniences imposed upon the Dakota people by this U.S.-sponsored, involuntary resettlement program. Resorting to American myths, such as "rugged individualism," and racially tainted connotations of social evolutionary development, Myer found it impossible to suspend his prejudices even when answering Bakewell's charges about the inconveniences of involuntary relocation:

> We realize that if the agency is moved to Chamberlain it may result in some inconvenience to individual Indians, but we feel strongly that the long range results from such a move would far outstrip any temporary inconveniences. If the agency were moved, too, there is the possibility that many of the Indians who now take all their problems, great and small, to the agency superintendent might through necessity have to start taking care of some of them [the problems] for themselves. It seems to us that the completion of Fort Randall Dam is going to become a starting point from which we can either lead the Indians toward more and more assimilation and integration, or allow them to retrogress to the narrow and inbred way of life which has been customary of reservation living.[12]

Myer's response impressed Berry sufficiently to inspire him to try to resell it to Bakewell. Remaining unconvinced about the whole relocation matter, Bakewell stated in a 17 September 1951 letter to Berry: "It is a heartless plan . . . I only wish someone with as facile a pen could tell to the world this final cruelty to the Sioux Indian on the Crow Creek Agency."[13]

For reasons entirely different from Bakewell's concern about disrupting the Crow Creek community, the whites residing in Chamberlain were also vigorously opposed to relocating the Fort Thompson agency headquarters to their community. Several months prior to HCR No. 108's enactment, Herschel V. Melcher, the white mayor of Chamberlain, and four white city commissioners—Willard A. Wristen, Gerrit Brink, Frank C. Knippling, and E. C. Martin—cited the city's inability to adequately absorb a population increase. Though the city welcomed thousands of tourists passing through en route to the Black Hills in numbers that placed far greater demands on the city's infrastructure than the relocated Dakota would, the city officials nonetheless unanimously adopted a January 1952 resolution opposing the relocation of the agency to Chamberlain.

Because Chamberlain remained the BIA's favorite relocation site, and despite HCR No. 108's much touted policy to make Native Peoples more American, the city's white officials remained adamant, and a truer picture of the community's attitude toward moving the BIA agency to their city began to emerge. Mayor Melcher's 30 March 1954 correspondence to Francis Case, a S.D. senator, did not mince words: the Dakota of the Crow Creek and the Lakota of Lower Brule were definitely unwelcome. Should they emigrate to Chamberlain because of the agency's relocation, the Dakota/Lakota People could in fact expect terrorism from their white neighbors:

> Some of the boys in the Community Club seem to favor it but the people in town are most all against it. If they come in here it will be necessary to declare an open season on Indians and Government Agents, we do not feel that we are entitled to this kind of abuse from the government and we do not intend to take it peacefully. . . . The people of Brule County do not feel that we should be saddled with a relief load for Indians, that is the job of the Federal Government, and we do not intend to let an Indian light around here at all. We do not want to live with them and we see no reason why we should, we don't want them in our schools, the hospital is plenty.[14]

With termination policy less than a year old, Mayor Melcher's threat of violence against Native people certainly strained HCR No. 108's credibility that the Dakota/Lakota could enjoy all the benefits of American citizenship, such as, in this case, the liberty to choose when and where to live without the threat of racial reprisal. Indeed, the white reaction to the relocation of Dakota/Lakota people to Chamberlain resembled what often happened in the deep South, where Black people chanced their lives when they entered a white community.

Zimmerman's second criterion for determining a Native Nation's termination-ready status was its economic state of self-sufficiency. In Lakota Country, any claim that the Lakota were ready to have their federal services eliminated was at terrible odds with the realities of reservation life. The little economic activity that did exist among the various Native populations had been documented by the Interior Department in its ten-year development program reports for each reservation throughout the United States.[15] Completed in 1944, these reports proved beyond a doubt that the overall state of many Native economies was dismal at best. The Dakota's condition at Fort Totten Reservation was typical among the Native economies of the Northern Plains:

> The standard of living and economic conditions among the Fort Totten Indians is below the rural non-Indians in this area. This, however, may be due to the fact that the Indian families have always been kept down to the lowest minimum in providing relief for the families; that is, they have never been allowed the adequate amount of relief so they could raise their standard of living.
>
> As further commentary on Tribal economy, it is important to point out that these Fort Totten Indians are living under a strong bondage to their historical wardship. It is evident to most of them that their meager incomes from land leases and relief can never provide an adequate standard of living, yet they cling tenaciously to the negative security of reservation living. For the most part they are reconciled to the most precarious kind of subsistence and they are deeply devoted to the guardianship of the Indian Service without any particular hope for an expanded government rehabilitation program. The more enterprising ones have a fair degree of income from farm and livestock units, while a few others regularly hire out to white farmers as farm hands. A conspicuous feature of Indian interest is the regular Friday parade of Indians to the Agency, who hope to collect some little sum of lease money. . . .
>
> Economically the tribe is in a most difficult position. It is true that there is some land resource which is not Indian used, but even if it were, there would still be a serious lack of economic opportunity. One can scarcely blame these Indians for the hopelessness and frustration which is reflected by their present lack of ambition.[16]

The report's mention of land leases indicated that the use of Dakota land was primarily serving white interests. Indeed, this white orientation of Fort Totten's land use reflected a general pattern of how Lakota lands were being used throughout the Northern Plains. Shortly after the 1944 ten-year program reports, another Interior Department–sponsored report, dated 15 October 1948, about Lakota "rehabilitation" on the Standing Rock Reservation graphically illustrated how, primarily through leasing, whites had acquired large tracts of Lakota land for their ranching (the area's primary industry) or farming purposes. On an acreage basis, from 1943 to 1947, Euroamericans dominated the use of three of the four Standing Rock land categories identified in the 1948 report (table 3).

Of the 729,324 acres of land in use for either grazing or farming on the Standing Rock Reservation in 1943, whites were using 607,529 acres (83 percent), while Lakotas were using only 121,795 acres (17 percent).[17] Five years later, on 1 October 1953, two other Interior Department reports presented similar statistics. The Lakota at Pine Ridge used less than half (46 percent) of the 1,349,010 acres of available range land and only 9,701 acres of 187,964 dry-farm acres,[18] while at Rosebud the Lakota used only 33 percent of their 1,094,776 reservation acres.[19]

Naturally, the Lakota were quite alarmed at losing bits and pieces of land and were actively expressing their anxiety over the loss-of-land trend. In her 10 May 1955 letter to E. Y. Berry, Mrs. Angelique Wilcox voiced her personal concerns about the effect that land sales were having on the already impoverished Pine Ridge Reservation:

> I am just wondering what they [the Oglala Lakota] will do, when they sell all their land to the whites, where will they set their tents? And what will they live on after the money is all gone. I think they [the BIA] made a big mistake when they [the BIA] let them sell all their land to whites. As soon as they sell their land[,] they go buy a car and get drunk, wrecked [*sic*] the car and that[']s the end of their money, and nothing to eat in their little old shabby log houses.[20]

After raising the troubling socioeconomic issues following a land sale, this Lakota woman further observed who the real beneficiaries of the land sales

Table 3. Land Utilization on Standing Rock Reservation, 1943

| Operator | Land Category in Acres | | | | |
	Native	Allotted	Government	Dry-Farm Trust	Total
Lakota	20,372	94,505	5,194	1,721	121,795
Euroamerican	105,854	456,674	2,640	42,361	607,529
Idle	31,462	266,155	3,130	30,215	330,959
Total	157,691	871,331	10,964	74,297	1,060,283

Source: Standing Rock Reservation Planning Board, 1948–1958, First Year.

were: "This land sale doesn't benefit us indians, as us small cattle man [*sic*] doesn't have a chance to buy their land when they put it up for supervised sale, as too many whites to bid against. I think the indians will be better off if they [the BIA] let them keep their land unless if its heirship land."[21]

Wilcox's observations were officially corroborated nearly a year before her correspondence with Berry, when Ben Reifel, the BIA superintendent of the Pine Ridge Agency, stated his concerns over the rate that Lakota lands were being lost: "At Pine Ridge . . . almost 320 acres are now being sold to non-Indians every day either by Indian owners or in response to their requests."[22] Given that such land constituted at least 80 percent of the Oglala Lakota's land base in 1950, the Oglala Lakota's economic prospects were grim. On the basis of Reifel's 1954 projected land alienation rate, if left unabated, by 1967, the Pine Ridge Reservation would no longer have any trust-allotted land.[23]

Furthermore, in January 1957, W. O. Roberts, a retired BIA official, outlined exactly how the alienation of allotted lands worked to Native people's detriment:

> Of course, it is technically true that every sale of Indian land originates with the application of the Indian owner himself. A sale could not be made without the Indian's signature. However, it is equally true that strong pressure is put on the Indian owner, in most cases, to sell his land. This pressure is artful, persuasive, and almost invariably successful. . . . The Indian petitions his Superintendent to advertise his land for sale if he, the Indian is "incompetent," and to grant a patent in fee if he is "competent." It is not at all unusual for the white would-be-purchaser or his attorney to work out an agreement with the Indian in advance, including a banker-like use of the money.[24]

But even with the aid of a "white would-be-purchaser," Roberts was quick to point out that, for a Native seller, the actual benefit realized from a land sale was exceedingly short term:

> The results rarely stack up with the plans, however. Invariably the Indian gets a good price for his land, because the land is in demand in Dakota; but just as surely, the Indian must use up the money for living expenses. In a few months it is gone, and the land is gone, together with the income he had been getting previously from leasing it. . . . Agency records show that as the Indians' land holdings grow smaller, the relief rolls grow larger.[25]

That a Native person could be successfully pressured into selling his or her land might suggest a lack of personal will to resist such pressure; yet for Natives mired in poverty, the thought of a possible land sale that would bring them a substantial return of money was hard to resist, especially since white capitalists charged Lakota people exorbitant prices for life's basic necessities.

Although Native Nations have always had the legal prerogative to purchase allotted lands, land-sale politics often did not favor a Native Nation committed to maintaining its land base. Again, Roberts's candor exposed how the United States used its influence to arrive at a favorable outcome for white would-be-purchasers:

> Tribes are empowered by act of Congress to acquire lands from individual Indians who wish to sell, taking title in the name of the tribe and paying for it from tribal funds. However, the success of this policy, like any other Government program, depends on the attitude of the administrative officers handling it. If a Commissioner favors a policy of withdrawal of Federal supervision of Indian Affairs, the best way to accomplish it is through the sale of the Indians' property. Obviously, allowing a tribe to buy land from its individual members is not withdrawal.[26]

Specifically, during the early termination period, Glenn Emmons, the commissioner of Indian affairs (1953–61),[27] released a disturbing 16 May 1955 memorandum to BIA area directors regarding a new policy of liberalizing the issuance of fee patents for individual trust property without weighing the property's importance to a Native Nation: "This policy [of taking into account any adverse impact a land sale may have on a tribe] is now modified by giving recognition to the fact that an individual Indian's right to the ownership of his land in fee simple need not be subordinated to the interests of his tribe nor to the management of the land as part of a timber or grazing unit."[28]

Prior to Emmons's memorandum, if land consolidation for economic development or other tribal purposes was a Native government's priority, and if there existed several key tracts of individual trust—that is, allotted land in an area designated for such consolidation—the BIA could ostensibly help facilitate a mutually desired land-consolidation program. It could, for example, either discourage the issuance of fee patents or perhaps administratively promote a land exchange between the Native individual and his or her nation. Or, if an allottee was determined to sell his or her land, the BIA could invoke a supervised sale, so that the preferred would-be-purchaser would be the Native Nation rather than a white. While not entirely preventing a Native Nation from acquiring fee-patent land through purchase, the fee-patent policy, especially Emmons's white-favoring policy, severely limited a Native Nation's ability to affect the sales of fee-patent land in ways that kept it part of the nation's land base.

In her address to the governor's 1957 Interstate Indian Council conference in Oklahoma City, Oklahoma, historian and writer Angie Debo painted an alarming picture of Native Country's general state of economic unreadiness:

> Compare[,] for instance, the Oglala Sioux Tribe of South Dakota. . . . Their reservation [the Pine Ridge] is checkerboarded, much of their best land is lost, and under current policy the rest is due to be lost with shocking rapidity. Thus any attempt to construct an economy for them is undermined in advance. Extreme poverty frustrates efforts to furnish both education and health. With impersonal, bureaucratic finality they are, in effect, being told that as a tribe they shall not be permitted a future, as a community they may not progress. . . .
>
> At Pine Ridge, the Oglala Reservations [*sic*], in the year 1955 alone . . . 23,000 acres were sold out of Indian ownership. Under the present administration, allotted land is being taken out of trust at the rate of approximately three percent per year, and sales of such land range from 500,000 to 250,000 acres per year. The sales bear directly upon any policy of improving Indian economy.[29]

For Native Country, maintaining a land base was obviously essential for any sustainable development, but as Debo and so many other Native advocates made clear, the land base of Native Nations, such as the Oglala Lakota, was dwindling fast due to a BIA policy that heavily favored whites in the purchase of allotted Native land. As Debo's speech suggested, the reason for this rapid loss had an all-too-familiar ring: a person's race almost always determined the outcome of the sale.

Naturally, any Native initiative to either minimize or reverse this destructive pattern of Native land use or purchase by whites encountered formidable resistance. Incorporated in 1943, for example, the RST's Tribal Land Enterprise (TLE) had the primary mission of stopping, either through purchase or the issue of certificates, the increasing fractionation (heirship) and alienation (fee patent or sale) of its land base caused by the U.S. allotment policy. To be sure, a Native organization like TLE faced its share of internal political turmoil, and this turmoil somewhat compromised its capacity to pursue its mission most effectively.[30] Nonetheless, a Native organization dedicated solely to land matters introduced a third variable, besides the BIA and individual Lakota landowners, that white would-be-purchasers or lessors of Lakota land had to face. After more than a decade of operation, in a July 1955 letter to a graduate student, Charles O. Jones, Berry summarized what his white constituents generally thought about TLE's presence:

> Fundamentally and originally, it [the 1934 Indian Reorganization Act] was a grand socialistic program. When John Collier took over as Commissioner of Indian Affairs [21 April 1933], it was his idea that the Indians should be retained as a museum piece so far as possible, and it was his idea to test out communistic programs on these Indian reservations. He established tribal government partly by law, partly by executive order, and partly by historical rights. . . .
>
> In this kind of set-up, they established on the Rosebud [Sioux] Reservation a separate organization for the purpose of handling land ownership, known as the Tribal Land Enterprise. This corporation issued shares of stock to anyone who wanted to sell their land to the Enterprise, and the shares of stock were partly negotiable in that the final transfer had to be approved by the TLE Board. The holder of the share of stock could in turn deposit it and demand a piece of land in exchange. He received no title to the land other than a surface right which could be inherited only once, then reverted to tribal ownership, which was intended at the end of one generation to make all property communally owned and separated.[31]

Obviously, whenever a Native effort, such as TLE's land-consolidation initiative, did not overwhelmingly favor the long-term economic well-being of the surrounding white community, whites got upset. Perceiving a threat to their interests, they called into question the very nature of such a program, often labeling it, as Berry did, "communistic," hence un-American. By contrast, in view of Berry's visceral condemnation of the Rosebud Sioux Tribe's TLE program, had the TLE made thousands of acres of Lakota land available to whites for their primary use, thereby stimulating their local or regional economies and increasing the whites' profit margins, Berry would have surely hailed the effort as a model of Native business savvy.

Native Country's approximate 54,556,000 remaining acres as of 1950 bore no relationship to the affluence or prosperity that would normally be associated with white property ownership. According to all reports, land-abundant people such as the Lakota were not described as being wealthy or even as making a reasonably decent living. Instead, various Interior Department records portrayed a picture of stark poverty. To cite the Lakota Nation's economic condition as evidence of its readiness for a reduction or termination of federal services invokes the fictional.

Of course, the cause of the Lakota's chronic poverty had nothing to do with incompetency on their part but was a direct result of a series of U.S.

policies, programs, and laws. Beginning in the late 1800s, U.S. national policy toward Natives first destroyed them and their existing economies as much as possible and then forcibly subjected the surviving Natives to culturally alien white schemes rigged to effect their eventual demise. Given this history that remained all too present for the Lakota in its devastating impact on daily life, terminationists would have a hard time claiming economic self-sufficiency as grounds for cutting off federal services to the Lakota.

Zimmerman's third criterion for evaluating a Native Nation's readiness to have their federal services reduced or eliminated was the Native Nation's willingness to have this happen. Needless to say, because the Lakota had been stripped of their previous economic resources and were now reduced to a state of high dependency, it is not the least difficult to understand why their federal and other services became so relief oriented or why the Lakota People were not at all inclined to forego federal assistance.

After acknowledging that Native Peoples were experiencing a widespread, post–World War II poverty crisis while the rest of the "United States as a whole [was] enjoying prosperity and virtually full employment,"[32] the Hoover Commission's Indian Task Force (ITF) addressed the scope of federal assistance to Native Country, revealing the magnitude of the crisis: "Federal appropriations for the Indian Bureau over the last 20 years have allocated more than 50 percent to welfare aspects of the Indian problem."[33] If at least fifty cents of every BIA dollar since the late 1920s went toward welfare services, it was an unrealistic expectation for Native Peoples to dispense with an already minimal social safety net.

According to the same October 1953 BIA report that had revealed the prevalence of white-oriented land use on the Rosebud Reservation, only 38 percent of the 1,440 Lakota families residing on the Rosebud Reservation were, in 1953, viewed as self-supporting and at least 661 received some form of welfare. Of the 548 Lakota families that were deemed self-supporting, nearly half (or 264) "obtained their income from a wage economy off the reservation."[34] Based on this employment figure, if the off-reservation economy were to experience a decline that brought layoffs, Rosebud's economy would not be sufficiently robust, given its bleak employment picture, to absorb a substantial number of these laid-off workers. Moreover, because Rosebud's export of labor was substantial, if just 60 of the 264 Lakota families depending on off-reservation jobs lost this source of income, the Rosebud Sioux Reservation would more than likely see a 4 percent increase, from 46 percent to 50 percent, in the number of families receiving welfare.[35]

Indeed, a 1956 study, "The American Indian Relocation Program," was conducted by the Association on American Indian Affairs (AAIA), a New York–based organization promoting Native interests. This study published a portion of the Bureau of Indian Affairs Manual (BIAM), which echoed the 1944 ten-year program report's assessment of pervasive poverty—a reality of reservation life documented in every economic report since:

> On many Indian reservations throughout the country and in certain other areas where there is a large Indian population, opportunities for self-support are inadequate. Land resources are insufficient either in quantity or quality, industrial development is negligible, and a considerable portion of the Indian population is faced with the alternatives of leaving the area to seek new opportunities, including adequate employment, or remaining to live in privation or dependent, wholly or partially, on some form of public assistance.[36]

Given that almost all the self-supporting economic activities on or near a reservation—such as the labor-intensive but seasonal farm-ranch employment or the leasing of land—could not provide for an extended family, it is no surprise that Native people were forced to seek various forms of public assistance to supplement their low-wage or nonexistent incomes. As a result, they strongly opposed the reduction, much less elimination, of federal services, because no matter how minimal these services were, they made all the difference between malnutrition and starvation. As for state-level programs, few, if any, existed that were willing to assume the responsibility for Native affairs if the federal government backed out.

Finally, since Native Peoples were not inclined to dispense with federal assistance (criteria 3), Zimmerman's fourth criterion, namely, a state's willingness or ability to assume total responsibility for Native affairs, raised the other side of the coin: Were the whites in South Dakota willing to have federal services to Natives withdrawn, knowing that they would be called upon financially to make up the difference?

The U.S. Indian Removal Act and the *Cherokee Nation v. Georgia* case demonstrated beyond a shadow of a doubt that the most popular and long-held position of states toward assuming the responsibilities associated with the country's "Native Question" has been not to assume any.[37] This unwillingness of states to address the needs of Native Peoples is even more categorical if the Native Peoples located in the state are autonomous from the state's sphere of influence.

The common nineteenth-century Euroamerican solution for a state if it chose not to assume responsibility was, of course, to physically remove—usually under military threat or escort—whole Native populations from a state.

While the en masse forced removal of Native populations has lost much of its appeal during the twentieth century, a state's extreme hostility toward Native populations has nonetheless motivated whites—at the local, state, and regional levels—to indulge in discriminatory practices against their Native neighbors.[38]

Whenever states were called to provide public services to their Native citizenry, they consistently displayed this vehement unwillingness to do so except under two conditions. In both circumstances, the states had little choice. First, states were sometimes forced to provide services by their own laws and constitution, as Arizona and New Mexico were in 1948 when they could no longer prohibit or discourage otherwise qualified Native people from exercising their right to vote in state elections. Second, states were in some cases bribed into providing services when the federal government wholly or substantially subsidized the cost of administering state services that happened to include Native recipients. The 1949 Hoover Commission report advised the second approach of financially subsidizing state services to Natives:

> The Commission recommends that, pending achievement of the goal of complete integration, the administration of social programs for the Indians should be progressively transferred to State governments. The States should receive appropriate recompense from Federal funds until Indian taxes can help carry the load. The transfer to States should be accompanied by diminishing activities by the Bureau of Indian Affairs.[39]

On 7 January 1953, several months before termination became official policy, Berry introduced H.R. 1220 to amend section 9 of PL 81-474—the Navajo and Hopi Rehabilitation Act. This section contained provisions that provided "for additional Federal contributions to the Arizona and New Mexico Departments of Public Welfare for public assistance grants [that is, Social Security assistance payments for the elderly, dependent children, the needy, the blind, and the disabled] to Navajos and Hopis."[40] Presumably, Berry's amendment would have also included a greater share of federal Social Security payments to South Dakota's Department of Public Welfare for the Lakota people who received state public assistance.

Berry's rationale for amending PL 81-474 was that South Dakota, like Arizona and New Mexico, had Native populations located within its borders, yet the two latter states received additional federal Social Security payments for "their Indians" who were receiving state public assistance. To bolster his arguments for increasing the Social Security payments to South Dakota, Berry uncharacteristically resorted to treaty law:

> In consideration for the acceptance by the Sioux of these vastly reduced areas [1851 and 1868 Sioux Nation boundaries, which included portions of the present states of Montana, Nebraska, North Dakota, South Dakota, and Wyoming], the federal government entered into the Treaty of 1877 which reads in part as follows:
>
> " . . . The United States does agree to provide all necessary aid to assist said Indians in the work of civilization; to furnish to them schools and instruction in mechanical and agricultural arts, as provided for by the treaty of 1868. . . . Such rations, or so much thereof as may be necessary, shall be continued until the Indians are able to support themselves."[41]

Having invoked the appropriate treaty language concerning U.S. aid to the Lakota, Berry then established what essentially amounted to a cost-sharing arrangement between South Dakota and the United States to provide the Lakota with public assistance:

> When the social security program was established in South Dakota and other Sioux nation states [that is, Minnesota, Montana, Nebraska, and North Dakota] the federal government disregarded its treaty with the Sioux and provided that social security benefits to members of the Sioux Tribe should be paid on a 50–50 basis, half by the state and half by the federal government, with the major costs of administration being borne by the states and this, in spite of the fact that the Indian treaty reads that such aid "or so much thereof as shall be necessary shall be continued until the Indians are able to support themselves."
>
> It is my contention that when an Indian applies for old age assistance or aid to dependent children, they are required to sign an affidavit that they are unable "to support themselves," and that it is the bounden obligation of the federal government and not the states to provide that assistance.
>
> It is my contention that when the Sioux Indian people, because of age, infirmity or other reasons are eligible for social security benefits, the federal government is obligated by virtue of its treaty to provide such benefits to them.
>
> Certainly, if the state governments of Arizona, Nevada and New Mexico are entitled to this additional assistance, the states in which the Sioux Indians reside are entitled to the same consideration.[42]

For a deep-seated, free-market conservative like Berry to justify a federal subsidy to South Dakota for public assistance programs for the Lakota population reeks of socioeconomic doubletalk and casuistry. Indeed, a closer look at the legislative history surrounding this particular measure shows that in fact South Dakota's white welfare recipients would be the real beneficiaries of H.R. 1220.

Matthew Furze, the director of South Dakota's Public Welfare Department, revealed in a 13 January 1953 letter to Berry that, irrespective of a welfare recipient's race, the cost-sharing split between the federal government and South Dakota for public assistance programs was actually 67 percent and 33 percent rather than the 50 percent and 50 percent that Berry proposed.[43] Because the federal government already contributed at least 67 percent of the money toward South Dakota's public-assistance programs, H.R. 1220's basic premise—that the state required a much larger federal share because of the Lakota who were receiving state public assistance—immediately became suspect.

Supporting H.R. 1220 and its misleading promise of *increased* federal subsidy to South Dakota, Furze essentially argued that the Lakota population—approximately 3.7 percent of the state's estimated 1950 population of 652,740—was receiving disproportionately greater amounts of state public assistance than their population warranted. As proof of this claim, Furze, in a previous 16 December 1952 memorandum to Berry (table 4) on the non-white recipients of public assistance, showed that the Lakota were receiving public assistance in far greater proportional percentages than were the state's white recipients who, after all, constituted at least 96 percent of the state's population. In making this claim, Furze's data included multiple statistics that were calculated to be misleading.

Specifically, according to Furze, the Lakota were receiving 33.8 percent of the aid to dependent children and 44.4 percent of the aid to the blind, leaving a strong but very wrong impression that the Lakota were "unfairly" receiving more public assistance than their numbers warranted. The state, according to Berry's "novel" treaty interpretation, deservedly merited a higher federal share than it currently received for an otherwise federal responsibility. The implication was that the state's current assistance to the Lakota was being carried out on a charitable basis rather than a statutory one.

Another significant statistical misrepresentation concerned the percentage of the Lakota population that ostensibly was being served by South Dakota. Furze's memorandum to Berry presumably included both on- and off-reservation Lakota populations, suggesting that the state was assuming responsibility for all the Lakota residing within it. In fact, the state's responsibility for Lakota people did not include those living within reservation boundar-

Table 4. Nonwhite Recipients of State Public Assistance for December 1952

Aid Category	Total	Native
Old age assistance		
Number of recipients	11,644	911
Amount	$508,619	$31,959
Average per recipient	$43.68	$35.08
Percentage of recipients		7.8
Aid to the blind		
Number of recipients	203	90
Amount	$8,680	$3,505
Average per recipient	$42.76	$38.94
Percentage of recipients		44.4
Aid to the disabled		
Number of recipients	292	11
Amount	$13,178	$363
Average per recipient	$45.13	$33.00
Percentage of recipients		3.7
Aid to dependent children		
Number of families	2,571	963
Number of adults	2,070	720
Number of children	6,352	2,150
Amount	$202,806	$69,143
Average per recipient	$24.08	$24.09
Percentage of recipients		33.8

Source: South Dakota Department of Public Welfare, 1952.

ies. Instead, the figures that Furze provided likely included only the Lakota who resided "in" South Dakota but off-reservations, thus making the total number of Lakota in South Dakota seem smaller than it actually was.

Essentially, Furze could have made two different arguments to get more money for South Dakota from the federal government. On the one hand, the state wanted to argue that it was struggling under the burden of providing a disproportionate percentage of aid to the Lakota, in which case a smaller number of Lakota would make a strong argument.

On the other hand, the state could have made a more robust case for increasing federal funding if it had admitted that the data perhaps applied to off- rather than on-reservation Lakota, in which case the state could have asked for more federal money to extend state support to the on-reservation Lakota as well. The fact that Furze did not argue the latter suggests his and Berry's real motives. Had he done so, he would have undermined H.R. 1220's general statewide application and thereby would have severely reduced the amount of cost-sharing dollars for welfare programs to whites that Berry and

Furze actually wanted. In making the first argument, Furze chose to make the Lakota look bad—disproportionately dependent and on the dole—in order to wangle more federal money for whites. As an added bonus, Furze's argument served to feed the already virulent hostility of white taxpayers toward the Lakota.

While South Dakota and Berry were busily depicting the state as a benevolent sponsor to the indigent Lakota, a closer examination of Furze's data shows that white welfare recipients received, on average, more public assistance money than did their Lakota counterparts. Since the application process for public assistance was uniform for all potential welfare recipients, this disparity implies—contrary to all the economic reports that identified the Lakota as being far more impoverished than any other segment of the S.D. population—that the economic circumstances of South Dakota's white welfare recipients were somehow being construed as more needy and extenuating than the Lakota's economic condition.

The statistics proved particularly deceptive concerning South Dakota's aid for dependent children (ADC) and old-age assistance (OAA) categories. South Dakota raised considerable alarm when it claimed that the Lakota constituted 34 percent of the ADC caseload but constituted less than 4 percent of the state's population. However, these claims fail to tell the whole story. While both Lakota and white welfare recipients averaged nearly the same amount—$24.09 and $24.08 per person, respectively—the average family size for whites was larger (3.45 persons per family) than for the Lakotas (2.98 persons per family). Therefore, white families were receiving on average more ADC ($83.07) than were Lakota families ($71.78).

As to the philanthropic images that Berry and others were promoting—making it seem as if South Dakota were generously providing public assistance to Lakota people because the federal government was failing to do so—the state's administration of its OAA program to Lakota Elders dispels all illusions that South Dakota was acting in any charitable capacity whatsoever toward the Lakota. The business dealings of organized crime more accurately fits the state's conduct. For example, in a 15 December 1952 letter to the elderly Lakota woman Mrs. Alice Straight Forehead, the Pine Ridge superintendent O. R. Sande denied her application for a supervised sale of her trust land outright because she was an OAA recipient:

> It [Mrs. Straight Forehead's application] is disapproved for the reason that you are 90 years of age, and, therefore, will probably be unable to make the best use of the money derived from the sale of the land. In addition to that

you are a recipient of Old Age Assistance at the rate of $39.00 a month, and you have received Old Age Assistance until the total amount is $2892. The appraised value of the land is $1760.00 and if the land is sold the State will expect to be reimbursed for the amount that is owed. If the land is sold for the appraised value there will not be enough money to pay the State, and when the money has been applied on your obligation to the State there will be nothing left for your use.[44]

Even beyond Sande's condescending and harsh attitude toward this elderly Lakota woman, his letter calls into serious question South Dakota's claims of looking after the best interests of needy Lakota individuals. Indeed, his letter unwittingly exposed exactly why South Dakota tolerated having individuals such as Mrs. Straight Forehead on its public assistance roles in the first place: an elderly Lakota's trust assets were being used to reimburse South Dakota for services rendered. More than that, the OAA payments were being used to divest the Lakota of their allotments. And while U.S. law did in fact expressly prohibit encumbering with debts, liens, or claims the allotted land held in trust status for Native people, the Secretary of Interior, by invoking his administrative authority, often circumvented this prohibition to satisfy the state's OAA claims against elderly Lakotas or their heirs.

Far from being charitable, then, South Dakota's services were functioning as an entrapping device for the Lakota, allowing the state to increase both white ownership and state control over yet more Lakota land. Not until the Lakota challenged this highly questionable "reimbursement" practice in *Running Horse, et al. v. Secretary of Interior Udall* was the U.S.-S.D. collusion fully exposed.[45] In a 7 July 1960 letter to his Native clients, Sonosky offered a legal opinion about this illegal and blatantly racist practice and gave some further examples of it:

> The question is clear. Trust property is not subject to any debt, claim, lien[,] or charge of any kind. The Secretary is aware of this. He does not attempt to force the sale of trust land to pay old age assistance claims but he does use the power to protect and preserve trust land to collect the rent or the proceeds from the voluntary sale of trust land and pay it to the State. I list some examples.[46]

> 1. The regulations provide that adult Indians may negotiate leases subject to the approval of the local superintendent (25 CFR 131.8). The approval . . . is required to insure that the rental is fair. But this power, given to protect trust property, is used as a device to collect old age assistance claims. In the case of inherited lands superintendents approve such

leases only on [the] condition that the rent is paid to the [local BIA] agency. Of course, the agency then sends the rent to the state for payment on the old age assistance claim.

2. When an Indian wishes to sell inherited land, the Secretary will approve only if the first money from the sale is paid to the State on the old age assistance claim.

3. Where there are Indian heirs and non-Indian heirs, the Secretary has no jurisdiction over the interests of the non-Indians. The practice of the Department is to collect the entire old age assistance claim out of the trust proceeds. The non-Indian[']s take [is] free and clear. Thus, the non-Indian get[s] the benefits because the Secretary uses his power to make the Indians' trust property pay the whole claim.

4. Where there is a will and each heir takes a separate tract of land and one heir rents or sells, the Secretary collects the entire amount of the claim from that heir.

5. The Secretary treats the old age assistance claims as a perpetual lien against the land. There never comes a time when the land is free and clear of the old age assistance claim unless it is paid or unless the property passes to non-Indian heirs. This means that if an heir sells inherited land 10, 20, or 50 years after he inherits it, the State's claim must be paid.[47]

When the Lakota successfully challenged in court the state's demand for reimbursement of OAA payments, South Dakota's disingenuous interest in the Lakota's elderly population was finally exposed. After the court case pulled the plug on the state's outrageous scheme, state officials feared the financial crisis that this highly profitable, twenty-three-year-old racket would have on the state's public welfare programs. They were afraid not because the court required the state to give back twenty-three years of stolen land and money, but only because the state could no longer depend on this source of income. Furze's 18 April 1963 letter to Archie Gubbrud, the governor of South Dakota from 1961 to 1965, reveals how profitable the OAA reimbursement had been for the state:

Collections resulting from claims filed in estates of deceased Indians for old age assistance payments are substantial. As pointed out in the [S.D. Public Welfare Commission] resolution, the average recovery per year from Indian estates from the past three fiscal years is over $98,880.00. Total collections beginning with July 1959 and ending June 30, 1962, came to $296,653.89.[48]

Knowing that this particular trough was soon to be empty, South Dakota devised other strategies to either stop or slow the expected cutoff of OAA reimbursement money from the individual trust funds of the Lakota. The most obvious strategy, of course, was for the state to claim financial ruin for its service program if it could no longer depend on OAA money. Noting that these BIA-approved OAA reimbursements "helped reduce state appropriations for Old Age Assistance and its administration,"[49] Gubbrud officially expressed his concern in a public statement, saying that a change in the status quo would cause "a serious breakdown in available funds for the South Dakota Old Age Assistance program, through depletion of moneys for Federal Matching funds."[50]

South Dakota then resorted to a poorly thought-out, highly reactive outburst. What the state previously touted as a charitable act of providing public assistance was now portrayed as a favor it did for the BIA all along. The state charged that, without its participation, "the total responsibility would fall to the Bureau of Indian Affairs."[51] Of course, the reality was the reverse: without the BIA's illegal collusion, South Dakota would never have received any reimbursement for its OAA claims against Lakota people.

Trying to justify its illegal conduct, South Dakota interjected a fairness issue, arguing that the real victims of *Running Horse* were white welfare recipients and taxpayers. Unlike the Lakota, the whites not only were subject to liens and claims against their property but also had to pay state taxes that contributed to the public assistance programs:

> The disallowance of OAA claims filed in Indian estates is unjust. Not only is this decision [that is, *Running Horse*] unfair to the non-Indian recipient whose property is subject to liens in addition to claims against estates—but [it] is also unfair to the taxpayers of South Dakota who contribute [to] the State's share of these programs.[52]

The property interests of a white and a Lakota, of course, were entirely different. On closer examination of that difference, the state's argument of inequity immediately collapses. First, compared with a Native allottee, a white person owned his or her property outright and had virtually unlimited power to do with it as he or she pleased. And though liens or debts could be placed against trust property inherited by whites, such liens or debts were never made by the Secretary of Interior to collect for OAA payments. Even in many of the OAA claim cases involving a Lakota recipient, South Dakota could not file a lien or claim against the property for the simple reason that, thanks to Marshall's *Cherokee Nation v. Georgia* opinion, the title of the Lakota's property was in the name of the United States. Thus, a Lakota technically was not a property owner until he or she was issued a patent-in-fee title for the trust land.

Secondly, much of the "property" in question was almost always located within the boundaries of a reservation where South Dakota had no authority to levy taxes anyway. By simply avoiding these basic politico-legal truths, South Dakota tried to depict itself and its white population as victimized.

South Dakota's maneuverings around its public assistance programs illustrate how Zimmerman's fourth criterion—the state's willingness or ability to assume responsibility for Native affairs—brought into focus the thinly veiled greed and racism that shaped the interactions between states and Native Peoples. In South Dakota, despite the treaty-based argument that Berry used when he introduced H.R. 1220 or South Dakota's initial contention that its public assistance to Lakota recipients was more of a charitable act than a legal responsibility, the real determining criterion for states turned out to be whether they could persuade the federal government to assume their welfare costs in ways that materially benefited whites. Two days after he introduced H.R. 1220, Berry revealed the measure's real purpose to Rex Terry, the lieutenant governor of South Dakota:

> It seems to me that this bill could do a lot for South Dakota. If the federal government would assume their legal obligation, as they did in the southwestern states, it would leave the state in a position to extend further and greater social security benefits to white recipients.[53]

For Berry and others, it was immaterial that South Dakota's white recipients already received greater amounts of public assistance than did their more impoverished Lakota neighbors. To serve their purposes, South Dakota's terminationists selectively manipulated information, reinforcing the already prevalent negative image that Lakota traditions, not American ones, were responsible for the extremely dismal state in which the Lakota found themselves. In other words, according to HCR No. 108, if the Lakota People could just embrace white American traditions and values, the so-called "Indian Problem" would readily resolve itself.

Given that the Lakota (and other Native Peoples) in no way met the four socioeconomic conditions that Zimmerman deemed critical before federal services could be reduced or withdrawn, Zimmerman's initial assessment that the Lakota were far from being termination-ready was vindicated. Executing the wholesale termination that Watkins, Berry, and others envisioned would likely require a minimum of ten years. Until then, the question of eliminating federal services to Lakota Country should not even be considered. Moreover, the white culturally-laden rationale (such as the purported law-and-order deficiencies in Native communities) that terminationists used to justify various aspects of their policy could not stand up to even a cursory analysis, as chapter 1 showed.

Given the specious quality of the terminationists' policy justifications and the obvious unreadiness of the Lakota People for termination, the Lakota theoretically should have had little to worry about from terminationist efforts, at least for a good while. But there was one "justification" remaining for a state like South Dakota that the Lakota knew all too well: the opportunity for the state's white community to pull off an overtly aggressive landgrab of Lakota Country.

Maintaining The Homeland

Zimmerman's 1947 groupings together with the provisions in PL 83-280 (see table 2, p. 51) mapped out how the landgrab was to be accomplished. Zimmerman had initially identified 129 reservations (Group I) as ready for the immediate reduction or elimination of federal services. In terms of land, that meant that approximately 3,014,687 acres of Native Country would be affected and could face having its jurisdiction transferred to a state.

But by 1953, Zimmerman's groupings had been drastically altered to terminate more or less all reservations immediately. PL 83-280's rough equivalent of Zimmerman's Group I—the mandated states—included 160 reservations, 43 of which were previously not in Group I. Twelve of the original Group I reservations were left out either because of PL 83-280's statutory language or because a Group I reservation did not fall within the boundaries of a mandated state. This increase of 31 reservations (from 129 to 160) according to PL 83-280 represented an additional 554,798 acres (from 3,014,687 to 3,569,485) that were not originally subject to state jurisdiction.

Though the increased number of Group I reservations now slated for immediate and mandatory termination by PL 83-280 added only 18 percent to the amount of acreage affected, that amount would increase considerably if a federal-to-state transfer of jurisdiction were to include Groups II and III as well. If these groups underwent termination—as PL 83-280 made clear provision for them doing—12,859,171 and 38,322,064 Native acres could soon come under state control. Moreover, since the 93 reservations of Group IV that had been omitted from all three groups were now also slated for termination, PL 83-280 was adding yet another 3,118,433 Native acres to the politics of state jurisdiction.

In other words, given the amount of land that could come under state control—adding nearly 57 million acres—it became clear to Natives that *the* motive for termination had little to do with American democratic ideals or Native well-being and everything to do with asserting control over Native lands. PL 83-280 was a landgrab, plain and simple.

For terminationists, the only remaining question was the timeline for doing this. Indeed, perhaps the most dramatic effect of PL 83-280 was its impact on Zimmerman's timelines for reducing or eliminating federal services to Groups II and III. According to Zimmerman, after an "incubation" period, ranging from two to ten or more years, Group II's 44 and Group III's 89 reservations might have been ready for either a partial or a full withdrawal of federal services. Zimmerman's plan reflected what he believed about Native assimilation into mainstream society: for an overwhelming majority of Native Peoples, assimilation would take time, and so termination could not happen all at once.

With the passage of H.R. 1063, however, termination was set to go forward regardless of a reservation's perceived readiness or degree of assimilation. PL 83-280 accurately became synonymous with the immediate transfer of jurisdiction to the states, thus casting a pall over a far greater range of Native territory. Within a decade, the original incremental approach of federal withdrawal that Zimmerman advocated in 1947 gave way to the pressure of immediate withdrawal. Instead of various "chunks" of Native land becoming subject to state control over time, a grand total of 57,314,355 acres of Native Country became automatically available to any state desiring to assert its control over Native Peoples.

Such was the case for the Dakota/Lakota People; PL 83-280's effects were felt immediately. Of the eighteen Dakota/Lakota communities located in the five states of Minnesota, South Dakota, North Dakota, Nebraska, and Montana (table 5), seven Dakota communities—six in Minnesota and one in Nebraska—were subject unilaterally to the jurisdiction of two mandatory states. In the three option-disclaimer states of Montana, North Dakota, and South Dakota, the remaining Dakota/Lakota communities had to wait and see whether a state legislative body would arbitrarily decide to invoke PL 83-280.

The Lakota in South Dakota did not have to wait long. South Dakota's state legislators moved swiftly to introduce termination bills, and the only barrier that stood between the millions of acres of Lakota land and the whites who wanted to control its ownership and use were the governing bodies of the Dakota/Lakota People.

As discussed in the last chapter, one of the obstacles to states that wanted to take over Native Country was the longstanding "ward-guardian" depiction of

Table 5. Dakota/Lakota Reservations Affected by PL 83-280, 1953

Group	Agency	Reservation	State	Land (acres)
Mandatory States				
IV	Pipestone	Lower Sioux	Minnesota	1,734
	Pipestone	Pipestone	Minnesota	532
	Pipestone	Prairie Island	Minnesota	534
	Pipestone	Prior Lake	Minnesota	258
	Pipestone	Upper Sioux	Minnesota	746
	Pipestone	Wabasha	Minnesota	110
	Winnebago	Santee Sioux	Nebraska	5,282
Option-Disclaimer States				
II	Fort Peck	Fort Peck	Montana	1,270,301
	Turtle Mountain	Fort Totten	North Dakota	55,344
	Cheyenne River	Cheyenne River	South Dakota	2,812,022
III	Crow Creek	Crow Creek	South Dakota	180,492
	Pine Ridge	Pine Ridge	South Dakota	1,874,611
	Rosebud	Rosebud	South Dakota	1,095,667
	Sisseton	Sisseton	South Dakota	109,094
	Standing Rock	Standing Rock	South Dakota	1,064,282
IV	Crow Creek	Lower Brule	South Dakota	146,695
	Flandreau	Flandreau	South Dakota	2,741
	Rosebud	Yankton	South Dakota	44,591

Source: H. Rpt. No. 2503 (1953).

the relationship between Native Peoples and the federal government. Nationally, though, termination forces did not advocate against ward status when that status suited or furthered their interests. A 1969 report, *Our Brother's Keeper,* issued by the Citizens' Advocate Center, based in Washington, D.C., reveals how the pragmatics of Marshall's 1830s wardship analogy invariably gave the BIA extensive influence in Lakota Country. Moreover, rather than promote the interests and welfare of the Lakota, as wardship should dictate, the BIA served the Euroamericans, especially when important Lakota land-management issues, such as leasing and selling, were involved. The report states:

> Nowhere is the BIA's authority better demonstrated than in its power over tribal and individual Indian trust property. The use of Indian land is controlled by the Bureau, as are sales, exchanges and other land transactions.... It approves leases, controls prices, terms and conditions. Often the leasing process is initiated not by the owner [the Native allottee] of the land, but by the person [most often a non-Native] desiring to lease it. Leases have been approved without the owner's consent and only the Bureau—not the tribe or individual owner—is empowered to cancel a lease....

The Indian can, however, count on being treated as "competent" for at least one purpose—to sell his land. He may not be competent to lease it or mortgage it, but if he needs money he will find the BIA most willing to help sell his land.[54]

The BIA's authority over land and leasing originated in 1891 when whites anticipated early on that Native allottees—because of U.S.-manufactured poverty; Native cultural factors, such as social organization; or environmental variables, such as access to water and so forth—would fail either to occupy or to materially improve their allotments as whites expected. Congress enacted the first of several laws authorizing the Interior Department to lease these so-called unoccupied or unimproved allotments.[55] Not surprisingly, then, land-use data for Lakota lands often reveals a clear pattern of greater white than Lakota use.

The United States' forced-allotment policy deliberately contained serious flaws, the most serious of which was a standard allotment size of 160 acres. In 1931, Walter Prescott Webb reflected on an appropriate size for an allotment relative to the environment and the economy of scale in the Great Plains. He observed:

> With the Federal government the Eastern tradition of a farmstead was too strong, and for the most part the government thought that every man ought to have 160 acres or, under hard conditions, 320, and eventually 640. It never recognized the fact that even this maximum amount ... only vouchsafed a precarious existence at best, and at worst meant starvation and eventual abandonment. The result was that the lands in the West inevitably and by a process of agglomeration of numerous "homesteads" and small holdings came into the hands of a comparatively few men. The wise men of the Senate and the House could never see why one man would need at least 2560 acres of free land with the possibility of acquiring 10,000 acres more.[56]

Webb was not the only Euroamerican to recognize the scale of economy that the Great Plains required, however. A decade prior to the U.S. allotment law, John Wesley Powell's 1 April 1878 study, "Report on the Lands of the Arid Region of the United States," recognized the economic folly of a land unit less than 2,560 acres. Webb credited this study, nor was he the only one who knew of it.

Thus, if 2,560 acres of land constituted a minimally adequate economic unit, then the Interior Department's policy of dividing up commonly held Lakota reservation lands into allotments of 320 acres to heads of families,[57] 160 acres to single individuals over the age of eighteen, and 80 acres to minors showed how out of touch Congress was with the environment and scale of the Great Plains. Clearly, the size of the allotments made it all but impossible for the Lakota to ever achieve any real level of self-sufficiency, as both Powell and Webb argued and as the historical experience of westering in the Northern Plains unequivocally proved as well.

Moreover, from 1900 onward, any white who had an interest in Lakota territory had multiple options for gaining some access to or control of it. Whites could agglomerate tracts of Lakota land either by leasing Native allotments or—once a patent-in-fee was issued to a Lakota allottee or when a BIA-supervised land sale was pending—by acquiring these allotments through "purchase."

In 1902, when the Interior Department first began leasing "un-utilized" Lakota land,[58] it was not unusual for large-scale, white-owned cattle operations to acquire many such leases and to form "super land tracts." Because Lakota land was held in common—that is, there were no individual Lakota property owners—and because ranching required large grazing areas, ranchers eagerly sought to create these super land tracts of Lakota land holdings.

For instance, from 1904 to 1914, the British- and Scottish-owned Matador Land and Cattle Company leased millions of so-called unused acres of the Cheyenne River Reservation to graze thousands of its cattle. Likewise, in the 1920s, Matador also leased a 350,000–acre tract on the Pine Ridge Reservation.[59] On the Standing Rock Reservation, which shares a common border with the Cheyenne River Reservation, thus making the two reservations among the largest contiguous grazing areas in western South Dakota, the cattle syndicate of Lake, Tombe, and Lemmon leased 865,529 acres for its large-scale cattle operation.[60]

Many of these highly profitable cattle operations were organizations that, like Matador and others, had sufficient capital to manage the massive scale that the livestock industry demanded. On the Cheyenne River Reservation, for instance, in order to create a direct route that could accommodate large cattle drives from westernmost South Dakota to the Chicago livestock markets, various white interests fashioned a six-mile-wide, 80–mile-long corridor complete with stock dams placed at regular intervals. This project required collusion among and the combined resources of the large white-owned cattle operations; the Chicago, Milwaukee, and St. Paul Railroad Company; and the Lakota's guardian, the Interior Department.

Notably absent from the decision-making process were the·Lakota, the obvious reason being their lack of money and clout. After the United States destroyed the Lakota's political economy in the late 1800s, the Lakota of the

Cheyenne River and Standing Rock reservations had no capital. And because they were wards of the United States, they had no position sufficiently influential to affect a project of that magnitude.

Just before the five newly established Lakota reservations were broken up into allotments, the whites' clamor for a greater use of Lakota land promised to drastically alter the Lakota land-tenure pattern—far more even than the super land tracts leased to the cattle operations ever could. The large cattle companies quickly realized that they could no longer politically justify leasing Lakota lands in super tracts if the eventual appropriation of the Lakota's finite land base were earmarked for homesteading. And it *was* in spades. According to the calculus of Manifest Destiny, the 865,529–acre lease of Lakota land held by the cattle syndicate of Lake, Tombe, and Lemmon could far better serve the interests of 5,409 whites if it were divided into 160–acre plots and used for homesteading. Yet the destructive impact of this homesteading policy on the Lakota went beyond the moral and ethical limits of decency. Whereas a lease contract legally recognized the validity of unceded Lakota land rights, homesteading unilaterally, arbitrarily, and forcibly vacated Lakota land rights in favor of "pioneering" homesteaders—the surrogates of U.S colonization.

After one hundred years of homestead invasion, the historian Patricia Nelson Limerick spoke with a refreshing but all-too-rare candor among most whites, unveiling the pernicious lie of self-perceived "innocence" that the pioneers maintained about what they were doing—that their westering was about rugged individualism and romantic ideals and not about genocide and land theft:

> Even when they were trespassers, westering Americans were hardly, in their own eyes, criminals; rather they were pioneers. The ends abundantly justified the means; personal interest in the acquisition of property coincided with national interest in the acquisition of territory, and those interests overlapped in turn with the mission to extend the domain of Christian civilization. Innocence of intention placed the course of events in a bright and positive light; only over time would the shadows compete for our attention.[61]

Moreover, the United States' post-1880 campaign of attrition against the Lakota Nation through undeclared war, massacres, executions, starvation, and so on invariably contributed to a low population of about 19,643 Teton Lakota (1889 est.). This radically reduced population size factored significantly in the allotment policy: the small numbers of surviving Lakota and the ensuing 80–, 160–, or 320–acre allotments obviously guaranteed that a substantial amount of acreage on each newly created Lakota reservation in western South Dakota would remain unallotted.

Rather than retain the unallotted portions for future Lakota needs, as logic would clearly dictate, and long before twentieth-century Germany would make genocide—prematurely foreclosing on the thought of any future Lakota existence—highly unpopular, the United States promoted an unpardonable program of land "redistribution," so to speak, that was pregnant with ethnic-cleansing features. Specifically, the United States' self-appointed role as guardian presumably authorized Euroamerica to declare the unallotted reservation lands to be "surplus" to Lakota needs. In a series of genocide-tainted legislative acts between 1904 and 1916, Congress "opened" these Lakota lands to white homesteaders:

> The first Rosebud opening [in 1904] initiated a series of similar land releases [that] stretched out over a period of eleven years. . . . In 1907 a 55,000–acre tract on the Lower Brule Reservation drew 4,350 applications for 343 homesteads available. During the following year 114,769 registrants flocked to Dallas, Chamberlain, Gregory, Presho, O'Neill[,] and Valentine (the latter two in Nebraska) in quest of 4,000 land units [of 160 acres each] in Tripp County.
>
> In October of 1909 there were 81,456 hopeful enrollees at Aberdeen, Pierre, La Beau, Mobridge, Lemmon[,] and Bismarck (North Dakota) for approximately 10,000 160–acre plots on the Cheyenne River and Standing Rock Reservations. A million and a half acres in Mellette, Washabaugh, and Bennett counties (Rosebud and Pine Ridge) attracted proportionately less applicants in 1911. . . . After a span of four years, a final opening of approximately 100,000 acres on the Standing Rock Reservation brought to close the wholesale dispersal of surplus Indian lands bought and then resold by the United States government to [non-Natives].[62]

What was once a contiguous area of unceded, commonly held Lakota reservation land was soon dispersed among thousands of whites spread out over each reservation. Often the homesteaders were placed adjacent to the allotted Lakota lands, and because of the economic impracticability of small tracts that Webb noted earlier, they began to agglomerate the surrounding Lakota allotments.

The initial form of agglomeration followed the precedent set by the large cattle companies, and many homesteaders simply anticipated the lease and eventual purchase of the numerous "unoccupied" or "unimproved" allotments available. Typical of this agglomeration-by-lease pattern throughout Lakota Country was John Anderson's situation on the Crow Creek Reservation. In 1902, Anderson had thirty leases, each for one year's use, on several Crow Creek Reservation allotments that ranged between 80 and 400 acres each.[63] After twelve years, Anderson successfully managed to arrange the lease and purchase of "allotments that bordered a tribal pasture and fenced the whole as a single ranch."[64] The length of time and resources involved with Anderson's lease project suggest that initial leasing of Lakota allotments proved a somewhat difficult but not impossible task under the existing law, thus requiring a person to have Anderson-like patience, discipline, and political connections to acquire a sufficient quantity of land for a viable ranch operation.

Not surprisingly, as so many whites rushed to establish homesteads throughout the Lakota reservations, they discovered, as Anderson did, that though leasing an allotment was possible, it was difficult to actually obtain. Leasing reservation lands became all the more difficult when able-bodied Lakotas, like those who were boarding school–educated or had served in the U.S. armed forces during the 1898 Spanish American War (and the many who eventually served in World War I), could not be easily classified as having a disability that theoretically prevented them from occupying or improving their allotments.

In response to this confounding situation of white pioneers not being readily able to lease thousands of "idle" acres of Lakota land, the Interior Department decided to make it much easier. Whereas the previous laws restricted the leasing of allotments to cases where an allottee had a debilitating condition, in 1910, Congress gave the Interior Department wide discretionary authority to lease any allotment regardless of whether a Lakota was in some way incapacitated or not.[65]

But the Lakota faced yet more hardships due to Euroamerican intrusions on their homelands. Besides having to cope with an increasing white presence on their reservations—made even worse by the recent 1910 leasing law—the Lakota were plagued by the U.S.-imposed heirship model, which "fractionalized" the Lakota's fixed allotments among their heirs. Michael L. Lawson (1991) describes what happened:

> The most problematic legacy of federal Indian land policies of the nineteenth century has been their peculiar rules and regulations regarding inheritance. Because physical partitioning of land allotments upon the death of an allottee was deemed inconsistent with the policy goal of establishing individual farms or ranches on reservations, allotted estates were merely divided on paper and continued in federal trust for the benefit of heirs. . . . The exponential growth

of the so-called undivided interests in trust allotments rapidly made it infeasible for most heirs to make practical use of the land themselves. They soon found they could only derive economic benefit from their inherited interests by agreeing . . . to lease out the land and/or its resources (most often, again, to non-Indians).[66]

With piercing accuracy, Lawson explains that inheritance laws were responsible for fractionalizing Lakota land. His two key phrases—the "death of an allottee" and the "exponential growth of undivided interests"—together named something more insidious: how the long-term U.S. attrition campaign against the Lakota invariably produced its intended result—extreme poverty, malnutrition, lowered immune systems, and high susceptibility to diseases. After only a few generations, the Lakota population, despite many being in their prime, experienced a high mortality rate that was unheard of in Lakota oral tradition.

For example, less than a dozen years before the five newly established reservations in western South Dakota were divided into allotments, numerous field reports clearly stated that, because of the U.S. attrition policy, which included the December 1890 massacre of the Lakota by American soldiers, many Lakota were starving and severely impoverished. The Episcopal priest W. H. Hare, for instance, wrote a letter on 7 January 1891 to Interior Secretary Noble:

> The evidence compels the conclusion that, among the Pine Ridge Sioux at least, *hunger has been an important element* in the causes of *discontent* and *insubordination*. . . . In the year 1890, drought, the worst known for many years, afflicted the western part of South Dakota, and the Indian crops were a total failure. There is ample evidence that, during this period, the rations issued lasted, even when carefully used, for only two-thirds the time for which they were intended. To add to their distress, this period, 1889 and 1890, was marked by extraordinary misfortune. The measles prevailed with great virulence in 1889, the grippe in 1890. Whooping cough also attacked the children. The sick died from want.[67]

Such death and impoverishment would, unabated, wreak more and more havoc on Lakota lands because of the heirship policy. In fact, among the many grave deficiencies of the allotment program, the federal government's handling of Lakota heirship illustrates the complete myopia of western culture. In this case, its blindness got in the way of its unbridled pursuit of greed.

Specifically, as each deceased allottee's estate was probated, numerous heirs eventually acquired an undivided but varied proportional interest in the original allottee's land. Indeed, imagine John Anderson's shock if he had tried to negotiate those same 1902 leases on the Crow Creek Reservation fifty years later. To complete the thirty leases, Anderson most likely would find that only 135,986 of the original 285,281 acres remained in Lakota ownership. Not only would there be less Lakota land available for him to lease, but of the 1,599 original allottees, only 415 people remained as single owners of an allotment, while 410 people had an undivided interest in 67,346 (or 52 percent) of the remaining allotted acres. In effect, because many allotments were now held in common by several Lakota heirs, and because each lease required each heir's consent, the heirship situation would likely frustrate even Anderson's efforts to secure a contiguous range of sufficient size.

Whereas leasing an allotment was initially a simple transaction that required the consent of a single-owner allottee (ward) and the approval of the Interior Department (guardian), the heirship problem grew to such proportions that consummating a lease agreement involved gaining the consent of all of a deceased allottee's heirs, who in turn were leaving second- and third-generation heirs of their own. Heirship of allotments was creating a monster for the "guardian" to properly administrate. By the 1950s, anyone viewing the postallotment landscape would be dumbfounded to find that, of the combined 12,396,390 original acres of the five preallotted reservations, approximately 5,546,177 acres (only 45 percent) remained in Lakota ownership. Of that Lakota-owned amount, 3,356,990 acres (60 percent) was allotted land, and 1,899,138 (57 percent) of those allotted acres had two or more heirs.

With time, the heirship arrangement prevented more and more whites from using Lakota land, since they had to secure the consent of every heir to legally lease an allotment. Many whites who came to rely heavily on leasing thousands of acres of Lakota land for their ranch or farm operations found this heirship situation increasingly intolerable. In response to the whites' distress and the dampening effect that Lakota heirship was having on white lessors, the Interior Department solved the problem by establishing range units throughout the Lakota reservations. Hence, during the 1930s, by invoking its power of attorney over its wards, the Interior Department leased to whites on behalf of the Lakota allottee or the allotee's heirs range units that were thousands of acres each and that consisted of unallotted, allotted, and patent-in-fee lands.

This range unit program worked exceedingly well for whites, and, as BIA and other reports showed, they used reservation land in far greater percentages than did the Lakota. Thanks to this range-unit arrangement, whites could conveniently maintain or consolidate their holdings without suffering any economic, legal, or bureaucratic hardships.

By contrast, despite the significant amount of real estate involved with Lakota ownership, the same reports did not describe the Lakota as particularly wealthy. The problem of dividing an allotment among several hundred heirs had caused such fractionalizing of lands that there was no foreseeable economic return to individual Lakotas except to continue leasing their small inherited allotments. Even under the most favorable circumstances, when the income generated from these leases might be substantial, because there were so many heirs, their pro rata shares (which were not equal) were often substantially less than the administrative costs involved.

While leasing range units provided non-Natives with a method of aggregating Lakota land, the long-term goal of outright white ownership was, for obvious reasons, seen as far superior to leasing. For one thing, once a Lakota allottee was issued a patent-in-fee for his or her allotment, the fee patent removed any restrictions that had been previously placed on the allotment, including restrictions on who could buy the allotted land. But more unconscionable were the consequences for the Lakotas who received a fee patent in lieu of a trust patent: fee-patent allottees became "subject to the laws, both criminal and civil, of the State or Territory in which they may reside."[68] Even so, despite the 1904–19 openings of the reservations, because the allotment of Lakota territory did not occur until the early 1900s, and because a twenty-five-year restriction on selling allotted land to non-Lakotas provided a formidable barrier against non-Natives, there seemed little possibility of any immediate land loss due to fee patenting.

For the Lakota, this patent-in-fee situation dramatically changed in 1906 when the ward-guardian relationship took a critical but yet-to-be-implemented policy turn. Charles H. Burke, a S.D. congressional representative who later became the commissioner of Indian affairs, successfully introduced an amendment to the 1887 allotment law. This amendment provided the Interior Department with unlimited discretion in determining whether a Native individual was competent for the sole purpose of issuing a patent-in-fee before the twenty-five-year restricted period expired.[69]

Hence, not long after the allotment and subsequent openings of Lakota territory occurred, in 1917, Cato Sells, the commissioner of Indian affairs, unilaterally proclaimed a very liberal policy pursuant to Burke's 1906 amendment. This policy epitomized mainstream society's attitude after *Cherokee Nation v. Georgia* regarding the correlation between a Native person's degree of white blood and the question of Native (in)competency:

A careful study of the practical effects of government policies for determining the wardship of the Indian of this country is convincing that the solution is individual and not collective. . . .

While ethnologically a preponderance of white blood has not heretofore been a criterion of competency, nor even now is it always a safe standard, it is almost an axiom that an Indian who has a larger proportion of white blood than Indian partakes more of the characteristics of the former than the latter. In thought and action, so far as the business world is concerned, he approximates more closely to the white blood ancestry.[70]

By believing that possessing white blood was sufficient for determining Native people's competency, Sells invoked a racist policy that not only measured competency according to the amount of white blood a Native person possessed but also arbitrarily linked this blood quantum to Native land-tenure:

To all able-bodied adult Indians of less than one-half Indian blood, there will be given as far as may be under the law full and complete control of all their property. Patent in fee shall be issued to all adult Indians of one-half or more Indian blood who may, after careful investigation, be found competent.[71]

The policy of forcing fee patents on Natives totally ignored Marshall's initial condition in *Cherokee Nation,* namely, that the state of pupilage ended whenever Native Peoples *voluntarily* ceded their land rights. The white historian Wilcomb E. Washburn and others, such as Debo and Tyler, have noted that, while issuing fee patents to Native allottees suggested that an allottee was competent enough to manage and administer his or her affairs, the overall policy brought disastrous results for many Natives:

In the reassessment of the policy, the Commissioner of Indian Affairs [the former congressional representative Charles H. Burke], in his report for 1921, noted that more than two-thirds of the Indians who had received patents in fee had been "unable or unwilling to cope with the business acumen coupled with the selfishness and greed of the more competent whites, and in many instances have lost every acre they had." The commissioner noted the frequency with which "those of one-half or less Indian blood—often young men who have had excellent educational privileges—secure patents in fee, dispose of their land at a sacrifice, put most of the proceeds in an automobile or some over extravagant investment, and in a few months, are 'down and out,' as far as any visible possessions are concerned." The loss of the exemption from [state] taxation of land held in trust by the government for the Indian was rarely fully anticipated or adequately prepared for.[72]

Between 1908 and 1916, before Sells's much-heralded 1917 policy, 9,005 patents-in-fee were issued nationally, resulting in the loss of 1,022,746 acres of Native land, mostly to non-Natives. From 1917 to 1920, when Sells's policy of forcing fee patents on Natives was in effect, 17,376 patents-in-fee were issued nationally, and Native land loss soared to 2,461,504 acres—a 93 percent increase from the patents issued during the preceding nine years.

For Lakota people, being issued a patent-in-fee had several repercussions. The most significant was the decrease in Lakota land ownership within the reservations. If almost two-thirds of the total fee patents were issued to Native allottees and their heirs between 1917 and 1920, then a significant percentage of the 6,414 patents-in-fee issued to Lakota allottees between 1906 and 1920 were likely issued during this brief period (1917–20) as well. Furthermore, in terms of the land involved, the 6,414 Lakota patents-in-fee represented 1,117,143 acres that invariably went to whites.

Given this experience of forcing fee patents on Natives with more white blood, Sells's much celebrated axiom, namely, that a Native person possessing more white than Native blood innately achieved a level of competency beyond that achieved by Natives with little or no white blood, proved disastrously false. If anything, the forced-fee policy actually proved the opposite of Sells's axiom.

Up to this point, the discussion concerning wardship or ward status that the 1831 Marshall court initially enunciated—wardship being an analogy that the United States immediately turned into a hard-and-fast rule of dubious social meaning and legality—shows the extreme lengths that Euroamericans would go to link their assessments of Native competency (pupilage/ward and guardian) to Native land tenure (domestic, dependent nation/right of occupancy and use only). Given the agenda of U.S. colonialism to claim Native lands, wardship gave the United States many opportunities to do this. By juxtaposing these two issues—competency and Native land tenure—wardship complicated every aspect of the latter, such as leasing and selling Native land, probating a deceased allottee's estate, determining the heirs, and so on.

The 1969 report of the Citizens' Advocate Center, for instance, showed how the BIA eventually assumed a far greater administrative presence in Native Country than was necessary:

> The [Bureau of] Indian Affairs Manual, which explains and sets forth the procedures and rules that govern Indians, fills 33 volumes which stack some six feet high. . . . There are more than 2,000 regulations, 389 treaties, 5,000 statutes, 2,000 federal court decisions[,] and 500 opinions of the Attorney General which state, interpret, apply[,] or clarify some aspect of Indian law.[73]

Hence, as long as the United States could invoke any one of these various prescriptions as a means or excuse for divesting Native communities of their political power and land, terminationists could find very little, if any, fault with such a status and system, favoring and promoting white interests as it did.

Yet terminationists were not above playing both sides to serve their interests. While Native Peoples were objecting to the Interior Department's stifling overregulation of Native affairs as nothing less than a blatant colonial effort to co-opt the decision-making power of traditional Native governance, Watkins, Berry, and other like-minded terminationists were taking full political advantage of the obvious overregulation, using it to justify their "freeing the Indian" program. In reality, this catchphrase was a euphemism for divesting Natives of their lands, either through short-term schemes (leasing that temporarily removed Native land from Native to non-Native use) or long-term divestiture (selling that permanently removed land from Native to non-Native ownership).

Arguably, the post-1934 Native affairs record discloses that Interior Department overregulation actually interfered with the terminationists' objective of "freeing the Indian" for landgrab purposes. In 1963, E. Y. Berry, who came to Congress in 1951 and had been primarily involved with Native affairs throughout his congressional career,[74] submitted a blistering written testimony to the House Indian Affairs Subcommittee that displayed his open hostility at how the Interior Department's overregulation was adversely affecting the Lakota's ability to be "free":

> There is so much talk in this country today about the Indian problem. However, I want to submit to this Committee the statement that there is no *Indian problem,* but rather a problem of bureaucracy in which the Indian is the victim. There is no Indian problem that could not be solved by the return in this country to the principle of individual rights and a return to the original concept of property rights.[75]

To be sure, few people would disagree with Berry's assessment that the Interior Department's bureaucracy was victimizing the Lakota, but how it was victimizing them critically depends, of course, on the source.

Rather than characterizing the BIA for what it really was—an overbearing colonial system that suppressed Lakota self-determination—Berry and his non-Native constituency in South Dakota defined the problem as one of big government. By raising the highly conservative battle cry against government regulation as severely stifling individual initiative, Berry appealed to the worst fears of a cold war–plagued country. For Berry, opposition to the big government panacea depended on a strict religious adherence to both individual and property rights. Pursuing these rights would ostensibly solve any Indian Problem that may exist.

Applied to Native affairs, what Berry meant by returning to the principles of individual rights and property rights is not what most Euroamericans normally envision. Concerning individual rights, between 1950 and 1970, mainstream society was reeling from the embarrassment of being globally exposed as a people who paid considerable lip service to individual rights while blatantly denying such rights to people of color.

Berry was by no means immune from this hypocrisy either. When Mrs. Kenneth E. Arnn, a former BIA employee, received some 1962 campaign-reelection literature from Berry in which he claimed that the BIA "has as its intent the depriving of Indians of their civil rights,"[76] Arnn personally challenged Berry by adroitly calling this particular civil-rights claim into question. In her view, far from being a statesman deeply committed to any profound social change, Berry was just another political opportunist:

> Thinking of civil rights[,] one reason you [E. Y. Berry] lack my support is your failure to back the amendment to outlaw poll tax as a qualification to vote in federal elections. Your news letter of September 10, 1962, states that the Commission reported two states using the poll tax to discriminate against voters, that tinkering with the Constitution for political purposes was "like using a sledge hammer to kill a gnat." Evidently the citizens of those two states were of no concern. If the gnat is the deprivation of citizens of their right to vote and a sledge hammer is the only thing available, why not use it? The rights of citizens in two states are as precious as the rights of citizens in the other forty-eight states. I have lived in a state using poll tax and experienced the loss of my vote because of that tax. It isn't funny.[77]

Indeed, for Berry, championing individual civil rights came down to making Lakotas choose between either leasing or selling their allotments, preferably to non-Natives. In terms of actual property rights, with the lone exception of a patent-in-fee recognizing absolute title to land, a Lakota individual had none that the United States was constitutionally bound to respect, thanks to a series of Marshall court decisions (*Johnson v. McIntosh, Cherokee Nation,* and *Worcester*) that affirmed a perverse form of Native land tenure. Not surprisingly, in the same 1963 testimony, Berry included, appropriately enough, a "Land Disposal" section that, while railing at the post-1934 bureaucracy problem, conveyed a rather stilted view of Lakota property rights:

Neither the stated policy of the Bureau or its direct actions tell the Indian owner or the public that the land cannot be sold. They hold out hope to the allottee that if he is competent, his land can be sold, and he can use the proceeds to improve his living standards. However, by red tape and delay, the Bureau [of Indian Affairs] completely discourages him and wears him down, in hope that he will eventually give up and let the Bureau continue to handle his lands and his affairs on down through the next several generations of heirship.

Of course, if the Bureau loses its jurisdiction, it loses its argument for annually increased appropriations from Congress, and for increased staffs and employees, and the planners lose one more argument that the ordinary [Native] individual is too stupid to be able to handle his own affairs and his own property, and that someone in government must make his decisions for him.[78]

According to Berry, should a Lakota individual decide not to lease his or her allotment, the Interior Department, through its self-serving bureaucracy, was interfering with the Lakota's only remaining property right: to sell the land. Given an interested bidder, the Lakota's inalienable American right was to either obtain a patent-in-fee that completely removed all restrictions and protections pertaining to the allotment or to have the Interior Department conduct the land sale on his or her behalf. For reasons apparent to white would-be purchasers of Lakota land, securing a patent-in-fee for an allotment was by far the preferred avenue, since the latter route necessarily involved Interior Department supervision replete with all the rules and regulations governing the sale of Native land.

With his Washington office now converted into a real estate firm sporting a contorted civil-rights banner that championed Lakota individual and property rights, Berry proceeded to apprise the House Indian Affairs Subcommittee of the alarming magnitude of the obvious "civil-rights" crisis perpetuated by the BIA's bureaucracy:

I have in my office some 200 files where Indian landowners, a large percentage of whom are competent, have been trying for years to get patents [-in-fee] to their lands or to sell their lands through sales supervised by the Bureau. Let me present just a few of the dozens and dozens of instances of confiscation by red tape delay and discouragement [a list of twelve pending patent-in-fee cases].[79]

Conceding that big government's bureaucracy leads to an indefinite hiatus (hence, Berry's "confiscation by red tape" statement) in processing either patents-in-fee or land sales applications, and thus accounting for the "discouragement" of the two hundred Indian landowners who wanted either a fee patent or a supervised sale, what would Berry's alternative scenario be? In other words, assuming that the two hundred patent-in-fee and supervised sales files in Berry's possession were miraculously spared from the jaws of bureaucracy, what would be the so-called civil-rights victory for the Lakota landowners?

To partially answer these questions—to imagine what kind of all-American, civil-rights outcome might await two hundred hypothetically BIA-free cases—we can look to a 1955 case that involved Berry's personal intervention. A white livestock owner named O. A. Hodson wanted to obtain lease privileges on Lakota land to graze his cattle. Hodson was a state representative (1955–1958) whose legislative-imposed district on Lakota territory included parts of both the Pine Ridge and the Rosebud reservations. Hodson was also an owner-operator of the Black Pipe State Bank of Martin, South Dakota (at the time a Euroamerican enclave on the Pine Ridge Reservation).

Eight years prior to Berry's 1963 testimony, Hodson wrote Berry several times after Ben Reifel, the BIA superintendent of Pine Ridge, notified Hodson in a January 1955 letter that without an Interior Department–approved lease to pasture his livestock on Mrs. Katherine McDonald's two quarters (or 320 acres) of trust land, Hodson was criminally trespassing. Furthermore, the land Hodson trespassed on was part of a range unit awarded to Mr. Gilbert Valandry, an Oglala Lakota rancher, who asserted his right of Lakota preference to secure the range unit for his own ranching operations.

Hodson could have accepted the BIA's determination of his obvious trespassing and then tried to perfect a settlement among the parties. Better yet, he could have simply accepted that a Lakota ranch operator had been awarded a legal lease on a range unit that included McDonald's two quarters of allotted land. Instead, Hodson resorted to measures that eventually led McDonald to apply for a patent-in-fee for her allotment so that, without any federal proscriptions, Hodson could use McDonald's land freely as a part of his ranch.

As a political measure, Hodson maintained early on that he in fact did lease the allotment from McDonald, an Oglala Lakota married to a non-Native. However, on 9 March 1955, Reifel wrote Berry to explain Hodson's case, stating that Hodson secured an invalid lease and thus was trespassing:

> This [letter] will acknowledge your letter of March 4 [1955] requesting information on the difficulty with Mr. O. A. Hodson concerning a grazing lease.

The land involved in this controversy lies within a range unit boundary permitted to one of our Indian livestock operators, Mr. Gilbert Valandry of Martin, South Dakota.

From the correspondence with Mr. Hodson, it appears that he has negotiated an outside lease with the landowner [McDonald] for the use of this land.

As you know, the regulations provide for Indian preference in the awarding of grazing permits on Indian land, and Mr. Valandry has indicated his intention of appealing any decision which would infringe upon this preference privilege given him in the regulations.

Mr. Hodson, on the other hand, surely must know that leases on Indian land need to be made out on approved lease forms and be approved by the Superintendent to be valid. We have advised Mr. Hodson that we do not have any record of a lease to him on the land and that we expect his cooperation in keeping his livestock off of the land involved. If we are to follow the regulations, it appears that this is the only action for us to take.[80]

Provided with Reifel's official, by-the-book explanation of Hodson's illegal conduct, rather than admit that the state representative and bank owner-operator had crossed the boundary of legal propriety by executing a lease outside the prescribed rules and regulations, Berry became an apologist for Hodson's criminal behavior. In writing to Hodson, Berry implied that it was somehow the Lakota's fault that a whole federal bureaucracy had purposely been built around administering the allotments and that individuals like Hodson were merely innocent victims of less-than-ethical Lakota dealings:

I imagine what has happened is that you [Hodson] have been stuck in the position that many [white] ranchers on Indian reservations have gotten into of having to deal with the Indian direct in order to get along with the Indian. The only trouble is, when we make these kind of deals, we take a chance of getting 'hooked.'[81]

Having been exposed by the Interior Department with his hand in the illegal-leasing cookie jar, yet encouraged by Berry's soft peddling of a serious matter—framing Hodson's conduct as merely getting "hooked" rather than caught and so not holding him criminally liable for his illegal transactions—Hodson next projected his frustrations and anger with the Interior Department onto the greater Oglala Lakota community:

For just a minute place yourself [meaning Berry] in my position. Nearly every day one or more educated ambitious promising young Indian boy or girl [sic] come to my desk for advise [sic] and a little financial help. They are more than anxious to do something for themselves and remind us of the accommodations their white neighbor has gotten here at the bank. . . .

Last week I reluctantly refused a Mr. George Twist[,] a promising young returned Indian soldier boy who asked for a small loan to enable him to take a job in a body shop in Rapid City. It seems that his wife already has a job in a store there. I came near opening my personal purse to help him and then the thought came to me of the many such deals I have financed in the past.

So don't let the matter trouble you further[;] with this letter I will consider the matter closed and in the future I'll try harder to look out for Hodson and let the poor indian [sic] do likewise.

I realize your hands are, like my own, are [sic] tied. You can guess what my attitude toward the future pertaining to the numerous Indian affairs brought to us here at the bank.[82]

Because the leasing affair was threatening Hodson's ability to keep the land for his own economic benefit, he unethically used the situation to justify discriminating against what he termed "ambitious and promising" Lakota people who, like the "promising young returned Indian soldier boy," would now be denied bank loans for purposes as basic as job relocation.

Having lost all perspective that Hodson was illegally trespassing, that he was interfering politically with a Native preference project designed to encourage greater Lakota use of their own land base, and that he was obviously engaging in deliberate discriminatory and illegal banking practices, Berry attempted to whitewash the whole Hodson matter with an illusion of legitimacy. He cited Hodson's impeccable credentials to Glenn Emmons, the commissioner of Indian affairs:

I am enclosing herewith a copy of a letter [18 March 1955] I have today received from O. A. Hodson, Blackpipe State Bank, Martin, who for twenty years has operated a bank on the Pine Ridge Reservation and who serves in the State Legislature. In addition, to operating a bank on the Pine Ridge Reservation, Mr. Hodson has a small farming operation near Martin, which is operated by his son.[83]

After establishing Hodson's credentials to Emmons, Berry briefly explained the injustice that his constituent Hodson was suffering at the colluding hands of both the Interior Department and the Lakota. In an all-too-familiar pattern, Berry characterized collaboration between Natives and whites favorably at the expense of all-Native enterprises. Repeating Hodson's assessment of McDonald as a competent Lakota person, Berry spoke dismissively about

Valandry and how he had taken away the land in question—albeit legitimately—from Hodson:

> In order to operate this farm, he [Hodson] has had two quarters of land under lease from an Indian woman who owns this land. He describes her as being reliable and capable, and my understanding is that he has for a number of years been leasing her land and paying her direct. It seems that now this land has been tossed into a grazing unit for the benefit of an Indian operator by the name of Gilbert Valandra. Since the Hodson lease is not through the office, the land has been taken away from him, in spite of the fact that he has the lease paid for a year in advance.[84]

With such "impeccably honest" individuals as Hodson and McDonald both conducting and concluding the lease transaction, Berry made a further effort to construct legitimacy from illegality. Reminding Emmons that Hodson had paid his lease to McDonald a year in advance, Berry implied that the exchange of money somehow transformed a highly questionable lease into a completely legitimate transaction. Moreover, Berry conveyed to Emmons how other whites in the surrounding Pine Ridge Reservation area were reacting to Hodson's situation: "I would like to have you read his [Hodson's] letter [of 18 March 1955], because it does indicate the feeling of a great many white people who deal with these Indians and have made a conscientious effort to assist them, but who can't assist them because when they do, they 'get stuck.'"[85]

If Hodson's behavior—trespassing, politicizing a regulatory and preference process, and economically discriminating against the greater Lakota community because of a personal transaction that could potentially go sour—represented a conscientious effort on the part of the white community to assist the Lakota, then the Lakota could indeed use some of the Interior Department's regulatory protection from all the white help. With Berry and Hodson behaving thick as thieves in masking Hodson's trespass, however, it seemed unlikely that the case would result in any BIA enforcement. Indeed, Valandry's nonuse of McDonald's two quarters in his range unit sent a signal to both the Lakota and whites that Lakota preference would now be subordinated to a white's singular economic interest in using trust land.

Through contact with the local BIA agency at Pine Ridge, Valandry evidently knew of Hodson's political activity about whether McDonald's land would remain part of his range unit. Valandry, much like Hodson, appealed to Berry over the use of the land in question. Explaining that after working fifteen years as a ranch hand for Tom Berry, a rancher and former S.D. governor, and having decided to raise livestock for a living, Valandry quit his employer, invoked Native preference for a range unit that included McDonald's two quarter sections, and subsequently became embroiled with Hodson over the use of the land:

> I quit there last spring and came to Martin, and found me a grazing unit . . . north of Martin. This said unit is located and joins O. A. Hodson, the banker at Martin.
>
> I took this unit through my Indian preference, I secured a[n] F.H.A. loan, and bought me a string of cows last fall. This spring I got a suppliment [sic] loan and bought more which more than fills my unit.
>
> In order to comply with the rules and regulations of the Indian Department at Pine Ridge, South Dakota, I must have more land. Joining me on the south is three quarters of Indian land and the Indian Department has considered putting this in my unit.
>
> However, I understand Hodson has went [sic] into politics over this matter, and claims he needs it worse than I do. I understand that an agreement on this land will be decided through the Department of Interior. In reaching an agreement on this, it no doubt will be brought to your attention, and I would like you to consider it seriously, because if a[n] Indian's preference rights does [sic] not hold in a case like this, all I have to say is all your work for the Indians has been done in vain.[86]

Valandry's appeal unfortunately did not produce the desired effect: Berry did not seriously reconsider the Hodson matter. Incredibly, despite knowing the illegal particulars of Hodson's lease, Berry responded to Valandry with a paternalistic lecture on the inviolability of a Lakota keeping his or her word and creditworthiness if "the Indian is to improve his lot in this hard business world in which he is required to live."[87] Never mind that Berry omitted from his lecture the all-important fact that having a politician in one's back pocket helps, too.

Perhaps Valandry's 12 May 1955 letter to Berry about the Hodson lease affair best illustrates why so many non-Native ranchers and farmers residing in the Pine Ridge area and other Lakota lands had, as Berry had alluded to, a keen, vested interest in Hodson's leasing matter and anxiously awaited its outcome:

> Received your letter [3 May 1955] some time ago. And after reading it, I could see that you had decided that Mr. Hodson should have the land.
>
> You are right to a certain extent[;] it is always a good policy to keep ever[y]body honest[,] I know. But I don't believe that you are taking into

consideration the existing rules & regulations that we Indians have to live by here on the Pine Ridge reservation.

There is no Indian that can legally lease his land unless he leases through [the] Indian office. And we all know it there has been circular's & phamphlets [*sic*] sent out from the office ever so often stating that fact. And Supt. Reifel has made many talks this winter telling the white man & Indians both that even if an Indian has applied for his fee patent[,] and if the white man should make him (the Indian) an advance on the strength of it [the fee patent application], it will not be recognized when the land would be sold.

Now this land that we are arguing over at the present time, it won't make much difference who gets it. Because it has been overgrazed so much that I know Pine Ridge won't let anyone use it this year. And that's pretty good proof that these verbal leases or contractual agreements[,] whatever you may call them[,] are trying to be put aside by the Indian office.

Now I kinda [*sic*] hate to see this particular case be decided in Hodson's favor. Not so much because I am interested in it. But there is just many more cases like it right around in the near vicinity. And there [are] liable to be a lot more of these people trying to get their problems decided on in Washington instead of Pine Ridge. The personnel in Pine Ridge try to have us understand that they are capable of settling our problems. And I think they are.

Now there is a man here in the country by the name of Edison Ward. He does a lot of business for the Indians & white men. Like drawing up lease & selling their land for them. He disregards Pine Ridge & goes contrary to all the rules and regulations. Now for instance he leased four quarters of land out of my unit last winter to O. A. Hodson, made out his own lease forms & even went as far as to file them in the court house at a cost of about $7.50 a quarter. Now when the agency office found it out, they came down & damn quick made short work of that kind of business. . . .

And there are many more deals similar to this one going on here all the time[,] and if your [*sic*] knew the truth about them instead of maybe believing just what someone says, you may change your views some.[88]

After five months of controversy about who would eventually use McDonald's land, Valandry resigned himself to not having it included in his range unit. By exposing outright the vested interests that so many whites who lived on or near Lakota lands had in the outcome of Hodson's bureaucratic problem, Valandry sheared away any veil of innocence that Berry had tried so hard to manufacture on Hodson's behalf.

Indeed, living in an area in which Lakota land, when not being sold to nearby whites, was mostly being leased to them, Hodson cannot credibly plead ignorance about the Interior Department's leasing rules and regulations. As Valandry stated, the Interior Department had been releasing information for some time condemning the very type of transaction that Berry, Hodson, and others were defending. Perhaps the most telling fact of this leasing controversy, though, was Hodson's occupations. Being a state representative, a banker, and a rancher, Hodson was undoubtedly accustomed to handling matters that required close attention to detail. In view of this occupational background, the pleas of innocence that Hodson tried to make about not knowing all the legal protocols for leasing Lakota land reeked of hyperbole.

Finally, when Berry expressed to Emmons that other non-Natives were getting hooked or stuck with "just another 'lousey' deal" (31 March 1955) by the Interior Department's bureaucracy, the Lakota People, or both,[89] he undoubtedly meant that Hodson's flouting of Native land tenure laws was not a singular event. If the Interior Department had required Hodson to comply with the rules and regulations governing the leasing of Native land, such BIA-enforced compliance would have exposed countless other questionable leasing or purchasing deals that whites had made with Lakotas.

Having had his illegal lease and his trespassing exposed, Hodson, by advising "Mrs. McDonald to take a deed [that is, patent-in-fee] to her land,"[90] invoked the only remaining measure to circumvent the Interior Department's policies and to avoid its penalties for both trespassing and failing to uphold Native preference. Within a few weeks of Hodson's fee-patent advice to McDonald, Berry and others obligingly paved the much-maligned bureaucratic highway so that McDonald could obtain a patent-in-fee. Her fee patent not only freed Hodson from the bureaucracy that challenged his unauthorized use of Lakota land but simultaneously illustrated that bureaucracy was a problem only when it prevented a non-Native from using or acquiring Native land.

Iron Crow

For the greater Lakota community, Hodson's case represented only a microcosm of a more serious land divestiture problem. Contrary to his righteous outcry over the two hundred files languishing in bureaucratic abyss, Berry was an active player in the bureaucratic game, consistently skewing it to white advantage. For example, during 1957, Berry routinely corresponded with Thomas F. Arnold, a rancher who either leased or purchased large portions of Lakota land. At least fifteen times in seven months, Berry shared inside information on a minimum of forty-six fee patents that were approved and issued to Lakota people residing on the Rosebud Reservation.[91] As a rancher who had "an interest in five separate range units [that] include[d] 210 individual tracts of Indian land [on the Rosebud Reservation] . . . totaling 39,822 acres,"[92] and as a local and regional real estate and livestock dealer who happened to be a member of the South Dakota Stock Growers Association (SDSGA),[93] Arnold had a major economic stake in the status of Lakota land.[94] Gaining regular patent-in-fee intelligence from Berry, Arnold could conceivably target these fee-patent Lakotas—individuals whose standard of living was often far below their non-Native neighbors—and begin to negotiate a private land sale on behalf of either himself or one of his white ranching clients.

Yet however much whites used the bureaucracy to white advantage, rabid termination-oriented politicians like Berry could see that the burgeoning rules and regulations governing Native land use and management were, albeit unwittingly, slowing the rapid pace of Native land divestiture. This so-called bureaucratic problem was obviously proving troubling for Berry's several hundred Hodson-like constituents who found it more and more difficult to gain outright control of Lakota territory. Insofar as ward status was presumably the reason for the bureaucracy, it did not further the termination advocates' short- or long-term interests, and so ending ward status quickly became the terminationists' cant.

While the United States was busily solving its self-created Indian Problem—first through a 1947 proposed withdrawal program and later through a duly adopted 1953 policy of termination—the Lakota decided, without much fanfare, to invoke the principle of self-determination as a viable alternative answer. Given that the federal government was determined to decrease BIA appropriations in the late 1940s, the Oglala Lakota understandably responded to this decrease by forming a plan to raise revenue. The tribal council decided to tax non–Oglala Lakota members who leased land on the Pine Ridge Reservation. Thus, during an April 1949 Oglala Sioux Tribal Council meeting, the council membership approved Resolution 34-49:

> Whereas, the non-member lessee enjoys the privilege of grazing and farming Indian and Tribal land at a minimum cost far below the rates charged for like lands off the reservation, and
>
> Whereas, the said lessees do not pay any taxes on the land they operate and the Oglala Sioux Tribal Council has the power to tax non-members, now therefore be it
>
> RESOLVED, by the Oglala Sioux Tribal Council that there shall be an assessment fee of 4¢ per acre for grazing trust land (allotted, heirship, and tribal),

and 6¢ per acre for land with water (grazing). There shall be an assessment of 15¢ an acre for dry farm land. These assessments are in addition to the lease fees, rentals, and these assessments shall be paid in to the Oglala Sioux Tribal Council and accounted for by the Treasurer on a commercial system of accounting. This fund shall be used for general purposes of the public to benefit the tribe.

FURTHER RESOLVED, THAT THE PROVISIONS OF THIS RESOLU-TION SHALL REMAIN in full force and effect until a certified copy or copies of a duly adopted resolution or resolutions effecting a rescission or amendment, as the case may be, shall have been furnished [to or by] the Secretary of the Interior, or his authorized representative.[95]

For whatever reason, a subsequent Oglala Sioux Tribal grazing resolution that outlined the sale of grazing privileges for a three-year period, beginning 1 November 1950 and ending 31 October 1953, either did not include this tax-assessment provision, or, if it was included, ignored it altogether. In 1953, however, the Oglala Lakota began to aggressively enforce their 1949 resolution to tax the non-Native ranch and farm operators bidding for the privilege of grazing their livestock on Lakota land. This Lakota initiative would soon provoke these very operators to fiercely resist any policy that involved Lakota management or control of reservation lands.

Beginning in the late fall of 1952, the Oglala Lakota turned their attention to the 31 October 1953 expiration date of their current three-year grazing resolution. On 8 January 1953, the Oglala Sioux Tribal Council (OSTC) passed a new grazing resolution affecting 239 range units that totaled 812,304 acres. Extending the grazing period from three to five years, the OST Resolution 1-53 authorized the Lakota to advertise grazing privileges to the ranchers, who had to submit their bids for the range units by the closing date of 12 June 1953. In addition, the grazing resolution stipulated: (1) an increased grazing rate fee from $6.25 to $8.75 per head of cattle and a $5.00 minimum grazing rate fee; (2) a required hay-cutting permit that the operator-lessee must obtain at a nominal fee; (3) an assessment of a $.03 per acre per year tax; and (4) required stock-water facilities developed for every two sections (1,280 acres) of land.

As the 12 June 1953 deadline approached for all interested operators to submit their bids, several white ranchers and farmers began to protest the stipulated conditions. On 16 May 1953, Merton Glover, a rancher living on the Pine Ridge Reservation and a member of the SDSGA's executive committee, wrote Berry about his concerns regarding the Oglala Lakota's 1953 grazing resolution. After stating his reasons for opposing it—such as the

recent decline in cattle prices since the fall of 1952, the uncertainty of climate
conditions from year to year, and the reluctance of bonding companies to
issue surety bonds to ranchers and farmers for long-term contracts—Glover
further vented about the Oglala Lakota's three-cent tax:

> After paying this increased rental we still are black mailed [sic] into pay [sic]
> this three cent tribal tax, and I mean that literally, for the [Interior] Depart-
> ment uses the authority of the United States Government to collect this. If
> the Department did not sanction this action, someone could take them to
> court and get a legal decision. You must know its [sic] hard to bring action
> involving the United States.[96]

Glover's viscerally hostile reaction to the Oglala Lakota's stipulations,
especially the tax, was shared by other stock growers and eventually led to
a series of summer meetings among the Oglala Lakota, the BIA, the white
ranchers, and South Dakota's congressional delegation.

On 29 May 1953, Louis Beckwith, chair of the SDSGA's Public Lands committee and a lessee of Lakota land on the Pine Ridge reservation, wrote Senator Case about the committee's concerns over the OST grazing resolution.
Noting the volatility of cattle prices and no tenure or compensation granted
for permanent improvements on Lakota land, the committee wanted the
five-dollars-per-head minimum and the water stock development requirement omitted from the resolution.[97]

Much like Glover in sentiment but with less strident language, Beckwith
offered a different anti–OST tax opinion: "An explanation of the tribal tax
I think is unnecessary as you are well acquainted that the [Oglala Sioux]
Tribal Council is in competition with the Government of the United States
when it levies its own taxes."[98] In other words, the Oglala Lakota were, in
his view, vying with the United States' presumably exclusive authority over
taxation; therefore, the OSTC's tax resolution was not only legally suspect
but also frankly invalid. According to the white ranchers, the OSTC had no
power or authority to levy taxes.

With a growing number of white stock growers firing off complaints to
Berry about the Oglala Lakota's grazing resolution, a first meeting of the
Oglala Lakota, the BIA, and members of the SDSGA was set for 9 June 1953
at the St. Charles Hotel in Pierre, South Dakota.[99] William Fire Thunder
and Samuel Stands, both Tribal Council members, officially represented the
Oglala Lakota. The BIA officials present were Sande, the Pine Ridge super-
intendent; Mast, the BIA agency's range manager at Pine Ridge; Cooper, the
BIA area director; and Carl, the assistant to the area director. Those present

who represented the white stock growers were the ranchers Ed Arnold, Tom Arnold, James Ramey, Merton Glover, Ralph Jones, Bud Thomas, and Woodrow Metzer.[100] Though Berry himself was notably absent from the Pierre meeting because of his Republican Party duties, he nonetheless arranged to be in Rapid City, South Dakota, on 13 June 1953 for the sole purpose of being debriefed by the stock growers on the Pierre meeting.

As far as the white ranchers were concerned, the Pierre meeting failed to produce the desired result of having either the BIA or the Oglala Lakota change the grazing resolution to suit their liking. Instead, the stock growers left the meeting with the distinct impression that the BIA's agency and area office—not the Oglala Lakota—were the culprits spearheading the new conditions for obtaining grazing privileges at Pine Ridge.

Not satisfied with the outcome of the Pierre meeting, the white ranchers met with Berry in Rapid City a few days later and expressed their view that the four major elements of the grazing resolution were wholly unfair: the grazing rate fee was too high and must be renegotiated; the minimum grazing fee was too inflexible and must be removed because the grass was already paid for in the grazing fee; the hay-cutting permit was redundant; the water development provision must be voluntary rather than mandatory, and a former lessee must be reimbursed or compensated for any water development. It went without saying that they refused to acknowledge the Oglala Lakota's authority to tax them.

Moreover, two days after the Pierre meeting and a day before the Rapid City meeting, Tom Arnold perhaps best expressed to Berry the white stock growers' fears about where the Oglala Lakota's resolution might lead: "I attended the meeting day before yesterday at Pierre on this Indian business. While most of the matters discussed there pertained particularly to the Pine Ridge Indian Reservation, yet the policies behind it would not be limited entirely to the Pine Ridge Reservation if they [the BIA] were permitted to go through as set up for the Pine Ridge Reservation."[101]

In other words, should the stipulations of the Oglala Lakota's grazing resolution remain intact and take effect, Lakota officials on the Cheyenne River, Crow Creek, Flandreau, Lower Brule, Rosebud, Sisseton-Wahpeton, Standing Rock, and Yankton reservations would undoubtedly change their respective grazing resolutions as well. With millions of acres of reservation grazing land involved and sizeable profits at stake, it is no surprise that the white stock growers—the United States' surrogates—panicked over the horrifying prospect of greater Lakota control in managing reservation land. Hence, immediately after the Rapid City meeting, Berry wrote a three-page letter to Barton Greenwood, the then-acting commissioner of Indian affairs, reiterating the stock growers' major complaints with OSTC's grazing resolution and personally offering his office to broker a deal on behalf of the stock growers.[102] Indeed, Berry's immediate political intervention showed that the OSTC's action was quickly evolving into a seminal case that would determine whose influence—the Lakota's or the white ranchers'—would prevail in controlling the fate of the Lakota's homeland.

Between 12 June 1953 (the deadline for all stock growers to submit their bids for the sale of grazing privileges) and 1 November 1953 (the beginning date of the five-year grazing permit), the white ranchers intensified their efforts to modify the grazing stipulations. With little or no results to show from their June meeting in Pierre, Berry convened a meeting on 6 July 1953 in Washington, D.C., of South Dakota's congressional delegation, including Representatives Berry and Lovre, Senator Mundt, Art Junke (representing Senator Case, who could not attend), and BIA officials Greenwood, Weaver, and Rudolph. The meeting was to discuss a possible compromise on the contentious issues surrounding the leasing of range units on Pine Ridge Reservation.

The Washington meeting, like the Pierre one, failed to produce any substantive change in the OST grazing resolution. The next day, Berry, in an apologetic letter to Beckwith, emphasized the BIA's intractability on the $8.75 grazing rate:

> I appreciate, Louie, that this isn't too helpful but we [South Dakota's congressional delegation and staff] used every argument at our disposal and put it on political, economic, and distress basis. Every time, they came back with an answer that since the rate had been established and since it was in conformity with an overall policy which had been put into effect on all the other reservations prior to this time and since the Indians had already signed powers of attorney definitely setting forth this amount of lease on allotted land, there was just nothing they could do. . . . Sorry I don't have a more favorable report to give.[103]

However, Berry and others did get the BIA to at least reconsider the water development stipulation, possibly modifying water development from a mandatory to a voluntary basis. Furthermore, rather than requiring the standard, albeit capital intensive, water development for every two sections, the BIA would allow greater flexibility in where to place the stock-water facilities.

Berry's largely unfavorable report on the 6 July meeting apparently made the stock growers even more anxious over the grazing resolution. In a desperate measure, the stock growers' leadership used its reservation-based contacts to call a general meeting among the BIA's agency and area office, the OSTC, the Lakota trust landowners, and the stock growers. The stock growers' leadership evidently believed that if they had a significant number of stakeholders present to explain their rationale for a lower grazing fee, the BIA's bureaucratic unreasonableness and "corruption" would be exposed before the everyday Lakota. However, as Beckwith noted to Berry, such a gathering was not without risk:

> We had a meeting of some of the same fellows that were at your meeting [13 June 1953] at Rapid [City]. . . . We talked them in to [sic] calling a meeting of all stockmen and Indian land owners on the Pine Ridge as in my wire. Maybe this isn't the thing to do. The Council is calling the meeting and we are going to have a hard time presenting our side as [William] Firethunder and Butch are going to try to control this meeting with Sande's help. They are quite solid behind the Department. Firethunder and [Charles] Underbaggage were the two Executive [Committee] members that amended the Councils [grazing rate from] 6.25 to 8.75.[104]

The stock growers' increasing impatience with the BIA over the grazing resolution obviously outweighed the risk of facing such an outcome. Beckwith, moreover, displayed an all-too-common white arrogance when he outlined the stock growers' most likely strategy at the upcoming meeting:

> At the above [stock growers] meeting in Kadoka yesterday [11 July 1953] we tried to decide what to try to bring out at the meeting. Every point of this contract [that is, the grazing resolution] to be discussed and a resolution from the assembly on each. . . . We thought first on the program should be a talk by someone from your Indian Affaires [sic] Committee if you could not attend. . . . This meeting may backfire, one never knows how a meeting of these Sioux will turn out. If we could get up and run the meeting[,] I believe we could handle the crowd but we are letting the Tribe run this show and are trying to guide them a trifle in the direction and matters we'd like them to discuss.[105]

By having a member or members of the House Subcommittee on Indian Affairs attend the 20 July 1953 Pine Ridge meeting at their behest, the stock growers wanted to give the Lakotas the impression that they wielded significant political power. Combining this image of political clout with the expectation of a large turnout of white ranchers at the meeting, the SDSGA leadership hoped to intimidate the Lakota participants into letting them commandeer the agenda and accomplish their objective of renegotiating favorable grazing terms. However, reports from the meeting showed the opposite; the stock growers' influence was effectively marginalized:

> The [Oglala Lakota] landowners who arrived first at the meeting on July 20th, elected as chairman James Roan Eagle, who is a stock grower as well as land-owner. The council members who are helping the [white] stockgrowers imme-diately staged a protest to the election of the chairman and attempted to get their own presiding officers for the meeting but this movement failed."[106]

Beckwith complained bitterly to Berry that although the OSTC called the meeting and a presiding chair was to be elected from the assembly—which comprised the stock growers, OSTC, Lakota allotted landowners, and BIA personnel—"the [department] working through Billy Firethunder, gathered several old Indians and a few good talkers that were part Indian, elected a chairman [James Roan Eagle] and decided how they were to control the meeting for the [department], using the old Indian landowner theme, as their weapon."[107] Beckwith's description of the well-attended but highly contentious gathering, in which "approximately 500 Indians, part Indian and white people, talking two languages, and shouting at each other for five hours,"[108] revealed that the Lakota-BIA coalition and the stock growers were worlds apart, and that no compromise on the five-year grazing resolution was on the horizon.

One can easily imagine that having failed miserably at controlling the meeting, at forcing a showdown with an intransigent BIA agency and area office, and at preventing the OSTC from closing ranks with the BIA agency, the white stock growers relied more than ever on Berry's office for assistance. Berry, of course, would not disappoint his stock grower constituency. Imme-diately after the 20 July 1953 Pine Ridge meeting, Berry penned a detailed, nine-page appeal to the Assistant Interior Secretary Orme Lewis that reiter-ated the major complaints of the stock growers:[109] that the lease price or graz-ing rate of $8.75 was excessive, that requiring the purchase of a hay-cutting permit for an already paid-for range unit was unfair, that compulsory water development created an undue hardship, and, finally, that the Oglala Lakota $.03 per acre tax was not within the Tribal Council's authority to levy.

Again, Berry hastily convened a meeting on 28 July 1953 in Washington, D.C., between South Dakota's congressional delegation, their staff, and Inte-rior Department officials Lewis, Greenwood, Weaver, and Rudolph. From this meeting, Lewis agreed to modify the grazing resolution's stipulations. On 12 August 1953, an Interior Department news release officially outlined the

BIA's position on the summerlong grazing resolution controversy. Notably, while mentioning the four major conditions that had fueled the white stock growers' protest, the Interior Department focused publicly only on the least contentious stipulation, the grazing rate:

> Secretary of the Interior Douglas McKay has announced departmental decisions and clarifications on questions recently raised by a number of South Dakota livestock operators about the sale of grazing privileges at the Pine Ridge Indian Reservation for the five-year period beginning next November 1.
>
> Following the advertisement for the sale of the grazing privileges at the Pine Ridge Agency in May and early June, four principle [sic] questions were raised with the Department. First, it was charged that the minimum rate of $8.75 per head for cattle yearlong for the first year of the permit period was too high in the face of declining livestock prices. Secondly, some of the stockmen objected to the requirement for payment of a tribal tax of three cents per acre for doing business on the reservation. Thirdly, some objected to the provision that no hay shall be cut on the permitted lands without the written approval of the Indian landowners and the agency superintendent. Fourthly, there was objection to the requirement for the development of stock-water facilities on the permitted lands.
>
> On the question of minimum rate for the first year, the Department has determined that the $8.75 rate figure is equitable as a basis for the first year's grazing fees and should be maintained. Thereafter, fees will be adjusted annually in accordance with the average price of South Dakota beef as reported by the Bureau of Agricultural Economics, Department of Agriculture.
>
> In their protests, some of the stockmen had contended that the rate should be $6.25 per head which is the figure established by the Pine Ridge Tribal Council for the grazing on tribal lands of the reservation and recommended by that body for the allotted lands. Under the applicable regulations[,] the Tribal Council has the responsibility for establishing the rates for tribal land[,] while the Bureau of Indian Affairs is responsible for prescribing the terms and conditions applicable to the allotted lands under grants of authority given to the given agency superintendent by the individual Indian owners. Over 90 percent of the grazing area on the Pine Ridge Reservation is allotted land. . . .
>
> On the question of the tribal tax, the Department held that collection of this tax is a responsibility of the Tribe rather than the Bureau and that it should not be included in the stipulations attached to the permits. The Bureau has been instructed to eliminate this requirement from the stipulations.
>
> On the question of hay cutting, the Department has upheld the Bureau's position that the authorizations to issue grazing permits granted by the land-

owners does not authorize the cutting of hay. Hay cutting permits must, therefore, be obtained from the Indian landowners with the approval of the agency superintendent.

Finally, the Department has determined that the stipulations on stock-water development should be fully clarified for each permittee before the start of the grazing season so that there will be no doubt as to the extent of his obligations. In the event that agreement cannot be reached, the permittee will be allowed to withdraw this bid and his deposit will be refunded.[110]

Judging from the Interior Department's news release, it could seem as if the Oglala Lakota had not been able to defend their four conditions against the stock growers' campaign to rewrite the entire grazing resolution. Yet despite the stock growers' best efforts, the struggle had actually produced mixed results.

While they may have lost on reducing the grazing fee and on eliminating the hay-cutting stipulation, the stock growers won their battle to remove the Oglala Lakota tax from the grazing resolution. The tax could not be a U.S.-endorsed condition for leasing Lakota land. As for the stock-water development stipulation, the two camps drew a tie.

However, unlike the grazing fee, hay-cutting permit, and stock-water development issues, the stock growers' victory on the Oglala Lakota tax was not so clear-cut. Though it was removed as a stipulation, it was described as not being subject to the BIA's regulatory discretion. In other words, it was simply not within the BIA's domain. Accordingly, its removal as a stipulation did not necessarily negate the Oglala Lakota's taxing authority as an independent government. Not surprisingly, a stock growers' news article that appeared three days after the Interior Department's news release suggested otherwise: "The three cent an acre tribal tax, which was taken out of the contract will save the leasees [sic] thousands of dollars yearly. It is now a matter between the Tribal Council and the operator, with no part being taken by the Department."[111]

The Interior Department's move to eliminate the Oglala Lakota's land-use tax from the grazing resolution did, though, directly raise the issue of Lakota self-governance and the implied question of whether white ranchers could get away with defying its policies. First, as the Interior Department itself acknowledged in its news release, because of the socially disastrous allotment policy that virtually eliminated commonly held land, an overwhelming percentage of Oglala Lakota land was held as individual trust allotments that were usually leased. A significant percentage of the lessees on all nine

Lakota/Dakota reservations were non-Native. Thus, if non-Native interests flouted or seriously interfered with the Oglala Lakota's ability to collect this land-use tax, an important governmental function of raising revenue for Lakota government-sponsored programs would be seriously undermined. More important, the U.S. tradition of economic hegemony over Lakota communities would continue unchallenged.

When the Oglala Lakota first passed the land-use tax in April 1949 and, a year later, amended the tax rate from four cents to three cents per acre,[112] their decisions generated considerable discussion among the Lakota on the reservations. Knowing how controversial the OSTC's action would be, C. H. Powers, the Pine Ridge BIA agency superintendent, sought legal counsel regarding its validity. In a 19 April 1950 letter to A. B. Melzner, the BIA area office's counsel, Powers raised the issue of the tax:

> We will appreciate having the comments of the Legal Division of the two latter resolutions [147-50 and 148-50] since it appears they are the key resolutions and will be the basis for the assessment of taxes. This procedure has come in for a lot of discussion at the reservation level. Tribal members are pretty well aware of what it means in terms of a collection problem and are, we believe, in a position to spend the funds so collected for the betterment of living conditions on the reservation.[113]

Although the legal division endorsed the tax, and the Interior Department found no objection to Resolutions 147-50 and 148-50, on 2 September 1950, Superintendent Powers received from the SDSGA a resolution officially announcing its position on the Oglala Lakota land-use tax: "the tribal councils have no constitutional authority to levy, impose or collect taxes or assessments on nonmembers [read non-Natives]."[114] Believing quite mistakenly that the Oglala Lakota lacked any legal authority to tax nonmembers, several of the white ranchers refused to pay the land-use tax throughout the entire three-year grazing period and, as a result of their refusal, were delinquent. Since the three-year grazing contracts were to expire 31 October 1953, in January 1953, the OSTC considered and adopted Grazing Resolution 1-53. Immediately thereafter, they also approved OST Resolution 4-53 regarding land-use tax delinquencies:

> Whereas: A number of white operators have refused to pay the tribal tax assessment on leases held on the Pine Ridge Reservations.
>
> Therefore Be It Resolved: That the Oglala Sioux Tribal Council recommend that the Superintendent disapprove of any leases or grazing permits

to a non-member of the Oglala Sioux Tribe who are delinquent on payment of [the] Tribal Tax Assessment until such time as the Tribal Tax Assessment is paid in full.[115]

Since Lakota lands are held in trust and "title" to them is held by the United States, it becomes painfully obvious that, while the Oglala Lakota could invoke a land-use tax, they would have trouble enforcing it if the United States did not stand behind their rightful powers of self-governance, which included taxation. As Powers's 1950 letter to Melzner and as the Oglala Lakota's 1953 recommendation to the BIA both implied, collecting the tax from the white ranchers would require U.S. backing. Through its BIA surrogate, the United States could choose either to ignore the Oglala Lakota by arbitrarily approving grazing permits despite white ranchers' tax delinquencies on Lakota land leases, or to accept the Oglala Lakota's recommendation, in which case the BIA would refuse to approve any new leases for delinquent lessees until they satisfied their outstanding tax bill to the Oglala Lakota.

When the Interior Department capitulated to the whites' demand in its August 1953 news release by eliminating the land-use tax from the five-year grazing resolution, the Lakota were left not only in a subordinate political position but, with PL 83-280 just on the horizon, in a highly vulnerable one as well. Buoyed by their success at having the OSTC's grazing resolution significantly modified, the white stock growers boldly claimed that the land-use tax did not apply to them.

In response to the Interior Department's unilateral action to modify the OSTC's grazing resolution, as well as to the stock growers' refusal to pay the OST lease assessment, the Oglala Lakota began mobilizing their limited resources to enforce the administratively omitted but nonetheless valid tax. They called a 19 August 1953 special meeting in which the OSTC authorized its president or vice-president "to proceed with the collection of the license fee [that is, the land-use tax] under the general direction of the Executive Committee."[116] In a 20 August 1953 memorandum, the BIA superintendent Sande, who attended the OSTC special meeting, explained to the BIA area director why the meeting was held:

> The meeting was called for the purpose of discussing the problem created by the decision of the Secretary [of the Interior] that the Department or any of its representatives could not assist in the collection of the 3¢ and 15¢ an acre tribal license fee, or so-called tribal tax. There was considerable resentment over the fact that an important conference had been held in Washington to deal with the matters of considerable concern to the Oglala Sioux Tribe, without letting

the officers and the council know that such a conference was to be held and without inviting the council to send a representative to hold forth the views of the tribe with reference to the problems under consideration.

It is fairly apparent that most of the permittees will pay the license fee for the first year, but since it is the announced position opinion of the officers of the [South Dakota] Stockgrowers Association that the license fee is illegal and that the permittees do not have to pay it, it is likely to be difficult for the tribe to make the collection for the second and following years of the permit without the compulsion that would come from a plan whereby the payment of the tax could be a condition precedent to the approval of the permit by the Superintendent.[117]

Maneuvered into the position of having to collect their own tax, the Oglala Lakota began issuing tax-collection letters to all permittees who had successfully bid on and been awarded a range unit. These tax-collection letters made it clear to the permittees that the land-use tax was not going to vaporize just because the BIA had acquiesced to the white stock growers' political pressure. Unquestionably, the white stock growers and the Oglala Lakota were each approaching a critical juncture over the larger issue of who, in fact, had the authority to manage and control reservation lands.

Upset by the Oglala Lakota's determined efforts to have them pay the tax and having exhausted their reservoir of political remedies over the tax controversy through the Interior Department's administrative channels, the white ranchers decided to seek a judicial remedy (see Glover's letter, p. 122) as another way to derail or nullify the Oglala Lakota's sovereignty. In pursuing a judicial solution, the stock growers had no reason to fear that any white court would be adverse to their antitax argument against the Oglala Lakota. After all, influential whites had, almost without exception, aligned themselves with the white stock growers throughout the grazing resolution controversy, agreeing in principle with the SDSGA's position that "the tribal tax is a discriminatory and unjustifiable tax and . . . the tribal tax should be abolished."[118]

The surprising exception to this rule was George T. Mickelson. Recently appointed to the U.S. district court in South Dakota, Mickelson would eventually preside over the tax question in *Iron Crow v. The Ogallala Sioux Tribe of the Pine Ridge Reservation*. Mickelson proved a surprising exception because his political biography reads like any other overachieving white from South Dakota. He served in the state legislature (1937–43) and was speaker of the House (1941–43). He also served as South Dakota's attorney general (1943–

47). Mickelson was first elected governor in 1946 and then reelected in 1948. Because of a statutory limit, he could not seek a third term in 1952. During his first term as governor, Mickelson provided state aid to distressed stock growers during a devastating January 1949 blizzard. Moreover, at the SDSGA's annual convention in June 1949, the membership passed a resolution commending Mickelson for his assistance.

Because Mickelson was a popular governor, a natural step for him would have been to seek a congressional seat. Had he done so, though, it would have been costly to the state's Republican Party. The state's first and second House congressional districts were not open to Mickelson as a Republican. Regarding the first district, because Mickelson was from the East River region, E. Y. Berry's West River congressional seat was secure. As to the second district, it too was already occupied by a Republican. Having served as governor, Mickelson had statewide rather than regional political appeal, and so one of the state's two senate seats seemed more in line with Mickelson's political ambitions.[119] Indeed, as the 1946 and 1948 gubernatorial election results showed, Mickelson's voter appeal was comparable to South Dakota's Senate Republican incumbents, Francis Case and Karl Mundt. Case was up for reelection in 1956, and Mundt's term would expire two years after Mickelson's governorship ended in 1952.

As of 1953, then, the Republican Party's major dilemma was determining what to do with a popular political figure and vote getter such as Mickelson. If he ran for the Senate, his candidacy would most likely have resulted in an acrimonious Republican primary, splitting the Republican ranks, bitterly dividing loyalties, and possibly allowing a Democrat to win in either the 1954 or the 1956 general elections. In order to avert such a nightmarish scenario and to appease Mickelson, South Dakota's Republican Party leaders evidently struck a political deal in which President Eisenhower nominated, and, on 4 January 1954, the U.S. Senate confirmed, Mickelson as a federal judge. Hence, with virtually nothing in Mickelson's political career to suggest any hint of pro-Lakota sympathies, the SDSGA with its basically all-white membership had every reason to believe that Mickelson would buy their argument about the illegality of the Oglala Lakota tax assessment against white ranchers.

Confident as they were, the white stock growers nonetheless wanted an Oglala Lakota to champion their cause and found a willing accomplice by the name of Thomas Iron Crow. Accordingly, though the white stock growers were the ones vigorously opposing the land-use tax, they devised a court strategy that had Thomas Iron Crow sue his nation indirectly on their behalf. Because Iron Crow was an enrolled member of the Oglala Sioux Tribe and an allottee who happened to lease his trust land to nonmembers, the white stock growers hoped to win this case, making it seem as if the Lakota themselves were divided on the issue. After all, what more could they ask than for an Oglala Lakota individual to go against his nation's own land-use tax policy? If successful, though, the real beneficiaries would be not the Lakota but the white ranchers and farmers who, in the majority of cases, were the permittees of allotted trust land on the Pine Ridge Reservation.

Anticipating the OSTC's January 1953 grazing resolution, John Farrar, the attorney for Iron Crow and the white stock growers' counsel and lobbyist, filed Iron Crow's complaint with the U.S. District Court of South Dakota in November 1952. Mickelson's subsequent appointment to the federal bench assured that he would be the presiding judge to hear Iron Crow's complaint and rule on its merits, especially on the tax issue. Several months after Farrar's initial filing, Mickelson, in the opening statement of his landmark decision, poignantly framed the conflict between the white stock growers and the Oglala Lakota in terms of self-government:

> In past years plaintiff [Thomas Iron Crow] has leased some of his land within the Pine Ridge Reservation for grazing purposes to non-members of the Ogallala [sic] Sioux Tribe and he plans to continue this practice in the future. The Ogallala Sioux Tribe, has, under the provisions of the Tribal Council Resolution 147-50, assessed a tax against plaintiff's lessee for the privilege of grazing livestock on land within the reservation, and it, in turn, plans to continue to assess the tax in the future. Plaintiff now brings this action to enjoin the tribe from proceeding with that tax assessment.
>
> The question presented is whether this Indian tribe may levy a tax on non-members of the tribe for the privilege of doing business on the reservation under the tribe's jurisdiction, title to which is held by the United States in trust for an individual member of the tribe.[120]

After reviewing the historical and politico-legal background that gave rise to the Oglala Lakota's land-use tax policy, Mickelson reasoned that an 1877 treaty provision as well as a 1934 federal statute provided more than sufficient evidence that the United States, even if unwittingly, endorsed Lakota self-governance. Citing the federal statute, Mickelson reiterated that the Oglala Lakota electorate had adopted a constitution on 14 December 1935 and that the Interior Secretary had approved it on 15 January 1936. Mickelson noted further that the adopted and U.S.-approved constitution contained a clause that authorized the Oglala Lakota not only to levy taxes on its own members but also to "levy taxes or license fees, subject to the review by the Secretary of the Interior, upon non-members doing business within the reservation."[121]

Satisfied that there was more-than-adequate evidence to show that the Oglala Lakota's land-use tax policy had a firm, U.S.-endorsed foundation in Lakota self-governance, Mickelson turned to the all-important question of whether the Oglala Lakota possessed the jurisdiction to impose their land-use tax on nonmembers:

> It is the plaintiff's contention that the imposition of the tribal tax assessment interferes with his freedom of contract. To a limited extent it may be said that every tax, federal, state, local[,] and tribal, indirectly affects an individual's freedom of contract. The real and only question is whether the Ogallala [*sic*] Sioux Tribe, as a matter of jurisdiction, has the power to levy this tax in accordance with its constitution.[122]

Citing precedence from an earlier Native tax case, Mickelson ruled that the tax was not compulsory if a white rancher did not obtain a range unit because he or she decided not to purchase grazing privileges or because he or she had failed as a competitive bidder to acquire a range unit. In other words, a white rancher who had difficulty accepting the tax condition stated in the Oglala Lakota's grazing resolution could always refrain from the bidding process and in that way avoid subjecting him- or herself to a "non-white" government tax. Ostensibly, the white could take his or her business elsewhere. Otherwise, since it was the Oglala Lakota who were offering grazing privileges for the use of their land, assessing a tax or fee on non–Oglala Lakotas was the price that nonmembers rightfully had to pay for enjoying that privilege. For Mickelson, therefore, the OSTC's tax policy was entirely justified; all governments have the authority to set the terms of transacting and conducting business within their political boundaries.

Thus, after nearly twenty-eight months of litigation, instead of issuing an injunction against the Oglala Lakota as Iron Crow had sought, on February 1955, Mickelson handed the white ranchers the first of several devastating legal decisions. Until Mickelson's decision, these ranchers had successfully used their political network to undermine the Oglala Lakota's exercise in self-governance in every way they could. Now, quite unexpectedly, they were sent reeling by this stunning turn of events.

Five months after the favorable *Iron Crow* ruling, however, the Oglala Lakota realized that, though some white stock growers had reconciled their delinquent tax bill following the Mickelson decision, others still refused to pay their taxes. The reason was that *Iron Crow* had been appealed to the U.S.

Eighth Circuit Court, and the ranchers were ostensibly making a show of defiance.[123] Obviously, the appeal was a desperate ploy by the white stock growers, since Mickelson's legal reasoning was solid. They were hoping either for a more sympathetic audience—one that would be more understanding of their white plight—or for a delay of the inevitable in hopes that some political miracle (à la Berry) might somehow rescue them from the shadow of Lakota self-determination.

In the appeal, Iron Crow's attorney argued that the federal district court had "erred in its findings that the defendants have [the] power and authority to levy tax on citizens of the United States and the State of South Dakota."[124] A three-judge panel of Gardner, Woodrough, and Vogel did not agree. In their 6 March 1956 ruling, the judges essentially reaffirmed the lower court's opinion on the Oglala Lakota's authority to tax nonmembers:

> Inasmuch as it has never been taken from it, the defendant Oglala Sioux Tribe possesses the power of taxation which is an inherent incident of its sovereignty. The tribe has seen fit to give orderly implementation to that power through the adoption of a constitution which, among other things, has specially provided for the levy of taxes. . . . We conclude from the original precept of tribal sovereignty and the fact that the power of the Oglala Sioux Tribe to impose the tax or license in question has not been pretermitted by any federal statute or agency ruling thereunder, but, to the contrary, has been implemented by the Indian Reorganization Act . . . that such power still exists.[125]

In their *Iron Crow* rulings, the two federal courts were definitely cutting against the grain of the United States' national policy of termination. Contrary to Congress's legislative rush to termination, culminating in HCR No. 108 and PL 83-280, these two courts upheld the core principles of Lakota sovereignty. With South Dakota's white community clearly afflicted with a rampant case of termination fever to solve its Indian Problem, the Lakota governments faced the white's fevered threat of politically abolishing them and forcing the Lakota People to be culturally "absorbed" into the surrounding white community. From these two federal courts, however, the white stock growers received a strong juridical jolt to their anti-Lakota sensibilities.

These court decisions raised the political ante around the extent to which the Lakota Nation could regulate almost any activity, commercial or otherwise, on its reservations. *Iron Crow* proved the seminal event that, for South Dakota's white community, emotionally catalyzed them to launch a decade-long campaign to invoke PL 83-280 and to try to crush all Lakota governments, hoping to acquire as termination booty any remaining Lakota lands.

For the Lakota, *Iron Crow* gave timely support to the Lakota's long tradition of staunch, unswerving resistance in defense of their homelands.

Notes

1. Taylor, *The New Deal*, 41.
2. Van Every, *Disinherited*, 58.
3. Ibid., 60.
4. Ibid., 60–61.
5. Purcha, *Documents*, 176. The United States finally acknowledged the cultural importance of Native languages when, in 1990, Congress enacted the Native American Languages Act (NALA). Compared with the 1990 act, Commissioner Atkins (1885–88) stringently required the use of only English in U.S. government–run Indian schools. The 1990 NALA, contrasted with Atkins's 1887 annual CIA report, allows for full appreciation of the culturally racist impact of his position and the social environment from which it emerged.
6. Schusky, "Political and Religious Systems," 142.
7. In particular, the community of White River, South Dakota—until very recently a predominately white enclave on the Rosebud Reservation—had two Catholic churches, one for non-Natives and another for Lakota People.
8. H. Rpt. 2503, 186.
9. Ibid.
10. Box 137, EYB Papers.
11. Ibid.
12. Ibid.
13. Ibid. Bakewell's wish to have the "final cruelty" told to the world would eventually materialize. In 1982, Michael Lawson's classic work, *Dammed Indians*, exposed the human story of how, fully mindful of the extreme hardships and community disruption a dam would impose on the impoverished Lakota living in the river valley, a termination-minded white society arbitrarily violated all standards of human decency in pursuing its desire to build a massive dam project on the Missouri River.
14. Ibid.
15. For information on this ten-year development program, see Tyler, *A History*, 162, and H. Rpt. 2503.
16. H. Rpt. 2503, 150.
17. Standing Rock Reservation Planning Board, "Standing Rock Rehabilitation Program, 1948–1958, First Year," 4, 15 October 1948, Box 238, EYB Papers.
18. U.S. Department of the Interior, BIA, "Background Data on Oglala Sioux of the Pine Ridge Reservation, South Dakota," Box 213, EYB Papers.
19. U.S. Department of the Interior, BIA, "Background Data on Indians at the Rosebud Sioux Reservation," Box 226, EYB Papers. See also Hoover, "The Sioux Agreement." Hoover reveals that the 1947 figures on Pine Ridge land use disclose

nearly the same percentages as the 1953 figures. Unlike the 1953 report, this report adds that while the Lakota on the Pine Ridge Reservation used less than half the land, "non-Indians occupied approximately fifty-four percent under contracts of lease" (90).

20. Box 251, EYB Papers. In her letter, Mrs. Wilcox mentioned that she was married to a white rancher on the Pine Ridge Reservation. Lakota People married to non-Natives presented other issues, especially regarding how the latter could derive Lakota-supportive benefits from the marriage. In terms of a competitive advantage, for example, a Lakota is eligible for Native preference regarding the use of reservation land, such as preference over non-Natives in the allocation of a range unit. Non-Natives or nonmember Natives married to Lakotas could arrange, in the form of a front, to have such preference favor them.

21. Ibid.

22. Reifel, "Future of South Dakota Indian," 2.

23. Fortunately, the eventual emergence of Lakota resistance would circumscribe this alarming process. When 1967 arrived, Pine Ridge had retained several significant tracts of allotted land.

24. Roberts, "The Vanishing Homeland," 3.

25. Ibid.

26. Ibid.

27. For an account of Glenn Emmons's controversial appointment as commissioner of Indian affairs, see Larry Burt's *Tribalism in Crisis: Federal Indian Policy, 1953–1961* (Albuquerque: University of New Mexico Press, 1982). For a short biography of Glenn Emmons, see Robert Kvasnicka's and Herman Viola's *The Commissioner of Indian Affairs, 1824–1977* (Lincoln: University of Nebraska, 1979).

28. Daniels, *American Indians*, 110.

29. Debo, "Address Delivered by Dr. Angie Debo," 3, LJC.

30. For the internal politics of the TLE Corporation, see Robert Burnette, *The Tortured Americans*.

31. Box 192, EYB Papers.

32. Hoover Commission, 59.

33. Ibid., 71.

34. "Background Data on Indians at the Rosebud Sioux Reservation," 2, Box 226, EYB Papers.

35. Ruth Hill Useem's and Karl K. Eicher's, "Rosebud Reservation Economy," in *The Modern Sioux: Social Systems and Reservation Culture* (1970) discloses the economic state of affairs on the Rosebud Reservation during the 1950s and 1960s. From the economic information presented by Useem and Eicher, there is little question that returning off-reservation labor would not find steady, if any, employment, which thus increased the number of people receiving welfare.

36. Madigan, "The American Indian," 3.

37. *Indian Problem* is a Euroamerican convention used to victimize Native Peoples.

Native Question is a convention used by Native Peoples to refer to all the political ramifications raised by their interaction with the U.S. government and Euroamericans, including sovereignty issues, land return, rights of existence, honoring treaties, and other fundamental concerns.

38. Indeed, U.S. Supreme Court Justice Miller, who delivered the opinion in *United States v. Kagama* (1886), admitted the existence of this racial state of affairs when, in order to reach the "appropriate" legal conclusion, the court contrasted the nature of Native-federal relations to that of Native-state relations.

39. Hoover Commission, 65.

40. Tyler, *A History*, 161.

41. "Extension of Remarks," 1, Box 272, EYB Papers. The provision he quoted is Article 5 of the 1877 Black Hills Treaty.

42. Ibid., 2.

43. Ibid.

44. Box 255, EYB Papers.

45. *Running Horse et al. v. Udall*, 211 F. Supp. 586 (1962). This case originally began on 17 October 1958 when an examiner of inheritance allowed a S.D. OAA claim of $3,774.50 against James Running Horse's estate.

46. Sonosky, "General Bulletin No. 14 (1960)," 1, LJC.

47. Ibid., 1–2.

48. Archie Gubbrud Papers (AG Papers). This resolution was unanimously approved on 18 March 1963 by the all-white Public Welfare Commission (Freeman F. Otto, Henry H. Lewis, Albert Keffler, Hazel Parkinson, and A. N. Brenden), urging the Secretary of Interior Steward L. Udall to appeal the case and to promulgate regulations favorable to the continued reimbursement of South Dakota for providing public assistance to Lakota recipients.

49. "Statement of Governor Archie Gubbrud of South Dakota," 1, Box 322, EYB Papers.

50. Ibid.

51. Matthew Furze, 3 June 1963 letter to E. Y. Berry, 1, Box 322, EYB Papers.

52. Ibid.

53. Box 272, EYB Papers. In his 13 January 1953 letter regarding H.R. 1220 to Hobart Gates (South Dakota's 1953–54 State House Speaker), Berry also mentioned the angle of more money for white recipients. Noting that if the "federal government would assume 80% of the state's present share," this large cost-share arrangement "would leave South Dakota in a position of being able to pay larger benefits to white recipients." Box 272, EYB Papers.

54. Cahn and Hearne, *Our Brother's Keeper*, 9.

55. The act of 28 February 1891 and subsequent acts authorized the Interior Department to lease allotted land subject to the regulations and conditions prescribed by the secretary. See also Mollie Z. Margolin's 20 April 1961 "Legislation since 1900 Which Authorized the Secretary of the Interior to Lease Individual Indian Trust Lands"

summary. While this Library of Congress Legislative Reference Service document is not a comprehensive guide, it is instructive about the myriad leasing laws that supposedly were enacted to benefit a Native allottee.

56. Webb, *The Great Plains*, 398.

57. The Dawes Act specifically fixes the acreage of an allotment (160 acres per head of family, 80 acres per single individual over eighteen years of age and orphans under eighteen years of age) unless a "treaty or act of Congress . . . provides for the allotment of lands in severalty in quantities in excess of those herein provided." The Fort Laramie Treaty of 1868, Article 6, provides for allotments up to 320 acres for the head of family; an allotment up to 80 acres for any single person over eighteen years of age but not the head of a family; and 160 acre allotment for other non-Lakota Native males over eighteen years of age.

58. Ike Blassingame, (*Dakota Cowboy: My Life in the Old Days* [Lincoln: University of Nebraska Press, 1958]), a white ranch hand from Texas who was employed by Matador and came to the Cheyenne River Reservation in 1904, noted that the "whole range was nearly as primitive as it ever has been" (37). Of course, Blassingame's description suggested that the Lakota of the Cheyenne River Reservation did not occupy their allotments but instead remained in kinship groups living along the reservation's many watersheds. This form of Lakota social organization and the tendency to locate their dwellings in environment-friendly areas contributed, in addition to the poor economic conditions experienced by the Lakota, to a U.S. colonial-tinted rationale for leasing or selling these unoccupied or "unimproved" allottments.

59. Lee and Williams, *Last Grass Frontier*, 231.

60. Schell, *History of South Dakota*, 251. Also, according to Mr. Lemmon, in the summer of 1902, he discussed the leasing of Lakota land on the Standing Rock Reservation with President Roosevelt. After the meeting, the president ordered the Interior Secretary to approve Lemmon's lease (see Lee and Williams, *Last Grass Frontier*, 221).

61. Limerick, *The Legacy*, 36.

62. Karolevitz, *Challenge*, 230–31.

63. Hoover, "The Sioux Agreement," 77.

64. Ibid.

65. See the Act of 25 June 1910 (36 Stat. 856, ch. 431, sec. 4) concerning the leases of land held in trust. Although this act provides that an allottee may lease his or her trust land, the United States had great latitude over the lease's terms and conditions.

66. Lawson, "The Fractionated Estate," 1.

67. Mooney, *The Ghost Dance*, 840.

68. General Allotment Act 1887 (sec. 6), U.S. Statutes at Large 24:388–91.

69. This amendment is known as the Burke Act of 1906 (U.S. Statutes at Large, 34:182–83). In addition to unlimited discretion over questions of a Native person's competency, it also provides for U.S. citizenship at the end of the twenty-five-year trust period when a patent-in-fee is issued to the allottee rather than at the beginning of the trust period.

70. Prucha, *Documents,* 213.

71. Ibid., 214.

72. Washburn, *The Indian,* 247.

73. Cahn and Hearne, *Our Brother's Keeper,* 11.

74. In *Termination,* Fixico notes that E. Y. Berry "attended more hearings on Indian Affairs than any other member" (100–101). That Berry attended more hearings than other committee members or representatives might attest to the uneasy dynamics transpiring between his Indian and white constituents. It was Berry's misfortune to represent a district that is geographically coterminous with the original Great Sioux Reservation. Many of the politically contentious issues between the Lakota, the United States, and South Dakota remained unresolved during his twenty-year career as a U.S. representative from South Dakota.

75. "Statement of EY Berry, Prepared for the House Indian Affairs Subcommittee," 1, AG Papers.

76. 19 October 1962 letter to E. Y. Berry, Box 193, EYB Papers.

77. Ibid.

78. "Statement of EY Berry, Prepared for the House Indian Affairs Subcommittee," 4, AG Papers.

79. Ibid.

80. Box 179, EYB Papers.

81. 15 March 1955 letter to O. A. Hodson, Box 179, EYB Papers.

82. 18 March 1955 letter to E. Y. Berry, Box 179, EYB Papers.

83. 22 March 1955 letter to Commissioner of Indian Affairs, Glenn Emmons, Box 179, EYB Papers.

84. Box 179, EYB Papers.

85. Box 179, EYB Papers.

86. 30 April 1955 letter to E. Y. Berry, Box 179, EYB Papers.

87. 3 May 1955 letter to Gilbert Valandry, Box 179, EYB Papers.

88. Ibid.

89. 31 March 1955 letter to Commissioner of Indian Affairs, Glenn Emmons, Box 179, EYB Papers.

90. 28 March 1955 letter to E. Y. Berry, Box 179, EYB Papers.

91. This seven-month period was from 15 May 1957 to 17 December 1957.

92. Rosebud Agency Superintendent Will J. Pitner, 8 June 1954 letter to E. Y. Berry, Box 119, EYB Papers.

93. Originally founded on 21 April 1892 as the Western South Dakota Stockgrowers Association. Renamed the South Dakota Stockgrowers Association in 1937, the SDSGA was an especially tight-knit organization composed mainly of non-Native, western S.D. ranchers. The SDSGA exercised a considerable amount of state-level political influence during the first seven decades of South Dakota's statehood.

94. When he first became a member of the SDSGA, former SDSGA president (1946–48) and former S.D. lieutenant governor (1955–59), L. R. "Roy" Houck observed

this about Tom Arnold's influence within the SDSGA: "three mighty Toms (Jones, Berry and Arnold) were always locking horns. They were like three old bulls. Every time they were in the same room they would start to paw the ground and begin bellerin'. . . . Tom Arnold was the third Tom. He was pretty powerful in his own right. He was a Republican with big holdings down on the Nebraska line. Arnold was a good thinker, but somehow he always ended up on the opposite side of issues from [Tom] Jones and [Tom] Berry" (83). Dale Lewis, *Roy Houck: Buffalo Man*, 3rd ed., (Fort Pierre, SD: Buffalo Press, 1992). For more information about Tom Arnold and his role in the SDSGA, see Lee and Williams, *Last Grass Frontier.*

95. Furnishing a copy of a duly adopted resolution to the Interior Secretary for final dispensation may seem odd, since the Oglala Lakota were exercising their powers of self-government. However, when the Oglala Lakota adopted a constitution and bylaws pursuant to the 1934 Indian Reorganization Act (IRA), inserted in the Oglala Sioux Tribe's constitution was a review clause that stated that the Interior Secretary or a representative thereof could arbitrarily override a duly approved resolution or ordinance of the Oglala Sioux Tribal Council. Ironically, if termination involved freeing the Native People, the United States did little to try to remove this clause found in almost every IRA-adopted constitution.

96. Box 166, EYB Papers.

97. Ibid.

98. Ibid.

99. See OST Resolution of the Executive Committee, Resolution No. 30-53 XB: "To appoint delegates to attend [a] meeting between the representatives of South Dakota Stockgrowers Association and the Indian Service at Pierre, South Dakota, on June 9, 1953." This resolution was duly passed on 5 June 1953 by the five-member committee. The vote was 3 Yes, 0 Opposed, 2 Absent and Not Voting.

100. Beckwith reported in a 15 July 1953 issue of the *South Dakota Stockgrower* (the magazine of the SDSGA) that "members of this [Public Lands] committee, about twenty stockmen from various Indian Reservations, the president and secretary and several directors of the South Dakota Stock Growers Associations . . ." (12) attended the 9 June 1953 Pierre meeting.

101. Thomas Arnold, 11 June 1953 letter to E. Y. Berry, 1, Box 166, EYB Papers.

102. E. Y. Berry, 17 June 1953 letter to W. Barton Greenwood, Box 166, EYB Papers. Interestingly, Berry chose not to include the highly contested Oglala Lakota tax matter in his letter to Greenwood.

103. E. Y. Berry, 7 July 1953 letter to Louis Beckwith, 2, Box 166, EYB Papers.

104. Louis Beckwith, 12 July 1953 letter to E. Y. Berry, 2, Box 166, EYB Papers.

105. Ibid., 2–3.

106. Fire Thunder, "Sioux Indian Uprising at Pine Ridge, S.D.," *Pine Ridge* (a monthly mimeographed newsletter of the BIA Agency at Pine Ridge, the Oglala Lakota reservation), August 1953, Box 166, EYB Papers.

107. Louis Beckwith, 22 July 1953 letter to E. Y. Berry, 1–2, Box 166, EYB Papers.

Also, the contentious Indian landowner theme alluded to by Beckwith, and the question the BIA contended with, distilled to how much the BIA should subsidize cattle operators at the expense of Oglala Lakota People. It is the latter whose individual trust and commonly held allotments made up a significant proportion of the more than four hundred range units that the white ranchers desired.

108. Ibid., 1.

109. See "Presentation of Appeal to the Assistant Secretary of Interior from the Bureau of Indian Affairs," Box 166, EYB Papers.

110. "Secretary McKay Announces Departmental Decisions on South Dakota Indian Range Lands," Box 166, EYB Papers.

111. *SDSG*, "Stock Growers Get New Contract on Indian Lands," 14.

112. OST Resolution 34-49 instituted the land-use tax. OST Resolution 147-50 amended the 1949 tax rate.

113. U.S. Department of Interior, BIA, *OST Resolutions Binder 1948, 1949, 1950*.

114. Ibid. See SDSGA Secretary W. M. Rasmussen's letter to C. H. Powers with enclosed SDSGA resolution.

115. U.S. Department of Interior, BIA, *OST Resolutions Binder 1951, 1952, 1953*.

116. Ibid. See OST Resolution No. 62-53.

117. Ibid., 1.

118. *SDSG*, "Resolutions Passed at the 62nd Annual Convention of the South Dakota Stock Growers Association," "Resolution No. 12: Recommendations to Government Agencies on Indian Reservations," 22.

119. In his 1992 biography, Roy Houck had this to say about Mickelson's ambition:

> I think Mickelson was the best qualified governor. Oh, I was provoked at him sometimes too because he was a politician and looking at the horizon ahead so that he could better himself. . . . When Governor George T. Mickelson went out of office, he would have liked to become a U.S. Senator. But Karl Mundt and Francis Case were the two Senators representing South Dakota. Both were good friends of Mickelson and he didn't want to run against either. Mickelson accepted an appointment by President Eisenhower to the position of Federal Judge and served until the time of his death. (94)

120. *Iron Crow v. Ogallala Sioux Tribe of the Pine Ridge Reservation* (herein *Iron Crow*), 129 F. Supp 15 (D.S.D. 1955), 24.

121. Constitution and Bylaws of the Oglala Sioux Tribe, Article 4, sec. 1(h).

122. *Iron Crow*, 25.

123. U.S. Department of Interior, BIA, *OST Resolutions Binder 1954, 1955, 1956*, OST Resolution No. 55-77.

124. *Iron Crow*, Eighth Circuit Court of Appeals, 98.

125. Ibid., 99.

3

The 1958 Lakota Referenda

Whereas the national mood in the 1950s made the United States' termination policy seem inevitable, the mood of the Lakota was toward greater political and economic activism, challenging the status quo of U.S. colonialism. Because termination's professed goal was to "emancipate" Native Peoples—an attempt to cover the real landgrab motives—a Termination Era law like PL 83-280 conveniently provided South Dakota with an effective means to suppress if not outright eliminate Lakota resistance and to promote even greater white encroachment into Lakota affairs.

South Dakota responded quickly and in sync with the national termination policy by invoking PL 83-280 as a final solution to its state Indian Problem. And just as the profile of the congressional legislators in Washington affected termination policy and its swift passage, so too the social composition of those making the decisions and holding political and economic power in South Dakota during the termination years of 1950–64 affected how the national termination policy was carried out in the state.

Almost without exception, the membership of South Dakota's most influential political and civic organizations—such as the state legislature, departments and agencies, the county board of commissioners and county state's attorneys, SDSGA, S.D. Bar Association, and so on—mirrored the membership profile of a pre–civil rights Congress. During the most virulent period of termination, emotionally charged racial stereotypes about Indians were rampant in South Dakota, and the state's legislators embraced this mentality. Of the 364 state legislators who served,[1] 359 were white males, 5 were white females,[2] and all were Christians.

Political pundits and others offer a series of at least four explanations to justify South Dakota's all-white political governing body. First, party affiliation, they note, affects how state House and Senate district boundaries are drawn to ensure a party's majority in state government. Second, party affiliation has a race and class basis that enhances or diminishes the influence of its rank-and-file membership. Third, demographically speaking, whatever racial group or class predominates at a local, state, or regional level is naturally reflected in politics as well. Fourth, in South Dakota's case, the state's unique geography plays a major role in determining its legislative membership.

Of the first justification for how an all-white political body held power in South Dakota, various political studies reveal that the Republican Party so dominated South Dakota that it actually did not need to carve out districts in order to ensure a Republican majority.[3] Indeed, throughout the 1950s up until 1964, nearly three-fourths of 364 state legislators belonged to the Republican Party. Nonetheless, by highly marginalizing Lakota participation, district alignments did contribute to an all-white, 110–member state legislative body that favored white political (as well as economic and cultural) hegemony. This white dominance would factor heavily in formulating the state's Indian policy. Indeed, the political reality of white dominance became sharply apparent when white agitation to settle the Indian Problem began to coalesce at the state level around *Iron Crow*.

As the more obvious means of political exclusion, the state's House and Senate districts were in fact drawn to favor a concentration of white voters and to dilute Lakota vote clusters by breaking up the nine reservations (Cheyenne River, Crow Creek, Flandreau, Lake Traverse, Lower Brule, Pine Ridge, Rosebud, Standing Rock, and Yankton). From 1953 to 1961, twenty of fifty-four House districts and fourteen of thirty-three Senate districts had a reservation as part of their boundaries.[4]

Yet gerrymandering was not solely responsible for ensuring white political control. Even in cases where a House district-alignment pattern might have arguably favored the Lakota and therefore had the potential to influence the outcome of an election,[5] over the years, election results never bore out that potential. Instead, they indicated that important factors other than district alignments were responsible for marginalizing the Lakota's participation. Statistically, the districts whose election results could have been influenced by the Lakota vote accounted for at least one-third (125 of 364) of the state legislators between 1950 and 1964.

Regarding the second explanation for South Dakota's all-white political control, pundits have reasoned that party affiliation correlates with race and class. Mirroring the national pattern of the time, the S.D. Republican Party was (and remains) overwhelmingly white. The Democratic Party, while itself largely white, attracted more people of color for registration because of its New Deal programs. According to this argument, Lakota people were perhaps registered with the less influential party. The obvious solution, of course, was for the Lakota to switch to the more influential Republican Party. Until 1950, however, state law prohibited the Lakota people from entitlement to the state franchise altogether—a detail that many who try to explain away Lakota marginalization in more conventional terms somehow fail to notice. Certainly, this disenfranchisement explains why South Dakota had an all-white legislature throughout much of the state's existence.

Given state disenfranchisement and other discriminatory practices (such as gerrymandering) in South Dakota, the odds of having a Lakota win a state House or Senate seat, regardless of party affiliation, were equivalent to a Black person being nominated, much less elected, for Congress between the post-Reconstruction years and 1960. Moreover, as the events discussed in chapter 2 amply demonstrate, whenever either race or race-related matters surfaced in South Dakota's political arena, the state's all-white government rushed to close ranks, making the much vaunted two-party system function de facto as one indistinguishable white party.

The third common explanation offered for South Dakota's all-white legislature is demography. Because the Lakota constituted less than 10 percent of South Dakota's population, the state legislature's white profile presumably reflected these demographics. In other words, if an overwhelming number of state residents were white, the candidates would most likely be white as well. Such a view, however, dismisses an important element: the Lakota population was sufficiently clustered so as to warrant sending at least one of its own to the state legislature. Yet as the first point argued, how the House and Senate districts were drawn virtually excluded any chance of a Lakota becoming a state representative or senator.

Finally, the Missouri River presents a unique geographical feature of South Dakota that has had a major impact on state politics. It cleaves the state into two nearly equally sized regions—commonly called the East River and the West River. However, because the two regions have always had a significant population disparity, the House and Senate numbers have always reflected that disparity, determining the number of state legislators from each region. Of the fifty-four House and thirty-three Senate districts, fifteen and nine, respectively, were located in the West River region. The region was assigned a total of twenty-nine state legislators (twenty representatives and nine senators) for each legislative session. A total of eighty-eight individuals served in that capacity through the Termination Era, 1950 to 1964.

Of greatest interest for understanding the politics behind termination, however, are the 125 state legislators statewide who had a reservation as part of their district. As it turned out, the East River not only sent a greater number of legislators to the state's legislative body, but also had a greater number of legislators who had reservations as part of their districts, even though the majority of Lakota lived in the West River region. Of the 125 state legislators who had a reservation as part of their district, seventy-three were from East River while fifty-two were from West River. Because of this clear East River majority, the East River region could exert a greater political influence over the direction of the state's Indian policy.

The East River's dominance in setting Indian policy did not, however, reflect Native demographics. The West River had a much larger Native population than did the East River because of historical forces that allowed the Lakota to retain a significant portion of the West River area as reservations. Indeed, fifty-two of the eighty-eight state legislators from the West River had significant portions of the Cheyenne River, Lower Brule, Pine Ridge, Rosebud, and Standing Rock reservations as part of their districts. Moreover, Rapid City, the largest West River community and second-largest S.D. community, was also a reservation border town with quite a large Lakota population. Certainly the thirteen state legislators whose districts included areas of Rapid City were as preoccupied with solving the "Indian Problem" as were those legislators with reservations in parts of their districts. Thus, sixty-five of the eighty-eight West River state legislators had a Lakota constituency as part of their district, and of these sixty-five legislators, a core group would singled-handedly commandeer the state's Indian policy. Nor was this core group—all white as it was—of diverse opinion. To a person, the implementation of PL 83-280 dominated their personal and political agendas.

Just as the legislature formed a virtually all-white, male, Christian club, so too the club's primary constituency was composed of white, male, Christian farmers and ranchers. Several of the legislators were themselves either farmers or ranchers or economically involved with South Dakota's farm and ranch economy through some related activity. The power politicking that went on around the Oglala Lakota's grazing resolution and that culminated in the *Iron Crow* case proved beyond question that these state (and federal) legislators were prepared to take immediate political, interdictive action on the farmers' and ranchers' behalf. They were determined to minimize any adverse effects that Lakota self-governance might have on their white, farm-and-ranch constituency.

In western South Dakota, the livestock industry—ranching—dominated, and the SDSGA represented the interests of the stock growers. An SDSGA profile, obtained from several of the SDSGA's annual convention committee lists, shows that its membership virtually mirrored the state legislature's profile, thus making it a nearly all-white, male, Christian club as well. Furthermore, over 80 percent of the committee membership and as much as 67 percent of its general membership resided in the West River area.[6] These factors proved highly significant in a period when South Dakota repeatedly attempted to invoke PL 83-280 to claim control over the Lakota's reservation lands. Even though the SDSGA often prided itself in being an apolitical organization, at least two dozen of its more well-known and active members were also state legislators, including notable S.D. political figures such as E. Y. Berry. As legislators, these men often promoted themselves as proud, card-carrying SDSGA members.

The Lakota fully appreciated the importance of the West River's influence in deciding how to settle South Dakota's Indian Question. Yet they had virtually no grounds for believing that the West River's influence would be at all favorable or supportive. All the power cards were stacked against them.

Specifically, to secure an all-white state legislature, the state's white political parties had gerrymandered the House and Senate districts, especially in the West River region, so that it was not uncommon to have one reservation split among several districts. A nearly all-white SDSGA membership resided in the West River area, and some individuals were both state legislators and SDSGA members. The primary constituency of these two bodies was white farmers and ranchers, and both bodies would carry more weight in setting the agenda for the state's future Indian policy than would the Lakota themselves. Termination was now a national priority in Indian affairs, and PL 83-280 had become law just when the Oglala Lakota were challenging white hegemony. With all this in view, the Lakota People realized that the socio-political climate of South Dakota in general and the West River in particular had primed whites to translate their racial hatred toward the Lakota into action by attempting drastic institutional change.

But there were obstacles. Prior to invoking PL 83-280, the white termina-tionists needed to manufacture some rationale that would lend a façade of respectability and legitimacy to their implementation of PL 83-280. The classic white pattern for doing this begins with demonizing a targeted community of color as "the problem" (such as the Negro problem, the Oriental problem, the "Indian Problem," and so on). South Dakota proved more than ready to adopt this stock rationale. Rather than seriously examine any genuine avenues for resolving the differences over termination-related matters between the Lakota and the whites, South Dakota insisted on treating the Lakota as the problematic "other." By so doing, the whites refused to acknowledge that the Lakota community's acts of self-determination were already effectively altering the status quo that the former enjoyed at the expense of the latter.

Refusing to concede that Lakota self-determination was in fact fundamentally changing the S.D.-Lakota relations, in May 1955, South Dakota began a process of defining the Lakota self-determination phenomenon as its major "Indian Problem." Moreover, the politically stronger and more economically developed South Dakota intended to define not just the problem but the solution as well. This "solution" was to completely dismantle the Lakota politico-cultural structures that were giving rise to positive acts of self-determination, thereby preventing future "problems" like the Oglala Lakota's 1953 grazing resolution or the 1955 *Iron Crow* case.

Pretermination Stirrings: Senate Bill No. 278

On 1 December 1950—thirty-two months before August 1953 when termination became U.S. national policy—a local group of West River whites (calling themselves the Merchants & Stock Growers Association of the Pine Ridge Reservation [MSGAPRR]) proposed in a four-page letter to S.D. governor Sigurd Anderson that, because of "lawlessness" on the reservations, the state should assume jurisdiction over Lakota territory.[7] Later, W. E. Kieffe, an MSGAPRR member and chair, disclosed in an 18 December 1950 letter to E. Y. Berry that the MSGAPRR membership had significant concerns about the Indians that went beyond reservation law and order. They were upset because of their pocketbooks and who they thought did or did not have the authority to tax them. As the previous chapter recounted, the Oglala Lakota had managed to impose a land-use tax on non-tribal members—white stock growers who leased Lakota lands—and the OSTC was collecting a nominal fee from licensed Indian traders, most of whom were non-Natives.

According to Kieffe, "These are the two things to which the Stockmen and the Traders principally object[,] as they doubt the authority of any group of people to levy taxes within the State except the State or one of its legal subdivisions."[8] Indeed, Kieffe further related to Berry that at an earlier 13 December 1950 MSGAPRR meeting in Batesland, South Dakota, the OSTC's secretary was present and outlined for the audience what must have been a white person's ghoulish nightmare—Lakota self-determination:

> During the course of his remarks he told the white people just what the council was going to do and if they didn't like it that they could get off or be put off the reservation. That anyone leasing land who did not pay the tax they had levied or paid it under protest would have their leases cancelled. He told the Traders that the council expected to put a tax on each building that the Trader owned and if he didn't like it he could get off or be put off.[9]

Through its chair, the MSGAPRR expressed the ingrained emotional antipathies and fears that whites had about being subject to the jurisdiction of a nonwhite government, such as that of the Oglala Lakota. To avoid being put under the rule of nonwhites, the whites who were most affected conveniently cast all acts of Lakota self-determination as law-and-order problems. As the MSGAPRR gathering illustrated, the white community was also fully prepared to act upon its antipathies and fears; otherwise, its white-minority rule, which demanded favorable terms for white ranchers when they leased Lakota land, would be in jeopardy. On the Pine Ridge reservation at least, their hegemony would be subjected to further acts of politico-legal erosion by the Oglala Lakota.

A month after South Dakota's thirty-second biennial legislative session opened on 2 January 1951, the MSGAPRR called a meeting to discuss the "Problems of law enforcement on the Pine Ridge and Rosebud Indian Reservations."[10] Approximately one hundred white ranchers attended the meeting at Martin, South Dakota—then a Euroamerican enclave located within the boundaries of the Pine Ridge Reservation—to hear a presentation by Joe Robbie, an attorney and the future owner of the Miami Dolphins football team, about how jurisdiction operated between the Native and non-Native governments. It was at this meeting that Robbie proposed the state's first jurisdiction bill, claiming that it would help clarify the complex problems of jurisdiction. The state senator Alex Olson, whose district included parts of the Pine Ridge and Rosebud reservations, attended the meeting and, not to disappoint his constituents, dutifully pledged to be the bill's primary sponsor.

Nine days later, on 10 February 1951, Olson introduced the proposed bill as Senate Bill No. 278 (SB No. 278, appendix B), and it was then referred to the eleven-member, all-white, male Senate Committee on Judiciary and Uniform Laws. From the beginning, Robbie's proposal was confusing. On the one hand, the bill recognized that the United States had exclusive criminal jurisdiction over all individuals residing on a reservation whenever the state ceded—as South Dakota did in 1901—and the United States accepted and assumed such jurisdiction. To make sure that the state would not be hit with any of the jurisdictional expenses since its 1901 cession, SB No. 278 disclaimed for South Dakota any financial liability for what the United States had spent in the past or would spend in the future while exercising criminal jurisdiction on reservations in South Dakota.

On the other hand, SB No. 278 claimed for South Dakota a concurrent (jointly held with the United States) criminal jurisdiction on reservations, but only over non-Natives. In the event that the United States were to relinquish its criminal jurisdiction to South Dakota, South Dakota would then accept full jurisdiction, but again, only over the non-Natives residing on a reservation. Finally, if a treaty or U.S. statute applied, that took precedence, and South Dakota would then not exercise any criminal jurisdiction over any individual who lived within the boundaries of a reservation.

For a bill supposedly written to clarify the jurisdictional scheme between a Native government (Lakota) and two white governments (South Dakota and the United States), SB No. 278 added no small amount of legal and political ambiguity to the already-complicated and often-volatile field of Lakota-S.D. relations.

In spite of its confusing nature, though, on 19 February 1951 the Senate Committee on Judiciary and Uniform Laws recommended that the Senate pass SB No. 278. On that same day, thirty-four of the thirty-five senators voted, with one senator absent, in favor of the bill. Two days later, on 21 February, the House received SB No. 278 from the Senate and referred the bill to its eleven-member, all-white Committee on Judiciary and Uniform Laws. Following its Senate counterpart, the House committee also recommended passage of SB No. 278. Thus, on 24 February 1951, the all-white House passed the bill; none of its seventy-five representatives opposed the measure.[11]

This particular voting pattern suggested several things about South Dakota. One was that the state's cultural environment and its institutions lacked any tolerance for diversity, racial or otherwise. Another was that a Lakota presence served to continually remind South Dakota's white community of another history, which Robbie had alluded to but had not elaborated in his presentation to the white ranchers. That other history, of course, occurred in the late nineteenth century and concerned the United States' massive group and individual human rights violations (most often in the form of congressional laws) of the Lakota Nation.

Many of these violations (such as the Wounded Knee Massacre, the con-fiscation of homelands, and so on) began in February 1889, when Dakota Territory became pregnant with the future states-to-be of South and North Dakota. Upon its birth in November 1889, South Dakota bore a birthmark of human rights violations so grotesque and festering that no political or historical cosmetic surgery since has been able to cover it. By the 1950s, this unaddressed legacy of white racism and violent, inhuman domination had produced a racially and culturally intolerant mainstream society who cor-rectly sensed in the Lakota's legitimate claim to nationhood a stinging rebut-tal to the melting pot myth. If anything, SB No. 278's passage only demon-strated further how white people were unable to perceive Native coexistence as a viable alternative to the latter's extermination.

Yet for the whites bent on terminating Lakota self-governance, the legal road was far from clear. Of critical importance to the whole jurisdiction question was the Enabling Act, passed by Congress in February 1889. Various sections of the act were incorporated into South Dakota's constitution on 1 October 1889. These two political documents each contained a clause that, at the state level, expressly prohibited the non-Native community from includ-ing Lakota territory as its own until such time as the United States would extinguish the trust status of Lakota land. Thus, as a condition for statehood, section 4 of the Enabling Act required prospective states to include in their constitutions a disclaimer clause to the effect that:

> [T]he people inhabiting said proposed states do agree that they forever dis-claim all right and title to . . . all land lying within said limits owned or held by any Indian or Indian tribes; and that until the title thereto shall have been extinguished by the United States shall be and remain subject to the disposi-tion of the United States, and said Indian lands shall remain under the absolute jurisdiction and control of the Congress of the United States.[12]

Not entirely comfortable with a nice-sounding federal clause demand-ing that whites abandon any and all intentions of ever claiming Lakota lands—presumably because such aggression would cause more trouble and cost more white lives at Lakota hands—Congress specified that the clause could be revoked, but only when both the United States and the future state of South Dakota mutually consented to its revocation. Theoretically, only then could whites overtly begin an outright landgrab. Consequently, as the state's constitution was being voted on by the Euroamerican population of the soon-to-be state of South Dakota, an article called the "Compact with the United States" that basically plagiarized section 4 of the Enabling Act was added to South Dakota's constitution and became part of the state's fundamental law.

According to the legislative history of PL 83-280, when this law was still a house bill, these disclaimer clauses with their precise and unqualified language found in several state constitutions, including South Dakota's, held the forces of termination temporarily in confused abeyance. First, as a party to these compacts, the United States had to consent as a necessary step to making the article revocable. As it turns out, the United States had not, except in very limited instances, given any such consent prior to August 1953.

Second, since South Dakota had a disclaimer clause built into its constitution, it would have to alter its constitution by omitting the termination-offensive language before it could move toward termination. Yet amending the state's constitution unambiguously required the consent of the people: a statewide referendum. This constitutional problem would prove a sore sticking point for South Dakota's terminationists. Throughout the 1950s, as the state legislature sought to assume both civil and criminal jurisdiction over Lakota territory, the wording of the state's disclaimer language and the conditions necessary for changing it would raise many thorny political and legal questions for the state's politicians and courts.

Unlike the post-1953 state laws, SB No. 278's language did not in fact contemplate a wholesale transfer of jurisdiction. As a result, the state's disclaimer clause did not come up. In other words, regardless of the rabid terminationists' desire to have their government assume jurisdiction over Lakota territory, SB No. 278—despite its ambiguity (which even lawyers would later have great trouble interpreting)—did not materially alter any federal Indian-law scheme.

State Termination: House Bills Nos. 721 and 892

With so much political controversy around the Oglala Lakota's 1953 grazing resolution, why did South Dakota not simply invoke PL 83-280 as a way of nullifying future acts of Lakota self-determination right then and there? The problem was timing. The August date of PL 83-280's federal enactment coincided with the most controversial months surrounding the Oglala Lakota's Grazing Resolution No. 1-53, but it was too late for the state's legislative body to act. During the 1950s, the South Dakota state legislature held biennial legislative sessions that began in January of an odd year and usually ended two months later in the first week of March. As a result, the state legislature had adjourned in March of 1953 and would not reconvene until January of 1955. Any clamor by terminationists for a state jurisdiction bill in 1953 was simply not an option. They had to wait until the state legislature came back into session.

For Natives, the delay was fortunate. The Oglala Lakota were politically shell-shocked by how the aggressive lobbying efforts of the white ranchers, with the help of Berry and others, had succeeded in modifying nearly all the conditions of their grazing resolution. As far as the white stock growers were concerned, they won that particular firefight. Angered by the Interior Department's arbitrary and autocratic decision to remove the land-use tax from the grazing resolution, at an August 1953 meeting, the OSTC countered that it would assign the difficult job of tax collection to one of its own offices. What followed was *Iron Crow:* the white ranchers responded to the OSTC's determination to collect the tax by suing the Oglala Lakota in federal district court, arguing that the land-use tax was an illegal assessment against nonmembers and therefore was invalid and inoperative.

While it was true that *Iron Crow* was being heard throughout much of 1954 and that Mickelson was not expected to render his opinion until sometime in 1955, the whites were buoyed by their recent political victory against the Oglala Lakota, and they had little reason to suspect that the outcome of *Iron Crow* would be any different from the favored treatment they had come to expect, delivering them another victory. Hence, as the 1955 biennial legislative session approached, almost all the whites involved with the Lakota jurisdiction matter were confident that they had their Indian Problem well in hand.

Iron Crow radically tipped the jurisdiction scale in favor of the Lakota. The ruling was announced on 24 February 1955 with fewer than ten days remaining in the state's thirty-fourth legislative session. Stunned whites had little choice but to wait two years until the next legislative session before they could initiate any "corrective" measures. In the meantime, the pro-state jurisdiction forces and their sympathizers immediately began scrambling to use various white institutions to build a strong case for South Dakota to assume jurisdiction within the legal framework established by PL 83-280.

For example, on 16 May 1955, seven weeks after the *Iron Crow* ruling, the Legislative Research Council (LRC) met to consider the state's 1955–57 biennial legislative program. At this meeting, the LRC would set the initial parameters of the Indian Problem by deciding which committee would be most appropriate to deal with it. At its organizational meeting, the LRC had established five standing committees: agriculture and conservation; assessment, taxation, and finance; education, health, and welfare; state and local government; and transportation. After the committees were organized and vacancies filled, the LRC assigned each committee areas to study and, if necessary, to develop or recommend appropriate legislation. Given that whites generally perceived the Indian Problem as one of a presumed lack of law and order on the reservations, and given that state jurisdiction had been proposed as a way to solve this Indian Problem, the issues associated with government-to-government relations between the Lakota Nation and South Dakota would seem to be the relevant area for exploration and dialogue. Accordingly, the appropriate committee for studying the Indian Problem should logically have been the State and Local Government Committee.

That did not happen. Instead, the Education, Health, and Welfare Committee (EHWC) was assigned "the relation of state government to the Indian problem,"[13] and the law-and-order definition of the Indian Problem was subsumed under it. Granted, when state services involve the greater Lakota community, the state has a legitimate interest, and human services become a relevant area to consider. That being so, how, then, did the EHWC members conceive of the state's Indian Problem?

The profile of the EHWC's members suggests the most likely direction that the committee would take in examining the Indian Problem. The EHWC comprised twenty-nine state legislators of which nine were senators and twenty were representatives.[14] Of the twenty-nine committee members, nine were from the West River. Because of the large concentration of Lakota people and land there, these nine would play an important role in determining Indian policy. Among the West River members, Senator James Ramey's district included both the Pine Ridge and the Rosebud reservations. The districts of state representatives Merton Glover, Howard Blake, and Ernest Covey included portions of either the Pine Ridge or the Rosebud reservations, while Senator Joe Schneider's district included the Cheyenne River Reservation.

As for the SDSGA's connection to the EHWC, three of its more virulent anti-Lakota members—James Ramey, Merton Glover, and Edgar Gardner—sat on the committee and at least six others were state legislators. Given the SDSGA's extremely anti-Lakota position, its presence would invariably be felt in formulating and implementing a state termination policy.

Other state legislators on the EHWC who may not have been SDSGA members but who lived in or near Lakota communities typically held racist views about Natives. For example, on 15 January 1956, several months after the EHWC was organized, EHWC committee member John E. Mueller wrote Loren Carlson, the director of the LRC, about the nature of the Indian Problem: "I wish we had some way to keep those Indians busy. It does not help much just to give them food, etc.; without giving them something to keep them busy at least a part of their time."[15] Mueller was expressing two racist stereotypes—that of the lazy Indian and that of Indians receiving free items on the "government dole" without having worked to purchase them. A month later, reflecting on a 20 February 1956 EHWC meeting he attended, Mueller conveyed to Carlson his view of Indians and a possible solution to the Indian Problem:

> I think we should try for bigger better Trade High School on the Reservations if possible. As a rule the Indians make very good Painters, Carpenters, Plasters [sic], and mechanics. I think most of them would rather work with the hands than the head. If most of the Indians out on the Reservations who are farming are misfits, it seems that we should try for a series of aptitude tests. Really our government goes to the far corners of the earth and carries on other experiments that at times seem more foolish than this might.[16]

Echoing the policy at the infamous Carlisle Indian School in Pennsylvania, Mueller voiced the common white view that a vocational education for Natives was suitable enough. Natives were to be taught a trade rather than a profession because, according to whites, they had a natural aptitude for working with their hands, not their minds. Promoting trade schools for Natives revealed the racist thinking that Native people, as a matter of genetics, lacked the intellect required for professional schools. Thus, not only did a trade-school education represent the evolutionary high end of Native intellectual achievement, but also a Native person was expected to apply his or her trade in the service of whites.

Other committee members, such as Representative Ernest Covey, were forthright about their racial attitudes toward Indians. On 4 April 1956, Covey wrote to Carlson: "I might be a trifle prejudiced along some lines of this Indian situation, having lived with them all my life, but [I] will try to be as unbiased as possible."[17] What these "trifle" prejudicial lines were for Covey is not difficult to imagine. Covey resided in a community located a few miles from Winner, South Dakota—a white enclave on the Rosebud Reservation noted for its extreme racism. He presumably shared various stereotypical views about Indians with Winner's law-enforcement officials, such as the prevalence of Native drinking. Moreover, the opinions of three whites involved with law enforcement (the state's attorney Melvin Talbot, the Winner chief of police Lewis Hespe, and the Tripp County Sheriff James

F. Shoemaker) were given wide circulation in a local newspaper, stating in general that Native drinking had increased since a 1953 federal law repealed Native prohibition. Marvin Talbott, a future state circuit judge, elaborated that drinking and the problems that followed resulted from "the peculiar inability of the Indian to handle his 'firewater.' With relatively little to drink, an Indian loses his sense of judgment and perspective."[18] This pervasive racial stereotype of a drunken Indian, combined with several other equally racist images of Indians, most likely formed Covey's views of the Lakota community, hence his admission of being a "trifle prejudiced" about Natives.

Had the LRC and other state legislators interested in the Indian Problem realized that, soon after their 16 May 1955 meeting, the University of South Dakota's Institute of Indian Studies was sponsoring its first annual Indian conference, they could have, either as panelists or attendees, availed themselves of the multitude of topics being presented. The conference discussions, all led by non-Native panelists, of course, included areas of ostensible interest to the EHWC. Far more significant, though, was the fact that the invited Lakota representatives were able to voice their views on government, law and order, education, welfare, and health, even though they were limited to doing so from the floor. By failing to participate in the conference, the EHWC botched an opportune moment to discuss its views with the Lakota.

At the opening of the conference, W. O. Farber, the director of the University of South Dakota's Government Research Bureau, expressed what non-Natives generally felt about the Indian as a problem: "in dealing with the Indian Problem, in many of our communities and in many of our state institutions[,] the incidence of whatever is involved is higher for Indians than for whites."[19] Indeed, each panel presented a bleak picture in which Lakota people, who made up less than 5 percent of the state's total 1950 population, had higher state-incarceration rates, participation rates in state welfare programs, and communicable disease rates, as well as lower academic achievement rates in the state's public school system than did their white counterparts.

Moreover, since the Lakota were perceived to be primarily a U.S. responsibility, not a state one, the general tenor of the non-Natives at the conference was that the state was unduly burdened by the cost of providing these services to the Lakota. Bob Lee, the personal secretary for Governor Joe Foss, more than adequately articulated how South Dakota felt about providing such services:

The treaties were made with the Federal Government, not with the State of South Dakota. It was felt that when the lands where taken away from the Indians the treaty was made with the entire United States, not with any particular state in which the land is located. So, if the Federal Government does turn over these services to the State, a study project such as this [that is, a cost study], to come up with the facts to show what it costs to provide these services to the Indians, is of utmost importance as far as the State is concerned. The State of South Dakota would simply have to turn around and bill the Federal Government, *until such a time as the Indian population is so assimilated into the white population that they would be entitled to the normal functions of State Government.*[20]

One can well imagine the shock of the Lakota attendees at the secretary's closing remarks: apparently being of the appropriate race—not state citizenship—was the primary criterion for receiving state services. By making race an integral part of the state's cost-reimbursement argument, Lee expressed the all-too-apparent racist thinking usually associated with the southern states: a white government for white people.

Conference attendee Frank Ducheneaux, the Cheyenne River Sioux tribal president, eloquently provided a rare Lakota perspective on the whites' definition of the Indian Problem. Conceding that, in general, the Lakota incarceration rate was higher than that of whites, Ducheneaux minced no words about the whites' political motivations in framing the Indian Problem as one of law and order:

> Somehow or another the idea has grown that Indian reservations are no-man's lands [*sic*] of lawlessness and that tribal councils are fostering that lawlessness by opposing state jurisdiction. Great significance is attached to the fact that the ratio of Indians and non-Indians in the State prison population is so out of proportion to the population of the State as a whole. The conclusion is that Indians are more criminally inclined than non-Indians."[21]

As Ducheneaux was clearly implying, such declarations by non-Natives were simply blatant appeals for termination. According to whites, the reservations were no-man's-lands, and if tribal councils would only let the white S.D. government have jurisdiction over reservations, the Indian Problem would be solved. Whites would cite the disproportionate Native state prison population and other law-and-order statistics as proof that they knew how to get such problems under control. Obviously whites "understood" the Indian Problem much more "thoroughly" than did the Lakota themselves.

Ducheneaux, however, went further in debunking the whites' racially tainted perception of the state's Indian Problem:

> The fact that the Indian population in the State prison is high, comparatively speaking, is in itself support of our contention that our people are not ready for state jurisdiction. The truth of the matter is not that Indians commit more crimes per capita than non-Indians but that the percentage of convictions is higher in cases involving Indians. The reason behind this fact is that the majority of our people who are brought into state courts do not have a full understanding of their rights under the law. Many are convicted of major offenses without having adequate legal counsel; whereas, if they had had such advantages[,] the case might possibly have resulted in an acquittal or, at least, conviction on a lesser charge.[22]

A decade later, Ducheneaux's insight that the lack of basic legal aid or protection contributed to a higher incarceration rate of Lakota people was vindicated by a 1966 U.S. Supreme Court opinion: the groundbreaking *Miranda* ruling. This court decision held that any individual arrested for an alleged crime had a right, among others, to have an attorney present when being questioned by law-enforcement authorities. Otherwise, any evidence obtained in violation of the *Miranda* ruling would not be admissible in court. One can only imagine how *Miranda,* if it had been applied throughout the 1950s, might have drastically reduced the arbitrary and rampant incarceration of Lakota in South Dakota.

Furthermore, many Lakota were too impoverished to afford an attorney, provided one could be found. White or not, attorneys rarely resided on a reservation, and the few who did were either county judges or state's attorneys. What Ducheneaux did not explicitly mention in his pre-*Miranda* argument, though it existed and was proven by the state's prison data, was a program of selective targeting—that is, racial profiling—of Lakota people by white law-enforcement personnel. In all likelihood, a substantial number of the imprisoned Lakota committed no crime other than being Native.

Besides law and order, conference attendees discussed factors such as parental indifference or poor school attendance, which resulted in low academic achievement among the Lakota. Almost all whites involved with educating Lakota children either relied on state-generated data or invoked various racial stereotypes to promote or substantiate the widely held view that a vocational education was most appropriate for a Native child because it represented the upper end of the Native intelligence scale (see Mueller, p. 155). Ducheneaux did describe, however, the physical and economic hardships and cultural barriers that plagued almost all Lakota families when they contemplated sending their children to a public school:

> We believe that since the State Course of Study has been adopted in the reservation schools, we have just as good a school system as any other community on the reservation. The only thing that could be desired in this connection would be some way to check to see if the schools are actually following the State Course of Study. It is probably true that integration of Indian students into the public school system might be desirable if the only objective was to accomplish integration. But if the purpose is to improve better education for Indian students, then there are several drawbacks that must be eliminated first.
>
> In the first place, there are not enough public school facilities on or adjacent to the reservation to take care of all the non-Indian students properly under existing circumstances, and it is doubtful that non-Indian communities would wish to make room for Indian students. The great distances from the centers of Indian life to the existing public schools make it necessary that some provision be made for board and lodging for Indian students if they are to attend these schools. Since 90% of the Indian families who are presently sending their children to school at the agency boarding school or the reservation day school have an extremely low income, it is out of the question for them to provide these necessities.
>
> Fifty per cent or more of the children who attend the reservation schools are not able to speak or understand the English language when they enter school. They must first be taught to think in English. This fact is taken into consideration by the teachers and other school personnel in the reservation schools, and special attention is devoted to those who must learn to speak English before they can start learning anything else. They would not get that special attention in public school, and, as a result, they would never get the basic knowledge that is needed if the child is to derive any benefit from his schooling. . . .
>
> Competition in the matter of dress and recreational activities is another factor that puts Indian students at a disadvantage with their non-Indian schoolmates. The [Lakota] parents feel quite strongly about their inability to provide as much for their children as the non-Indian parents do and as a result they are reluctant to send their children to a school where the difference would be apparent.
>
> The lack of dependable roads and an adequate bus system make public school attendance difficult for our people since most of them are forced by reason of economy to live away from the non-Indian communities. There are no employment opportunities in or near these communities that would

make it possible for the head of the family to maintain a home in town so the children might attend public school.[23]

In short, the lack of adequate space in white public school facilities to accommodate Lakota students, the lack of facilities for boarding Lakota students so that they could attend a public school, English having been a second language for a significant percentage of Lakota students, inadequate resources to afford even minimum necessities that most whites took for granted, and the lack of off-reservation employment opportunities for a Lakota head of household all conspired to make any transition to a public school exceedingly difficult, if not impossible, for Lakota families.

Of course, the educational deficiencies of Lakota children were linked to welfare, especially to aid to dependent children (ADC). The welfare panelists, T. S. McPartland, the head of the University of South Dakota's sociology department, and Matthew Furze, observed that ADC and old-age assistance (OAA) were the two programs in which the Lakota were disproportionately "over" represented. McPartland and Furze went on to speculate that, rather than being intermediate measures, such assistance programs—especially the former—might evolve into a way of life. In making this disproportionate-services argument, these officials revealed not only the state's unwillingness to assume the cost of human services to Natives but also more than a few white value judgments about the welfare recipients.

Furze told the attendees, for example, about an earlier BIA bulletin directed at Natives that included information on personal hygiene or care "so common-place to the non-Indian that we [state welfare] have overlooked them in trying to work in the area of welfare services."[24] To Furze and others, the BIA bulletin expressed what they believed to be the Indian Problem: by providing everyday, commonplace, or commonsense services, the United States was preventing Indians from helping themselves. Welfare was becoming a way of life and leading to program abuses, such as having several in- or out-of-wedlock children to increase ADC benefits. But Furze and McPartland's concerns—the disproportionate welfare services to the Lakota, welfare as a way of life, and alleged program abuses—provided only the non-Native view. The Lakota attendees expressed valid welfare-related concerns of their own.

Melvin Robertson, the Sisseton Wahpeton president, explained to the welfare panelists that ADC abuse had a white element as well. The males who associated with Lakota women on welfare were not always Lakota men; white men were involved too—men who, for social reasons, "don't go with a [Lakota] woman because they [white males] like her; they just like her checks."[25] South Dakota's welfare system, through Lakota women, was actually supporting not only the extracurricular activities of white males but also their offspring.

Nearly a generation after this first Indian conference, an event on the Lake Traverse Reservation drove home this point. In 1974, approximately five hundred people, mostly white, assembled in an auditorium to protest the jurisdiction that the Sisseton-Wahpeton Dakotas were exercising over the whites residing on their reservation. One white male went up to the microphone and raged that the Dakota should be removed westward across the Bering Strait: "All they're doing is having kids, and being on unemployment and welfare anyway."[26] Immediately after he finished his racist tirade against the Dakota people—giving what Senator Abourezk described as easily worth a senator's yearly salary if his diatribe and what happened after had been videotaped for posterity—a woman from the audience commandeered the microphone and pointing in the direction of the whites, exposed the stench of their hypocrisy:

> "Youuu want to know whyyy we have kids . . . and whyyy we're on welfaaarrre. I'llll tell you why." Then she swept her right hand, index finger pointed, grandly around the auditorium. "It's because you white men . . . are screwing us Indian women . . . and we're having your kids . . . and you're not supporting them. That's why we're on welfare." Then came her thunderbolt, causing, I suspect, more than one family disruption that day. "I could name eight or nine of you right here in this auditorium," she again swept her index finger over the audience, "who refuse to support the kids you've fathered." There was noticeable discomfort among some of the white males.[27]

Throughout the Termination Era, whites consistently invoked ADC as a pro-state jurisdiction argument. Yet many Lakota leaders pointed out that the whites who made these charges—like the white male a generation later who railed at Dakota women and their children for being on welfare—seemed oblivious to the white fathers of these children and somehow "overlooked" the need to prosecute them for delinquent child support payments, if indeed the state was so concerned about its welfare costs to the Lakota.[28]

Finally, the health panel raised three concerns, two of which involved communicable diseases, tuberculosis and venereal disease, while the third concern involved infant mortality. C. M. Vaughn, the head of the University of South Dakota's zoology department (not the head of its school of medicine), disclosed health figures from the state health laboratory. Regarding the two communicable diseases, the Lakota had a reported rate of infection that was five times that of whites, and approximately half of all communicable diseases reported were Lakota. Infant morality among the Lakota was three times greater than that of whites. Amazingly, Vaughn made only one reference to the correlation between poverty and its effect on health. As with other panels, these panelists reiterated the all-too-common theme of inverse proportions (that is, high rates for a comparatively small population), strongly suggesting that a cultural, perhaps even genetic—and not necessarily economic—deficiency existed among the Lakota.

After the health panelists provided the white view of the state's Indian Problem, the Lakota attendees responded by drawing in the more inclusive social context, which once again revealed critical but overlooked aspects of the problem. Similar to Ducheneaux's and Robertson's responses to the panel discussion on welfare, attendee Abe Crawford observed that the comparative health data on whites and Lakotas were incomplete and needed considerable refinement:

> The percentage of venereal disease as stated is quite high as compared with the whites. The Indian has only one place to go to get treatment—that is the agency doctor. The white man, being a man of means, has ways to hide his sins. Often times they go by numbers instead of names. Had they been screened through like the Indians through reservation hospitals and doctors, I don't think the showing of Indian venereal disease would be as high.[29]

A white with the economic means and a personal family physician might, for reasons involving family and/or community standing, persuade his or her doctor not to report his or her venereal disease to the state health department. Hence, the health information on venereal diseases might not, as Crawford asserted, reflect an accurate picture of the comparison of white and Native sexually transmitted disease rates.

In discussing the venereal disease rate further, Crawford pointed out correlations not unlike Robertson's observations about the white male's extracurricular activities being subsidized by Lakota women who received ADC. Specifically, Crawford described a more than possible vector of disease transmission that the health panel might have preferred to overlook: the sexual behavior of the white males who lived in border-town communities adjacent to the reservations:

> Another thing, this is a known fact around the Sisseton area—that while many of the so-called white men will not date the Indian women in daylight, as soon as the sun goes down and an ADC contract comes in, they date them.

They usually drop them [off] before the sun rises and most of this venereal disease comes through those datings with the white friends. As one who has worked in a personnel office of the CCC [Civilian Conservation Corps] days back in the 30's, it was my job to screen the Indian work applicants through a physical examination. By this method I happened to know a lot of this dark history that is back there that a lot of you perhaps never knew.[30]

One can readily imagine a scenario in which a white male of moderate or even modest means who, wanting to keep his extracurricular activities secret because of strong community disapproval, would very discreetly make a habit of associating with Lakota women. Many white males maintained such intimate relations with Lakota women, as Crawford, Robertson, and many others since have pointed out. Often entire white border towns knew of these sexual dalliances but would fail to hold the men accountable. This community collusion among whites would allow health care providers, among others, to withhold information regarding communicable diseases, skewing the data to give whites a deceptively lower communicable disease rate.

About six months after the May 1955 quarterly executive board meeting, the EHWC was charged with investigating the relation of state government to the Indian Problem. The EHWC's first general meeting on this subject was convened on 24 October 1955. Twenty-eight of the twenty-nine state legislators attended, and at least twenty-five other individuals, representing several state and private agencies, were invited to discuss the state's Indian Problem. Examining the list of invited guests suggests that the Indian Problem was not actually about law and order but about human services: eight individuals were directly involved with some aspect of public and private welfare,[31] seven were associated with public instruction,[32] three worked in the public health field,[33] and the remainder represented various state and federal agencies.[34] Like the University of South Dakota's June 1955 conference on Indian affairs, during which the whites set the agenda, the committee discussion was again largely dominated—with the exception of John Artichoker and Ben Reifel—by the whites' view of "their Indian Problem."

As the committee meeting drew to a close, its only major action was to appoint from within the all-white EHWC a five-member Indian subcommittee. This subcommittee, which comprised EHWC members Ray E. Barnett, John E. Mueller, Merton Glover, Ellen E. Bliss (who was later replaced by Ernest A. Covey), and Robert A. Oden, was to arrange the next EHWC meeting with "particular interest in hearing the viewpoints of tribal officials, local law enforcement bodies, county education and welfare officials and others who have a close practical view of the problem."[35] This subcommittee was further "delegated [the] power to decide what areas should be studied as well as tak[e] steps to get different points of view represented at the next meeting."[36]

However, with many of the EHWC members having failed to attend the University of South Dakota–sponsored conference and then with the EHWC having failed to invite the Lakota leaders to the first general meeting in October, it is no surprise that the EHWC floundered in its initial discussions of the Indian Problem. From that first meeting, all they managed to do was appoint an Indian subcommittee and then leave the direction of the state's Native policy to that subcommittee, all the members of which had a known anti-Native bias.

With 1956 fast approaching and no program formulated for addressing the Indian Problem, the Indian subcommittee pushed for a second EHWC meeting on 20 February 1956 to pursue the goals outlined at the committee's October gathering. Besides the state legislators, the Indian subcommittee invited several state administrative officials,[37] BIA officials,[38] and Lakota officials from the Cheyenne River, Crow Creek, Flandreau, and Pine Ridge reservations.[39]

According to the less-than-detailed committee minutes, this meeting demonstrated how highly charged the issue of whether the state should assume jurisdiction over Lakota territory would be, especially given the various state's attorneys' efforts to frame the Indian Problem as one of law and order—that reservations were no-man's-lands of lawlessness. Because many of the county state's attorneys who attended the meeting had offices located on or near a reservation, they were regularly engaged in representing the state's interests in various politically contested jurisdiction issues. As a result, their view of solving the Indian Problem naturally favored some form of aggressive state intervention.

More important, because these state's attorneys were also members of the S.D. Bar Association (SDBA), their participation in the ongoing matter of the Indian Problem eventually drew the SDBA—another powerful yet predominately white-male institution—into the jurisdiction fight. With such close linkages between the state and the SDBA, the former viewed the latter as a future ally, and, indeed, the SDBA would not disappoint the terminationists.

Near the conclusion of the EHWC's February meeting, the EHWC's Indian subcommittee was given the task of studying three areas: law enforcement problems, higher education scholarships for Native students,[40] and the Minnesota plan for Native policy—a plan that used a racial quota argument to justify federal subsidy.[41] With the state's Indian Problem framed within the human services realm, the first area of study would undoubtedly be to link the state's human services to Lakota people with its regulatory and law enforcement activities involving Natives. In this context, the contentious issues surrounding welfare and its alleged abuses would invariably be seen as further evidence of the purported lawlessness that supposedly prevailed throughout Lakota territory.

This February committee meeting was a microcosm of the June 1955 conference on Indian affairs, in that it showed the extent to which whites were either unwilling or unable to think about the Indian Problem more than one-dimensionally. Their mantra was simple: the Lakota were the problem, and a rigorous dose of white governance in the form of state jurisdiction would solve it. By contrast, the Lakota understood more clearly than the whites the real cause of the Indian Problem: the whites' unending obsession with extending their hegemony over Lakota affairs. Of course, convincing the whites that their solution of white domination actually meant subjecting the Lakota to racism, greed, injustice, or worse fell largely on deaf ears.

Iron Crow notwithstanding, until about 1 March 1956, the terminationists could assess their gains in corralling the Indian Problem rather favorably. First, they halted the OSTC's Grazing Resolution No. 1-53—the land-use and management initiative that was designed to give the Oglala Lakota greater control over their reservation's land base. Second, the terminationists' immediate reaction to the devastating February 1955 *Iron Crow* ruling was to appeal Mickelson's decision to the Eighth Circuit Court, further delaying the collection of the OST's tax. Third, by rallying the resources of its all-white government, the terminationists initiated a program that was concerned far more with offsetting the possible effects of Lakota self-determination on white hegemony than it was with addressing the human needs and well-being of the Native population residing in South Dakota. Indeed, it became all too apparent to the Lakota leadership that the state's program of solving the Indian Problem often meant portraying the Lakota as a burden and the state as a victim of that burden. Framed this way, the state's "obvious" solution was to assert greater state control over the lawless Lakota not only outside but also inside the boundaries of the reservation—in other words, termination.

Except on rare occasions when the Lakota protested, the overall state program to assume jurisdiction was proceeding without a hitch. Then came a second legal shock: on 6 March 1956, the Eighth Circuit Court of Appeals upheld Mickelson's *Iron Crow* ruling. The higher court's affirmation of Lakota sovereignty and self-determination drastically changed the politico-economic equation in the Lakota's favor. Rocked by the appeals court's ruling, the pro-state jurisdiction forces rapidly escalated their efforts to terminate the Lakota.

With ten months remaining before the opening of the thirty-fifth biennial legislative session (January 1957), the pro-state jurisdiction forces were, because of *Iron Crow* and its unsuccessful appeal, feeling considerable urgency about proposing a state measure that would invoke PL 83-280. Not surprisingly, many of the county state's attorneys, county judges, and other attorneys residing on or adjacent to reservations promised the state's jurisdiction advocates that they could count on the SDBA as a natural ally. Since the EHWC's Indian subcommittee had been directed to study, among other things, the problem of law enforcement both on and off reservations, at its first meeting on 18–19 June 1956, the subcommittee wanted to explore the political and legal limitations and ramifications were South Dakota to assume jurisdiction over Lakota land. They wanted to know, for example, the pragmatics of implementing such jurisdiction as well as the existing costs to the Lakota and the federal government incurred by the status quo jurisdiction.

After its first meeting, the EHWC subcommittee sought the opinion of Phil Saunders, the S.D. attorney general, on whether South Dakota was currently exercising criminal jurisdiction on any reservations. More important, they asked Saunders whether "the Constitution of South Dakota prevent[ed] the state from assuming criminal and civil jurisdiction . . . as provided by Public Law 280[.]"[42]

Thus, in July 1956, the SDBA officially threw in with the termination effort. Responding to the questions of the EHWC subcommittee, the SDBA's five-member criminal law committee—all white men—of Phil Saunders; Phil Hall, South Dakota's Fifth Circuit judge; Robert Bakewell Jr., a soon-to-be appointed county state's attorney; Clark Gunderson, an attorney in private practice; and Clinton Richards, the U.S. attorney for the S.D. district, addressed the political and legal aspects of the Indian Problem and of termination as a solution. In its report, the SDBA's committee recommended that, because "there have been a number of criminal actions recently reflecting the uncertainty of jurisdiction over crimes involving Indians near and upon parts of the Indian reservations in South Dakota,"[43] the state should accept and assume "criminal and civil jurisdiction of all areas formerly Indian country in the State of South Dakota except the territories within such describe[d] areas [that is, the reservations]."[44]

A more telling indication of the state-level position regarding PL 83-280 was that, in its report, the SDBA committee advocated state assumption of jurisdiction pursuant to section 7 and not section 6 of PL 83-280—section 6 clearly being the more applicable category for South Dakota. Applying to states that had a disclaimer clause embedded in their constitutions, section 6 required these states to first change the constitutional language that forbade their citizens from ever making claims on Native lands. Without such a constitutional amendment process, termination was not legally possible.

Section 7 applied to states that had no such constitutional disclaimer clause but only a statute to that effect. For these states, PL 83-280 required their state legislatures to simply repeal the statutory disclaimer clause. After repeal, the way was then clear for section 7 states to enact a law assuming jurisdiction over Native Country. In these states, therefore, assuming jurisdiction was a much less messy and burdensome process. Though laws could sometimes be put to a statewide referendum, amending a state constitution always required a higher degree of participation.

In 1889, like eight other soon-to-be states seeking admission to the Union, South Dakota agreed with the congressional mandate stating that its disclaimer clause was revocable only by mutual consent. That is, the United States and South Dakota both needed to agree on whether the absolute jurisdiction of the United States over Lakota territory was to be relinquished.

Despite the legislative history of PL 83-280, which explicitly named South Dakota as a section 6 state, terminationists found in the language of South Dakota's constitution about the irrevocability of the disclaimer clause a slight ambiguity that, they argued, made it subject to political interpretation. The constitution stated that the disclaimer "shall be irrevocable without the consent of the United States and the people of the state of South Dakota expressed by their legislative assembly."[45] To be sure, the United States gave its consent in PL 83-280, but South Dakota's political and legal communities believed, conveniently enough, that simply enacting a state measure to assume jurisdiction was sufficient for PL 83-280 to become operative under section 7.

Obviously, this was highly debatable. Indeed, the legal argument is far more convincing that South Dakota had to proceed according to section 6 provisions. That is, before the legislative assembly could act on its desire to assume jurisdiction over Lakota land, it first had to remove the disclaimer clause through the formal process of amending its constitution. In South Dakota, the road to termination had to start with a constitutional amendment that said, "Yes, not only the United States but also the people of South Dakota do hereby give their consent to revoke that particular disclaimer language." Only after the disclaimer clause was removed could the state legislature, as a further expression of the people, enact a state jurisdiction measure.

Two months after its official entry into the termination effort, on the morning of 7 September 1956 at its 24th annual meeting, the SDBA membership heard Richard Clinton articulate the law-and-order version of the Indian Problem as simply a matter of defining the state's jurisdiction in relation to Indian Country. According to Clinton, the SDBA criminal law committee's jurisdiction plan was straightforward: it involved obtaining a map of the current reservation boundaries from the BIA, identifying both "former" reservation land and white enclaves within current reservations, and then encouraging the state legislature to enact a jurisdiction measure regarding the questionable areas during its 1957 session.

The SDBA members then asked questions. They inquired about the added costs associated with the state's assumption of criminal jurisdiction; Clinton claimed there were none. They raised the issue of the uncertainties around the understanding of the term *Indian Country;* Clinton stated that it was problematic but solvable with both map and jurisdiction law in hand. They inquired about the types of crimes that would be subject to the state's jurisdiction; again, he viewed this as somewhat problematic but solvable with map and law in hand. Finally, they raised the issue of who was Indian; Clinton said this matter had already been defined by Congress and the courts. Their inquiries satisfied, the SDBA membership approved the committee's recommendation that the state move to assume criminal and civil jurisdiction over the so-called former Lakota territory.

In effect, the SDBA was actually retreating from its July 1956 recommendation that the state assume total jurisdiction over Lakota territory; by September 1956, the SDBA recommended instead that the state seek to assume circumscribed jurisdiction over limited portions of Lakota land. This retreat suggests that the SDBA members were becoming increasingly aware of the legal thin ice the terminationists would be on if they acted as if South Dakota were a section 7 state. Indeed, as the state jurisdiction question intensified over the next few years, the issue of whether state jurisdiction should be assumed pursuant to section 6 or section 7 became critical for both the Lakota and the white community.

Other white institutions were also using the time before the 1957 legislative session to formulate their support for termination. After four meetings between May 1955 and June 1956, the EHWC published a September 1956 document, "Report of the Committee on Education, Health, and Welfare to the Executive Board," on its findings on the Indian Problem in relation to state government. In this document to the LRC executive board, the EHWC members listed six official recommendations, of which only one concerned law and order:[46] "that study be given toward the end that the state assume jurisdiction over law and order in Indian Country under P.L. 280 (83rd Congress)."[47] Realizing the complex issues surrounding the interpretation and application of PL 83-280, the EHWC could at best recommend a study of the politically volatile subject.

Although the issue of PL 83-280 jurisdiction was fraught with legal and political confusions among the terminationists and their supporters, the committee's report was perfectly clear about what invoking PL 83-280 would mean for Lakota self-determination: "The 83rd Congress enacted P.L. 280, an act which empowers any state to impose on tribes its own civil and criminal codes and enforcement machinery, *thus eliminating tribal codes and tribal authorities.*"[48] With fewer than four months remaining before the state legislature convened, terminationists were anxious to move as quickly as possible in asserting complete state dominance. They wanted to preclude any future Lakota initiatives of self-determination, especially if these Lakota initiatives meant politically and economically managing their own reservation land bases. South Dakota stood poised to virtually destroy the Lakota's political and legal infrastructure that, more often than not, had held the whites in abeyance.

The First State Jurisdiction Attempt under PL 83-280

Not long after South Dakota's legislature opened its thirty-fifth legislative session on 8 January 1957, George Malone, a white Indian trader on the Pine Ridge Reservation and a rabid state jurisdiction advocate, informed Berry that, on 23 January 1957, "a group [of whites] from the reservation met with the attorney general and the committee on Indian Affairs of the House and through John Farrar put a bill into the hopper to have the State take over the law and order set up on the reservation here."[49] By 1957, South Dakota's political climate and racist social environment converged to promote any measure that would impose white governmental authority over Lakota territory.

Politically, S.D. Attorney General Saunders had already made his views known when he recommended state jurisdiction at the SDBA's September 1956 convention. In addition, the membership profile of both the House and the Senate Committees on Indian Affairs revealed, almost without exception, that the members were representing districts that either included a portion of Lakota Country or had a significant Lakota population in an off-reservation border town as part of their districts (table 6).

Some of the state legislators who served on either the House or the Senate Indian committees, such as Ellen Bliss, Nels Christensen, Joe Schneider, Hilbert Bogue, and C. O. Peterson, also served on the EHWC. The gatherings of these all-white institutions gave whites the opportunity to bring their racism to their positions of power, unchecked by any Native perspective. Hence, when the EHWC as well as other state institutions, such as the University of South Dakota, convened meetings to collect testimony and information on the state's Indian Problem, extremely denigrating racist stereotypes about Native people emerged from all quarters of the state's white community.

It is not hard to imagine, then, the automatically positive response that this Pine Ridge–based group of whites received from state government officials. Yet despite this favorable environment, pro-state jurisdiction forces could not anticipate the volatility of the jurisdiction issue and how the ensuing controversy would produce unexpected developments on all sides. For the terminationists, what followed was a comedy of tactical political and legis-

Table 6. Membership of State House and Senate Committees on Indian Affairs, 1957

	Name	District	Reservation
House	Roy Armstrong	17	Flandreau
	Eldon Arnold	34	Lake Traverse
	Ellen Bliss	10	—
	Nels Christensen	32	Lake Traverse
	O. A. Hodson	42	Pine Ridge
	Don L'Esperance	45	—
	Joe Schneider	51	Cheyenne River
Senate	James Abdnor	29	Lower Brule
	Hilbert Bogue	6	—
	C. T. DeNeui	5	—
	Fred Hunter	30	Cheyenne River Standing Rock
	C. O. Peterson	1	—
	James Ramey	26	Pine Ridge Rosebud
	Alfred Roesler	33	—
	Don Stransky	10	Crow Creek
	O. J. Tommeraason	12	Flandreau

Sources: Proceedings of the House of Representatives, Thirty-fifth Legislative Session, State of South Dakota; Proceedings of the Senate, Thirty-fifth Legislative Session, State of South Dakota.

lative errors that, over the next several years, would plague South Dakota's ill-fated struggles to assume jurisdiction. The initial draft of a measure generated by the non-Natives from Pine Ridge called for a straightforward state acceptance of both civil and criminal jurisdiction over Lakota lands (HB No. 721, appendix C), and it was no surprise to anyone.

Many Lakotas were quite surprised, however, when the Lower Brule Sioux Tribal Council (LBSTC) suddenly came out in favor of applying state criminal jurisdiction to their reservation. According to Raymond Hieb, a solicitor for the BIA's Aberdeen area office at the time, in late January 1957, the BIA "received from the Lower Brule Sioux Tribal Council a request that we cooperate in making it possible for them to transfer their jurisdiction . . . to the state."[50] To ensure that the BIA would not be criticized for providing any kind of assistance on such a sensitive matter as termination, the BIA most likely sought a formal declaration of the LBSTC's intention. Hence, on 6 February 1957, the LBSTC passed Resolution No. 56-109 requesting that South Dakota enact a law to assume criminal jurisdiction over the Lower Brule Reservation.

Because the BIA had assigned Hieb to assist the LBSTC, he drafted their first measure. Hieb was ready to present it to the House Committee on Indian Affairs, when questions arose about treaty rights on the one hand and the state legislators' willingness to accept the LBSTC's measure on the other. Regarding treaty rights, since the banks of the Missouri River comprised the shoreline and major watershed of the Lower Brule Reservation, the LBST needed a guarantee that the Lakota's hunting, trapping, and fishing rights would remain intact, since these were of critical importance to their subsistence economy. In response, Hieb incorporated a "hold-harmless" disclaimer that protected these rights for the Lakota of Lower Brule.

Regarding the state legislators' readiness to accept the measure, the costs of assuming jurisdiction became an issue. According to Hieb, in a meeting between the LBSTC and the state legislators whose districts included the Lower Brule Reservation, the legislators said that, while they favored the LBSTC's measure, they had major concerns about the costs of assuming jurisdiction, and these concerns tempered their outright endorsement. To gain their support, Hieb provided language in which "jurisdiction will not be assumed by Lyman or Stanley County unless and until the county commissioners of the county pass a resolution accepting it and unless and until a contract has been entered into between the federal government and the respective county."[51]

The LBSTC's proposed bill (HB No. 892, appendix D) certainly represented an anomaly within the Lakota's widespread opposition to any form of state jurisdiction. Nonetheless, the LBST believed it was acting in its own best interests. At a 14 June 1957 gathering held at Lower Brule for the purpose of deciding whether to accept state jurisdiction, one Lower Brule tribal member revealed the LBSTC's reasons for sponsoring HB No. 892:

> Now, before I go any further I wish to take you back to about January, 1957[;] at this time there was a bill [HB No. 721] introduced at the State Legislature and if it were passed it would mean that the State would take over on Law & Order on all reservations in the State of South Dakota[;] you would not be allowed to retain your hunting and fishing rights, there was no provision for the Bureau of Indian Affairs to help finance such a change over, there was no provision allowing the Indians to vote on whether they would want it or not.
>
> Your Tribal Council as well as other Tribal Councils in the State became very much alarmed over the enactment of such legislation, we immediately investigated the matter and what we found happening was that which I just mentioned. It was our opinion that rather than have our Tribe come under such jurisdiction without our consent and without the aforementioned provisions that it would be the best strategy for us as one Tribe to ask for separate legislation whereby we could retain our hunting and fishing rights and whereby the Bureau would help finance the change over.
>
> Therefore, we introduced Bill [892][;] we now had two bills before the State legislation [sic], one where State Law & Order over Indian country would have been a blanket affair and one by the Lower Brule Tribe asking for certain provisions[;] we did this solely because we wanted to retain our hunting and fishing rights and have the bureau partially finance this change over and garantee [sic] Law & Order in this Community.[52]

For fear of being marginalized in the state's political process and thus having to settle for a state termination bill not of their choosing, the LBSTC offered HB No. 892 as an alternative to HB No. 721. By involving itself in the state's legislative decision-making process, the LBSTC had—to everyone's complete surprise—managed to influence the formulation of the state's termination policy.

On 12 February 1957, the House Committee on Indian Affairs (HCIA) officially introduced both controversial measures as separate bills from two different interests. As the Lakota had come to expect from the white community, the stench of white racism immediately engulfed the state's legislative process. For example, the HCIA arranged two hearing dates for HB No. 721 and none for HB No. 892, blatantly showing the committee's bias for the white-sponsored bill. Moreover, the hearing's protocol specified that the opponents of HB No. 721, who were almost without exception Lakota, present their case at the first hearing (18 February 1957), while the second hearing (20 February 1957) was reserved for the proponents of the bill. This order, contrary to standard protocol, revealed the committee's willingness to manipulate the legislative process in order to minimize or even neutralize Lakota opposition.

To the uninitiated, the HCIA's two hearings on HB No. 721 may not appear racially biased; after all, each side was allowed to present their arguments for or against the bill. However, Hieb, a former state legislator familiar with the legislative procedure in question, was savvy about how the HCIA was intentionally influencing the decision-making process in favor of state jurisdiction:

> We [the BIA] felt there was something peculiar about the hearing in that the opponents of the measure . . . were called first. It is traditional in the American system that the proponents first advance their reason for something, and then it is met by the opponents. . . . There was publicity given to the hearing, and then there was publicity given to the later hearing when the proponents came in. Somebody said that publicity given to the proponents received wider distribution than that given to the opponents.[53]

For obvious propaganda purposes, arranging the hearings this way gave the white-dominated media a choice of which view to cover. Confident of the media's support, the proponents of state jurisdiction and their sympathizers knew that neither the Lakota's objections nor any other potentially embarrassing information or incidents that might damage the image of the terminationists or their campaign would be reported to the public.

For instance, Alex Chasing Hawk, a delegate from the Cheyenne River Sioux Tribe, reported to his tribal council a rather disturbing exchange at the first hearing:

> We went to the State Legislature and there was a woman who was the Chairman of [the] House Committee On Indian Affairs of South Dakota[,] she stated that she did not want anyone to t[a]mper with the Jurisdiction bill [HB No. 721] and "if you do, I'm going to raise hell," . . . and she was angry, red in the face and that is an example of the way they are coming at us."[54]

Bliss's open contempt for the Lakota and her angry threats toward them should they "tamper" with the whites' bill would certainly call into question the committee's carefully crafted image of acting in a balanced and democratic fashion. Because Hieb was the HB No. 892 point person for the BIA, he often accompanied the LBSTC to the committee hearings. However, Bliss told Ben Reifel, the BIA Aberdeen area director, that Hieb's presence was no longer welcome at Pierre. Moreover, Loren Carlson observed that the atmosphere of the HCIA hearings was highly acerbic:

> These bills, particularly House Bill 721, were hotly contested, and in the hearing on 721 on Wednesday, February 20, it seemed to me, particularly vitriolic comments were exchanged. One of the proponents for House Bill 721 argued that the ranchers in Shannon County [the Pine Ridge Reservation] would be glad to assume the additional burden of cost in order to get good law and order. Various allegations were made as to the operation of the Indian tribal courts and Indian police system.[55]

Carlson appeared to be referring to the white community's poster child Edison Ward, an Oglala Lakota rancher who provided testimony on behalf of the state jurisdiction effort. On 20 February 1957, Ward delivered what amounted to a emotionally charged tirade not only against his government, the OSTC, but also against Lakota governments in general. First, Ward viciously attacked the current state of Lakota self-governance as unduly oppressive:

> There exists on the Pine Ridge Reservation a situation more insulting to the ideals of American freedom and liberty and justice than that exists in Hungary or Poland. I am sure that you are unaware that a police state exists on every organized Reservation in the State of South Dakota. The astounding part of it is that these Police States have been organized and perpetuated by the Executive Branch of the Federal Government through the Bureau of Indian Affairs and enforced by its Puppets, the Executive Committees of the various Tribal Councils.
>
> Under the guise of the Indian Reorganization Act, the Bureau of Indian Affairs is depriving the Indian citizens of the State of South Dakota living on the Reservations, of every freedom and right of citizenship sacred to White citizens except the right to vote.
>
> Through the connivance of the Bureau of Indian Affairs and its control over the Tribal, Jurdicial [sic][,] and Governmental Systems, we Indians are deprived the right of Habeas Corpus. We are thrown into filthy jails without cause, without complaints, without warrants and at the pleasure of Indian Police, the members of the Executive Committee, or at the request of the Superintendent. We are denied the right of representation by competent legal

counsel. We are denied the right of trial by jury. The so-called Judges of the Tribal Court are under the complete control of the Executive Committee and, of course, the Committee is subject to the control of the Superintendent of the Reservation.[56]

Ward's testimony characterizing Lakota governments as police states obviously gave the Lakota far more political clout than they deserved or certainly exercised. Indeed, a University of South Dakota study, *Indians, Law Enforcement, and Local Government,* released three months after Ward's testimony, seemingly supported the general contention or perceptions of whites that reservations were a no-man's-land of lawlessness; however, the study unwittingly revealed that, in many instances, it was actually white governance that was responsible for promoting an uneasy, if at times fearful, social climate against Lakota people.

Continuing with his testimony, Ward went on to name a major deficiency, as he saw it, of Lakota government compared to that of whites. This deficiency, he believed, made Lakota governance no different from that of third world juntas:

> There is no division in Tribal Government between the Legislative, the Judicial and the Executive branches as there is in our Federal and State Government. The Government which we do have is merely an extension of the Bureau of Indian Affairs. No Gestapo or Communist Dictatorship has more authority or less responsibility than the organization operated by the Bureau of Indian Affairs under the Indian Reorganization Act.
>
> Never since its inception has a Tribal Government accounted to the members of the Tribe for the millions of dollars which had been expended by the Tribal Executive Committee. These funds or moneys of the Indians did not come from appropriations of the Congress but was taken from the Indian landowners by the Tribal Executive Committees and from the leases of Tribal owned lands. . . .
>
> We have no protection from Police brutality, false arrest, arbitrary and dictatorial action on the part of the Bureau and the Executive Committees. Any time an Indian attempts to assert his rights as an American citizen[,] he suddenly finds that his lease money is held up for some vague reason, surplus commodities suddenly become scarce. Members of the Executive Committee and their friends are immune from prosecution in Tribal Courts.[57]

The reference to Indian landowners and the leasing of Lakota lands, of course, indicated that the state's white stock growers were still smarting from the effects of the *Iron Crow* decision. Indeed, at the third annual conference on Indian affairs, Moses Two Bulls treated the audience to a luminous political history of Ward's testimony, the introduction and eventual enactment of a state jurisdiction law (HB No. 892), and *Iron Crow:*

> The Public Law 892 came about in this manner. Several years ago the Tribal Council of the Pine Ridge Reservation adopted a resolution to tax or assess a fee on a non-Indian doing business with the reservation. . . . But when they start[ed] to tax or assess a fee on the stockmen in the reservation, there [was an] objection. Then we had to go through the courts [that is, *Iron Crow*] to bring about a correction to that. . . . The stockmen didn't want to pay, stating that the tribal council had no authority to do other things. But that was ruled in favor of the Indian. . . . Well, these fellows then went to work. They got a bunch of Indians and used them to bring about this House Bill 892. They furnished transportation and money to bring this stuff before the state legislature. I understand that this bill was in the hopper, but they smoked it out in order to take action on it before the time expired.[58]

Comparing Ward with Two Bulls, the motivation behind HB No. 721 and later HB No. 892 becomes obvious: by invoking PL 83-280, terminationists wanted to politically neutralize the future of Lakota self-determination, which would curb white hegemony.

Moreover, Ward's testimony further revealed that whites' feelings were so strident against Lakota self-determination that any individual who publicly opposed state jurisdiction was painted as a traitor to the white community. Ward stated:

> I recently read in the paper that the County Superintendent of Shannon County Schools came to Pierre together with the officers of the Executive Committee of the Oglala Sioux Tribal Council in opposition to the State taking Civil and Criminal jurisdiction on the Reservations. This person is an officer of the State Government of the State of South Dakota, sworn to uphold the Constitution and laws of the State of South Dakota. . . . To me, this is akin to treason, for a person sworn to enforce the laws of the State of South Dakota in Shannon County to purposely resist the State taking over Civil and Criminal jurisdiction so that she [South Dakota] could effectively enforce its laws.[59]

To blunt Lakota objections that, because of ignorance, they were not ready for state jurisdiction, Ward countered by invoking the principle of equality. Speaking as an Oglala Lakota, he used arguments that echoed Berry's and Watkins's:

A claim was made by Mat[t]hew High Pine that the Indians are too ignorant to be subjected to State laws. To me, an Indian, this is an insult to our entire Indian population. I want to assure you that the Indians as a whole are no more ignorant than our White brethern. It is true that many of us are poor and it is true that we live in a condition of servitude akin to slavery, and it is true that these conditions have been brought about by the theories of communal living and the Socialistic policies set up by the Bureau of Indian Affairs under Mr. Collier and which are still being advocated, developed and pushed down our throats by the Bureau of Indian Affairs with the help of the Executive Committees of the Tribal Councils, under the guise of self-determination.

We want to be on the same footing as the White citizens. We do not like the segregation policy of the Bureau of Indian Affairs and the Executive Committees. We are willing to assume our fair share of the cost of State and Local Government. We want to get out of bondage. We think that House Bill 721 will help us accomplish this purpose.[60]

Conceding that the Lakota were poor, Ward's statement about ignorance widely missed its mark. While it was true that the Lakota were not any "more ignorant" than whites, ignorance—as understood by the Lakota—meant a serious lack of economic parity with their white neighbors. This condition of economic impoverishment was the root of the Lakota's claim of ignorance. Hence, though Ward's argument of equality with white citizens was a theoretically laudable idea, in practice, without economic parity, the Lakotas were often at the mercy of a racially hostile white community.

Despite Carlson's claim that there were some people willing to assume the added costs of state jurisdiction, these people were in the minority. HB No. 892's cost-reimbursement provision was in keeping with the EHWC's recommendation that "the state be reimbursed for the administering of law and order on the reservation."[61] Even staunch pro-jurisdiction supporters balked at having the state assume the costs. Marvin Talbott, one such supporter, strongly recommended to Bliss that "no action be taken on House Bill No. 721 unless and until advance arrangement is made with Congress for a Federal subsidy to assist in the costs of providing additional law enforcement required."[62] Because whites had these cost concerns about HB No. 721, the LBSTC's bill was quickly becoming far more palatable to South Dakota's decision makers than was HB No. 721. Ingeniously, the LBSTC's option left white leadership somewhat in a quandary. They had to weigh their overwhelming desire to have jurisdiction over Lakota territory against their overwhelming fear of having to pay the costs of that jurisdiction.

Obtaining reimbursement for the costs was one condition that worried terminationists, even the most fervent. Another hotly contested issue—one raised by the LBSTC's bill—was that of the Lakota's consent. As sovereign people, the Lakota naturally expected that their political consent was central, without which no action should be taken. From a Lakota perspective, their consent seemed all the more necessary since the move to termination was couched in the rhetoric of democracy—of "freeing the Indian" and of according Indians all the rights and privileges of every other citizen of the United States. Whites, however, had no such expectations. Instead, most expressed a deep aversion to establishing Lakota consent as a condition for state jurisdiction.

Berry's earliest statements indicated a personal belief that the Lakota people should be given an opportunity to determine whether or not state jurisdiction would apply on their reservations.[63] Indeed, since PL 83-280's enactment, the Lakota had made clear to South Dakota's legislators on several occasions their determined view that the law be amended to include a consent provision.[64] However, according to a 7 February 1957 bulletin, Sonosky told his Native clients that from 5 January 1955 to 27 August 1956 (the Eighty-fourth U.S. Congress), though several consent bills had been introduced to amend PL 83-280 and the Senate had managed to pass one of them (S. 51), the House Subcommittee on Indian Affairs had failed to act on any of the consent measures.[65] Sonosky's review of the Eighty-fourth Congress's legislative record on Native affairs showed that Berry politically refused to act on his professed beliefs about consent, thereby leaving the principle of Lakota consent to the arbitrary whim of South Dakota.

According to local terminationists, Lakota consent reduced the chances of the state assuming jurisdiction considerably, hence for them, HB No. 721's strongest appeal was its omission of any consent language. By actually requesting state jurisdiction—albeit criminal jurisdiction—the LBSTC's HB No. 892 sufficiently contradicted the conventional wisdom about Lakota consent and effectively forced, however unwittingly, the pivotal question of consent into the legislative process. Three days before the HCIA officially introduced both HB No. 721 and HB No. 892, Berry suggested to Farrar and company that, because of the LBSTC's bill, they might want to amend their proposed bill in order to "provide that the state accepts jurisdiction of criminal and civil causes of action on reservations where such tribe has requested such jurisdiction."[66]

Farrar's predictable response to Berry's suggestion was to continue lobbying for the passage of HB No. 721 regardless of what the LBSTC proposed, believing that the LBSTC's proposal was insignificant and without political weight compared with the terminationists' own measure. Indeed, as late as 26 February 1957, while still firmly believing that the HCIA committee was "favorably inclined to give our Bill a do-pass" recommendation to the full House,[67] Farrar was more than slightly unnerved by the HCIA's favorable reception of HB No. 892. He bitterly confided to Berry, "The Bill submitted by the Bureau on the Lower Brule is nothing more or less then [*sic*] pure smoke screen. It would be worse than nothing to adopt the Bureau's Bill."[68]

A stunning turn of events for the Lakota came between 26 and 28 February 1957, when, according to the reports of Farrar, Hieb, and Carlson, the HCIA committee requested a meeting with Saunders and Reifel. As a result of this meeting, two amendments were added to HB No. 892. The first amendment expanded the range of the bill beyond Lower Brule to include all nine Lakota reservations in South Dakota. The second amendment was a referendum clause, requiring the consent of the Lakota for state jurisdiction to become law on each specific reservation.

To the referendum clause, however, the HCIA committee imposed a major condition: if the Dakota-Lakota of any of the nine reservations failed to hold such a referendum between the dates of 1 October 1957 and 1 October 1958, then "it shall be deemed that the referendum has been dispensed with and that the tribe has consented to and does approve the assumption of jurisdiction."[69] In other words, if a reservation failed to hold a referendum that defeated jurisdiction, the state would assume jurisdiction for that one particular reservation.

With these two amendments to the LBSTC's bill, on 1 March 1957, the HCIA committee's report to the full House made no mention of HB No. 721, in effect letting it perish in committee,[70] while HB No. 892 was reported out of committee. Moreover, the HCIA sent a do-pass recommendation to the full House, and, on 4 March 1957, the House complied by passing HB No. 892 by an overwhelming margin.[71]

This unexpected turn of political events left the state jurisdiction forces in a state of shock for the fourth time—first with the *Iron Crow* ruling, second with its appeal denied, third with the LBSTC's surprise bill, and now fourth with the vigorous passage not only of the LBSTC bill but also of its Lakota consent-by-referendum amendment.

On 2 March 1957, the Senate received HB No. 892 and referred it to the Senate Committee on Indian Affairs (SCIA). However, with the legislative session to officially end on 8 March 1957 (at 12:01 A.M.), there was not much time to consider the bill. Given this severe time constraint, the state jurisdiction forces, in their final, desperate attempt to amend HB No. 892, so manipulated the state's decision-making process that it spun out of control. Ethel Merrival, appointed by the Oglala Lakota to serve on its anti-state jurisdiction delegation, submitted a four-page "Pierre Legislation Report," detailing how, on the very last legislative day, the pro-state jurisdiction forces tried adding an amendment to HB No. 892 that would allow whites to vote in a Lakota-sponsored referendum, not a state one:

> Word was received by telephone that the Lower Brule House Bill 892 was to be amended at the request of certain stockgrowers and others for the state of South Dakota to take over civil and criminal jurisdiction. The above delegates [of Merrival, James Iron Cloud, Matthew High Pine, and Alfreda Janis] were delegated to protest the amendment in Pierre which would give the County the right to vote with the Indian on this bill at a referendum election.[72]

Throughout much of the final legislative day, the pro-state jurisdiction advocates of John Farrar, Clair Coomes, Halley, Merrill, Orvil Schwarting, Fred Gerber, Art Vitalis, John Linehan, Mert Glover, James Ramey, and Edison Ward lobbied the state senators to include whites in HB No. 892's referendum amendment. Interestingly, HB No. 892's language was explicit about voter qualifications: if a person voted in a Lakota election, that person was eligible to vote in the referendum (section 5). Including white voters would have meant one of two things. Either it would have required striking the amendment's language that specifically permitted only Lakotas to vote and replacing it with language that permitted all affected county residents, which included mostly whites, to vote. Or the legislators would have had to amend the bill's language to allow a county to hold a concurrent election.

The principal danger of both alternatives was that many Lakota had never voted in state elections. County officials would probably not recognize any noncounty or nonstate voter registration list. To define those qualified to vote on the question of jurisdiction, any amendment must recognize Lakota voter registration as equivalent to state, county, or local voter registration, otherwise the state would be requiring dual voter registration for Lakotas but not for whites. Even if a massive county voter-registration drive were organized to make the Lakotas eligible to vote in a state or county election, there were no guarantees that the Lakota would in fact turn out and vote. Being a county election, county polls and reservation polls were not always located in the same places. Because a significant number of Lakota were poor, transportation to the county polls was also a significant factor in turnout. Hence, in all fairness, the amendment would have had to address the geographical differences and resource deficiencies that would affect Lakota voting.

As to the second way to bring in the white vote, the suggestion of holding concurrent elections—whereby the Lakota and the whites would vote separately on the same question—was not so clear-cut either. There was no guarantee that the Lakota and county governments would agree to a same-day vote. Even if they did, the voter-registration question would reemerge. If a Lakota individual voted in previous state, county, and tribal elections, arbitrarily denying that person a vote in either a county or a Lakota election simply because of his or her political status would considerably muddy the legal waters.

Had John Farrar and company succeeded in convincing the Senate to amend HB No. 892 so that "the County could vote with the Indian population on this jurisdiction [question],"[73] it would most likely have derailed HB No. 892, as Merrival pointed out: "If this bill had been amended[,] then it would have had to go back to the House for concurrent consent. At this late date[,] however, we were told that the bill would probably die on the floor of the house[,] being that this was the last day of the 60 day session."[74]

Since Farrar and others felt that HB No. 892 was worse than nothing, one could speculate that derailing the bill was in fact their political strategy. However, Merrival's report suggests otherwise. While the 1957 Senate journal records only that HB No. 892 passed, Merrival's report tells a more lurid story—one of intense political wrangling, especially in the last hours and even minutes of the legislative session. Merrival reported that HB No. 892 was not even marked on the Senate calendar, which meant that it was going to die in committee without ever reaching a floor vote. Had that happened, pro-state jurisdiction advocates would have had to wait two more years until the legislature convened before another jurisdiction measure could be introduced.

It seems, then, that the senators who were sympathetic to the pro-state jurisdiction forces got desperate. They decided to take some last-minute interdictive steps on behalf of state jurisdiction that caused the legislative decision-making process to collapse, abandoning all semblance of integrity:

> When the Senate recessed for lunch [6:30 P.M.] in the evening, Senator Roessler called the State Legislation Committee together for about five minutes. . . . After the Senate resumed their meeting in the evening [7:30 P.M.] the Calendar was deviated from by motion to smoke out Bill 892 by pressure of the delegation that Edison Ward was with. They placed this Bill on the calendar by vote right after the Scholarship Bill to the Indian[,] which was on the very last item of the calendar.[75]

Having successfully smoked HB No. 892 out of committee, the Senate leaders allowed debate on the remaining bills to continue until about 11:25 P.M. when, incredibly, they halted the chamber proceedings to indulge in gift exchanges for fifteen minutes. With all of ten minutes left in the session, the Senate had two measures yet to be considered: the Indian scholarship bill and HB No. 892. As the senators debated the Indian scholarship bill, time ran out. It was now midnight. At sixty seconds past midnight, the thirty-fifth biennial legislative session would officially conclude, and the question of state jurisdiction would have to wait another two years.

So the Lakotas in attendance at Pierre thought. However, Merrival's report goes on to describe an outrageous incident. At 12:01 A.M., someone in the Senate chamber threw a coat over the Senate clock. This somewhat melodramatic and certainly unethical maneuver supposedly "allowed" the senators to continue their now extralegal session. At 12:10 A.M., the Indian scholarship bill was approved and thirteen minutes later, HB No. 892 was passed. To be sure, Merrival's report expressed her thorough disgust and outrage over the coat incident: "The trick of throwing the coat over the clock after the legal limit of the session has never been protested or taken issue with. What is the legal sense of covering the clock after midnight[?] Are the senators children that such play should go on?"[76] Yet after more than five hundred years of dealing with whites, Natives have learned that whenever whites become involved with Natives, the former feel no moral obligation to the latter, and therefore anything goes. Had it been otherwise, the presiding officer of the Senate would have adjourned, or Governor Joseph Foss would have vetoed HB No. 892 and refused to sign it. But sign he did, and HB No. 892 became law (appendix D-1).

When the political dust settled, the law outlined three primary conditions for the state to assume jurisdiction. First, "the Board of County Commissioners of any county containing Indian Country" (section 4) must formally adopt a resolution to assume and accept jurisdiction. Second, before adopting such a resolution, the county commissioners had to negotiate a cost-reimbursement contract with the BIA for any added expenditures associated with a county's assumption of jurisdiction. This language, which was in the LBSTC's initial proposal, resolved the state's dilemma over costs. Third, the Lakota/Dakota of each of the nine reservations could, if they desired, hold a referendum to accept or reject the imposition of state jurisdiction. Failure to conduct such a referendum within one year would mean that the Lakota on that reservation gave their automatic consent to state jurisdiction.

For the Lakota, it was not hard to imagine how these three conditions might lead to unanticipated outcomes when it came to actually implementing the law. Regarding the first two conditions, the law stated that if whites wanted jurisdiction over Lakota territory, then their boards of county commissioners would have to negotiate the all-important cost-covering contract with the BIA themselves. If they were successful in these negotiations, then they would have to pass a resolution to assume jurisdiction. With twenty-two counties charged with deciding the jurisdiction issue locally, the process of acceptance was not without complications.

For example, the Pine Ridge Reservation included parts of Bennett, Shannon, and Washabaugh counties, and this raised all kinds of logistical problems. Shannon and Washabaugh counties were unorganized counties and so did not even have a board of county commissioners who could act directly on the first condition. These two counties were attached, however, to organized counties for obvious administrative purposes; Shannon was attached to Fall River and Washabaugh to Jackson. Yet neither Fall River nor Jackson counties contained Lakota territory. Even so, their administering boards of county commissioners could ostensibly argue that, despite the fact that neither Fall River nor Jackson counties contained Lakota territory, they had the authority to invoke the first condition. Afraid of being sacrificed on the alter of state jurisdiction, the white residents of the unorganized counties might equally argue that their counties should get organized so that their own boards of county commissioners could decide whether and how to comply with HB No. 892.

Organized or not, though, Fall River, Jackson, and Bennett counties offered no guarantees that they would act in unison on the jurisdiction question. Any one of the three counties may, after reviewing the social factors and economic costs involved with assumption, conclude that the price of jurisdiction was prohibitive, especially if they failed to negotiate a favorable reimbursement contract with the BIA. The five other multicounty reservations—Rosebud, Cheyenne River, Lower Brule, Crow Creek, and Lake Traverse—faced similar logistical nightmares. The three reservations that were not multicounty— Standing Rock, Flandreau, and Yankton—faced their own problems. The boards of county commissioners in these counties were certainly not immune from the vulgarities that might arise in negotiating a reimbursement cost contract.

Finally, should any one of the twenty-two county commissions succeed in fulfilling the first two conditions—that is, in negotiating an acceptable cost reimbursement contract and enacting a resolution to assume jurisdiction—a Lakota referendum that rejected state jurisdiction would make the efforts of a county board moot. For all the stakeholders involved with the question of jurisdiction, the Lakota referenda became all-important.

Matthew High Pine v. South Dakota: "Persons Other than Indians"

Although the state legislature passed HB No. 892, as with any South Dakota law, it would not take effect until 6 June 1957, a full ninety days after the adjournment of the legislative session.[77] Moreover, one of the most important questions remained unanswered: Would South Dakota, as a disclaimer state, have to amend its constitution before it could assume jurisdiction? That question and the entire question of whether South Dakota would assume jurisdiction were soon to be answered. On 23 April 1957, Art Vitalis, the Shannon County deputy sheriff, arrested both Matthew High Pine and Paul Woman Dress for public intoxication. These arrests were made forty-three days before HB No. 892 was to take effect and several months before the Lakota referenda. Obviously, South Dakota was acting prematurely in assuming unilateral jurisdiction—not only without the authority of its recently passed law but also without the implementation of the law's two critical conditions.

Neither were any of these individuals unaware of the legislative process and HB No. 892. Both High Pine and Vitalis had been active in the state jurisdiction controversy. High Pine had given anti-state jurisdiction testimony, and Vitalis had been among the terminationists responsible for smoking out HB No. 892 on the last day of the legislative session. For Vitalis to arrest High · Pine indicated just how personal the jurisdiction issue had become.

The next day, both High Pine and Woman Dress appeared before the justice of the peace, Antoine G. LaDeaux. Each pleaded guilty, were required to pay court costs and a fine, and were given a ten-day jail sentence. However, shortly after their sentencing, Harold R. Hanley of the law office of Hanley, Costello, and Porter filed a writ of habeas corpus in the Seventh Circuit Court, demanding that High Pine and Woman Dress be released from state custody. The circuit court judge George Lampert issued the writ on 26 April 1957 and set a 10 May 1957 habeas corpus hearing. Ethel Merrival, the Oglala Lakota delegate who attended the May hearing, reported that High Pine and Woman Dress had protested their arrest and trial to LaDeaux on jurisdictional grounds, stating "that the state had no authority to arrest and try an Indian in any State Court."[78] Nearly 195 days after the 10 May 1957 hearing, Lampert agreed with Hanley's legal argument that the state indeed lacked jurisdiction and finally issued a 21 November 1957 court order releasing High Pine and Woman Dress from their initial sentence of incarceration. Of course, the state pro-jurisdiction interests were not at all happy with this ruling. Still hot with their desire to gain state jurisdiction, the terminationists immediately appealed Lampert's decision to the S.D. Supreme Court.

The appeal, however, placed the state in a most awkward legal and political position. At the time of the arrests, HB No. 892 and hence the assumption of jurisdiction by the state had not yet gone into effect. Contesting Lampert's habeas corpus ruling—a decision Lampert made on the grounds that the state lacked jurisdiction—meant that the state had to manufacture some outright fictitious arguments claiming that it did in fact have the necessary criminal jurisdiction.

For its first argument, the state devised an elaborate claim that can best be described as an "idle acts theory"—an argument that we will explore at some length. Mindful of the shaky legal ground of this idle acts argument, though, the state mounted a second and frankly incredible argument that neither High Pine or Woman Dress were in fact Indians and therefore were not exempt from state jurisdiction. The state's third and final argument, which actually made much more legal sense than the other two, was that a writ of habeas corpus was an improper remedy; High Pine and Woman Dress should have invoked a writ of error or an appeal instead.

For both the state and the Lakota, the most critical and important argument was, naturally enough, the first one. If the state could prove convincingly that, despite HB No. 892, it had always had criminal jurisdiction over Lakota territory, then HB No. 892 would become questionable, if not moot. Indeed, the S.D. Supreme Court framed the appeal exactly in these terms: "Whether the State of South Dakota has jurisdiction to punish an Indian . . . is the principal question presented by this appeal."[79] If so, then HB No. 892's most significant conditions would become irrelevant.

In its 1 October 1958 appeal, the state contended that state courts had concurrent criminal jurisdiction with Lakota and U.S. courts and therefore that the Shannon County justice of the peace had the authority to impose a sentence on High Pine and Woman Dress. To justify this claim, the state used the historical record to construct an "idle-acts" theory supporting its contention that the state already had criminal jurisdiction. Invoking pre-1953 statutes relating to the criminal jurisdiction question, the state attempted to thread the tiniest of jurisdictional needles and, in effect, resurrect the politically dead HB No. 721 without even having to pass it into law.

Central to the debate that followed was the notion of "idle acts," yet this term took on various meanings over the course of the appeal. Sometimes the term was used to mean that an act that had been passed was legitimate but had been dormant; it had not been implemented or used for decades. Though it had lain idle, it could nonetheless be called into effect at any time. Other times the term "idle act" was used to suggest that a law that had been passed was not done so idly; it must have had some purposeful use, otherwise the legislators would not have bothered with it. Sometimes the term was used to argue that the state's failure to implement a law or act rendered it useless. Yet other times "idle act" meant that a law had no legitimacy whatsoever—implemented or not—and therefore was truly useless.

According to the state's argument, in Chapter 106 of the Session Laws of the State of South Dakota for 1901, South Dakota ceded to the United States its criminal jurisdiction over any and all criminal offenses that occurred within Lakota territory:

> There is hereby relinquished and given to the United States of America and the officers and courts thereof exclusive jurisdiction and authority to arrest, prosecute, convict[,] and punish all persons whomsoever who shall, upon any Indian reservation within the state of South Dakota, commit any act in violation of the penal laws of the United States.[80]

The state's counsel then argued that, before 1901, the state legislature must have believed that it held such authority. Moreover, the United States must have thought so too. When Congress officially accepted South Dakota's relinquishment in 1903,[81] the legislators must have been satisfied that the state possessed the jurisdictional authority in order to give it. Otherwise, argued the state, why cede and then reaccept what it did not originally have? Using this 1903 relinquishment as part of its argument, South Dakota readily conceded that, until 1948, when the United States removed that particular 1903 statute from its federal code, South Dakota in fact did not have exclusive criminal jurisdiction over any individual residing within the boundaries of Lakota territory.

To explain how South Dakota, from 1948 onward, reassumed its previously ceded jurisdiction, the state's counsel evidently built its entire argument on a spring 1957 *South Dakota Law Review* article, "Federal Jurisdiction over Criminal Matters Involving Indians," written by Clinton Richards, the U.S. attorney for South Dakota:

> In the 1948 Federal Code revision . . . the special statute [the Act of 1903] was dropped and the general statute became applicable to South Dakota as elsewhere. The following year the South Dakota Supreme Court held [in State ex rel. *Olson v. Schumacher*[82]] that the effect of this repeal was to restore to South

Dakota the jurisdiction ceded to the United States under the Act of 1903, and that the general law as to Indians and Indian reservations existing elsewhere was now applicable in South Dakota. The legislature, in effect, confirmed this action of the Supreme Court in Chapter 187, S.D. Laws 1951 [SB No. 278].[83]

The state's counsel based its reasoning on Richards's account of how South Dakota had reacquired criminal jurisdiction from the United States. Outlining the legislative history of how South Dakota had relinquished criminal jurisdiction to the United States in 1901 through Chapter 106 and then reassumed it in 1948, the state noted that Chapter 106 was subsequently carried forward and changed. In 1929, the state amended it so that the state could reserve with the United States concurrent criminal jurisdiction "to arrest any person committing any offense under the laws of the state . . . even though the acts constituting such offense may also constitute an offense under the laws of the United States of America [Chapter 158 1929]."[84]

Of course, as Hanley later pointed out, although South Dakota may have believed in 1929 that its amendment to establish concurrent jurisdiction was effective over Lakota territory, it could not legitimately base that claim on the 1903 federal law for the simple reason that Congress did not repeal the law until 1948. Until that repeal happened, the federal government and not South Dakota had jurisdiction in Lakota Country, and no amendment could change that. In a nutshell, changing the state law but not the federal law was not sufficient to establish joint jurisdiction.

Moreover, as the S.D. Supreme Court noted in *Schumacher*, the 1948 repeal of the 1903 federal law, when the United States supposedly transferred criminal jurisdiction back to South Dakota, it was required that the state legislature reaccept jurisdiction through an affirmative legislative act; otherwise, the state could not be said to have legally reassumed it. In response to this requirement, the state's counsel pointed to the 1951 SB No. 278 as providing the required affirmative act. Hence, the state argued, barring a treaty or U.S. statute to the contrary, South Dakota had in fact possessed the jurisdiction to punish any person on any Indian reservation or in Indian Country who violated state criminal laws ever since 1951.

This was the essence of the state's idle-act argument. Presumably, jurisdiction was automatically vested in South Dakota; otherwise, if South Dakota had no jurisdiction, then neither it nor Congress had any power to engage in the transfer of criminal jurisdiction one way or the other. Of course, the next legal hurdle for the state's counsel to explain was how, in transferring criminal jurisdiction back and forth between South Dakota and the United

States, South Dakota's actions came to include the Lakota People. Certainly South Dakota had no grounds in any treaty with the Lakota for assuming some kind of original default jurisdiction. In fact, the very need for HB No. 892 showed that, as of 1957 at least, the state had no legitimate criminal jurisdiction over Lakota territory.

To address this highly embarrassing political question, the state invoked PL 83-280 as its legal source of authority. After quickly mentioning sections 6 and 7, which provided for how states were to assume jurisdiction in view of their constitutions, the state's attorneys offered their explanation for how South Dakota acquired criminal jurisdiction:

> It is our interpretation that Public Law No. 280, Chapter 505 enables "any other State" to assume jurisdiction of criminal offenses by amending its Constitution or laws notwithstanding any legal impediments contained in the Enabling Act or any previous Act of Congress. This condition has already been complied with as far as the State of South Dakota is concerned by the amendments contained in Chapter 158, Laws of 1929 and Chapter 187, Laws of 1951.[85]

Therefore, citing the 1901 Chapter 106 as its primary criminal jurisdiction law and then following the legislative history to the amendment of that law in 1929 as well as the passage of SB No. 278 in 1951, the state concluded its oral argument by claiming that it was already exercising criminal jurisdiction over Lakota territory. Though some of these laws may have been "idle" and not implemented by South Dakota, they remained in force nonetheless. Accordingly, since South Dakota became a state in 1889, it possessed first total jurisdiction (1889–1901), then no jurisdiction (1901–1929), then joint jurisdiction with the United States (1929–1953), then total jurisdiction again (1953 on) over Lakota territory. In other words, South Dakota could claim some jurisdiction even before 1953 when the United States gave its official legislative consent for states to do so fully. So went the state's argument. Could it withstand the Lakota's defense?

On 15 January 1959, H. R. Hanley, the counsel for High Pine and Woman Dress, countered the state's appeal on three major points. First, as a clear-cut disclaimer state, South Dakota was required to follow section 6, not section 7. Second, state assumption of jurisdiction had to follow and not precede PL 83-280. The claim that South Dakota already had jurisdiction over Lakota territory was far outside the body of accepted legal opinion, otherwise why would Congress and South Dakota's legislature need to pass any termination bills? Third, the 1901 state law and its later amendments applied only to non-Indians.

Of the first point, Hanley argued that the Enabling Act clearly made South Dakota's admittance as a state conditional on its willingness to disclaim any and all jurisdiction over Lakota territory. He argued that South Dakota readily complied by having such a disclaimer statement written into its constitution. Moreover, Hanley effectively employed a 1906 S.D. Supreme Court decision, *Peano v. Brennan,* which amplified the state's constitutional disclaimer language. The outcome of that case stated with even further clarity that the people of South Dakota had agreed never to try to claim Lakota lands or to impose any of their laws on Lakota Country. The explosive implication of Hanley's first argument was that South Dakota needed to amend its constitution before it could even consider exercising jurisdiction over Lakota territory.

In view of the extensive contextual evidence reinforcing the state's disclaimer language and the illegality of brushing it aside or treating the constitutional disclaimer as if it were only a law or statute, Hanley observed with some sarcasm that the state's counsel had advanced a novel legal theory that PL 83-280 "automatically vested jurisdiction in the State by bringing into full bloom a State statute [chapter 158, Session of Laws 1929] . . . which had lain partially dormant for twenty-four years."[86] As a result, he continued, "unbeknownst to the Congress of the United States, the Legislature of the State of South Dakota, and the law enforcement agencies of the Federal and State governments,"[87] the state had supposedly possessed criminal jurisdiction over Lakota lands for decades.

Having established that South Dakota's constitution prevented it from automatically assuming criminal jurisdiction under PL 83-280, Hanley moved to the second point: South Dakota had to intentionally change the disclaimer clause in its constitution before it could pass a law to assume criminal jurisdiction over the Lakota People. Because PL 83-280 specified precisely what a section 6 state must do before it could assume jurisdiction, Hanley focused on section 6's language and the legislative history behind it. For Hanley, the language of section 6 was explicit: "the law contemplates State action *after* the effective date of the Act,"[88] not before. Examining the legislative intent of section 6, Hanley showed that, despite a state's desire to assume jurisdiction, if a state had either a constitutional disclaimer clause or a statute to that effect, the state had to remove that constitutional clause or statute *before* it could enact any state jurisdiction legislation.

Hanley adroitly pushed the argument that PL 83-280 required the consent of the people in a section 6 state *before* that state could assume jurisdiction. Even though South Dakota had not removed its disclaimer language before enacting HB No. 892, Hanley observed that two of HB No. 892's three conditions—a county's assent and the Lakota's consent—provided further evidence that South Dakota could assume criminal jurisdiction only *after* it had obtained the support and consent of the people involved. After all, the state's white people were the ones who had agreed in the state's founding constitution never to encroach on Lakota lands.

Moreover, with HB No. 892, South Dakota went beyond what Congress required by seeking the consent not only of the white county commissioners but also of the Lakota people. South Dakota's legislature, Hanley said, "vested the ultimate decision as to the extension of State jurisdiction in the entities directly concerned, the counties and the Indian tribes."[89] In other words, in spite of the state's glaring oversight in not amending its state constitution, the legislature had nonetheless managed to pass the one and only law—HB No. 892—that could conceivably fall within PL 83-280's statutory framework. None of the previously enacted criminal jurisdiction laws even remotely fulfilled section 6's public-consent requirement and hence were null and void—inapplicable.

Hanley's third argument was perhaps his best and strongest. After showing how South Dakota could not possibly have accepted criminal jurisdiction over the Lakota People, what did the state's 1901 law and its amendments actually mean? What jurisdiction were they actually assuming and to whom did they actually apply? Addressing these questions, Hanley conceded the state's point in its idle-act theory: neither South Dakota nor Congress had passed "idle" (in the sense of useless) criminal jurisdiction laws; instead, these laws applied "solely to non-Indians."[90]

Going back to the 1901 state law, Hanley argued that South Dakota could not have included the Lakota when it relinquished criminal jurisdiction to the United States. To do so would have contradicted not only treaty law but also an existing federal statute, the Enabling Act of 1889, as well as the state's constitutional disclaimer which clearly denied the state any and all jurisdiction over Lakota territory. Hanley summarized his argument: "The State could not relinquish what it did not have. The inescapable conclusion must be reached that what the State relinquished and the Federal government assumed was jurisdiction over non-Indians."[91]

Hanley found overwhelming support for his legal insight in the 1882 U.S.

Supreme Court case, *United States v. McBratney*, in which the court ruled that a state's criminal jurisdiction applied only to the non-Indians on a reservation. As a matter of settled case law, *McBratney*'s impact loomed large behind the state's disclaimer language and thus shed considerable light on the appropriate interpretation of South Dakota's 1901 act of transferring its criminal jurisdiction to the United States. Reviewing the legislative history of the United States' 1903 acceptance, Hanley showed that federal preemption of a state's criminal jurisdiction involved only those who were "other than Indians" in Lakota territory. Moreover, Hanley argued, this was not an obscure but a widely understood policy:

> Once the fact is recognized that the 1901 [state] statute applied to "other than Indians," all other pieces fall into place. The 1929 law, Chapter 158, was an assumption of concurrent jurisdiction over non-Indians by the State. If it had done any more, it would have been in conflict with the Enabling Act and the Constitution of the State of South Dakota.[92]

Having demonstrated that the 1901 Chapter 106 and its 1929 amendment involved only non-Indians, Hanley then showed how the 1951 amendment, or SB No. 278, also fell to the logic of his argument. Unlike the state's counsel, who intentionally overlooked all the language in SB No. 278 that contradicted a termination agenda, Hanley cited a critical paragraph in which South Dakota unambiguously acknowledged its circumscribed criminal jurisdiction. Specifically, the 1951 law mentioned pointedly that the state, in accepting the 1948 U.S. relinquishment of criminal jurisdiction, realized that this jurisdiction applied only to "persons other than Indians for the commission of crimes upon Indian reservations."[93]

Having skillfully dismantled South Dakota's idle-act theory, Hanley established that federal law and state constitutional law necessarily preempted any pre–PL 83-280 state jurisdiction over Lakota territory. Moreover, because the state's appeal was filed on the ending date for the Lakota referenda, Hanley showed how HB No. 892's three conditions for implementing jurisdiction underscored his argument that South Dakota was indulging in utter fantasy when it claimed any pre-1953 criminal jurisdiction over Lakota territory.

Citing the three main conditions that HB No. 892 required for the state to assume criminal jurisdiction—negotiated contracts for the United States to reimburse counties, the official consent of a county's administrative body, and the consent by referenda of the Lakota People—Hanley observed that in several counties, two of the three conditions remained unfulfilled:

[T]here is no showing that Fall River County has passed the required resolution, nor that it has reached a subsidy agreement with the Federal government[.] (In fact, at present there is no legal authority for Federal agencies to conclude such a subsidy agreement.) Moreover, the Oglala Sioux Tribe has specifically vetoed any extension of State jurisdiction over the Pine Ridge Reservation.[94]

In his summation, Hanley concluded that PL 83-280 provided no automatic force or effect to South Dakota's claim of having assumed criminal jurisdiction over the Lakota People—either before or after 1953. If anything, state officials were legally obligated to adhere to HB No. 892, otherwise they had no grounds at all for claiming criminal jurisdiction over Lakota territory.

After the state's final oral argument was filed with the S.D. Supreme Court on 13 March 1959, everyone would have to wait eight more months before the state's five supreme court justices would render their fateful decision. Ironically, beginning with *Iron Crow,* the judicial trend of South Dakota's federal and lower state courts was to favor Lakota self-determination—a trend that flew in the face of the federal and state intention to terminate Native Nations. As the Lakota waited for the ruling, the burning question was, would the state's highest court follow that trend as well?

On 2 November 1959, the five justices of the S.D. Supreme Court unanimously concurred with Hanley, ruling that South Dakota did not have, nor did it ever have, criminal jurisdiction over Lakota territory. In effect, this ruling upheld Lampert's reasoning in his initial habeas corpus decision. A further analysis of the justices' ruling reveals that, in addition to Hanley's solid legal argument, the five justices had been influenced by a recent U.S. Supreme Court case, *Williams v. Lee* (12 January 1959), and by an *Arizona Law Review (ALR)* article, "Criminal Jurisdiction over Indian Country in Arizona," which examined the legal impact of *Williams.* On the question of whether South Dakota had the authority to punish a Lakota, the five S.D. justices led off their opinion by referring to *Williams,* saying that the case would govern their analysis.

Williams involved a civil suit in which a white Indian trader filed in an Arizona court to have a Dine couple pay an $81.22 credit bill they owed. Predictably, the Arizona court, despite the Dine couple's motion for dismissal because the Dine and not the Arizona court had jurisdiction, entered a decision in favor of the trader. Eventually, the lower court's decision was appealed to Arizona's Supreme Court and it, too, affirmed the lower court's ruling, citing that, "since no Act of Congress expressly forbids their doing so[,] Arizona courts are free to exercise jurisdiction over civil suits by non-Indians against Indians[,] though the action arises on an Indian reservation."[95]

Since non-Native versus Native jurisdiction was and remains an all-important matter, the Arizona high court's opinion was appealed to the U.S. Supreme Court. The Supreme Court reversed the Arizona high court's decision, concluding that, without a clear grant from Congress, no state could arbitrarily assume jurisdiction over Native Country. Moreover, in support of Dine (and therefore Native) self-determination, the court stated further:

> There can be no doubt that to allow the exercise of state jurisdiction here would undermine the authority of the tribal courts over Reservation affairs and hence would infringe on the right of the Indians to govern themselves. . . . The cases in this Court have consistently guarded the authority of Indian governments over their reservations. . . . If this power [of self-government or jurisdiction] is to be taken away from them, it is for Congress to do it.[96]

Without question, the S.D. Supreme Court's opinion borrowed heavily from *Williams*. Quoting it at length, the state's supreme court boldfaced critical phrases in which Native and U.S. criminal jurisdiction were recognized as exclusive, and their exclusive authority could be changed only by Congress, as happened with PL 83-280. Having adopted the reasoning in *Williams,* South Dakota's high court next framed a crucial part of its opinion. As with *Williams,* the essential question that South Dakota put before the high court was, did Congress grant the state criminal jurisdiction over Lakota Country?

In formulating its answer, South Dakota's high court referenced not only *Williams* but also the 1959 *ALR* article that commented on its implications. The article was written by Laurence Davis, the attorney employed by the Dine Nation as its general counsel. Davis outlined the spheres of criminal jurisdiction among the United States, individual states, and Native Nations as it existed in the late 1950s. Analyzing how sections 6 and 7 of PL 83-280 applied to the states accepting jurisdiction over Native Country, Davis examined the legislative history of PL 83-280 to uncover congressional intent:

> It is thus clear that Congress intended section 6 of the act to apply to Arizona and to other states having disclaimers of jurisdiction in their constitutions; if such states wish to assume jurisdiction over Indian country, an amendment is required. Section 7 applies to states such as Nevada, which never had a disclaimer in its constitution; mere legislation is sufficient for such states to extend their jurisdiction. To date, the writer is informed that Washington, South Dakota, and Nevada have purported to accept the invitation of Congress to extend their jurisdiction to Indian country. Despite the fact that the

first two states have disclaimers in their constitutions, all three have acted by legislation only.[97]

Concluding that it was Congress and not the states that ultimately would decide whether a state could assume any type of jurisdiction over Native Country, Davis also inferred that, because South Dakota's constitutional disclaimer had not been repealed, its most recent law, HB No. 892, was of questionable validity.

Faced with the recent *Williams* opinion, Davis's article in a respectable law journal, and the post–HB No. 892 developments (especially the Lakota referenda), the justices of the South Dakota's high court faced the most difficult task, politically speaking, of having to go against an overzealous state-level policy designed to eliminate Lakota self-determination altogether. Reviewing PL 83-280's legislative history with respect to South Dakota, the high court interpreted the termination law in the context of the existing political compact between the United States and South Dakota—a compact established when South Dakota entered the Union as a state. Unfortunately that academic interpretation would be as close as the high court would come to agreeing with Hanley or Davis on the section 6 issue. The justices fell short of stating outright that unless South Dakota removed its disclaimer language by amending its constitution, which section 6 required, none of its state jurisdiction laws were valid or would ever be so.

After painstakingly sidestepping the full constitutional implications of how Hanley and Davis had deconstructed the terminationists' claims to legal authority, the high court turned its attention to the initial matter raised by the pro-state jurisdiction forces. Was SB No. 278 the affirmative state law that, pursuant to PL 83-280, accepted from the federal government criminal jurisdiction over Lakota territory, such that High Pine and Woman Dress were not illegally detained but rightfully punished?

The high court began by admitting that PL 83-280 had at least the cloak of a political compact between the federal government and the state governments, especially given the specific provisions it made for states with disclaimer language in their constitutions. The court went on to reason that the 1953 federal law (PL 83-280) did not offer states a simple or automatic transfer of power but instead offered "a grant of power to any state which would indicate its acceptance of that offer through appropriate future action."[98] To augment its reasoning, the high court invoked the highly controversial 1957 HB No. 892 as evidence of what appropriate future action might mean: "The act [PL 83-280] was so interpreted by our Legislature. In tendering a conditional acceptance . . . the state of South Dakota assumes and accepts jurisdiction of all criminal and civil causes of action arising in Indian Country under the provisions of this Act [HB No. 892] as hereinafter set forth."[99]

When the high court named HB No. 892 as the state law by which South Dakota could potentially accept jurisdiction from the United States, South Dakota's legal reliance on the earlier 1951 law—SB No. 278—as having given the state blanket jurisdiction over Lakota territory was considerably undermined. Without saying so explicitly, the court was in effect agreeing with Hanley's argument that the 1901 law and its two subsequent amendments (1929 and 1951) had to do with state and federal jurisdiction over non-Indians only. That being so, the court inadvertently and indirectly strengthened the contention of anti-state-jurisdiction forces that, as a disclaimer state, South Dakota had to amend its constitution before its all-white legislature could pass a law accepting jurisdiction over the Lakota People.

In other words, the court was ruling that all of South Dakota's jurisdiction laws previous to HB No. 892 applied to whites only. Accordingly, South Dakota had no law on the books that applied its jurisdiction to Natives—no law, therefore, that could now be overruled by passing a new law. South Dakota's only legally established statement regarding jurisdiction over Indian Country lay in its founding constitution, and that language expressly forbade South Dakota and its citizens from claiming such jurisdiction. To try to claim jurisdiction over Native Country now, the state had no choice legally but to amend its constitution. Simply passing a law would not suffice.

Finally, the court drew its attention to an inherent contradiction in the state's argument between SB No. 278 and HB No. 892. While the former law presumably expressed the state's unconditional acceptance of criminal jurisdiction, the latter made the transfer of jurisdiction conditional on whether the counties could arrange a way to pay for it. In the justices' view, it made no sense for the legislature to pass the latter law if the former already applied to Lakota Country, hence their ruling that it did not:

> The assumption of jurisdiction over all crimes committed by tribal Indians within the Indian reservations of South Dakota involves no inconsiderable financial burdens for the affected counties. That our Legislature is aware of the magnitude of that burden is indicated by the fact that . . . it insisted upon a Federal subsidy for the benefit of those counties as a condition to its acceptance of such jurisdiction. To yield to the advocacy of the sheriff would be to charge the Legislature with indulging in the useless act of agreeing . . . to conditionally accept that, which according to his view, it had theretofore

acquired under its earlier unconditional offer of 1951. As we have stated, we deem the sheriff's contention untenable."[100]

By viewing PL 83-280 as a political grant of power that the states could accept through some future act of their legislatures, the justices agreed with the state's argument that there existed an "idle" law that could be put into effect—"idle" in the sense of being legitimate but dormant, ready to be acted on. However, in spite of all the legal hair-splitting that the state's counsel had done to try to claim that the state possessed criminal jurisdiction over Lakota territory and had for quite some time unbeknownst to everybody— the Lakota, Congress, the state legislators, and the public—Hanley's argument prevailed. Every pre-1953 criminal jurisdiction act passed by the state and the United States were not idle acts (in the sense of being useless), insofar as they affected non-Indians only. If, however, the state tried to construe these laws as applying to the Lakota as well, then they would indeed be idle laws—"idle" in the sense of being illegitimate and hence useless.

As the case progressed, the pro-state jurisdiction advocates seemed more and more like bumbling, even comical first-year law students, legally straining to convince the court that SB No. 278 gave the state jurisdiction over Lakota Country—the Enabling Act, the state's constitution, PL 83-280, and HB No. 892 all notwithstanding. Confronted with the state's absurdly strained argument, the justices had little choice but to affirm Judge Lampert's writ of habeas corpus.

To be sure, the S.D. Supreme Court's decision blocked the state's backdoor judicial attempt to assume criminal jurisdiction over Lakota territory, but it did not address the fundamental issue that South Dakota was actually a section 6 state, not a section 7 one as the terminationists wanted everyone to believe. Although the congressional record clearly identified South Dakota as a section 6 state, the state's high court alluded to that record but remained silent on South Dakota's actual classification as an option-disclaimer state. The court's silence suggests that South Dakota's five justices were unwilling to challenge the state's terminationists and their expedient political contention that South Dakota was a section 7 state. This court challenge would have to come later.

The 1958 Referenda

Hit with yet another adverse court ruling a year after the 1958 referenda, state jurisdiction forces no doubt experienced mounting frustration. Still, they had the entire all-white political apparatus at their disposal as well as the overwhelming preponderance of resources, which together guaranteed that the state jurisdiction battle was not over yet. For instance, a second jurisdiction measure—a clear indication of the terminationists' failure to achieve any political and economic control over Lakota territory—would be introduced in the forthcoming thirty-sixth legislative session. Because of the extraordinary length of time that the state's high court had taken to render its *High Pine* decision, several other developments had unfolded that were now powerfully influencing the politics of state jurisdiction. *Williams* was, of course, one such development, and the Lakota referenda required by HB No. 892 was yet another.[101]

However, three earlier and less encouraging statewide developments occurred before the referenda and sent shocking reminders to the Lakota/ Dakota People just how deep white hostility was toward them. First, in June 1957, the University of South Dakota released its study on the law-and-order "Indian Problem." Second, whites vehemently opposed a federal transfer to the Lakota of federally held submarginal lands lying inside the boundaries of Lakota territory. Third, the white stock growers angrily objected to various Lakota/Dakota rehabilitation programs that were upsetting the economic status quo that they had enjoyed since statehood. The pervasiveness and intensity of white hostility convinced the Lakota/Dakota that state jurisdiction was not in their Nation's best interests.

Notwithstanding federal law and the state courts' rulings on state jurisdiction over Lakota territory, both the white and the Lakota communities realized that the whole question of state jurisdiction rested on the referenda. For the white community, it made more sense for county officials to wait until after the state-imposed deadline for each Lakota community to hold its respective consent referendum before trying to negotiate contracts to cover jurisdiction costs. The counties' reluctance to start the process of accepting state jurisdiction was understandable for two reasons.

First, as Raymond Hieb, the legal representative for BIA's area office, explained to attendees of the University of South Dakota's 1957 June conference, counties could expect a difficult contract process with the BIA over cost reimbursements. Though that in itself would not deter South Dakota, what would cause the state to hesitate was to go to all that trouble and then face a Lakota rejection of state jurisdiction. Such a rejection would obviously render moot any prereferendum deals that South Dakota had successfully negotiated with the United States.

Second, counties waited for the outcome of the referenda because HB

No. 892 contained a self-executing consent clause. According to that clause, should any of the nine reservations fail to hold a referendum, that particular reservation would automatically be treated as if it had consented to state jurisdiction. In that case, counties would carry more political weight in their negotiations with the BIA. For example, the BIA was very sensitive to mainstream charges of overmanaging Native affairs. By raising the usual howl of BIA self-interest, a county could conceivably exert greater negotiating leverage against the BIA. To exploit this advantage during federal-state contract negotiations, all a county had to do was wait for the deadline to pass. From all angles, then, the entire question of the state jurisdiction fell squarely on Lakota shoulders.

While Lampert was hearing *High Pine,* on 6 June 1957, HB No. 892 became effective. The white players in this high-stakes game of state jurisdiction—the stock growers, the terminationists, and the state—were intensely interested in how the Lakota would respond. Not ones to miss an opportunity to express their racism, both the all-white state government (e.g., the LRC's interim EHWC) and the largely white business and professional organizations (such as the SDSGA and the SDBA) launched campaigns against the Lakota by promoting racist images of them. This racist campaign eventually exploded during the thirty-fifth legislative session when HB Nos. 721 and 892 were being considered. The promise of being handed a law that so favored further white encroachment into Lakota territory made various quarters of the white community unable to resist having a last say on South Dakota's Indian Problem. These white voices were especially shrill because the outcomes of both *High Pine* and HB No. 892 were at that time so uncertain.

Three months after HB No. 892 passed, on 16–17 June 1957, the University of South Dakota held its third annual conference on Indian affairs. And it is no surprise that the one aspect of the Indian Problem raised over and over at the conference reflected the ever present white preoccupation with law and order, namely, civil and criminal jurisdiction. For the whites, too much was at stake, namely, Lakota lands, and too much was happening beyond their control. HB No. 892 had just passed, yet it included conditions that could jeopardize jurisdiction. As of April 1957, High Pine and Woman Dress had just been arrested by county law officers, putting the question of state jurisdiction once again before the courts. Ever since *Iron Crow,* the terminationists realized that they could not depend on the courts, white-run though they were, to defend this latest landgrab scheme. Finally, 1 October 1957 was the opening date of the Lakota referenda window, and that was less than six months away.

Before the conference, the university's Institute of Indian Studies set the agenda in its May 1957 newsletter, stating that high priority would be given to discussing the controversial jurisdiction law, HB No. 892. Resembling the profile of the earlier HB No. 892 February legislative hearings, one conference panel, with the exception of Ray Hieb of the BIA, was made up exclusively of pro-state jurisdiction supporters and sympathizers: Edward Baron, South Dakota assistant attorney general; Loren Carslon, former LRC director; W. Blair Roberts, member of the State Commission of Indian Affairs; and Clinton Richards, the U.S. district attorney for South Dakota. Already racially and politically biased, these panelists were given the responsibility of discussing the "proposed program for assumption of jurisdiction over Indian lands." One panel did consist mostly of Lakota participants: Moses Two Bulls, Frank Ducheneaux, Robert Burnette, William O'Connor, Gloria Wells, and William Benge. This group was assigned the job of discussing the "Indian view of the present and prospective system of law and order."

The conference organizers gave the opening address of the session to Berry, obviously a strong pro-state advocate. Although unable to attend the conference, Berry nonetheless submitted a copy of his address. Outlining what he believed were the legal impediments that prevented the full termination of Native Peoples' ward status, Berry appealed to the standard "white-American manifesto" and on this basis concluded that all the impediments that had created a confused politico-legal landscape could be rightfully resolved only through termination:

> So, we find that this last great hurdle—the legal hurdle—is probably the most definite and the most difficult of all. Foreigners from other countries have come here and have integrated into our society and economy, but with a part of their heart remaining back in their home land. The Indian has no home land other than the reservation where a part of his heart by nature must remain.
>
> A home land which is both part of the United States and *not* a part of the United States. A home land which makes him both a citizen and a quasi-foreigner. A home land having the right of self-government and yet lacking in authority to make that government effective. A home land with some attributes of sovereignty and yet encompassed and entwined with state and federal authority. A home land "which is neither fish nor foul [*sic*]," which he cannot understand and which few others comprehend. A home land situated in the heart of a free nation, founded upon the rights of the individual but which is shackled and bound by bureaucratic regulations and control. A home land revered by the older members of the tribe but which holds few opportunities for its youth of today.

It was into this picture of confusion, chaos, and hopelessness that Glenn Emmons moved five years ago. He brought with him the idea that the Indian people were not too much different from their white neighbors. He brought with him a leadership which Congress has been happy to accept—a leadership based upon the concept that our free enterprise system can function for the benefit of all; that the thing these people need is an opportunity to take advantage of the opportunities offered by this great country. This is what Congress has been attempting to put into law; this is what the Commissioner has been attempting to put into effect.[102]

The Lakota who read a copy of his speech recognized classic Berry—a self-righteous American extolling the virtues of the great white experiment while omitting its most serious failures, crimes, and contradictions. But to a highly termination-minded community bent on destroying the Lakota politically, his address was heard as a none-too-subtle endorsement of the state's jurisdiction movement.

Adding to the swell of terminationist voices, W. O. Farber, a University of South Dakota professor, debuted at the conference his recently completed 1957 study, *Indians, Law Enforcement, and Local Government*. Since the issue of termination through the state's assumption of criminal jurisdiction dominated S.D.-Lakota relations, the release of Farber's study proved more than a little strategic. In terms of timing, the study likely originated at the 1955 conference on Indian affairs when the university's Institute of Indian Studies outlined a general proposal to investigate South Dakota's Indian Problem. Law and order was one of eight areas to be investigated—along with culture, demography, government, economics, health, education, and welfare—that together would address the Indian Problem. Farber's study was also triggered by the EHWC and its own series of 1955–56 meetings to investigate the Indian Problem. Farber attended these earlier meetings, and one meeting in particular may have persuaded him to focus on law and order.

At the 20 February 1956 EHWC meeting, in which several state legislators and officials, other white community members, and the Lakota met to discuss the state's Indian Problem, Farber was treated to an emotionally charged exchange over the contentious issue of state jurisdiction. State law enforcement officials gave reports on the presumably deplorable conditions of Indian law and order (a no-man's-land of lawlessness), while the Lakota fired back incisive rebuttals (racial discrimination by whites). The confrontation led, as mentioned earlier, to the formation of an Indian subcommittee to further study and make recommendations on law and order.

With funding from the University of South Dakota and the Social Science Research Council, a Washington-based foundation, Farber and his student assistants spent the summer of 1956 gathering information and interviewing at least 150 individuals involved with some aspect of law enforcement. By selectively interviewing this group, Farber conducted his study from an exclusively white perspective, namely, from the white institution of law enforcement. But his selectivity went further.

Much of the heated debate over state jurisdiction, especially criminal jurisdiction, concerned its application to reservations. Yet Farber's study focused on off-reservation law-and-order problems. As close to the debate as he was, it is hard to fathom Farber's unorthodox decision to interview people off rather than on reservations. His decision is all the more perplexing in view of the September 1956 EHWC report, which observed in one of its several recommendations that, "The status of law and order on the Indian reservations was acknowledged by many who testified to the full Committee to be somewhat less than satisfactory.... It is acknowledged by the Committee that an improvement of law and order on the reservations is long overdue."[103] To those familiar with the nature of Lakota-S.D. relations, South Dakota's use of the term *improvement* was code for white control with respect to state jurisdiction.

In outlining the main purpose of his study, Farber justified his study of off-reservation law-and-order problems with his unsupported contention that the off-reservation variables could equally apply to reservations:

> The primary objective of this study has necessarily been limited: to assess the magnitude of the impact of the off-reservation Indian Problem on local government with respect to law enforcement and to point out the implications of this impact. The study thus assays the needs of local government and the extent to which federal assistance would be warranted if the so-called withdrawal program is put into effect.[104]

Clearly, Farber addressed the EHWC's major concern that "the state should be reimbursed for the administering of law and order on the reservation.... Neither should the state bear the cost, which in the Committee's opinion is a federal obligation."[105] If Farber could show the magnitude of the off-reservation impact, he reasoned, it would justify South Dakota's argument for a federal subsidy whenever the state assumed on-reservation jurisdiction.

Of course, the inherent deficiency in Farber's study came from its racially biased assumptions about a state's responsibility to its citizens: should a state citizen's race or national origin be a factor? For the Lakotas living off-reservation, being under the color of state citizenship and subject to state jurisdiction, South Dakota could not, on account of race, legally distinguish among citizens who received state services. Yet Farber and others were implying that an individual's race should be a cogent factor in deciding whether a Lakota was entitled to receive state services.

As Farber was compiling his study, a 14 January 1957 federal measure, called the "four-states bill" (S. 574), was introduced that bore striking parallels to Farber's final recommendation of a race-based subsidy. The bill was sponsored by Edward J. Thye, the Republican senator from Minnesota; Alexander Wiley, a Republican senator from Wisconsin; William Langer, a Republican senator from North Dakota; Karl E. Mundt, a Republican senator from South Dakota; Francis Case, a Republican senator from South Dakota; and Hubert H. Humphrey, a Democratic senator from Minnesota. The bill proposed race-related federal subsidies to Minnesota, Wisconsin, North Dakota, and South Dakota for providing state services to Native people who, regardless of their on- or off-reservation residency, were state citizens.

Natives opposed this bill (and others like it) on the grounds that it distinguished them from other state citizens on a racial basis.[106] In his 27 March 1957 letter to James Murray, chair of the Senate Committee on Interior and Insular Affairs, and to Clair Engle, Chair of the House Committee on Interior and Insular Affairs, Sonosky outlined the Native opposition to the four-states bill, because it would distinguish Native people having state citizenship from non-Indians having the same citizenship:

> The major objection to these bills is the fact that they separate Indians out as a class wherever they are. Special lists would be established defining "Indians." . . . The bills give no recognition whatsoever to the fact that Indians are citizens of the United States and of the States in which they reside, that they have the same rights as any other people in the United States, and that the States and the United States owe them the same duty and obligation that they owe to any other citizen. There is no reason to classify by race or to impinge on the State rights of Indians. There is no valid reason for distinguishing Indians from other people under general laws of the United States applicable to all. We have not reached the stage where any class of our citizens must carry a card defining his race to prove his eligibility for benefits under general laws.[107]

To put the bill in practical perspective as well as to clarify how the notion of "same duties and obligations" would give rise to gross inequities under the four-states bill, Sonosky juxtaposed the indiscriminate payment of state taxes by Natives with the racially discriminate allocation of benefits. Whites would become the obvious beneficiaries, subsidized by Native taxpayers:

> South Dakota's and North Dakota's share of public assistance funds are paid out of general funds of the States. Those general funds of the States come from revenues from all sources, including sales taxes, tobacco taxes, alcoholic-beverage licenses and taxes, gasoline taxes, etc. . . . If the States collect from Indians, they have no basis for avoiding their obligations to Indians. If Indians are recognized as residents and citizens of the States for the purpose of paying State taxes, they should be recognized for the purpose of receiving the benefits for which those taxes were collected. Otherwise, the Indian tax money would go to pay the benefits of non-Indians.[108]

Sonosky's exposure of South Dakota's blatant maneuverings to have it both ways called into question the real intent and motives behind Farber's study. Indeed, Farber's work turned out to be anything but an objective, unbiased study. Instead, his conclusions represented an open attempt to lend academic respectability to the terminationists' positions, stating, for example, that South Dakota was a section 7 state and that the United States should subsidize the full cost of state jurisdiction within Lakota territory. In other words, he tried to give terminationists academic ammunition for having control over Lakota territory but not having to pay for it.

Because he believed that the Indian law-and-order problem had its greatest impact on white communities on or near the reservations, Farber selected the white enclaves and border towns of Sisseton (Roberts County), Mobridge (Walworth County), Chamberlain (Buffalo County), Pierre (Hughes County), Fort Pierre (Stanley County), Kadoka (Jackson County), Martin (Bennett County), Lake Andes and Wagner (Charles Mix County), Winner (Tripp County), and Rapid City (Pennington County) as study samples. When the EHWC released its September 1956 report and recommendations on the Indian Problem, Farber likewise issued a September progress report of his study:

> Data already collected shows clearly that some South Dakota communities have been shouldering a considerable and increasing burden. While final figures will not be available for several months, preliminary tabulations reveal that in Tripp and Todd Counties, 80.9% of the arrests are Indian. In Bennett County, the rate is 76% and in Roberts County the percentage is 54. City data is comparable. In Pierre, for 1953, white arrests exceeded Indian arrests 165 to 161; in 1955, Indian arrests exceeded white 433 to 329. In Rapid City, where

the Indian population is about 10% of the population, 43% of the arrests are Indian if traffic violations are excluded.[109]

When the final figures were made public, they revealed a clear trend of considerably more Lakota arrests than white arrests and a higher incarceration rate of the former than the latter. At the June 1957 conference, Farber explained to the audience that the high incidence of arrest and confinement of Natives was due to what he termed "significant weaknesses in our South Dakota legal system."[110] The system weaknesses that he named were poverty, uncertainty of the law, and inadequate rehabilitation facilities. Of the first, Farber pointed to how the impoverished economic status of the Lakotas usually led to their incarceration because they were unable to pay court costs and fines. While poverty might explain a correlation between crime and imprisonment, it does little to explain why the arrests of Lakota were so disproportionate.

Farber's study was quick to eliminate race as a factor. The white law enforcement officers of border towns that he interviewed uniformly denied that race was a factor in their arrests or in the convictions of Lakota people. Arguably, even if race were not a factor, certainly a Lakota's political status might have been. After all, the Lakota had been successfully challenging state and local hegemony. As Farber's study was unwittingly revealing, the subsequent anti-Lakota political backlash—beyond the jurisdiction bills and court cases that whites initiated to neutralize Lakota self-determination—likely included the increased harassment of the Lakota by the state's law enforcement apparatus.

Continuing to try to account for the disproportionate arrest and incarceration of the Lakota, Farber used the argument that hundreds of additional laws and regulations applied to Native people and that this bewildering array of laws and regulations left state judges somewhat uncertain about how to apply the law. To the Lakota conference participants, the argument's obvious flaw was that state—not federal or Lakota—laws apply off the reservation.

In an honest moment that held far greater explanatory power than his appeal to the complexities of Native-specific laws and regulations, Farber referred in passing to the common human element of subjectivity that even judges are not immune to: "I understand that there was once an interesting experiment conducted among the circuit court judges in this state. They used a test case and put on slips of paper what sentence they would impose in the particular case; it varied from two years to life."[111]

The implications of Farber's too-brief comments about sentencing are fairly damning for state or county judges who are unable to tolerate racial and cultural diversity. As for the all-important question of Lakotas serving as jurors in state court proceedings, one circuit court judge wrote Farber that he knew of no Lakota ever having served as a juror in his court, and other judges reported the same. Given that this particular judge held an extremely dim view of the Lakota, he most likely would have seen little benefit in having a Lakota juror or in finding a Lakota innocent:

> Many of the Indians who are not living on reservations are not educated, and still practice many of the Indian customs. Constitutionally, the Indian is inclined to be shiftless, and he is unable to cope with the white man's liquor for which he has a craving. Every effort is being made by this state and the government and by the churches . . . to educate the Indians to become good, useful, law-abiding citizens, and no doubt these efforts will in the end accomplish that purpose. Ordinarily the white man will lean over backwards to help and protect the Indian in this state, and the Indian is in no way oppressed, although as a rule the white people are averse to inter-marriages.[112]

Farber's study pointed out, further, that many of the offenses committed by the Lakota who were sent to the state's prison were against property and not persons—that is, they were poverty-related crimes. If jury trials were involved, no Lakota served because, as one judge had told Farber, "jury selectors apparently overlook Indian names and the fear exists that Indians would not vote for the conviction of Indian offenders."[113] Given the high arrest, conviction, and incarceration rates of the Lakota compared with those of their white counterparts,[114] any Lakota being tried in any justice of the peace, county, or circuit court had every right to question and every reason to be afraid of whether S.D. justice was at all fair.

Much to Farber's credit, he raised—again, unwittingly—crucial questions about racially selective arrests and judicially racist sentences. However, since a racially tainted legal system was not the object of his study, Farber could treat most of these disturbing findings casually as only incidental to the study's main point.[115] What concerned Farber was that the increasing, off-reservation, Indian law-and-order problem was financially debilitating to the state and would become only more so if the state assumed jurisdiction over reservations as well:

> This sort of data can be duplicated with respect to other South Dakota communities. With the rise in the number of arrests, law enforcement costs have likewise increased, and especially do the boarding costs for prisoners reflect

the rise in arrests. Thus in Bennett County there has been an increase in annual board costs from 1951 to 1955 of $345 to $1,604.

The significance of the increased burden on local government is enhanced by the growing costs for state government. At the time of the survey, of the 452 inmates in the State penitentiary, 140 were Indian. If the withdrawal policy is further implemented so that the state's responsibility is augmented, then the state must be concerned with the potential financial burden.[116]

With HB No. 892 coming into effect and the question looming about federal cost reimbursement to the state or county should it assume criminal and civil jurisdiction, the release of Farber's study added to the terminationists' arsenal of arguments. Several other white-biased official reports had provided similar ammunition: the February 1957 testimony on HB No. 721 presented before the HCIA; the University of South Dakota's June 1955 and 1957 conference proceedings; and the EHWC's September 1956 report. Now the termination-ists could point to Farber's study, despite its overt racism, as evidence that the Lakota were indeed a social and financial burden to the state.

Of course, the state's flagship university was only one of various white institutions in the state that had the Lakota in its jurisdictional crosshairs. The SDSGA had its ongoing land and lease disagreements with the Lakota. The SDSGA's intense but failed lobbying effort to have HB No. 721 enacted during 1957, far from demoralizing the association, seems to have strength-ened its resolve. Its members continued to refuse to pay the three-cent-per-acre tax, despite the SDSGA's legal setback in *Iron Crow*. The SDSGA also issued in 1957 two policy statements against proposed transfers of land to the Lakota. The first land transfer involved submarginal lands within the reserva-tions. The second involved U.S.-sponsored land consolidation programs for displaced Lakota families who lost their homes because of the damming of the Missouri River. The SDSGA's opposition to both clearly indicated that its intention to derail Lakota self-determination remained steadfast. Indeed, because of economic self-interest, the SDSGA railed against any land reform effort beneficial to the Lakota.

For example, in March 1956, the Oglala Lakota won a legal victory over the SDSGA when the federal appeals court affirmed the Oglala Lakota's tax-ing power over non-tribal members in *Iron Crow*. However, most of those same non-tribal members involved in the case adamantly refused to pay the tax—many since 1953, the year the Oglala Lakota fully implemented it. By refusing to pay their tax bill, the white ranchers were again challenging the Oglala Lakota's sovereignty. This time, though, they were challenging the

Lakota's use of the federal courts to compel them to pay their delinquent taxes. Of the many white tax delinquents and staunch tax evaders, the Oglala Lakota eventually sued five for collection: Albert J. Barta and John E. Barta, Charles K. Failing, Clair Coomes, and A. R. Davis. On 8 November 1956, eight months after the *Iron Crow* appeal was decided, Mickelson ruled once again in the Oglala Lakota's favor in *Oglala Sioux Tribe v. Barta*. He stated that the OST not only had the legal authority to assess taxes against nonmembers but also could employ the federal courts to sue for the collection of delinquent taxes owed by nonmembers.[117]

The significance of Mickelson's ruling in *Barta* was not lost on the greater Lakota community. In a 29 May 1957 confidential memorandum to his tribal clients, Sonosky cited in full an Interior Department press release that stated that the Interior Secretary Hatfield Chilson had recently approved a Rosebud Sioux Tribal Council resolution that not only levied a three-cent-per-acre land-use tax but also included a clause canceling grazing privileges to nonmembers who failed to pay it.[118] Fully mindful of the recently enacted HB No. 892, the ongoing *High Pine* suit, and the now-appealed *Barta* case, Sonosky drew out the clear implications of the Interior Department's press release, namely, that if it were presented with a reasonable tax program, the department would not refuse to approve similar grazing resolutions:

> This principle laid down by the press release points to the availability of "reasonable tax programs" to Indian tribes. This is meaningful on many reservations where the tribe must pay for law and order. Outsiders doing business on the reservation, as a matter of civic pride, should be glad to pay a modest tax for police protection alone, apart from other benefits derived from the orderly government provided by a tribal council.[119]

Whites, however, could never perceive or relate to Lakota self-determination in terms of civic pride. When the Lakota responded to the tax evasion through various legislative efforts designed to achieve compliance with Lakota land-use and management policy, the prospect of state jurisdiction became all the more attractive to the tax-dodging whites. Moreover, as expected, the stock growers' legal counsel John Farrar immediately filed an appeal of Mickelson's *Barta* decision to the Eighth Circuit Court. After nearly two years, on 15 October 1958, the appeals court again affirmed Mickelson's ruling,[120] yet the whites still refused to pay their land-use taxes. Instead, as 1958 opened, the SDSGA intensified its termination campaign against the Lakota.

As a result of these unnerving developments throughout Lakota Country, on 16 January 1958, the *Bennett County News* printed a vitriolic editorial on

Oglala Sioux Tribe v. Barta and its appeal. After commenting on the East Coast conviction of two mobsters for extortion, the editorial compared the Oglala's governmental authority to tax nonmembers with organized crime syndicates' extortion or blackmailing of law-abiding citizens:

> On the other hand, tribute under almost any other name often times goes barely noticed and many times receives the approval of judicial branches of our government. Such was the case when eleven South Dakota West River [white] ranchers were ordered by a federal court last September to pay more than $16,000 in grazing taxes on Indian land they lease on the Pine Ridge reservation.[121]

Alluding to the Mickelson court in which decisions often ran counter to what the white stock growers had come to expect from other whites,[122] the emotionally charged editorial made a backhanded plug for state jurisdiction and then let loose in spitting both political and white racist venom at the Oglala Lakota:

> The catch, of course, is that there is no provision for tribal enforcement of tribal laws against non-members, nor is there any penalty for violation of tribal laws by non-members. And there is no state or federal law providing for enforcement of tribal laws on non-members of the tribe, nor is there any penalty for violation. . . . The only alternative then is to refuse to grant leases on Indian land to any one who refuses to pay the tax. In other words: Pay up or else be black-listed! . . . Leasing of Indian land is supposed to be open to competitive bidding under the supervision of the [B]ureau of Indian Affairs. The tribal government is not supposed to have the control over who can and who cannot bid on Indian leases. . . . But "extortion" and "blackmail" are extremely dirty words. Out here in South Dakota on the reservation it[']s regarded as a legal, legitimate governmental function to help the Indians "retain their Native culture in Native surroundings."[123]

The editorial's most telling statements reveal the response of whites to the ever changing nature of S.D.-Lakota relations from one of complete white hegemony to greater degrees of Native self-determination. The litmus test of this change was—and is—the degree of Native control over Native lands, and in this case, the Lakota's control over who leased reservation land. Whites sensed that, despite their national termination policy and the all-white state government to implement it, they were on the wrong side of a long-term trend that spelled their ever waning influence in Lakota affairs. As the court conflicts, the state jurisdiction laws, the voluminous correspondence with

S.D. congressional representatives, the SDSGA resolutions, and the 1958 editorial show, whites fought Lakota self-governance tooth and nail. Rather than accept the reality that their involvement would no longer be a significant part of the Lakota decision-making process, whites found the very idea of losing such control so offensive that they thought and acted compulsively in extremely hostile ways.

Two examples of the whites' extreme hostility were, first, the SDSGA's opposition to a simple federal transfer to the Lakota of submarginal lands within the boundaries of various reservations and, second, the whites' opposition to various Lakota land-consolidation programs for Lakota families displaced by the federal government's decision to dam the Missouri River.

Regarding the first, the total lack of environmental stewardship on the part of white ranchers and farmers had not only destroyed the natural prairie ecology but also resulted in highly erodible and therefore unproductive land. During the dust bowl of the 1930s, these lands were designated as submarginal and then purchased by the federal government for conservation purposes. Of the thousands of acres deemed submarginal in South Dakota, nearly 122,000 of them lay within Lakota territory: Pine Ridge (46,522), Rosebud (28,730), Crow Creek and Lower Brule (34,733), Standing Rock (6,879), and Cheyenne River (5,111). On 15 April 1938, by presidential Executive Order 7868, the Secretary of Agriculture Henry A. Wallace had transferred the administration of these submarginal lands from the Agriculture Department to the Interior Department "with a view to their ultimate administration by the Office of Indian Affairs for the benefit of Indians."[124]

Ever since 1938, however, the Lakota had routinely but unsuccessfully lobbied Congress to have these submarginal lands on their reservations placed in trust status as Lakota lands. Finally, in a May 1957 meeting with Berry, the RST President Robert Burnette suggested in frustration that the Rosebud Sioux Tribe purchase the submarginal lands—without any of the usual trust restrictions that often apply to Native lands—from the United States. Berry's office complied by having two bills drafted, one for the RST (H.R. 7626) and the other for the OST (H.R. 7631), both of which incorporated Burnette's suggestion. As fate would have it, though, in an April or May letter to Harold Geersen, a white constituent from the vicinity of Pine Ridge, Berry inadvertently included two previous congressional bills that provided for the submarginal lands on the Rosebud and Pine Ridge reservations to be held in trust for the Rosebud (H.R. 6826) and Oglala Sioux Tribes (H.R. 6958). These bills did not incorporate Burnette's proposal.

As word spread among the white community about Berry's plan to place substantial amounts of submarginal lands in trust for both the Rosebud and Oglala Sioux Tribes, reaction was swift. Wendell E. Long, the publisher of the *Bennett County Booster II,* protested bitterly to Berry: "Frankly, we were shocked that you were sponsoring any such legislation. As far as we can see[,] this legislation would help the individual Indian about as little as if a law were passed giving them title to all grazing lands on Mars."[125] Moreover, on 30 May 1957, Long ran a lengthy and inflammatory editorial that undoubtedly sent Berry reeling politically:

> The bills provide that this land, purchased by the federal government from taxpayers, with tax money, is to be GIVEN "lock, stock, and barrel" to the Indian tribes of the Pine Ridge and Rosebud reservations. Not to the INDIVIDUAL INDIANS—it is to be given to the TRIBE—to be owned and controlled by the tribal councils of these respective reservations.[126]

Intentionally playing to the emotions of the white ranchers who knew from experience that Lakota governance was far more resistant to their manipulations than Lakota individuals could sometimes be, the editorial immediately ignited letters to Berry's Washington office. Many of the letters were filled with howls of protests from the whites, essentially saying that the two bills were worse than bad legislation; they bordered on treason. Indeed, Merton Glover's 25 May 1957 letter to Berry indicated how deeply Berry's white constituency felt betrayed:

> I am sure you are missing the point in that people surely would like to see this land back [on the] tax rolls, but as your bills read[,] it would go in trust for tribe[s] to play with from now on.
>
> The one dealing with lands on Reservations was enough to stir up a lot [of] fuss by itself but the ones letting them have adjacent lands was the straw that broke the camel's back. Don't you realize this could take a large part of Fall River, Pennington, Custer and some in Jackson Co. There is a universal feeling that the tribe's high-handed activities should be curtailed rather than expanded.
>
> If there is some mistake in these two bills you had better do something fast, if not then you are in trouble I'm afraid. I've tried several times in the past, if you'll recall, to warn you about this Indian give away stuff. People all over the state are fed up with them, they've got so far out of line interfering or attempting to in so many things not of their business they've about hung themselves with their own rope.
>
> All comment I've heard tends to the belief they (tribe) should be the last people in the world to lay claim to submarginal lands. . . .

I certainly do not intend to be overly critical but I have heard much bitter comment in regard to what many people feel is your undue concern and efforts to promote this tribal gangster mob-set on the reservations.[127]

Having been part of SDSGA's leadership when they were continually losing cases in Mickelson's court, Glover felt no qualms about expressing his hatred and contempt for Natives and using his position to attack them and anyone who supported them. His advice to Berry that he do some quick damage control or face election consequences prompted Berry to place some distance between himself and the transfer-to-trust bills H.R. 6826 and H.R. 6958. At the same time, Berry sought to put the best possible political spin on the sell-to-the-tribes bills H.R. 7626 and H.R. 7631.

Of the two former bills—the trust bills—Berry explained to his white constituents that, ever since 1945, bills to have submarginal lands placed in trust were handled largely as minor legislative routines to placate the Lakota. Beyond being introduced, these two bills, as several others before, were inconsequential because, first, "No one has ever paid any attention to them before,"[128] and, second, "South Dakota ranchers opposed them."[129] In other words, nothing would ever really come of them.

As for the latter two bills, Berry still favored them and sought a spin that would appease the enraged whites. He tried to convince them that, since the federal government—presumably because of the 1938 executive order—had been reluctant to transfer any submarginal land into individual private ownership, and because Congress might now be favorably disposed to selling submarginal land to the Lakota Nation as taxable property free of any trust restrictions, in the long run, these submarginal lands sold to the Lakota as fee-patent land would probably end up white owned anyway. The reason was that many individual Lakotas were too poor to pay the property taxes on their fee patent land, and so they often ended up losing it, usually to whites. Relying on this pattern for his political spin, Berry was obviously playing to white people's insatiable historical desire to take over Native lands.

Berry even turned the well-worn white complaint that trust lands contributed nothing to a county's tax base to his advantage, stressing that the submarginal lands to be acquired by the RST and the OST pursuant to H.R. 7626 and H.R. 7631 would be taxable property and thus would help pay the county's expenditures for law and order, schools, and so forth.

Yet despite Berry's best spin on the sale of submarginal lands to the Lakota—lands on their own reservations no less—Louie Beckwith thoroughly castigated Berry for even listening to the Lakota. As chair of the

SDSGA's Public Lands committee, Beckwith knew full well that the SDSGA had proposed a very similar idea to Congress some years earlier. Even so, he categorically condemned the plan now that the Lakota suggested it:

> Now, we have suggested long ago for such a bill to apply to all states[,] to sell this land to these associations in *all states*. And they in turn to sell or dispose of the lands to the present users. Now, that sounded impossible and we know it is impossible and we are not contemplating such a move—but, a representative of the Tribal Council comes along and recommends the idea we put forth, beginning, several years ago and you think the idea is wonderful. . . . It is getting to the point where we feel here, that the Council influence in Washington and within the Department is great enough to get that bill on the floor. Every Council on every Reservation will jump on the wagon for their share. . . . We are not standing by to see the Council force the operators off these Reservations through excessive taxation and a prohibitive sale price on these lands.[130]

Beckwith's vitriolic denunciation of the Lakota's ever expanding political influence and his threat that the white operators would not stand by idly while the Lakota used their influence to establish a pro-Lakota land-management policy disclosed how much control Beckwith and company believed they were losing to the rising tide of Lakota self-determination. Hence, in a move designed to publicly reprimand Berry for what they perceived as his pro-Lakota leanings, seventeen taxpaying farmers, ranchers, and business people from the Pine Ridge Reservation area adopted a 27 May 1957 document objecting to both H.R. 7626 and H.R. 7631. These seventeen people included some familiar terminationist names: Wendell E. Long, Art Vitalis, Clair Coomes, Ed M. Arnold, Alvin Brown, Merton Glover, Alex Olson, Cecil L. McCue, Harold L. Genes, Paul Guise, Ralph Anderson, Ira E. Allowed, William Porch, Bruce B. Hudson, F. Rot, Charles J. Putsch, and Robert J. Shell.

The document argued that the submarginal land "covered in these two bills should be returned to control of the Secretary of Agriculture from the Secretary of Interior at the earliest possible date for leasing directly to present users."[131] To make sure that Berry understood his constituents' anti-Lakota feelings, the document was submitted as a resolution to the SDSGA's sixty-sixth annual convention and approved by its membership in June 1957. In effect, Berry had been publicly tarred but not yet feathered.

Another SDSGA resolution passed at the convention concerned a second example of the extremely hostile reactions that whites were having to Natives. The resolution vehemently opposed how the Cheyenne River Sioux Tribe's Rehabilitation Program for displaced Lakota families was, in effect, "displacing many white people and thereby curtailing the farming ranching, pasturing and grazing of cattle in certain areas."[132] The Cheyenne River Sioux Tribe's program was a response to the disastrous and devastating damming of the Missouri River by the U.S. Army Corps of Engineers. Michael L. Lawson described what the Lakota of the Cheyenne River, Standing Rock, Lower Brule, Crow Creek, and Yankton Sioux reservations had suffered because of the United States' callous and colossal 1944 dam project:

> Army [Corps of Engineers] dams on the Missouri inundated more than 202,000 acres of Sioux land. Approximately 580 families were uprooted and forced to move from the rich, sheltered bottomlands to empty prairies. Their best homesites, their finest pastures, croplands, and hay meadows, and most of their valuable timber, wildlife, and vegetation were flooded. Relocation of the agency headquarters on the Cheyenne River, Lower Brule, and Crow Creek reservations seriously disrupted governmental, medical, and educational services and facilities and dismantled the largest Indian communities of these reservations. Removal of churches, community centers, cemeteries, and shrines impaired social and religious life on all five reserves. Loss not only of primary fuel, food, and water resources but also of prime grazing land effectively destroyed the Indians' economic base. The thought of having to give up their ancestral land, to which they were so closely wedded, caused severe psychological stress. The result was extreme confusion and hardship for tribal members.[133]

For the Lakota of the Cheyenne River Reservation, the construction of the Oahe Dam—one of six built on the Missouri—drastically affected their lifestyle. The Oahe Dam was "deeper than [Lake] Erie and longer than [Lake] Ontario" and was, "next to Fort Peck Dam, the largest earth dam in the world. Stretching 250 miles northward to Bismarck, North Dakota, its reservoir, Lake Oahe, became the largest on the Missouri."[134] In terms of the incalculable human cost to the Cheyenne River Lakota, Lawson stated:

> The Oahe Dam destroyed more Indian land than any other public works project in America. The Standing Rock and Cheyenne River Sioux lost a total of 160,889 acres to this project, including their most valuable rangeland, most of their gardens and cultivated farm tracts, and nearly all of their timber, wild fruit, and wildlife resources. The inundation of more than 105,000 acres of choice grazing land affected 75 percent of the ranchers on the Cheyenne River Reservation. . . .
> Cheyenne River lost 104,420 acres to the Oahe deluge. Cheyenne Agency, the largest town on the reservation, and two other smaller communities

were completely submerged. BIA and tribal facilities were moved sixty miles inland to the desolate prairie town of Eagle Butte, South Dakota. . . . Over 180 families, about 30 percent of the tribal population, were forced to leave their homes.[135]

With massive social and economic disruption on the Cheyenne River Reservation, and with the hard-won but grossly inadequate $10.6 million 1954 settlement to the CRST ($13 million less than the CRST's figure) from a tight-fisted United States, the Lakota leadership initiated a rehabilitation program specifically designed to reestablish displaced Lakota families.

Lawson's work provided a comparative pre– and post–Oahe Dam account of how the CRST's program to help the displaced Lakota families fundamentally altered the white stock growers' long-standing land-use patterns:

> Prior to the inundation caused by the Oahe reservoir, tribal members on Cheyenne River had only been able to make use of 41 percent of the reservation land base. Most of the remaining land was leased to white ranchers for as little as ten cents per acre. With the implementation of new land and livestock programs following the final settlement in 1954, tribal officials began canceling those leases and consolidating ever larger areas of land through the use of exchange assignments. Despite the bitter attacks and angry cries of neighboring white cattlemen, the Indians were able to reclaim over 600,000 acres of grazing land for their own use within five years. Between 1957 and 1965 the tribe was able to purchase or consolidate an additional 170,000 acres. Consequently in 1972 tribal members were able to claim use of 87 percent of their own land.[136]

Indeed, in a letter to the editor in the 15 November 1956 issue of the *South Dakota Stock Grower,* a white male who called himself a Dewey County taxpayer angrily expressed what most white people were evidently feeling about the CRST's rehabilitation program and similar programs on the Standing Rock, Lower Brule, and Crow Creek reservations:

> Did you know that the present Indian Rehabilitation program is crippling the economy of both Ziebach and Dewey counties? . . . Did you know that approximately 700 white families in Dewey County alone are having their economic way of life disrupted? . . . Did you know that many of these white operators will be reduced to the status of peons? . . . Did you know that these same "ruined" white operators will still be expected to bear the tremendous added tax burden being thrust upon them by the flood of non-taxpayers? . . . Did you know that before long our fine court houses, churches, and hospitals will be vacant and left for the occupancy of the swallows?[137]

Using a series of questions designed to catch the interest of the SDSGA membership and others, the writer next pointed out that the rehabilitation program was the driving force behind the inevitable ruin of its innocent victims, namely, white farmers, ranchers, and businesspeople:

> The Indian Rehabilitation program has become a creeping paralysis to our economy and a mill stone around the Indian's neck! . . . It is, in the hands of an unscrupulous few, being used as an unfounded reprisal against the white man. ALSO—as a means to an END—Against the Indian—namely—the gaining of possession of the Indian people's allotments![138]

Of course, whenever the Lakota moved toward greater self-governance or self-sufficiency that in any way reduced a white community's control or influence, the whites would attack the Lakota leadership, suggesting that they were somehow betraying their people. Here, the "unscrupulous few" alluded to were Frank Ducheneaux and the CRST Council members, since they had planned and overseen the direction of the rehabilitation program. Just as the *Bennett County News* editorial had tried to group Lakota individuals with white stock growers as common victims of the excesses of Lakota government, so too this taxpayer's tortured charges exposed the all-too-common, one-sided relationship between the Lakota allottee and the white stock grower. Feigning friendship, a white stock grower would deceive and manipulate a Lakota allottee into giving the stock grower extremely favorable lease terms—far below the going rate anywhere else.

Finally, exhorting his peers to resist the rehabilitation program, the Dewey County taxpayer invoked Manifest Destiny and Americanism. Whatever gains their ancestors had made in their westward movement, the whites now needed to protect against the ever rising tide of Lakota influence:

> This country [western S.D.] was thrown open for homesteads. We were invited here! Our fathers, forefathers, came here, lived, worked and died here. THEY carved out this civilization which BOTH white man and Indian now enjoy. The day of annihilation ended with the Custer Massacre. The weapon being used against us today is our own tax dollar. Let us refuse to be clubbed to death with our own pocketbooks! WAKE UP BOYS! Let's demand some attention from Washington, D.C.![139]

Many Lakota of the time would likely take exception to being named as beneficiaries of white civilization. Indeed, as this discussion about jurisdiction has repeatedly shown, the Lakota were at the bottom of just about every socioeconomic indicator. Moreover, far from sharing in the outcomes of the westward movement, the Lakota vigorously resisted them. By invoking the westward-movement theme, the writer not only placed the Lakota outside the movement's pale but also cast them as antagonists in the whole westering experience. In short, with vitriolic contempt for the Indians and arrogant presumption of superiority, the white community perceived itself as the innocent victim of imagined Lakota atrocities.

A month later, Ducheneaux wrote a stinging rebuttal in the 15 December 1957 issue of the *South Dakota Stock Growers (SDSG)* magazine. He challenged James J. Matthews—who turned out to be the Dewey County taxpayer—to defend his unfounded assertions that the whites were facing complete economic ruin. Using the then-current figures on the rehabilitation program, Ducheneaux showed that 86 percent of the white ranchers did not entirely lose their grazing privileges on Lakota land:

> Let us examine some of Mr. Matthews' statements. There are now in operation in the two counties [Ziebach and Dewey] 177 non-Indian ranchers using Indian lands. Of these, there are 25 from whom a complete withdrawal of Indian lands has been made, 49 from whom a partial withdrawal has been made, 77 from whom no withdrawal has been made, and 26 who have had less than 640 acres of Indian land to begin with. Mr. Matthews would have you believe that every non-Indian rancher in the two counties has been subject to withdrawal of all his Indian land holdings.[140]

Matthews's charge that white operators were being reduced to peonage and his professed concerns about the Lakota's plight gave Ducheneaux the opening to skillfully recast Matthews's words in favor of the Lakota. Ducheneaux not only defended the rehabilitation program but also exposed Matthews to be little more than a demagogue, stirring up South Dakota's deep reservoir of white supremacy and racism:

> Where, we wonder, was Mr. Matthews when these Indians about whose plight he expresses so much concern were losing their lands and their homes, and the fruits of a lifetime of labor as a result of the taking of their lands for the Oahe Dam? Where was he when those Indians who are now benefitting from the Rehab[ilitation] Program were ekeing out a miserable existence around a reservation sub-station, supplemented by an occasional lease payment from a non-Indian rancher in the magnificent sum of $19.20 a year for a quarter of land? Where was he when our old people were living in dirt-roofed log houses, with nothing but the bare earth under their feet? These were his neighbors. What did he do to improve their lot—he who is so concerned about their plight?[141]

Because many whites who leased Lakota land knew about the squalid housing conditions that existed on reservations, Ducheneaux's questions and vivid descriptions likely made more than one white wince with guilt or shame as he reminded them about who, in fact, had been most unjustly dispossessed.

But that was not the end of Ducheneaux's rebuttal. In no sparing mood after Matthews's assault on the CRST's rehabilitation program, Ducheneaux went on to attack one of the whites' most sacred cows—the one that Matthews invoked—namely, the westward movement:

> Mr. Matthews makes reference to the good old Homestead Act. We were invited here, he says, with exclamation points. Who invited him? Did he see the names of any members of this Tribe on the invitation? He did not, and for a very good reason. Our lands were simply declared surplus and opened to homestead entry. We got in payment a fraction of the real value of those lands on which our "invited guests" built the "fine courthouses, churches, schools, and hospitals" that are supposedly doomed to the tenancy of swallows and all because the nasty Indians want to use for their own benefit the few acres of land that are left to them after all these takings, instead of leasing it to some non-Indian ranchers for the princely sum of $.33 per acre.[142]

While the historical "taking" of Lakota reservation land began with the U.S. law that first "opened" the Great Sioux Reservation in 1889 and then "created" the Cheyenne, Standing Rock, Rosebud, Pine Ridge, and Lower Brule reservations, the "takings" to which Ducheneaux referred were the homesteads that whites took possession of when the five reservations had been divided into individual allotments between 1904 and 1919. After the land had been allotted to Lakota individuals—imposing a model of private ownership and displacing the traditional model of shared land stewardship by the tribe—the United States declared the remaining unallotted lands within the reservations to be "surplus" and opened them to white homesteaders.[143]

Knowing that it was an election year for state and federal offices, Ducheneaux framed Matthews's letter as nothing more than a backhanded campaign ploy to use the CRST program against Matthews's incumbent Republican opponent, Fred J. Hunter:[144]

> It appears that what started to be a sincere effort on the part of the Tribal Council to bring a better way of life for the people of the Cheyenne River Sioux Tribe, through its Rehabilitation Program, has become a political football for local and state politicians. The Tribal Council has from the beginning, scrupulously avoided political controversy on the theory that what was good for

the white man was good for the Indian, and vice versa, and it was hoped that we could continue to work for the benefit of our people without incurring the ill-will that our Rehabilitation Program seems to have brought about.[145]

In a Republican-dominated state, Hunter easily defeated his Democratic challenger, Matthews. Interestingly, since Matthews's letter was printed in the *SDSG* not before but after the 6 November 1956 state elections, it had no use as a campaign advertisement but served instead as a propaganda tool for whites against the Lakota. Just as the whites had been tarring Berry for ostensibly being pro-Lakota in his handling of the submarginal land bills, so too the whites were "righteously" up in arms against the rehabilitation program and were pressing Berry to be a better champion of white interests. In a letter to Berry, one white constituent expressed the general indignation that whites felt about his supposedly overgenerous support of the program: "if he would work for the White people as he is doing for the Indians, he would be a good Congressman."[146] Of course, many whites knew perfectly well that Berry was doing much more *to* the Indians than *for* them as they claimed. Such caustic statements served to warn Berry in no uncertain terms not to "go Native" on them.

For the Lakota, it was painfully clear that any action on their part to take care of their people and their lands would be construed by whites as hostile and threatening. When, for example, the Oglala Lakota had developed a simple and otherwise standard and reasonable post-1953 grazing program to eventually develop their own reservation lands for Lakota use, the whites went ballistic. Now once again, no matter how hard the CRST tried to keep its program politically neutral, because the program diminished the whites' control and influence on the Cheyenne River Reservation, the whites were outraged.

By January 1957, patterning the mindset of their late 1800s circle-the-wagon ancestors, whites became paranoid about the Lakota's increasing assertions of self-government and saw threatening silhouettes of the Lakota's power everywhere. Whites who shared this paranoia felt driven to preserve their economic interests and their political hegemony over the Lakota. For them, the 1953 passage of the federal termination law was a godsend. They jumped on PL 83-280 and wanted to enact a state jurisdiction law as soon as possible. The opportune moment to strike was during South Dakota's upcoming thirty-fifth legislative session.

Indeed, from January 1953 to the summer of 1957, whenever the Lakota leadership from various reservations compared their intelligence about South

Dakota's white community, they discovered disturbing patterns of hostility toward Lakota self-determination: the more the Lakota exercised their self-governance, the more the whites became angry and enraged.

To summarize the events that the Lakota leaders were witnessing, in January 1953, as we have discussed, when the Oglala Lakota initiated a major land-management policy by enacting a grazing resolution that called for, among other things, a land-use tax, the white ranchers, many of whom were SDSGA members, vigorously resisted. They not only called on Berry to provide ongoing political interference on SDSGA's behalf but also took legal action with *Iron Crow* and *Barta* to oppose the Lakota and challenge their authority as a nation. The SDSGA's May 1953 resolution against the OST land tax gave further unmistakable evidence of the depth of white resistance.

In January 1955, when the Lakota of the Cheyenne River Reservation reluctantly accepted the U.S. Oahe Dam settlement and subsequently initiated a rehabilitation program that affected established land-use patterns that had long favored white stock growers, these stock growers, like those at Pine Ridge, resisted with venom and outrage. Unlike the OST grazing resolution controversy, however, Berry did not directly interfere with the eventual outcome of the CRST's rehabilitation program. He did, however, encourage and fan the bitterness over white "displacement." Not surprisingly, the SDSGA's June 1957 resolution disclosed an extremely high level of white animosity toward the CRST's program.

In February 1955, when the LRC's Education, Health, and Welfare Committee decided to examine South Dakota's Indian Problem, it used indicators that depicted the Lakota as a "lawless" people who imposed a social and economic burden on South Dakota. Other predominantly white organizations, such as the University of South Dakota's Institute of Indian Studies and the S.D. Bar Association, established agendas that mirrored the state's termination-serving analysis of its Indian Problem. The institute's June 1955 and 1957 conferences on Indian affairs, for example, focused on themes that reflected the standard white perception of the Indian Problem as one of lawlessness. Similarly, in 1956, the SDBA recommended greater state intrusion into Lakota affairs to solve the Indian law-and-order problem. Lending academic ammunition to the whites' political and economic agenda to maintain dominance over the Lakota, Farber's June 1957 study on off-reservation Indian law and order reinforced whites' negative image of the Lakota and thereby justified not only the recently passed state jurisdiction law but also its contention that the United States subsidize the state.

In January 1957, when the state government opened its thirty-fifth legislative session, the two state jurisdiction bills introduced—HB No. 721 and HB No. 892—were the culmination of these post-1953 white hostilities toward the Lakota People. The former bill (which fortunately died in committee) proposed to have South Dakota accept unconditionally all civil and criminal jurisdiction over Lakota territory. The latter bill—amended in committee without the participation of the Lakota—proposed to accept jurisdiction through forced consent. Both bills came about because of the whites' fear of the Lakota's emerging political influence and hence were nothing less than a direct political assault on Lakota self-determination.

In April 1957, when Matthew High Pine and Paul Woman Dress were arbitrarily arrested by a white state law enforcement officer, after which both men were released on a writ of habeas corpus, South Dakota appealed the writ and fought the Lakota in state court, arguing that, HB No. 892 notwithstanding, the state actually possessed previous criminal jurisdiction over Lakota territory. More than two years later, in November 1959, the S.D. Supreme Court handed down a surprise ruling in favor of the Lakota. This ruling, like that of *Iron Crow*, only intensified the whites' growing resentment over losing their control on Lakota reservations.

In May 1957, when Berry introduced two somewhat routine bills that would relinquish submarginal lands to the Lakota on both the Rosebud and the Pine Ridge reservations, the white stock growers and their supporters automatically closed ranks to vehemently chastise Berry for trying to "give" the Lakota more land. Their fierce opposition ignored the fact that the Lakota would not only purchase the submarginal lands (rather than have them transferred) but also obtain a fee patent (rather than a trust title) to the lands in question, thus allowing the land to be placed on the county's property tax rolls. Regardless of these facts, the SDSGA's June 1957 resolution categorically opposed the bills, asking instead that such lands be available for purchase by its members who were leasing the submarginal lands.

This 1953–57 history convinced the Lakota in no uncertain terms that, because of their unanticipated political and judicial successes against local white hegemony, their white neighbors were now in an especially ugly mood.[147] The introduction of HB No. 721 in particular and its subsequent hearing gave ample evidence of just how ugly the state's mood was toward the Lakota. Over the course of the next four legislative sessions—in 1957, 1959, 1961, and 1963—new state jurisdiction legislation was successively introduced, proving just how persistent the anti-Lakota feeling was in South Dakota.

With very little evidence to support its claim, the state nonetheless contended that if only its jurisdiction were allowed on the reservations, conditions for the Lakota would automatically, if not drastically, improve. The Lakota throughout the state knew otherwise and needed no convincing. Although HB No. 892 authorized the state's takeover, the Lakota still had the crucial proviso requiring a reservation-by-reservation referendum to obtain Lakota consent.

Pondering their vote on the bill, the Lakota only needed to ask themselves the all-important question, Would I or my relatives be better off under state jurisdiction? To answer that question, besides reflecting on the 1953–57 series of interactions with whites, a Lakota could simply travel off reservation or to a border town and experience firsthand the application of "state jurisdiction" several times over. Such forays into white governance were usually more than enough to convince any otherwise undecided Lakota of the extreme shortcomings of state jurisdiction. Almost without exception, the Lakota's answer to the question was a simple but emphatic "no." Yet despite their general consensus on the issue, by state law, they still had to conduct their referenda by 1 October 1958, otherwise they would automatically lose their political voice and their chance to say "no" to a state-mandated "yes."

Among the first to hold a referendum—and be the exception—were the Lakota of the Lower Brule Reservation. Ninety-seven days after HB No. 892 was approved, the LBSTC called a 14 June 1957 community meeting for the sole purpose of "deciding of whether or not we want State Law & Order on this reservation."[148] After reciting the LBST's involvement with HB No. 892 as a primary countermeasure to HB No. 721 and explaining the provisions of the former to community members, various LBST members addressed the matter of state jurisdiction; a community vote immediately followed. Of the Lakota who attended the community meeting, thirty-five voted for and thirty-three voted against the application of state jurisdiction. Thus, on 3 July 1957, the LBSTC adopted a resolution to accept "the results of the election as the desire of the Tribe for state jurisdiction . . . and request[ed] the Indian Office to take the necessary steps to negotiate and contract with the Board of County Commissioners for assumption and acceptance of jurisdiction of all civil and criminal offenses committed on the Lower Brule Reservation."[149]

Not all Lakota from the Lower Brule Reservation agreed, however, with how the referendum was handled. They were also concerned about its outcome, which seemed anomalous to many Lakota throughout the state. A month after the LBST formally adopted the July resolution in favor of state jurisdiction, Elmer Pretty Head wrote Berry about his concerns regarding the referendum "election":

On [14 June 1957], we the whole tribe had a general meeting at the community hall. The delegates that went to Washington D.C. made their reports
on [a] new proposed [Missouri River] settlement plan. Then the members
of the tribal council discussed on House Bill 892. . . . After the discussion
they had [an] election on H.B. 892. The result of the votes, by small margin,
accepted the tribe to go under State Law and Order. . . . As for myself I am
against the State Law and Order. . . . I did not vote on State Law and Order.
Because I had in mind we was going to vote at our general tribal election on
October 1958.[150]

As Pretty Head noted, the LBST could have employed an election process
for its referendum that was more formal than a town-hall type meeting,
even though this was the more traditional way. In any case, the 14 June 1957
vote of the LBST turned out to be not in compliance with HB No. 892, since
the timing parameters of the referenda were narrowly defined. As the law
was written, if the Lakota did not want state jurisdiction, they had to vote
to reject it, and such a vote had to take place between 1 October 1957 and
1 October 1958. Otherwise, "if the Tribe has failed to take action as above
prescribed [that is, holding a referendum], within one year from and after
October 1, 1957, it shall be deemed that the referendum has been dispensed
with and that the tribe has consented to and does approve the assumption
of state jurisdiction herein provided."[151]

Because the LBST referendum was outside the timeframe established by
HB No. 892, the state, as much as it wanted to, could not officially accept
the LBST referendum as conclusive. However, since the LBST initially voted
to accept state jurisdiction, both the LBST and South Dakota could simply
wait for the deadline to pass. The state could then safely announce that the
LBST had legally accepted state jurisdiction. As the first, somewhat perplexing, Lakota referendum, the LBST vote forced the remainder of the Lakota
to look elsewhere in their nation for leadership in defeating HB No. 892.

The LBST's initial vote for state jurisdiction did not yet put the state in a
position to accept or assume it. Additional conditions had to be met. Specifically, because the LBST opted for state jurisdiction, the board of county
commissioners of both Stanley and Lyman counties were now obliged to
fulfill the other condition for the state's assumption of jurisdiction: they
had to enact a resolution of acceptance, but only after they had negotiated
a cost reimbursement contract with the BIA. The existing records indicate
that neither county fulfilled this statutory obligation. Three years after the
1957 LBST referendum vote, Ramon Roubideaux, the Stanley County state's

attorney, while attending the sixth annual conference on Indian affairs in June 1960, described how the county's poor infrastructure, especially its grossly inadequate road system, posed a serious obstacle to providing state law enforcement for the LBST:

> On our particular reservation in Stanley County we have a situation that's pretty current, I think, throughout the state. The [Lower Brule] reservation is located in the easternly most corner of the county. In fact, a part of the reservation is in Lyman County, a very small part of it is in Stanley County, and we have good transportation to other parts of the county, but if you ever get in the car and try to get down to Lower Brule going straight over, you're liable never to get there, especially if it's raining. In order to get there on good roads you have to go way around a distance of some 80 or 90 miles. Straight across distance is maybe 20 miles. It's a practical matter more than anything else. I think that if the Federal government is going to preserve this myth of tribal enforcement of its own laws, then let the Federal government give the tribes sufficient money in order to properly do the job which they are supposed to do. . . . Let's either make the tribal setup work or let's put it under state control and let state officials administrate and enforce the law.[152]

Poor infrastructure notwithstanding, when asked why, as the county state's attorney, he did not enforce state jurisdiction even on the small part of the Lower Brule Reservation that was "in" Stanley County, Roubideaux invoked the state's much-heralded complaint about the costs of assuming jurisdiction: "Because we don't have the money to do it. . . . Now if they asked us to come down to help on isolated instances we certainly would do it without any question, but as a continual matter say of having a deputy down there—who would pay the deputy? That would be the whole thing."[153] At most, the county was willing to provide a form of law enforcement comity to the LBST on a limited basis, but that was not what HB No. 892 proposed.

At it turned out, the town-hall vote notwithstanding, the Lower Brule Reservation evidently never came under state jurisdiction. When, for example, the state later passed additional jurisdiction laws in 1959, 1961, and 1963, their provisions did not distinguish between the LBST and the other Lakota/Dakota whose referenda votes rejected state jurisdiction. Moreover, comparing the provisions spelled out in HB No. 892 with what actually happened after June 1957 in Stanley and Lyman counties reveals that these two counties never took the steps necessary for the state to assume jurisdiction over the LBST.

Other Lakota who found the idea of state jurisdiction untenable opted for a more formal election process to express their opposition. Within weeks after the state passed HB No. 892, at its 8 April 1957 meeting, the RST Council was presented with a resolution from the Rosebud community that the community had approved a few days earlier. This resolution recommended "that a general referendum be held for the people of the Rosebud Reservation so that the people could decide if they want to turn law and order over to the State of South Dakota or remain as is."[154] Robert Burnette, the RST president, opened the council floor for discussion on the community's resolution. After some brief remarks by council members that tribal members may need some information and education about HB No. 892 before they cast their vote in the referendum, the RSTC voted to adopt the Rosebud resolution and authorized its executive committee to set a date for the referendum.[155]

Between April 1957 and the soon-to-be decided RST referendum date, it became clear that the RST did not need to engage in a large-scale education program on the pluses and minuses of state jurisdiction. The whites' own conduct—such as the racial and political animosity that the whites had directed at the Lakota during the February 1957 hearings on HB No. 721, the midnight drama of unethical behavior by the white legislative leadership to make sure that HB No. 892 was enacted, Farber's 1957 biased and one-sided study, and the EHWC committee's depiction of reservation Lakota as lawless people—provided more than enough evidence of how life for the Lakota would change dramatically under state control. To maximize voter participation, the RSTC set the date for the referendum to coincide with its January 1958 general election.

On 7 January 1958, the Lakota of the Rosebud went to the polls and voted. When the election returns came in, eighteen reservation communities spread throughout a four-county area rejected state jurisdiction.[156] The vote count was 227 for and 811 against state jurisdiction. Like the LBSTC, the RSTC later adopted a resolution (18 July 1958) that officially informed the board of county commissioners for Todd, Tripp, Mellette, Gregory, and Lyman counties that "the members of the Rosebud Sioux Tribe disapproved of the assumption of [S.D.] civil and criminal jurisdiction over the members of the Rosebud Sioux Tribe."[157]

While the RST referendum was the second one held, it was the first to resoundingly reject state jurisdiction. By so doing, the RST referendum carried special significance as an expression of the will and desires of the Lakota People. It provided the first of many acid tests proving that the LBST vote was an anomaly and did not mirror a trend. Whatever euphoria the state jurisdiction advocates might have felt from the outcome of the LBST vote, the RST referendum summarily dampened.

Three other referenda were held in early September 1958 by the Cheyenne River Lakota, the Standing Rock Lakota, and the Oglala Lakota at Pine Ridge. Again, to maximize voter turnout, the CRSTC, whose rehabilitation program had provoked such strong anti-Lakota feelings among white neighbors, set the referendum date to coincide with its 2 September 1958 general election. For these Lakota, the devastating disruption of their daily lives, especially the lives of the 180 displaced Lakota families due to the damming of the Missouri River; the callous insensitivity to Lakota suffering of institutions such as Congress, the Army Corps of Engineers, and the BIA; and the attack from local whites on the CRST's rehabilitation program because of how it was adversely affecting the whites' livelihood all provided more than ample proof that, despite white claims to the contrary, state jurisdiction would mean only more degradation of the Lakota's human dignity.

Thus, on 2 September 1958, the Lakota of the Cheyenne River Reservation went to their polling places in thirteen districts dispersed over two counties and voted both for their council representatives and for whether they wanted state jurisdiction.[158] As the referendum results came in from each district (Agency, Bridger, Cherry Creek, Red Scaffold, Eagle Butte, Four Bear, Green Grass, Lantry, LaPlant, Promise, Robertson, Thunder Butte, and White Horse), all but one, White Horse, rejected state jurisdiction. The final referendum tally showed that 291 Lakota were in favor of and 595 were against state control.

On 6 September 1958, four days after the CRST referendum, the Standing Rock Sioux Tribe (SRST) held its referendum. Because a significant portion of the reservation lay in North Dakota, only those who lived on the South Dakota side of the reservation were permitted to vote. Like South Dakota, North Dakota was a section 6 disclaimer state, which meant it had to amend its constitution before it could move toward assuming jurisdiction. However, unlike the S.D. Supreme Court in its *High Pine* decision, the N.D. Supreme Court did not equivocate on the section 6–section 7 issue. In a case involving state jurisdiction over Native territory, it handed down an unambiguous 18 February 1955 ruling for *State of North Dakota v. Lohnes* that required the state to modify the disclaimer language in its constitution.[159] If it did not, any N.D. or U.S. law that authorized jurisdiction over Native Country would be viewed as invalid. Hence, with North Dakota failing to assume jurisdiction over the N.D. portion of the SRST,[160] the SRST needed to provide a referendum only for that part of its reservation that lay in South Dakota.

On 26 August 1958, the SRST Council called a special meeting to discuss with its legal counsel, Sonosky, the likely implications of South Dakota state jurisdiction. After a brief discussion of the referendum, the SRST selected the judges and clerks for the four districts, established the polling places, and agreed on the wording of the referendum question: "Do you wish to have criminal and civil jurisdiction of the State of South Dakota extended over the Standing Rock Indian Reservation in Corson County, South Dakota?" After the Lakota of the Standing Rock Reservation voted, the referendum results showed that all four SRST districts—Bullhead, Little Eagle, Wakpala, and Kenel—rejected S.D. jurisdiction with a final vote of 19 for and 216 against.

On 23 January 1958, soon after the RST referendum vote, the Oglala Lakota discussed holding their referendum as well. Peter Janis urged the OSTC to give serious thought to the upcoming but yet-to-be determined referendum. Two months later, in a 21 March 1958 special session, the OSTC adopted Ordinance No. 85, which authorized a 9 May 1958 referendum on the state jurisdiction question. To conduct the election, the council selected a three-member election board: William Young Bear, James Roan Eagle, and Chester Red Kettle. For whatever reasons, the referendum election did not take place. In a 9–10 June 1958 special session, the OSTC discussed setting a second referendum date. After some deliberation about scheduling so as to allow sufficient time to educate the public on HB No. 892 as well as to ensure greater voter participation, the OSTC settled on 26 August 1958 as the date for the referendum.

At its 11 July 1958 regular meeting, the Kyle Livestock and Landowners Association (KLLA), organized the year before in June 1957, initiated a program to discuss the pros and cons of state jurisdiction. According to its president, Leo Vocu (who incidentally was also the OSTC's treasurer), the KLLA's purpose was to bring together 120 Lakota operators who shared a strong commitment to promoting a program of Lakota use of reservation resources. These KLLA members knew firsthand how their white counterparts had used their SDSGA influence to successfully challenge the OST's 1953 grazing policy and to lobby first for HB No. 721 and then for HB No. 892. They undoubtedly understood how disastrous state control would be for the Lakota Nation and how severely it would undermine their goal to achieve greater Lakota control over reservation land.

In preparation for its July regular meeting, Vocu sent a 20 June 1958 invitation to various individuals to participate on one of two panels: one favoring and the other opposing state jurisdiction:

> The Oglala Sioux Tribe, within a few weeks, will vote YES or NO for State Jurisdiction on Law and Order, and in order to prepare the people on this important matter, a two (2) panel group discussion has been scheduled.

Outstanding leaders who are opposed to State Jurisdiction will be fully represented on the *No Panel*, and every effort is being made to set-up the other
panel in favor of state jurisdiction.

We feel, that as an organized group, it is our duty to sponsor this educational
feature for the benefit and welfare of our people—the Oglala Sioux Tribe.[161]

As the KLLA meeting approached, the association posted flyers announcing that, while it had established a "no" panel of Lakota leaders, the "yes"
panel remained incomplete. Since there are no extensive records of the meeting, the panel members remain unknown as does the number of people who
actually attended this important forum.

On 18 July 1958, a week after the KLLA conducted its education program
on state jurisdiction, the OSTC met in a special session to discuss the upcoming referendum, particularly who was to conduct the election. Some OSTC
members suggested that its five-member executive committee could act as
the election board and that perhaps other council members could act as precinct judges and clerks. After a short recess called by the presiding president,
Samuel Stands, the OSTC decided to consult its legal counsel. Following the
legal advice they received, they agreed that the executive committee would
establish the election rules. Interestingly, the OSTC also decided to bill South
Dakota for the expenses incurred while conducting the referendum.

With less than two weeks to go before the referendum, the OSTC met again
in a 14 August 1958 special session and decided to rescind the 26 August 1958
referendum date. While the record is unclear as to why they did this, most
likely the council felt they needed extra time to finalize the election rules and
to get fully organized for the referendum. Of course, with the state-imposed
deadline of 1 October 1958 only a few weeks away, any further delay of the
referendum by the OSTC would place the Oglala Lakota dangerously close
to being automatically subject to state control. Therefore, for a third and
final time, the OSTC set the referendum date for 10 September 1958.

A few days prior to the referendum, an unsigned, four-page, anti–state
jurisdiction letter circulated throughout the Pine Ridge Reservation. The
letter reminded the Oglala Lakota that HB No. 892 represented a long line of
laws—both state and federal—that ultimately proved harmful to the Lakota,
no matter how vehemently the supporters of each of these laws had at the
time claimed otherwise. In the letter's closing, the anonymous writer characterized the status of Lakota-U.S. relations as dismal at best:

The forces allied to induce our people to accept state jurisdiction are a few in
number. To mention a few, they are: a small number of disgruntled members

of the tribe, a handful of land hungry non-Indian stockgrowers, a few non-Indian people who have lived on the reservation so long that they think they own the reservation and a few do gooders and well wishers who think they can change the way of life for an Indian with the stroke of a pen. . . . If the non-Indian population of South Dakota . . . are so interested in us to want us to become equals to themselves for economic reasons, the Stockgrowers Association of South Dakota could have urged Congress to pass the 14 million dollar Rehabilitation measure we requested in 1951. In its stead, they implored upon [sic] members of Congress to defeat the Bill and it was so defeated [see April 1953 issue of the Stockgrowers Association publication]. Such a Rehabilitation Program on the Pine Ridge reservation would have ended plum picking for the Stockgrowers in Indian country. For the other group who wants us to become equals to themselves, they must remember that adjustment by Indians to non-Indian civilization cannot be hasten[ed] by compulsion.[162]

As a final plea for Oglala Lakota unity, the writer requested that, despite the internal conflicts or malaise that may have led to factions or differences among the people, in this particular case, they must set aside those conflicts for a greater purpose, namely, to stop white encroachment:

Selfishness, ignorance, and jealousy amongst our own people have caused disunity and indifference to the point where we cannot all defend our rights in one group for the common good of every member of the tribe. However, in this case it is important that every member of the tribe who is of voting age go to the polls on September 10 and defeat House Bill No. 892 with a strong majority.[163]

After the Oglala Lakota went to the twenty-two precincts located throughout three counties and voted, the election results showed that they had indeed heeded the plea for unity. In all precincts without exception, the Oglala Lakota rejected state jurisdiction by a wide margin. When each precinct reported in, the final count came to 154 in favor and 1,095 against state jurisdiction. The Oglala Lakota referendum decisively laid to rest the subject of state control on the Pine Ridge Reservation and by so doing drove a political stake through the heart of the most rabid proponents of state jurisdiction.

When HB No. 892 was being discussed during the 16–17 June 1957 Institute of Indian Studies conference, Gloria Wells informed attendees that the Crow Creek Sioux Tribe (CCST), much like the LBST, had convened an 11 June 1957 general meeting of its members, or General Council,[164] and had debated HB No. 892. Wells went on to explain that the CCST president had translated the bill into Dakota, and that much of the discussion about state jurisdiction concerned the discriminatory treatment that the Dakota people had received at the hands of the white community. After the discussion was closed, a motion was passed in which thirty-six of the forty people in attendance rejected state jurisdiction.

Although this was an official CCST meeting, the motion rejecting state jurisdiction did not count as a referendum because, like the vote that the LBST conducted at its town-hall meeting, the vote fell outside the bill's specified timeframe. Even so, the motion clearly showed how displeased the Dakota were with the surrounding institutions' failure to address crucial race relations in any constructive way. When the CCST eventually held its official referendum, the result was consistent with its previous action; the CCST rejected state jurisdiction by a vote of twenty in favor and ninety-four opposed.

As for the Sisseton-Wahpeton Sioux Tribe (SWST), Yankton Sioux Tribe (YST), and Flandreau Sioux Tribe (FST), only the SWST held a referendum and rejected state jurisdiction by a vote of six for and 31 against. While it is uncertain whether the YST and FST held referenda of their own—and if they did not, acquiesced to state jurisdiction by default—their circumstances were not unlike that of the LBST. Respectively, the Charles Mix and Moody boards of county commissioners never fulfilled the statutory responsibilities outlined in HB No. 892, thus rendering invalid any claim whatsoever by the state that it had assumed criminal and civil jurisdiction over the YST and the FST.

When the 1 October 1958 deadline arrived, with the questionable exceptions of the LBST, the YST, and the FST, the Lakota/Dakota had conclusively rejected state jurisdiction through their respective referenda and hence had successfully stopped South Dakota's outright attempt to abolish Lakota governance. In political terms, the Lakota viewed the referenda as definitive, and it is not hard to imagine why.

First, based on events in the five mandatory states, the Lakota saw PL 83-280's application as being an all-or-nothing proposition. In other words, the United States gave its unconditional consent for all states to assume the total, not partial, jurisdiction that the federal government was relinquishing over Native Country. Moreover, since PL 83-280 did not provide for retrocession, once a state had accepted the United States' offer, it could not give back to the United States the jurisdiction it had assumed. Termination was irrevocable. Indeed, South Dakota's HB No. 892 mirrored PL 83-280's one-time, all-or-nothing terms by allowing the Lakota only one chance to reject state jurisdiction.

Second, the Lakota viewed their referenda as definitive because of South Dakota's political tradition of using referenda to decide important issues. Within the first decade of statehood in South Dakota's political history, its citizens had reserved for themselves through a duly approved 1898 constitutional amendment[165] the power of the initiative and the referendum. This Populist Movement–inspired amendment of political reform allowed people to either propose new laws or to refer already enacted measures to a statewide vote.[166] South Dakota understandably prided itself in being the first state to provide these means for direct democracy and routinely accepted the outcomes of referenda as law. Between 1898, when the initiative and referendum amendment was approved, and 1958, sixteen initiatives and thirty-one referendum questions had been referred to voters and decided upon by them. Out of this rich S.D. political tradition, if any aspect of HB No. 892 was to be honored as conclusive and recognized as binding, it was the hard-fought-for Lakota referendum provision and the referenda's outcomes.

Given the force and magnitude of these various U.S. and S.D. factors, the Lakota had every reason to believe that they had buried the state jurisdiction question once and for all.

Or so they thought.

Notes

1. In this termination period, I have included those state legislators who served in 1951, two years before termination became official policy. In 1951, these state legislators enacted what can be considered the first attempt to exercise state jurisdiction: SB No. 278.

2. Indeed, the state senate was an exclusively white male body.

3. See, for instance, James G. Abourezk's *Advise & Dissent: Memoirs of South Dakota and the Senate* (Chicago: Lawrence Hill Books, 1989); Robert Sam Anson's *McGovern: A Biography* (New York: Holt, Rinehart and Winston, 1972); and the South Dakota Legislative Research Council's *Biographical Directory of the South Dakota Legislature, 1889–1989* (Pierre: South Dakota Legislative Research Council, 1989).

4. The following nine reservations were part of the following House and Senate districts, abbreviated as HD and SD, respectively (the relevant counties are in parentheses):

Lake Traverse Reservation (now called the Sisseton–Wahpeton Dakota Nation): HD30 (Codington), HD 31 (Grant), HD32 (Roberts), HD33 (Day), HD34 (Marshall), SD18 (Codington), SD19 (Grant and Duel), SD20 (Roberts), and SD21 (Day, Roberts).

Flandreau Reservation: HD17 (Moody), HD53 (Moody, Lake), and SD12 (Moody, Lake).

Yankton Reservation: HD5 (Charles Mix, Brule, Aurora) and SD3 (Charles Mix, Bon Homme).

Crow Creek Reservation: HD21 (Buffalo, Hand), HD22 (Hyde, Sully), HD23 (Hughes), SD10 (Buffalo, Aurora, Brule, Jerauld), SD16 (Hughes, Hyde, Hand, Sully).

Lower Brule Reservation: HD 47 (Lyman, Stanley, Jones) and SD29 (Lyman, Stanley, Jones, Haakon).

Standing Rock Reservation: HD52 (Corson) and SD30 (Corson, Dewey, Ziebach).

Cheyenne River Reservation: HD51 (Dewey, Ziebach) and SD30 (see Standing Rock Reservation).

Pine Ridge Reservation: HD42 (Bennett, Mellette), HD43 (Shannon, Fall River), HD46 (Washabaugh, Jackson, Haakon), SD26 (Bennett, Washabaugh, Jackson, Mellette, Todd), and SD27 (Shannon, Fall River, Custer).

Rosebud Reservation: HD40 (Gregory), HD41 (Tripp, Todd), HD 42 (see Pine Ridge Reservation), SD25 (Gregory, Tripp), and SD26 (see Pine Ridge Reservation).

5. The Standing Rock Reservation was unique in that a House district was coterminous with the reservation. Like the House district, a Senate district not only was coterminous with the Standing Rock Reservation but also included the Cheyenne River Reservation. The Cheyenne River Reservation had three House districts that were coterminous with the reservation in 1951, but they were later consolidated into one. Also, the eastern half of the Pine Ridge and the western half of the Rosebud reservations comprised a Senate district.

6. These figures were derived from the South Dakota Stockgrowers' convention committee lists of 1950, 1952, 1954, 1955, 1956, 1957, 1958 (partial), 1962, and 1964.

7. W. E. Kieffe, MSGAPRR chair, to S.D. Governor Sigurd Anderson, Box 213, EYB Papers.

8. W. E. Kieffe to E. Y. Berry, 2, Box 213, EYB Papers.

9. Ibid., 3.

10. *Martin Messenger,* "Traders' Problems Discussed at Martin Meeting Wednesday," February 1951, 1, Box 213, EYB Papers.

11. The House vote on SB No. 278 was 63 Yes, 0 No, 2 Absent and Not Voting, and 10 Excused. On 27 February 1951, Governor Sigrud Anderson signed SB No. 278 into law.

12. U.S. Statutes at Large, 25:676.

13. LRC Executive Board, 16 May 1955 minutes, 2, LJC.

14. The listing of the committee is Representative John Buehler, chair, and Senator C. O. Peterson, vice chair. The senators are Ray E. Barnett, Hilbert Bogue, L. F. Ericsson, L. A. Johnson, Joe E. Lehmann, John E. Mueller, James Ramey, and Chester W. Stewart. The representatives are Thomas O. Bergan, Howard E. Blake, Ellen E. Bliss, Fred A. Boller, Paul E. Brown, Nels P. Christensen, Ernest A. Covey, Joe R. Dunmire,

Edgar Gardner, Merton Glover, O. A. Gustafson, Ralph O. Hillgreen, Theodore W. McFarling, Harry H. Martens, J. C. Noonan, Robert A. Oden, Merle Pommer, David Pulford, and Joe Schneider.

15. LJC.

16. Ibid.

17. Ibid.

18. *Winner Advocate*, "Officials Express Opinions on Increased Indian Drunkenness," 1 September 1955, 1, Box 192, EYB Papers.

19. Institute of Indian Studies, *Program and Proceedings, 1st Annual Conference on Indian Affairs* (herein *PPCIA-I*), 3.

20. Ibid., 7 (emphasis mine).

21. Ibid., 32.

22. Ibid., 33.

23. Ibid., 35–36.

24. Ibid., 11.

25. Ibid., 42.

26. Abourezk, *Advise & Dissent*, 221.

27. Ibid.

28. Indeed, Frank Ducheneaux, the CRST president, gave a blistering, four-page testimony on 20 February 1963 before state legislators on the matter of jurisdiction and ADC:

> The State Welfare Department of South Dakota has made a lot of ballyhoo about Aid to Dependent Children because they say they cannot prosecute Indians because of illegitimate children and broken homes. The record shows at Cheyenne Agency [i.e., the Cheyenne River Sioux Reservation] that about 60% of the illegitimate children are [from] white fathers and 30% of the broken homes [involve] white fathers. Why hasn't the state prosecuted them when they have jurisdiction over them regardless if they live on the reservation or not? It seems to me that they [the welfare department, state's attorneys] don't care about the white father but would like to prosecute the Indian father (3).

29. Institute of Indian Studies, *PPCIA-I*, 15.

30. Ibid.

31. The public and private welfare participants were Fern L. Chamberlain, S.D. Department of Public Welfare; Public Welfare Commissioners E. H. Everson, Freeman Otto, and Florence M. Lee; Grace Martin, Division of Child Welfare; Matthew Furze, director of the Department of Public Welfare; E. J. Colleran, S.D. Social Welfare Conference; and Rev. E. H. Hirrschoff, S.D. Council of Churches.

32. The public instruction participants were F. R. Wanek, S.D. Department of Public Instruction; J. W. Deacon, Associated School Boards of South Dakota; M. L. Reynolds, Pierre Public Schools; John Artichoker, South Dakota Director of Indian Education; Wesley R. Hurt, director of Over Museum, University of South Dakota;

W. O. Farber, director of Government and Government Research Bureau, University of South Dakota; and E. W. Harrington, dean of arts and sciences, University of South Dakota.

33. The public health participants were R. J. Morgan, Rapid City Health Department; the state health officer Dr. G. J. Van Heuvelen; and H. L. Stricklett, S.D. Public Health Association.

34. The other participants were Ephriam Hixson, Division of Agriculture, South Dakota State College; Floyd F. Collins, Extension Service, South Dakota State College; George I. Gilbertson, Director of Extension Service, South Dakota State College; Frank Dwyer, County Commissioners Association; Bishop Blair Roberts, S.D. Indian Affairs Commission; Phil Saunders, S.D. attorney general; and Ben Reifel, Bureau of Indian Affairs.

35. EHWC, 24 October 1955, minutes, 3, LJC.

36. Ibid.

37. The state officials included individuals involved with various aspects of the state's education program: John Artichoker Jr. and Fern Wanek were both from the state's Department of Public Instruction; A. E. Mead was executive secretary of the S.D. board of regents; Cordelia Shevling was with the state's Division of Vocational Rehabilitation; and W. O. Farber, Philip Odeen Jr., Robert A. Tschetter, James C. Johnson, and Thomas McPartland were all from the University of South Dakota. Others were Fern L. Chamberlain and Jerry Gardner from the Department of Public Welfare; the state treasurer Ed T. Elkins and the state auditor F. A. Allbee; G. J. Van Heuvelen, State Department of Health; John C. Farrar, the assistant state's attorney; E. D. Mayer, Hughes County state's attorney; Allen G. Wilson, Fall River and Shannon County state's attorney; G. W. Wuest, S.D. assistant attorney general; and Rol Kebach, Chief Law Enforcement Office of the Attorney General's Office.

38. Representing the BIA were Ben Reifel from the Aberdeen area office and Norman Gregory and C. H. Beitzel from the Pierre agency.

39. Lakota officials attending the committee meeting were Frank Ducheneaux, president of the Cheyenne River Sioux Tribe; Lawrence Mayes, general manager of the CRST's rehabilitation program; Robert Philbrick, president of the Crow Creek Sioux Tribe; George L. Allen, president of Flandreau Sioux Tribe; Richard K. Wakeman, secretary of the Flandreau Sioux Tribe; Antonine G. Ladeaux, justice of the peace at Pine Ridge; Moses Two Bulls, president of the Oglala Sioux Tribe; and Henry Black Elk, OSTC.

40. See HB No. 612, "Scholarships in State Educational Institutions for Persons of Indian Blood." Already approved by the state House of Representatives, the state Senate concurred on 8 March 1957.

41. This Minnesota policy eventually became known as the four-states bill. According to Marvin Sonosky's 5 February 1957 memorandum to his Native clients, the purpose of these bills, S. 574 and H.R. 3362, was "to require the United States to pay the actual cost and administrative expenses for services rendered by the States to

'Indians' under contracts with the United States and to pay additional sums to the States for social security and health, education and welfare benefits given by States to 'Indians.'" In other words, the four states of Minnesota, North Dakota, South Dakota, and Wisconsin all wanted a federal subsidy in return for assuming jurisdiction over Native affairs from the United States.

42. L. M. Carlson, 28 June 1956 letter to Phil Saunders, LJC.

43. South Dakota Bar Association, *South Dakota Bar Journal* (*SDBJ*), July 1956, vol. 25, no. 1, 43.

44. Ibid.

45. *Constitution of the State of South Dakota,* art. 22, sec. 2, "Compact with the United States."

46. Four recommendations concern Indian education: increasing the dollar amount of higher education scholarships to Native students, allocating the scholarships more efficiently, expanding vocational training programs for Native students at Southern State Teachers College, and initiating a more extensive guidance and counseling program for Native students at institutes of higher education to prevent a Native student from withdrawing. The other committee recommendation, of course, was to have the federal government financially assist the state when the state provided welfare services to Native people. This was initially called the Minnesota Plan, but later became the four-states bill.

47. EHWC, "Report of the Committee on Education, Health, and Welfare to the Executive Board" (herein EHWC Report), 11.

48. Ibid. (emphasis mine).

49. George Malone to E. Y. Berry, 25 January 1957, Box 168, EYB Papers.

50. Institute of Indian Studies, *Program and Proceedings, 3rd Annual Conference on Indian Affairs,* 33 (herein *PPCIA*-III).

51. Ibid.

52. Lower Brule Sioux Tribe, "Bill No. 892," 1, LJC.

53. *PPCIA*-III, 34.

54. Cheyenne River Sioux Tribal Council, Regular Session, minutes, 5–7 March 1957, LJC.

55. *PPCIA*-III, 30.

56. "Speech by Edison G. Ward in Support of State Jurisdiction before the Indian Affairs Committee of the State Legislature," 20 February 1957, 1, Box 252, EYB Papers.

57. Ibid.

58. *PPCIA*-III, 52.

59. *PPCIA*-III, 1–2.

60. Ibid., 2.

61. EHWC Report, 11.

62. Marvin Talbott to Ellen E. Bliss, "House Bill No. 721," 4, 23 February 1957, LJC.

63. For example, at a S.D. State Commission of Indian Affairs meeting on 24 November 1953, Berry explained the recently passed PL 83-280 and how any state law to assume jurisdiction over Lakota territory would not apply unless or until Lakota consent were obtained (Minutes of Meeting, 2, Box 168, EYB Papers).

64. See, for example, OST Resolution No. 55-30 (14 January 1955) and No. 57-23 (28 January 1957); SRST Resolution 9-57 (6 March 1957); and RST Resolution No. 64-05 (27 January 1964).

65. Marvin J. Sonosky to Tribal Clients, "General Bulletin No. 4," 2, LJC. See also Daniels, *American Indians,* in which a National Congress of American Indians mimeograph, "U.S. Government Policy Towards American Indians; A Few Basic Facts, Revised October 1, 1956," notes that S. 51 was "postponed without prejudice" by the House Committee on Interior and Insular Affairs on 16 July 1956.

66. E. Y. Berry to John C. Farrar, 9 February 1957, Box 183, EYB Papers.

67. John C. Farrar to E. Y. Berry, Box 183, EYB Papers.

68. Ibid.

69. HB No. 892, sec. 5, 429.

70. The pro-state jurisdiction forces could take consolation in the fact that the language of HB No. 892's section 1 was the entire HB No. 721.

71. The House vote was 71 Yes, 1 No, 1 Absent and Not Voting, and 2 Excused.

72. Ethel Merrival, "Pierre Legislation Report," 1, Box 252, EYB Papers.

73. Ibid.

74. Ibid., 2.

75. Ibid. In the *Proceedings of the Senate, Thirty-Fifth Legislative Session,* the journal records that, "Mr. Abdnor moved that the rules be suspended and that House Bill No. 892 be placed on the calendar to follow House Bill No. 612 [Indian scholarship bill]" (939). A two-thirds majority was required to suspend the rules, and thirty-one of thirty-five senators voted to do so. James Abdnor's senate district included the Lower Brule Sioux Reservation.

76. Ibid.

77. See art. 3, sec. 22, of South Dakota's constitution.

78. Ethel Merrival, "Delegation Report," 1, Box 165, EYB Papers.

79. *Petition of Matthew High Pine et al.,* 122.

80. Chapter 106 of the Session Laws of the State of South Dakota for 1901, sec. 1, 132.

81. The U.S. law in question is the Act of 2 February 1903 (32 Stat. Chapter 351), which, after listing the crimes, states that "this Act is passed in pursuant of the cession of jurisdiction contained [in] chapter one hundred and [six], Laws of South Dakota, nineteen hundred and one."

82. *Ex rel.* stands for *Ex relatione:* "Upon relation or information. Legal proceedings which are instituted by the attorney general (or other proper person) in the name and behalf of the State, but on the information and at the instigation of an individual

who has a private interest in the matter, are said to be taken 'on the relation' of such person." *Black's Law,* 5th ed. West., 522–23.

83. Richards, "Federal Jurisdiction," 54. In addition, the SDBA's September 1956 official recommendation was confusing, as was the previous 1951 state law that outlined the conditions under which the state supposedly could assume criminal jurisdiction over the Lakota People and their land. In an attempt to further elucidate the SDBA Law Committee's recommendation for its membership—and perhaps as an attempt to either educate or influence the 1957 state legislature in its drafting of a jurisdiction measure—in spring 1957, the *South Dakota Law Review* printed an article by Richards about the state's assumption of jurisdiction.

From the Law Committee's recommendation that South Dakota accept total jurisdiction over former areas of Indian Country, Richards had only this to say: where a crime is committed "outside the 'closed' portion of the reservation, even though within the original territorial limits of the reservation, but on [fee] patented ground to which the Indian title has been extinguished, it is held that the state court does have . . . jurisdiction" (*SDLR* 1957, 51). In other words, when the Great Sioux Nation was rearranged into six separate reservations in 1889, the remaining portion was declared surplus land. This surplus land was opened for white settlement and, with some exceptions, is now mostly considered "former" Indian Country. Apparently, as the SDBA's September 1956 discussion and Richards's article disclosed, there were a sufficient number of crimes committed in these "former" Indian Country regions that, in the course of enforcing state laws, were troubling enough to various county state's attorneys, county judges, the state's attorney general's office, state circuit judges, and local law enforcement personnel to warrant some form of state intervention. From a Lakota perspective, however, the state's intent seemed more sinister, as if the state were acting on a compulsive desire to incarcerate an even greater percentage of Lakota people than were already in prison.

Closely connected to the criminal jurisdiction debate are two more issues: the type of crime in question and who is actually Native. Regarding the first issue, Richards's analysis focused only on whether the crime was committed on- or off-reservation within Indian Country. Richards also revealed that, other than the congressional acts that preempted state control, crime typing is, at best, an inexact science and so should not be used to determine who gets to prosecute an alleged crime—the United States, South Dakota, or the Lakota.

Much of the confusion around determining jurisdiction is non-Native in origin, stemming presumably from whites' fear of entrusting their fate to non-whites. Imagine a scenario in which a white person has to go to a Lakota court to answer for an alleged criminal act that he or she committed. For most whites, such a scenario is outrageous. Consequently, many U.S. laws and court cases assure white people that this will not happen.

As for the second issue, determining who is Native obviously depends on who has jurisdiction: the United States, South Dakota, or the Lakota. Richards is most concerned with establishing the fate of the "emancipated Indian," one who severs his or her tribal relationship and fully adopts the habits of white civilization. If such an individual can be construed to be non-Native, the state has a greater interest in what such an "emancipated" Native does, regardless of whether that person is residing on- or off-reservation.

84. *Petition of Matthew High Pine et al.*, 12. Appellant's brief.

85. Ibid., 14.

86. *Petition of Matthew High Pine et al.*, 7. Respondent's brief.

87. Ibid., 6.

88. Ibid., 9.

89. Ibid., 12.

90. Ibid., 13.

91. Ibid., 15.

92. Ibid., 16.

93. SB No. 278, sec. 1.

94. *Petition of Matthew High Pine et al.*, 12–13. Respondent's brief.

95. *Williams v. Lee*, 218.

96. Ibid., 223.

97. Davis, "Criminal Jurisdiction," 87.

98. *Petition of Matthew High Pine et al.*, 127.

99. Ibid.

100. Ibid., 129.

101. Recall that a year before the *High Pine* opinion was finally handed down, these referenda had already taken place by 1 October 1958. Indeed, most likely influenced by the outcome of the referenda, the court had observed that HB No. 892's conditions for acceptance of state jurisdiction were, to one degree or another, not met and had not been performed.

102. *PPCIA*-III, 23.

103. EHWC Report, 11–12.

104. Farber, Odeen, and Tschetter, *Indians*, iv.

105. EHWC Report, 11–12.

106. In addition to S. 574, Berry, on 22 January 1957, introduced a companion bill to S. 574—H.R. 3362—and on 1 February 1957, Case introduced S. 1015, a bill to more equitably apportion the costs between South Dakota and the United States. Finally, Otto Krueger, on 24 January 1957, introduced H.R. 3634, which was not unlike H.R. 3362.

107. LJC.

108. Ibid.

109. Institute of Indian Studies, "Law Enforcement," 2.

110. *PPCIA*-III, 3.

111. *PPCIA*-III, 4.

112. Farber, Odeen, and Tschetter, *Indians*, 67.

113. Ibid.

114. Interestingly, Farber, in his presentation at the June 1957 conference, had this to say about the profile of a Lakota offender: "But there was a significant thing about the statistics that we had not anticipated, and that was this: the average Indian offender is young, he is ordinarily not well educated, and he has been guilty of offenses that are less serious in character than many. Usually, he has been arrested for such things as theft, but not crimes against persons" (3).

115. For example, Farber remarks that the absence of Lakota jurors is not a major defect in the state's legal system nor should the state's judges be held responsible for the lack or absence of Lakota jurors.

116. Institute of Indian Studies, "Law Enforcement," 2–3.

117. In not dismissing the suit as motioned by John Farrar, Mickelson found a significant federal question raised by the Oglala Sioux Tribe's tax controversy. According to the annotated *Oglala Sioux Tribe v. Barta et al.,* "When action involves controversy respecting effect of act of Congress, federal District Court must assume jurisdiction to determine if claim is well grounded" (917). Mickelson cited the 1934 Indian Reorganization Act and his previous *Iron Crow* decision as controlling.

118. Indeed, the acting treasurer, William LaPointe, of the Rosebud Sioux Tribe sent a 2 August 1956 letter to the Pine Ridge BIA agency saying that, much like Pine Ridge, the RST was "experiencing some difficulty in the collection of our tribal tax. . . . We have started legislation here in our Tribal Council to levy a tax of .03¢ an acre on grazing land and a tax of .15¢ an acre on farming land. Perhaps you could also give us some information as to how this is progressing [on Pine Ridge]" (LJC).

119. LJC.

120. See *Barta v. Oglala Sioux Tribe of Pine Ridge Reservation,* 259 F. 2d 553 (1958). When the five white ranchers appealed the federal district court's decision, six more white ranchers joined the lawsuit: John Glover, Merton Glover, Jack Lewis, Marvin Spracklin, Cyrus Porch, and William Porch. In addition to these eleven white ranchers who leased Oglala Lakota land, others refused to pay but were not parties to the lawsuit. These included J. J. Linehan, Lee Harrison, Wesley Harrison, William Deckert, Bud Thomas, Gilbert Norman, Charles F. Rock, Peter J. Rock, Claude A. Berry, John Hageman and sons, John L. Hageman, James Olge, Alva Woods and sons, and Senator James Ramey (letter from Richard Schifter to OST President James Iron Cloud, 13 November 1956, Box 252, EYB Papers).

121. 2, Box 214, EYB Papers.

122. See, for example, Edison Ward's 20 June 1957 letter to Berry in which Ward writes, "The tax case [*Barta v. Oglala Sioux Tribe*] will be tried at Deadwood within the next few days. Tom Arnold and Mickelson had a p[u]blic scene at Pierre[;] guess the sparks flew fast. Very undignified to say the least for a Federal Judge to enter into such a public argument. May have a tendency to make him realize that the citizens of the State do not appreciate his pampering the Bureau. It appears that this will be very embarrassing for him through the years to come."

123. See note 118.

124. H. A. Wallace, 19 February 1938 letter to President Roosevelt, 1, Box 299, EYB Papers.

125. Wendall E. Long, 17 May 1957 letter to E. Y. Berry, Box 299, EYB Papers.

126. "Potentially a Huge Landgrab," *Bennett County Booster II*, 30 May 1957, 1, vol. VII, no. 46, Box 299, EYB Papers.

127. Ibid.

128. E. Y. Berry, 30 May 1957 letter to Merton Glover, Box 299, EYB Papers.

129. E. Y. Berry, 25 June 1957 letter to Mr. and Mrs. C. W. McCormick, Box 299, EYB Papers.

130. Louis Beckwith, 7 June 1957 letter to E. Y. Berry, Box 299, EYB Papers.

131. White constituents' 31 May 1957 letter to E. Y. Berry, Box 299, EYB Papers.

132. SDSGA Resolution No. 1, 5 June 1957.

133. Lawson, *Dammed Indians*, 29.

134. Ibid., 50.

135. Ibid., 50–51.

136. Ibid., 169–70.

137. Matthews, "Attention," 14B.

138. Ibid.

139. Ibid.

140. Ducheneaux, "Frank Ducheneaux's Rebuttal," 10.

141. Ibid.

142. Ibid.

143. In Herbert S. Schell's *History of South Dakota*, Schell notes of the takings: "The surplus lands on the Indian Reservations supplied the principal stimulus for the intense activity in the trans-Missouri region. Between 1904 and 1913 the government negotiated a series of agreements with the Teton subtribes on the Rosebud, Lower Brule, Pine Ridge, Cheyenne River, and Standing Rock reservations whereby over half the reservations, a total of over four million acres, were made available for purchase by white settlers" (253). It is these agreements that James J. Matthews, like so many other whites, calls "invitations" in order to justify their illegal occupation in Lakota territory.

144. In a letter to Rasmussen, the SDSGA administrative secretary, the rancher H. H. Hunt wrote, "The article 'Attention Fellow Taxpayers' was mailed out over the signature of John Matthews in the mistaken idea it would help him in his campaign to unseat Fred Hunter. If you want to be fair, you'll print F. Ducheneaux's answer to him. It will be interesting to watch and see if Matthew's predictions come true" (*SDSG*, December 1956, 10).

145. Ibid.

146. Warren J. Knipfer, 7 August 1956 letter to E. Y. Berry, Box 130, EYB Papers.

147. See David R. Mayhew's *Divided We Govern: Party Control, Lawmaking, and Investigations, 1946–1990* (New Haven: Yale University Press, 1991) in which he ascribes

five social features of a public mood that, among South Dakota's white community, seemingly describes the state jurisdiction phenomenon:

> First, much of at least the politically aware public, inside and outside of Washington, shares a certain outlook about what can and should be done right now on a wide range of political issues. Second, a large number of people who possess that outlook bring considerable intensity to it; they are not lukewarm. Third, to the extent that the outlook calls for it, an appreciable number of people go on to engage in . . . citizen action. They actually do things: They may form organizations, persuade others, go to meetings, give money, write letters, join protests, approach members of Congress, in general make themselves heard and felt. Fourth, the outlook in question is in some sense dominant: Non-sharers of it have a hard time wholly resisting its intellectual or political appeal or mustering intensity or action against it. Fifth, a "public mood" has a beginning and end. The outlook, the intensity, and the citizen action emerge or balloon at some detectable juncture, and then several years later, at another juncture, they deflate or disappear (160).

148. See note 51.

149. LBST Resolution No. 57-207.

150. Elmer Pretty Head, 2 August 1957 letter to E. Y. Berry, Box 168, EYB Papers.

151. HB No. 892, sec. 5.

152. Institute of Indian Studies, *Program and Proceedings, Sixth Annual Conference on Indian Affairs* (herein *PPCIA-VI*), 47.

153. Ibid., 47–48.

154. Rosebud Community Resolution No. 5726, 2 April 1957, LJC.

155. See 8 April 1957 Rosebud Sioux Tribal Council Minutes. Narcisse Brave made the motion to approve the Rosebud community resolution and Opie LaPointe seconded the motion. The vote count was 13 Yes, 3 No, 4 Absent. Brave also made the motion (seconded by Wellman Collins) to have the executive committee set a referendum date. The motion passed 16 Yes, 0 No, 4 Absent.

156. Because of population shifts, by 1958, four of the communities (Upper and Lower Ponca, Little Crow, and White Thunder) no longer held elections for tribal council representation. The Rosebud agency was a nonrecognized community with tribal council representation. Three other communities, He Dog, Ideal, and Horse Creek, had polling problems and new elections were scheduled. Thus, there was no initial record of how they voted on state jurisdiction. On 27 March 1963, the RST adopted Resolution No. 63-23, which eliminated the Little Crow and White Thunder communities; consolidated Upper and Lower Ponca communities into a newly established community, Milk's Camp; formally recognized the agency as a community, Rosebud; and established a new community, Antelope. The four-county area in question was Tripp, Todd, Mellette, and Gregory.

157. Rosebud Sioux Tribe Resolution No. 58-50.

158. The two counties were Dewey and Ziebach.

159. This case formally is cited as 69 N.W. 2d 508.

160. According to Laurence Davis, the N.D. voters initially rejected such an amendment on 26 June 1956, but another similar amendment was resubmitted and subsequently approved in June 1958. However, Davis also noted that "as of February 6, 1959, the North Dakota Legislature had taken no action to avail itself of its newly created authority to extend state jurisdiction to Indian county" (88).

161. Kyle Livestock and Landowners Association invitation letter to potential panelists, 20 June 1958, LJC.

162. "A Few Things to Remember before Making a Decision on September 10, 1958, Regarding the Jurisdiction Matter," Box 214, EYB Papers.

163. Ibid.

164. At that time, a general council meeting of CCST members could be called by the president, with a written request of five of the six CCST council members, or with a petition signed by at least 10 percent of the eligible resident voters. It took 20 percent of the eligible voters to constitute a quorum (art. 7, sec. 2, Constitution and Bylaws of the CCST).

165. The 1898 statewide vote for the initiative and referendum question was 23,816 yes and 16,483 no.

166. See South Dakota State Historical Society's quarterly, *South Dakota History* 22 (1992), for an account of the populist movement in the state's political history. For a general reading of the populist movement, see Lawrence Goodwin's *The Populist Movement: A Short History of the Agrarian Revolt in America* (Oxford: Oxford University Press, 1978).

Afterword

For the terminationists and their sympathizers who had been either heavily lobbying for or supporting complete state jurisdiction over Lakota territory since 1953, the Lakota referenda proved a stinging setback. Indeed, it was hard to believe. After all, the termination forces controlled the state's entire political apparatus. The LRC, the EHWC, the state health and education departments, the county board of commissioners, the state's attorneys, and so on—all in full collaboration with their respective constituencies—forged a Native policy whose main goal was to destroy the Lakota politically by eliminating their self-determination.

When HB No. 721 was introduced in February 1957, South Dakota was poised to "solve" its pressing Indian Problem. Yet the terminationists sensed that victory was far from certain. As the events surrounding HB No. 721 and HB No. 892 reveal, termination forces were audacious enough to manipulate the legislative process in order to salvage a jurisdiction bill that neither suited their taste nor satisfied their liking; they were that desperate to defeat the Lakota and to force through their termination agenda. Hence, the terminationists' shock that, despite all the advantages that they enjoyed at the state level, the referenda delivered yet another defeat at the hands of the Lakota—a defeat originally set in motion by the 1953 OST grazing resolution. The terminationists had the state's entire political apparatus under their control, yet they somehow managed to let the jurisdiction ball slip through their hands.

Moreover, with each defeat the state suffered, the Lakota gained in political strength and leverage. This was especially true when the state and federal courts became involved and handed down rulings that unexpectedly cut against the grain of the state's anti-Lakota policy. These court rulings dramatically reinforced the reservations' political status by recognizing Lakota jurisdiction, thus angering many whites who were doing everything they could to abolish Lakota self-governance.

At the state judicial level, the courts unwillingly found themselves embroiled in the bitterly controversial and legally challenging politics of state jurisdiction. The pressure the justices felt was most evident, for example, in the *High Pine* ruling. Yet much as the S.D. justices may have wanted to side with the state, they faced multiple factors that prevented them from handing down explosive decisions favoring state jurisdiction over Lakota territory. For example, they had no clear legislative mandate (such as the legislatively dead HB No. 721) from the state itself to go on. They were presented with robust, insightful, and compelling legal arguments by Lakota-hired attorneys. Moreover, federal and state courts throughout the United States were ruling unambiguously against state jurisdiction over Native Country. In the end, the justices found it more politically expedient and practical to rule against state jurisdiction.

Rulings in support of South Dakota's termination policy could have been adverse to the terminationists' long-term interests. Given the federal juridical trend, the justices understood that, had they handed down a pro-state jurisdiction decision, an appeal to the federal courts could have had debilitating consequences for the terminationists. South Dakota may have been required to amend its constitution before enacting any jurisdiction measure, thus accentuating a legal barrier that would further complicate the state's efforts to cement its hegemony.

Hence, when the referenda deadline was still five months away, and with only the LBST having voted to accept state jurisdiction, many terminationists were becoming increasingly fearful of the referenda's outcome. In his July 1958 monthly *SDSG* column, the SDSGA president Louis Beckwith expressed what many frustrated whites were feeling about Lakota self-determination:

> The Indian problem is moving into the top bracket in State Affairs. . . . It is time that the white people and part Indian realize this is America and not a socialistic State whereby we segregate the Indians in Communities and keep dictating to them what they should and should not do. This providing for a State within a State whereby the Indians are separate from all other people is nonsense. . . . The Indian people while on the Reservation need no license for anything. They make their own laws, divorce their own people, levy their own

taxes. They can require all white people on the Reservation to obtain permits to leave their lands or to cross the Reservation as was done many years ago. This is progress at a standstill.[1]

Beckwith's bombastic editorial against Lakota self-determination left no doubt in anyone's mind that the five-year state jurisdiction movement—culminating in HB No. 892 (a highly compromised version of HB No. 721)—was in serious political trouble. As the 1950s were drawing to a close, much to the disquiet of S.D. terminationists, three events hot on the heels of the Lakota referenda bode ill for the future of the country's termination policy.

First, the incumbent Senator Watkins was defeated in his 1958 reelection bid. The rabid terminationist duo of Watkins and Berry had been halved, and, while Native Country breathed a sigh of relief, residual termination fever would linger for quite some time, particularly in South Dakota.

Second, in a radio address from Flagstaff, Arizona, on 18 September 1958, Interior Secretary Fred A. Seaton supported what Native Nations had lobbied for vigorously ever since PL 83-280 became law, namely, that Native consent be a prerequisite for a state to assume jurisdiction, hence that Native consent must be secured before any termination law could be imposed. Seaton's statement would not immediately affect South Dakota, but it nonetheless inched PL 83-280 closer to incorporating Native consent.

Given the outcomes of the Lakota referenda, the state rightly realized that a consent amendment to PL 83-280 would put state jurisdiction over Lakota territory far beyond their reach. Moreover, ever since *Iron Crow*, the economically impoverished Lakota were pursuing aggressive land use and management programs that not only increased the amount of land-generated revenue that they received from white permittees but also promoted greater Lakota use and expansion of their own reservation land bases.

For the whites whose politico-economic interests were being acutely affected by the Lakota's increasing self-determination, the situation was becoming more intolerable with each passing year. Beckwith's July 1958 editorial rant accurately expressed the sentiments of many whites. Although the Lakota might have viewed Seaton's 1958 statement as positive, its actual bearing on South Dakota's Native policy was minimal. If anything, it might have spurred S.D. terminationists to move faster in trying to force the state jurisdiction question before PL 83-280 could be amended to include Native consent.

Third, on 10 February 1959, the House Subcommittee on Indian Affairs scheduled a routine congressional hearing on H.R. 3737 that unexpectedly erupted into a scathing indictment of—and national scandal about—South Dakota's racist history, policies, and institutions. This bill to amend the Johnson-O'Malley Act of 1934 would have authorized the Interior Secretary to enter into contracts with states for the purpose of funding the enforcement of a state's criminal laws in Native Country.[2] Fortunately, the RST president Burnette happened to be in Washington, D.C., on RST business. When he learned of the bill's hearing, he made arrangements to appear before the subcommittee. In preparing for his appearance, Burnette described what moved him to give his politically explosive testimony:

> I knew if this amendment [H.R. 3737] became law, all Indians on reservations would be at the complete mercy of state authorities, whose primary aim would be to divest the Indian of his land and to destroy the tribal system. I imagined Indians in state courts, facing a jury of whites; Indian children taken from their parents and placed in foster homes; Indian children in schools dedicated to the eradication of their heritage; wholesale discrimination against Indians and the Indian way of life. I decided to make my testimony a report of the injustices that had occurred since Public Law 280 had been enacted. . . . [I] knew that such testimony would have lasting reverberations at home. Nevertheless, five years of open and vigorous fighting had brought results, and it would be not only cowardly but unwise to shrink at this time from a direct assault on a legal weapon that whites had fashioned to harass, subjugate, and ultimately devastate the reservation Indian.[3]

Focusing on the whites' racial hatred of the Lakota in South Dakota, Burnette concluded that any U.S. subsidy made available to the state for the purpose of criminal or civil law enforcement "would be used in the service of discrimination, not justice."[4] Afterward, James Haley, chair of the subcommittee, commented to Burnette that he wished Berry could have been present at his testimony because "Northerners were always charging the South with discrimination, while they discriminated against the Indian."[5]

At a time when the burgeoning civil rights movement was exposing mainstream society to its own debilitating racism, the news media readily carried Burnette's testimony. His words dropped a public relations bombshell that sent the state of South Dakota reeling with embarrassment. In the state, an immediate backlash followed. On the one hand, the whites vehemently denied that any racial discrimination existed in South Dakota; on the other hand, they simultaneously punished the Lakota for having one of their people expose the racist reality and speak out against racial discrimination and its history.

As the 1960s began, these unsettling developments for South Dakota made the state's jurisdiction issue take on an even greater sense of urgency and emotional intensity. Rather than respect and abide by the 1958 referenda that, paradoxically, the state had forced upon the Lakota, frantic terminationists had their state legislators repeatedly introduce three state jurisdiction measures. During three successive legislative sessions, SB No. 210 (appendix E),[6] HB No. 659 (appendix F),[7] and HB No. 791 (appendix G)[8] were put forth, whereupon the state legislature would either unanimously or overwhelmingly approve them into law.

The least ambitious of these bills was SB No. 210, according to which South Dakota, without raising its usual cost-reimbursement argument, accepted only concurrent police jurisdiction over highways passing through Lakota territory. All the other post–HB No. 892 laws shared the following characteristics: they were all introduced by state legislators who had a significant Lakota presence in their districts; the laws accepted and assumed complete criminal and civil jurisdiction over Lakota territory; they completely ignored PL 83-280's section 6 stipulation that South Dakota first amend its constitution before any termination laws could be considered valid; and, most notably, the laws glaringly omitted any language requiring Lakota consent, despite Lakota desires to the contrary. This last feature obviously shows how deeply frustrated, angry, and resentful whites had become over the Lakota's politico-economic gains during the 1950s.

For the Lakota, 1961 proved a pivotal year for eventually settling the state jurisdiction question. In the beginning of that year, the thirty-seventh state legislative session adopted HB No. 659—a bill that would lead South Dakota closer to accepting fiscal responsibility for its would-be jurisdiction. In a determined but somewhat symbolic display that the state was serious about termination, the bill expanded on SB No. 210's provision of concurrent police jurisdiction over reservation highways. With HB No. 659, the state would not only assert complete criminal and civil jurisdiction over all reservation highways but also commit to paying the costs of that jurisdiction.[9]

As for nonhighway jurisdiction, just as HB No. 892 required the condition of a federal subsidy, so too the final version of HB No. 659 would not be considered effective until the United States agreed to reimburse South Dakota for the cost of assuming total criminal and civil jurisdiction over Lakota territory.[10] Without a U.S. subsidy, South Dakota refused to accept jurisdiction. In the unlikely event that the United States would agree to subsidize South Dakota's jurisdiction over Lakota territory, HB No. 659 would repeal HB No. 892.[11]

The question of obtaining a U.S. subsidy to fund a state responsibility was predictably the major difficulty with HB No. 659. A 23 March 1961 Interior Department news release stated that—despite the best efforts of the S.D. congressional delegation to persuade the Interior Department otherwise—the United States was, and always had been, reluctant to finance a would-be state responsibility: "The Department of the Interior today announced its opposition to legislation now pending in Congress (S. 381) which would provide for Federal subsidies to States to finance the costs of law enforcement on Indian reservations." Alluding pointedly to South Dakota's recently passed (3 March 1961) HB No. 659, the news release stated further: "At present, however, it appears that certain State legislatures are being influenced to adopt similar legislation [to S. 381] by the prospect or possibility that Federal subsidies will be provided to finance law enforcement costs on the Indian reservations."[12]

Convinced that no U.S. funds were forthcoming, in a 27 March 1961 letter, Governor Gubbrud notified the commissioner of Indian affairs that HB No. 659 would not go into effect. South Dakota was left with having to finance all the costs of assuming criminal and civil jurisdiction over narrowly defined portions of the reservations, namely, the highways. Most significantly, HB No. 892 remained in effect, which meant that the "no" of the Lakota referenda held fast as state law.

Even more damaging to South Dakota's efforts to assume control was a December 1962 Seventh Circuit Court decision that invalidated the section of HB No. 659 that specifically provided for reservation highway jurisdiction. In circumstances similar to the *High Pine* case, on 4 August 1962, Julia Hankins was arrested by a S.D. Highway Patrol officer, charged with driving under the influence on the Pine Ridge Reservation, and then imprisoned. Despite the fact that the state had asserted jurisdiction over reservation highways with the passage of HB No. 659, Hankins's attorney immediately filed in Lampert's court for a writ of habeas corpus, and she was released that same day. After the hearing on Hankins's habeas corpus writ, on 7 December 1962, Lampert upheld the argument by Hankins's attorney that jurisdiction pursuant to PL 83-280 must cover all and not just parts of the Pine Ridge Reservation. Lampert ruled that South Dakota had, in fact, no jurisdiction over reservation highways.

The state immediately appealed Lampert's December decision to the S.D. Supreme Court. Twelve months later, the justices published their 30 January 1964 opinion, *South Dakota v. Hankins*. Not only did they rule that the state's highway jurisdiction law was invalid, but also, unlike the *High Pine* ruling, they stated unequivocally that South Dakota was a section 6 state. Accordingly, any state law claiming jurisdiction over Lakota Country was invalid without a prior change in South Dakota's constitution.

Without question, the 1964 *Hankins* ruling, like all the court decisions since *Iron Crow*, stunned the state and its terminationists. The pro-state jurisdiction advocates had only to review the record of the last seven years—three unsuccessful legislative attempts (HB No. 892, 1957; SB No. 210, 1959; and HB No. 659, 1961), two adverse state supreme court decisions (*High Pine*, 1959 and *Hankins*, 1964), and an equally adverse U.S. Supreme Court ruling (*Williams*, 1959)—to realize that they were far from achieving the political objective that they had announced in 1956, namely, of politically destroying the Lakota. The irony is that the whites' lust for Native lands and for the profits to be gained through jurisdictional takeover was stopped by South Dakota's adamant unwillingness to pay for the very jurisdiction it so doggedly craved.

Because South Dakota consistently refused to assume the full costs of its would-be criminal and civil jurisdiction and instead lobbied for a U.S. subsidy, whites faced the real prospect of never gaining any control over Lakota territory. But the deadlocked positions of South Dakota and the United States over who should pay for jurisdiction were not the only obstacles. Given the *Hankins* rulings, South Dakota's judicial policy regarding PL 83-280 was that state jurisdiction had to be all or nothing. The state could not assume complete jurisdiction over a limited portion of Lakota territory, neither could it assume a limited or piecemeal jurisdiction over all of Lakota territory. Arguably, Lampert's December 1962 *Hankins* habeas corpus ruling may well have convinced the state that the only way to assert control over Lakota homelands was to assume the full cost of both criminal and civil jurisdiction, and the state was simply unwilling to do this.

Shortly after the thirty-seventh legislative session adjourned in March 1961, a 1961–62 interim investigating committee was established to conduct hearings about the state's Indian Problem, much as the EHWC had done back in 1955–56. This new committee was authorized to investigate the misuse and abuse of the state's welfare program. Of course, focusing primarily on the state's ADC program,[13] the seven-member, all-white committee used the ADC to voice yet more racist stereotypes and white-biased judgments about the state's "Indian population." After meeting on twelve separate occasions between 15 July 1961 and 25 July 1962, the committee released, in August 1962 (ironically the same month Hankins was arrested), its official forty-seven-page report on the "irregularities," "inefficiencies," and "abuses" of public

welfare. Not surprisingly, a significant portion of its report concerned Native
ADC recipients:

> The investigation revealed that about 45 per cent of the ADC cases arise
> among the Indian population, which constitutes only about 5 per cent of
> the population of the state. . . . The Welfare directors and workers, as well as
> the State's Attorneys and other law enforcement officers are inclined to label
> this problem as "hopeless." Many of the Indian Welfare recipients are on the
> rolls because they tend to be irresponsible, lacking in foresight, dependent
> (probably because they have so long been wards of the federal government),
> and they do not care very much whether they are in jail or out.[14]

On top of this racially tainted profiling of Native welfare recipients, the
report implicated Lakota governance in fostering Native apathy toward white
American values of responsibility, foresight, independence, and respect and
fear of the law. According to an attorney in the state's welfare department,
because Lakota self-governance preempted state jurisdiction, such governance made it difficult, if not impossible, to enforce state penalties against
Lakota welfare recipients who were allegedly abusing the program and then
using their homelands to shield them from state prosecution.

Again, not surprisingly, the committee recommended "passage of appropriate legislation by the 1963 Legislature to accept criminal and civil jurisdiction over Indian Country in South Dakota with regard to the public welfare
program and the related areas of juvenile affairs, commitments, and domestic
relations."[15] In a radical departure from the state's long-standing position on
cost reimbursement, the committee took the bold stand of recommending
that the state bear the cost of civil (but not criminal) jurisdiction.

With this high-profile welfare investigation conducted by the committee
throughout most of 1961 and 1962, the release of the committee's August
1962 report, and the 1962 appeal of the *Hankins* case, other state institutions
again rushed to enter the "Indian Problem" debate. On 26 February 1962,
the advisory council to the state commission on Indian affairs convened and
passed a motion by state senator Ramey to make civil jurisdiction the topic
of the council's next meeting. On 15 November 1962, with approximately
six weeks to go before the January opening of the 1963 state legislative session, the state commission on Indian affairs held a conference on state civil
jurisdiction.

Typical of such gatherings sponsored by whites, the civil jurisdiction
agenda followed a predictable format: it allowed the whites to define the
Indian Problem (name who or what is out of line), explain the problem

(present white-biased analyses and statistics), and then solve the Indian Problem (advocate state jurisdiction), while leaving the Lakota attendees on the sidelines to contest the white-skewed definitions, explanations, and solution. Indeed, since the committee had already made its preliminary 26 July 1962 recommendation that the state assume civil jurisdiction, the Lakota knew a few months before that the November 1962 conference would be a cursory, not a genuine, solicitation of Lakota input. In a 20 August 1962 memorandum, Sonosky wrote:

> When the South Dakota Legislature meets, they will again take up the extension of State jurisdiction in Indian Country under Public Law 83-280. There is every reason to believe that the Legislature will be thinking in terms of extending this jurisdiction without first obtaining the consent of the Indian people on the reservations as was done when the Legislature voted to take concurrent jurisdiction over highways through Indian reservations [SB No. 210].[16]

Moreover, on 22 October 1962, two months after the committee report and three weeks before the civil jurisdiction conference, the LRC staff released a twenty-one-page, pro-state jurisdiction report, *Jurisdiction over Indian Country in South Dakota*. While acknowledging that the state had not yet managed to achieve the inevitable, namely, state jurisdiction over Lakota territory, the document rehashed the familiar stable of terminationist arguments, such as denying that South Dakota was a section 6 state; claiming that, compared with South Dakota, the Lakota had an inferior jurisdiction claim or status, despite overwhelming evidence to the contrary; and, by omitting from the report any discussion about Lakota consent, marginalizing consent as if it were little more than a trivial argument made by the Lakota.

Back in 1957, the state and its terminationists had devoted tremendous resources to dismantling Lakota governance—all under the disingenuous guise of solving the Indian Problem. Now in 1962, the Lakota observed a similar mobilization of resources to solve, once again, the "Indian Problem." For a fourth time, the Lakota anticipated yet another jurisdiction bill to be introduced during the upcoming 1963 state legislative session.

The Lakota would not be disappointed. On 8 February 1963, a month after the thirty-eighth state legislative session opened, Representative Olsen introduced a fourth jurisdiction measure, HB No. 791. This measure substantially amended HB No. 659 by abandoning the state's long-held position that made acceptance of jurisdiction over Lakota territory conditional on a federal subsidy. The bill even went beyond the investigating committee's recommendation by accepting the costs not just of certain aspects of civil jurisdiction but of the entirety of both civil and criminal jurisdiction.

When the bill was finally adopted on 3 March 1963, the one major hurdle besides Lakota consent—namely, the U.S. financing of a would-be state responsibility—was a thing of the past. As to the Lakota consent hurdle, not since HB No. 892 had any other state measure, including this one, made jurisdiction conditional on Lakota consent. HB No. 791's repeal of HB No. 892 meant that the 1958 Lakota referenda that conclusively rejected state jurisdiction would now, incredibly, no longer hold.

With all the conditions that had for a decade prevented South Dakota from achieving its elusive goal of terminating the Lakota removed from HB No. 791, the Lakota faced the greatest threat to their nationhood. How they responded through a series of maneuvers that ultimately defeated HB No. 791 in 1964 remains the single, most stunning political upset in U.S.-Native relations in the twentieth century, meriting far more print than this discussion allows.

The basic facts of what happened in 1964 are remarkable. Electorally out numbered, fiscally out-resourced, and living in a state well-known for its hatred of Native people, the Lakota—using highly risky political strategies and tactics to defeat HB No. 791—were awe inspiring, if not brilliant. Invoking the state's referral law, the Lakota eventually collected 20,231 signatures and presented them to the state's secretary on 4 June 1963.[17] By so doing, they adroitly maneuvered the white community into holding a statewide referendum on HB No. 791 that would prevent the law from going into effect until 3 November 1964, the exact date of the referendum.

Approximately seventeen months before the referendum, the Lakota initiated a highly tactical public relations campaign. Since this time the whites would be allowed to vote in the referendum to decide jurisdiction, the Lakota's major focus was to persuade the state's white community to rethink the financial consequences of HB No. 791 and to realize that assuming jurisdiction over Lakota Country was not in the whites' best interests.

The referendum's results proved just how successful their public relations campaign was: 77.6 percent of the 259,678 voters who went to the polls decided against HB No. 791 (58,289 people voted to sustain, while 201,389 voted to reject). Stunned and frankly overwhelmed by the election's results, the state jurisdiction forces were shocked into admitting how severely they had underestimated the Lakota's political savvy and initiative.

Practically speaking, the referendum put an end to further attempts by state termination forces to propose jurisdiction measures. For one thing, as a result of the 1964 referendum, South Dakota became the only state in which its citizens had directly participated in determining whether their government should assume civil and criminal jurisdiction over Native territory. After such a decisive outcome on the state jurisdiction question, it was highly unlikely that the state jurisdiction forces—as covetous as they were of Lakota lands—would have the nerve to submit another jurisdiction bill, since, in all probability, such a bill would subject the electorate to yet another referendum.

In addition, South Dakota's politico-historical pattern had never favored "referred laws"—laws that were so controversial that they had been put to a referendum. Prior to 1964, thirty-one laws passed by the state legislators had been referred to the people since 1908, and the last referred law occurred in 1956. During those forty-eight years, only eight of the thirty-one referred laws were approved. For the state jurisdiction advocates, the chances of political success if a law was referred to the people were obviously not favorable to begin with, but given their defeat in the 1964 referendum, the idea of putting a similar bill to the electorate held them in abeyance.

Finally, the state termination forces have never fully recovered from the 1964 Lakota-engineered upset, especially since PL 83-280 was amended in April 1968 to include a Native consent provision.[18] That is not to say that the ongoing self-determination struggle between the Lakota Nation and South Dakota is settled. It has raged on ever since and on multiple fronts: the 1973 Wounded Knee Conflict, the Black Hills Land Returns bill, the contentious gaming compact negotiations between the Lakota and South Dakota, and the Lakota-S.D. litigation over taxation powers and natural resource management and use.

Yet the days are long past when whites could arbitrarily introduce a bill to assume state jurisdiction. Indeed, as the ongoing story of the Lakota Nation since the 1960s readily shows, the principle of Lakota consent is now an expected norm. For some, it may not be any less controversial, but, like it or not, Lakota consent is an established reality in South Dakota state politics. For this, we have the Lakota People and the Lakota leaders of the 1950s and 1960s—the generations of our parents and grandparents—to thank.

Hecetu welo

Notes

1. Beckwith, *South Dakota Stock Grower*, 3.

2. The act authorizes the Interior Secretary to enter into contracts with states or territories to provide education, medical, and social services to Native Peoples.

3. Burnette, *Tortured Americans*, 58.

4. Ibid.

5. Ibid., 59.

6. SB No. 210 was introduced on 30 January 1959. On 9 February 1959, the state senate approved SB No. 210 with 35 Yes votes, 0 No, 0 Absent and Not Voting, and 0 Excused. On 2 March 1959, the state representatives approved SB No. 210 with an amendment by a vote of 70 Yes, 0 No, 4 Absent and Not Voting, and 1 Excused. Later, on 6 March 1959, the senate concurred with the house's amendment with 34 Yes votes, 0 No, 0 Absent and Not Voting, and 1 Excused.

7. HB No. 659 was introduced on 19 January 1961. On 22 February 1961, the house passed HB No. 659 by a vote of 72 Yes, 0 No, 1 Absent and Not Voting, and 2 Excused. On 2 March 1961, the senate passed HB No. 659 by a vote of 33 Yes, 0 No, 1 Absent and Not Voting, and 1 Excused.

8. HB No. 791 was introduced on 8 February 1963. On 27 February 1963, the house passed HB No. 791 by a vote of 61 Yes, 9 No, 2 Absent and Not Voting, and 3 Excused, while the senate passed HB No. 791 by a vote of 22 YES, 11 NO, 0 Absent and Not Voting, and 2 Excused.

9. Sec. 4 of HB No. 659.

10. There were three proposed amendments to the original HB No. 659 bill: 1) assume only criminal jurisdiction over Lakota territory irrespective of costs; 2) assume complete criminal and civil jurisdiction over Lakota territory but conditional on a U.S. subsidy; and 3) incorporate Lakota consent. While some degree of the first two amendments can be found in the approved version of HB No. 659, the Lakota consent proposal was never seriously considered.

11. Sec. 3 of HB No. 659.

12. Interior Department News Release, 23 March 1961.

13. For example, a S.D. newspaper [*Sioux Falls Argus Leader*] reported that the interim investigating committee "decided at its inception that welfare on Indian reservations was the Welfare Department's biggest headache" (26 July 1962), Box 176, EYB Papers.

14. Interim Investigating Committee, 9.

15. Ibid., 17.

16. Marvin Sonosky, Memorandum No. 32, "Preparation to Oppose Extension of State Jurisdiction over South Dakota Indian Reservations," 1, LJC.

17. South Dakota's constitution provides that 5 percent of the qualified electors is required to invoke either an initiative or a referendum. State statute defines the calculation of this number as 5 percent of the total votes cast for governor at the last

gubernatorial election. Thus, because the total votes cast in the 1962 gubernatorial election was 256,120, the Lakota needed at least 12,806 signatures to refer HB No. 791. They exceeded that number by 7,425 signatures.

18. That is not to say the 1968 Indian Civil Rights Act (ICRA) corrected all the political damage that PL 83-280 incurred on Native Nations. In their treatment of federal Indian law, David H. Getches and Charles F. Wilkinson examined a few of the ICRA's more significant deficiencies or limitations with respect to PL 83-280:

> The beneficial impact of the 1968 amendments to PL 83-280 should not be overemphasized, however. The Indian consent provision was not made retroactive, and thus earlier assumptions of state jurisdiction over Indian objections were not affected. Moreover, it did not enable Indians who had consented to state jurisdiction under a state-initiated consent provision to reconsider their decisions (*Federal Indian Law,* 357).

Having stopped South Dakota from successfully assuming criminal and civil jurisdiction over their territory, the Lakota fell within the pale of the 1968 ICRA, at least on the issues of termination and self-governance.

Public Law 83-280

An Act

To confer jurisdiction on the States of California, Minnesota, Nebraska, Oregon, and Wisconsin, with respect to criminal offenses and civil causes of action committed or arising on Indian reservations within such States, and for other purposes.

Be it enacted by the Senate and House of Representatives of the United States of America in Congress assembled, That chapter 53 of title 18, United States Code, is hereby amended by inserting at the end of the chapter analysis preceding section 1151 of such title the following new item:

"1162. State jurisdiction over offenses committed by or against Indians in the Indian country."

Sec. 2. Title 18, United States Code, is hereby amended by inserting in chapter 53 thereof immediately after section 1161 a new section, to be designated as section 1162, as follows:

"§ 1162. State jurisdiction over offenses committed by or against Indians in the Indian country

"(a) Each of the States listed in the following table shall have jurisdiction over offenses committed by or against Indians in the areas of Indian country listed opposite the name of the State to the same extent that such State has jurisdiction over offenses committed elsewhere within the State, and the criminal laws of such State shall have the same force and effect within such Indian country as they have elsewhere within the State:

State of	Indian country affected
California	All Indian country within the State
Minnesota	All Indian country within the State, except the Red Lake Reservation

Nebraska	All Indian country within the State
Oregon	All Indian country within the State, except the Warm Springs Reservation
Wisconsin	All Indian country within the State, except the Menominee Reservation

"(b) Nothing in this section shall authorize the alienation, encumbrance, or taxation of any real or personal property, including water rights, belonging to any Indian or any Indian tribe, band, or community that is held in trust by the United States or is subject to a restriction against alienation imposed by the United States; or shall authorize regulation of the use of such property in a manner inconsistent with any Federal treaty, agreement, or statute or with any regulation made pursuant thereto; or shall deprive any Indian or any Indian tribe, band, or community of any right, privilege, or immunity afforded under Federal treaty, agreement, or statute with respect to hunting, trapping, or fishing or the control, licensing, or regulation thereof.

"(c) The provisions of sections 1152 and 1153 of this chapter shall not be applicable within the areas of Indian country listed in subsection (a) of this section."

Sec. 3. Chapter 85 of Title 28, United States Code, is hereby amended by inserting at the end of the chapter analysis preceding section 1331 of such title the following new item:

"1360. State civil jurisdiction in actions to which Indians are parties."

Sec. 4. Title 28, United States Code, is hereby amended by inserting in chapter 85 thereof immediately after section 1359 a new section, to be designated as section 1360, as follows:

"§ 1360. State civil jurisdiction in actions to which Indians are parties

"(a) Each of the States listed in the following table shall have jurisdiction over civil causes of action between Indians or to which Indians are parties which arise in the areas of Indian country listed opposite the name of the State to the same extent that such State has jurisdiction over other civil causes of action, and those civil laws of such State that are of general application to private persons or private property shall have the same force and effect within such Indian country as they have elsewhere within the State:

State of	Indian country affected
California	All Indian country within the State
Minnesota	All Indian country within the State, except the Red Lake Reservation
Nebraska	All Indian country within the State
Oregon	All Indian country within the State, except the Warm Springs Reservation
Wisconsin	All Indian country within the State, except the Menominee Reservation

"(b) Nothing in this section shall authorize the alienation, encumbrance, or taxation of any real or personal property, including water rights, belonging to any Indian or any Indian tribe, band, or community that is held in trust by the United States or is subject to a restriction against alienation imposed by the United States; or shall authorize regulation of the use of such property in a manner inconsistent with any Federal treaty, agreement, or statute or with any regulation made pursuant thereto; or shall confer jurisdiction upon the State to adjudicate, in probate proceedings or otherwise, the ownership or right to possession of such property or any interest therein.

"(c) Any tribal ordinance or custom heretofore or hereafter adopted by an Indian tribe, band, or community in the exercise of any authority which it may possess shall, if not inconsistent with any applicable civil law of the State, be given full force and effect in the determination of civil causes of action pursuant to this section."

Repeal.

Sec. 5. Section 1 of the Act of October 5, 1949 (63 Stat. 705, ch. 604), is hereby repealed, but such repeal shall not affect any proceedings heretofore instituted under that section.

Sec. 6. Notwithstanding the provisions of any Enabling Act for the admission of a State, the consent of the United States is hereby given to the people of any State to amend, where necessary, their State constitution or existing statutes, as the case may be, to remove any legal impediment to the assumption of civil and criminal jurisdiction in accordance with the provisions of this Act: *Provided,* That the provisions of this Act shall not become effective with respect to such assumption of jurisdiction by any such State until the people thereof have appropriately amended their State constitution or statutes as the case may be.

Sec. 7. The consent of the United States is hereby given to any other State not having jurisdiction with respect to criminal offenses or civil causes of action, or with respect to both, as provided for in this Act, to assume jurisdiction at such time and in such manner as the people of the State shall, by affirmative legislative action, obligate and bind the State to assumption thereof.

Approved August 15, 1953.

Senate Bill No. 278

Relating to Jurisdiction of Crimes on Indian Reservations

AN ACT Entitled, An Act Amending SDC 34.0502, Relating to Jurisdiction Upon Indian Reservations Within the State of South Dakota.

Be It Enacted by the Legislature of the State of South Dakota:

Section 1. That SDC 34.0502 be, and the same is hereby amended to read as follows:

34.0502 Exclusive jurisdiction and authority to arrest, prosecute, convict, and punish all persons who shall commit any act in violation of the penal laws of the United States upon any Indian Reservation within this state shall be given and relinquished to the United States and the officers and courts thereof, whenever such jurisdiction shall be assumed by the United States, but no costs or charges, incurred in the United States courts, in the prosecution of offenses committed upon any Indian Reservation shall be chargeable to this state, but whenever any of said acts committed by any person upon any Indian Reservation within this state shall constitute a crime under any law of the state of South Dakota, concurrent jurisdiction is hereby expressly reserved to the state of South Dakota to arrest, prosecute, convict, and punish any person committing any offense under the laws of the state of South Dakota even though the acts constituting such offense may also constitute an offense under the laws of the United States of America.

Whenever the United States has assumed jurisdiction to arrest, prosecute, convict, and punish all persons who shall commit any act in violation of the penal laws of the United States upon any Indian Reservation within this state, as a result of this cession of such jurisdiction by the state of South Dakota, and shall later relinquish such assumed jurisdiction, such jurisdiction shall revert to the state of South Dakota, and this act shall operate to accept the relinquishment by the United States of jurisdiction over persons other than Indians for the commission of crimes upon Indian Reservations contained in 18 United States Code Annotated, Section 1153, and to reinvest such jurisdiction in the state of South Dakota.

In the absence of treaty or statute of the United States, the state of South Dakota shall have jurisdiction to arrest, prosecute, convict, and punish any person committing any offense under the laws of the state of South Dakota on any Indian Reservation or in the Indian Country.

Approved March 2, 1951

House Bill No. 721

Introduced by Committee on Indian Affairs

A BILL

FOR AN ACT ENTITLED, An Act relating to the Indian Country and assuming and accepting jurisdiction by the state of South Dakota of all civil and criminal causes of action arising therein.

Be It Enacted by the Legislature of the State of South Dakota:

Section 1. The state of South Dakota, in accordance with the provisions of 67 Statutes at large, page 589 (Public law 280), hereby assumes and accepts jurisdiction of all criminal and civil causes of action arising in Indian country, as Indian country is defined by Title 18 USCA [U.S. Code Annotated] section 1151, the provisions of Chapter 106 of the Session Laws of the State of South Dakota for 1901, as amended, or any law to the contrary, notwithstanding.

House Bill No. 892
(as originally introduced)

Introduced by Committee on Indian Affairs

A BILL

FOR AN ACT ENTITLED, An Act relating to assuming jurisdiction by the State of South Dakota of all criminal offenses in violation of state law committed in the counties of Stanley and Lyman, which contain the Lower Brule Indian Reservation, and preserving existing hunting and fishing rights and providing for Federal Assistance.

Be It Enacted by the Legislature of the State of South Dakota:

WHEREAS, there is contained within the borders of Stanley and Lyman Counties in the state of South Dakota the Lower Brule Indian Reservation; and

WHEREAS, the state of South Dakota does not have jurisdiction of crimes committed on the trust or restricted lands within said reservation when committed by or against the Indians; and

WHEREAS, Congress of the United States has heretofore passed enabling legislation whereby jurisdiction with respect to criminal offenses may be conferred on the states as provided in Sections 6 and 7 of Public Law 280 of the 83rd Congress (67 Stat. 588): and

WHEREAS, the Lower Brule Tribe of Sioux Indians, a duly constituted and organized tribe under the Indian Reorganization Act otherwise known as Public Law 383, enacted June 18, 1934 (48 Stat. 984), has through its governing body expressed a desire that state jurisdiction of criminal offenses committed on said reservation be assumed by the state of South Dakota;

therefore,

Section 1. That the state of South Dakota shall assume jurisdiction over all criminal offenses on Indian land within the counties of Stanley and Lyman in the state of South Dakota, the counties which contain within their borders the Lower Brule Indian Reservation.

Section 2. All criminal offenses occurring on Indian lands within such counties shall be dealt with and proceeded against in like manner as if they had occurred on other lands within such respective counties.

Section 3. Nothing in this act shall deprive any enrolled member of said Tribe of any right, privilege, or immunity afforded under Federal Treaty, agreement, or statute with respect to hunting, trapping, or fishing or the control, licensing, or regulation thereof.

Section 4. Authority is hereby given to the County boards of said respective counties to assume such criminal jurisdiction by resolution spread upon its minutes or to enter into any permitted contract with the Bureau of Indian Affairs of the United States Department of Interior whereby such counties might be reimbursed for added costs in connection with the assuming of jurisdiction. The rates or terms of any such contract shall so far as possible be on the basis of and take into consideration the untaxed Indian lands and the proportion such land bears to the total land area of said re[s]pective counties and the propertion [sic] the law enforcement costs bear to the total government costs of said respective counties. This act shall not be effective unless a resolution on the part of the affected county is spread on the minutes of its County board proceedings to the effect that it has assumed jurisdiction and if such jurisdiction is based on a negotiated contract with the Bureau of Indian Affairs its terms shall be adequately set forth.

Chapter 319
(House Bill No. 892 as signed into law)

Assumption of Civil and Criminal Jurisdiction in Indian Country

AN ACT Entitled, An Act relating to the Indian Country, the assumption and acceptance of jurisdiction by the state of South Dakota of all civil and criminal causes of action arising therein, providing procedure before such assumption and acceptance by tribes and certain counties becomes effective, and protecting tribal members with respect to their hunting, trapping, and fishing rights.

Be It Enacted by the Legislature of the State of South Dakota:

Section 1. In accordance with the provisions of 67 statutes at large, page 589, Public Law 280, and as Indian Country is defined by Title 18 USCA, Section 1151, the provisions of Chapter 106 of the Session Laws of the State of South Dakota for 1901, as amended, or any law to the contrary, notwithstanding, the state of South Dakota assumes and accepts jurisdiction of all criminal and civil causes of action arising in Indian Country under the provisions of this Act as hereinafter set forth.

Section 2. All criminal offenses occurring on Indian lands within such counties shall be dealt with and proceeded against in like manner as if they had occurred on other lands within such respective counties.

Section 3. Nothing in this act shall deprive any enrolled member of said Tribe of any right, privilege, or immunity afforded in Federal Treaty, agreement, or statute with respect to hunting, trapping, or fishing or the control, licensing, or regulation thereof.

Section 4. Jurisdiction shall not be deemed assumed or accepted by this state in any county of South Dakota unless and until a resolution assuming and accepting the same is adopted by the Board of County Commissioners of any county containing Indian Country. Prior to the adoption of such a resolution, the County Commissioners shall negotiate and contract with the Federal Bureau of Indian Affairs of the United States Department of Interior for reimbursement of any authorized and appropriated federal funds for the added costs to any county in connection with the assumption of said jurisdiction. The rates or terms of any such contract shall so far as possible be on the basis of and take into consideration the untaxed Indian lands and the proportion such land bears to the total land area of said respective counties and the proportion of the law enforcement costs bear to the total governmental costs of said respective counties.

Section 5. Be it further provided that no assumption of civil or criminal jurisdiction shall become effective under the provisions of this Act until the Tribal Council of a Tribe over which state jurisdiction is to be taken, shall have considered a referendum in which all persons eligible to vote at elections held for the purposes of electing officers of such Tribe, shall have been given an opportunity to approve or disapprove such assumption of jurisdiction. A majority of the persons so voting in such a referendum must cast affirmative votes in favor thereof before such approval shall be given, and the Tribal Council shall then notify the Board of County Commissioners of the counties concerned as to the results of such referendum. Provided, however, that if the Tribe has failed to take action as above prescribed, within one year from and after October 1, 1957, it shall be deemed that the referendum has been dispensed with and that the tribe has consented to and does approve the assumption of jurisdiction herein provided, and that the county or counties concerned may then proceed as set forth in Section 4 of this Act.

Approved March 18, 1957

Chapter 144
(Senate Bill No. 210)

Accepting Concurrent Police Jurisdiction Over Certain Highways as Ceded by the United States

AN ACT Entitled, An Act accepting concurrent police jurisdiction over certain public highways located in the state of South Dakota.

Be It Enacted by the Legislature of the State of South Dakota:

Section 1. The United States of America having ceded to the state of South Dakota concurrent police jurisdiction excepting the ten major crimes as defined by 18 USCA Section 1153, unless automobile accidents are involved, over all public highways or portions thereof, including rights-of-way, located within the state of South Dakota:

(1) which are established through any Indian Reservation or through any lands which have been allotted in severalty to any individual Indian, under any laws or treaties, but which have not been conveyed to the allottee with full power of alienation, and;

(2) which were established or which are maintained by the joint participation of the United States and the state of South Dakota.

Section 2. The state of South Dakota hereby accepts such jurisdiction.

Approved March 11, 1959

Chapter 464
(House Bill No. 659)

Assuming Jurisdiction of Offenses and Actions Arising in Indian Country

AN ACT Entitled, An Act relating to the Indian Country and assuming and accepting jurisdiction by the State of South Dakota of all criminal offenses and civil causes of action arising therein, and authorizing certain county commissioners and the State Board of Finance to contract and receive funds for additional costs of such assumption, and to repeal sections 65.0805, 65.0806, 65.0807, 65.0808, 65.0809, and 65.0810 of the Supplement to the South Dakota Code of 1939.

Be It Enacted by the Legislature of the State of South Dakota:

Section 1. The State of South Dakota, in accordance with the provisions of 67 Statutes at Large, page 589 (Public Law 280), hereby assumes and accepts jurisdiction of all criminal offenses and civil causes of action arising in the Indian Country located within this State, as Indian Country is defined by Title 18 United States Code Annotated, section 1151, and obligates and binds this State to the assumption thereof, the provisions of Chapter 106 of the Session Laws of the State of South Dakota for 1901, as amended, or any other law of this State to the contrary, notwithstanding.

Section 2. The county commissioners of those counties of this State in which there is located Indian Country as affected by this Act, and the State Board of Finance shall be, and they are hereby authorized to accept grants-in-aid, and to negotiate, and contract with the Federal Bureau of Indian Affairs of the United States Department of Interior for reimbursement of any authorized and appropriated federal funds for the added costs to such counties and this State in connection with such assumption of jurisdiction.

Section 3. That SDC 1960 Supp., sections 65.0805, 65.0806, 65.0807, 65.0808, 65.0809, and 65.0810 be, and the same are, hereby repealed.

Section 4. Except as to criminal offenses and civil causes of action arising on any highways, as the term is defined in SDC 28.0101, the jurisdiction provided for in Section 1 herein shall not be deemed assumed or accepted by this State, and Sections 1 and 3 of this Act shall not be considered in effect, unless and until the Governor of the State of South Dakota, if satisfied that the United States of America has made proper provision for the reimbursement to this State and its counties for the added costs in connection with the assumption of said jurisdiction, has issued his proper proclamation duly filed with the Secretary of State declaring the said jurisdiction be assumed and accepted.

Approved March 9, 1961

Chapter 467
(House Bill No. 791)

Assumption by South Dakota of Unrestricted Jurisdiction in Indian Country

AN ACT Entitled, An Act to amend Chapter 464 of the South Dakota Session of Laws of 1961 relating to jurisdiction in Indian Country.

Be It Enacted by the Legislature of the State of South Dakota: That Chapter 464 of the South Dakota Session of 1961 Laws be amended to read as follows:

Section 1. The State of South Dakota, in accordance with the provisions of 67 Statutes at Large, page 589 (Public Law 280), hereby assumes and accepts jurisdiction of all criminal offenses and civil causes of action arising in the Indian Country located within this State, as Indian Country is defined by Title 18 United States Code Annotated, section 1151, and obligates and binds this State to the assumption thereof, the provisions of Chapter 106 of the Session of Laws of the State of South Dakota for 1901, as amended, or any other law of this State to the contrary, notwithstanding.

Section 2. The county commissioners of those counties of this State in which there is located Indian Country as affected by this Act, and the State Board of Finance shall be, and they are hereby authorized to accept grants-in-aid, and to negotiate, and contract with the Federal Bureau of Indian Affairs of the United States Department of Interior for reimbursement of any authorized and appropriated federal funds for the added costs to such counties and this State in connection with such assumption of jurisdiction.

Section 3. That SDC 1960 Supp., sections 65.0805, 65.0806, 65.0807, 65.0808, 65.0809, and 65.0810 be, and the same are, hereby repealed.

Approved March 15, 1963

Bibliography

A. Papers References

Berry, E. Y. Papers (EYB Papers). Black Hills State University, Spearfish, S.Dak.

Gubbrud, Archie. Papers (AGP). University of South Dakota, Vermillion, S.Dak.

Lakota Jurisdiction Collection (LJC). Rosebud, S.Dak.: Rosebud Sioux Reservation, 1950–1965.

Valandra, Cato W. Papers (CWV Papers). Vermillion, S.Dak.: University of South Dakota.

Valandra, Edward C. Papers (ECV Papers). Rosebud, S. Dak. Rosebud Sioux Reservation.

B. Government Documents

Atkins, J. D. C. House Executive Document No. 1, Fiftieth Cong., 1st Sess., Serial 2542, 19–21. Quoted in Frances Paul Purcha, ed. *Documents of United States Indian Policy.* Lincoln: University of Nebraska Press, 1975, 176.

Constitution of South Dakota.

Education, Health, and Welfare Committee. Minutes of the Education, Health, and Welfare Committee, South Dakota Legislative Research Council, Pierre, S.Dak., 24 October 1955.

———. *Report of the Committee on Education, Health and Welfare to the Executive Board,* South Dakota Legislative Research Council. Pierre, S.Dak. September 1956.

Hoover Commission. *Social Security and Education: Indian Affairs.* Eighty-first Cong. 1st Sess., H. Doc. No. 129, Report No. 15, 21 March 1949.

Interim Investigating Committee. *Report to the 1963 South Dakota Legislature: A Report of an Investigation of the South Dakota Department of Public Welfare.* Pierre, S.Dak.: Executive Board of the State Legislative Research Council, 1962.

Lower Brule Sioux Tribe. Lower Brule Sioux Tribe Resolution No. 57–207. Lower Brule Sioux Reservation: Office of the Secretary of the Lower Brule Tribe, July 1957.

Oglala Sioux Tribe. Oglala Sioux Tribe Resolution No. 34–49. Pine Ridge, Pine Ridge Reservation: Office of the Secretary of the OST, 1949.

———. Oglala Sioux Tribe Resolution No. 147–50 Pine Ridge, Pine Ridge Reservation: Office of the Secretary of the OST, 1950.

Rosebud Sioux Tribe. Rosebud Sioux Tribe Resolution No. 58–50. Rosebud, Rosebud Sioux Reservation: Office of the Secretary of the RST, July 1958.

———. Rosebud Sioux Tribe Resolution No. 86–34. Rosebud, Rosebud Sioux Reservation: Office of the Secretary of the RST, 1986.

Senate Subcommittee on Indian Education of the Committee on Labor and Public Welfare. *The Education of American Indians: The Organizational Question.* November 1969, Ninety-first Cong. 1st Sess., Vol. 4. Washington, D.C.: GPO, 1970.

South Dakota House Bill No. 106. An Act Ceding to the United States of America Jurisdiction over Criminal Offenses Committed upon Indian Reservations within the State of South Dakota [chapter 106, Session of Laws, 1901]. Seventh Session (1901), Legislative Assembly, State of South Dakota.

South Dakota House Bill No. 721. An Act Relating to the Indian Country and Assuming and Accepting Jurisdiction by the State of South Dakota of all Civil and Criminal Causes of Action Arising therein. Thirty-fifth Session (1957), Legislative Assembly, State of South Dakota.

South Dakota House Bill No. 892. An Act Relating to Indian Country, the Assumption and Acceptance of Jurisdiction by the State of South Dakota of all Civil and Criminal Causes of Action Arising therein, Providing Procedure before Such Assumption and Acceptance by Tribes and Certain Counties Becomes Effective, and Protecting Tribal Members with Respect to their Hunting, Trapping, and Fishing Rights [chapter 319, Session of Laws, 1957]. Thirty-fifth Session (1957), Legislative Assembly, State of South Dakota.

South Dakota House Bill No. 659. An Act Relating to the Indian Country and Assuming and Accepting Jurisdiction by the State of South Dakota of all Criminal Offenses and Civil Causes of Action Arising therein, and Authorizing Certain County Commissioners and the State Board of Finance to Contract and Receive Funds for Additional Costs of Such Assumption, and to Repeal Sections 65.0805, 65.0806, 65.0807, 65.0808, 65.0809, and 65.0810 of the 1960 Supplement to the South Dakota Code of 1939 [chapter 464, Session of Laws]. 37th session (1961), Legislative Assembly, State of South Dakota.

South Dakota Senate Bill No. 278. An Act Amending SDC 34.0502, Relating to Jurisdiction upon Indian Reservations within the State of South Dakota [chapter 187, Session of Laws]. Thirty-second Session (1951), Legislative Assembly, State of South Dakota.

South Dakota Legislative Research Council. Minutes of the Legislative Research Council, No. 21. 16 May 1955.

————. *Jurisdiction over Indian Country in South Dakota.* Staff Report, 22 October 1962.

U.S. Code Congressional and Administrative News. Eighty-third Cong., 1st sess. 2:2409–14. St. Paul, Minn.: West Publishing and Brooklyn, N.Y.: Edward Thompson, 1953.

U.S. Code Congressional Service. Eightieth Cong. 2d sess.2:983–end. St. Paul, Minn.: West Publishing and Brooklyn, N.Y.: Edward Thompson, 1948.

U.S. Congress, House. *Report with Respect to the House Resolution Authorizing the Committee on Interior and Insular Affairs to Conduct an Investigation of the Bureau of Indian Affairs.* Eighty-second Cong. 2d sess. Report No. 2503, Calendar No. 790. Washington, D.C.: GPO, 1953.

U.S. Interior Department, Bureau of Indian Affairs. Commissioner of *Indian Affairs Annual Report,* 1920.

————. *OST Resolutions Binder 1948, 1949, 1950.* Pine Ridge Sioux Reservation, S. Dak.: Pine Ridge Agency.

————. *OST Resolutions Binder 1951, 1952, 1953.* Pine Ridge Sioux Reservation, S. Dak.: Pine Ridge Agency.

————. *OST Resolutions Binder 1954, 1955, 1956.* Pine Ridge Sioux Reservation, S. Dak.: Pine Ridge Agency.

————. "Interior Department Opposes Bill Providing Federal Subsidy to States for Law Enforcement on Indian Reservations." News release, 23 March 1961.

U.S. Public Law 280. 1953. 83rd Cong., 1st sess. (15 August 1953).

U.S. Statutes at Large 24 (1887): 388–91. *General Allotment Act.*

U.S. Statutes at Large 25 (1889): 676. *Enabling Act of 1889.*

C. Court Cases

Cherokee Nation v. Georgia. 1831. 30 U.S. 1, 8 L. Ed. 25, quoted in David H. Getches and Charles F. Wilkinson, *Federal Indian Law: Cases and Materials,* 2d ed. (St. Paul, Minn.: West Publishing Company, 1986), 46–50.

Iron Crow v. Ogallala Sioux Tribe of the Pine Ridge Reservation. 129 F. Supp. 15 (D.S.D. 1955).

————. 231 F. 2d 89 (1956).

Oglala Sioux Tribe of the Pine Ridge Reservation v. Barta. 146 F. Supp. 917 (1956).

Petition of Matthew High Pine et al. Appellant's Brief, Docket No. 9708, 1958. McKusick Law Library, University of South Dakota, Vermillion.

————. Respondent's Brief. Docket No. 9708, 1959. McKusick Law Library, University of South Dakota, Vermillion.

————. 78 S.D. 121, 99 N.W.2d 38 (1959).

Rosebud Sioux Tribe v. State of South Dakota. 900 F.2d 1164 (1990).

United States v. Kagama. 118 U.S. 375, 6 S.Ct. 1109, 30 L.Ed. 228, quoted in David H.

Getches and Charles F. Wilkinson, *Federal Indian Law,* 2d ed. St. Paul, Minn.: West Publishing Company, 197.

Williams v. Lee. 358 U.S. 217 (1959).

D. Publications

Abourezk, James G. *Advise & Dissent: Memoirs of South Dakota and the U.S. Senate.* Chicago: Lawrence Hill Books, 1989.

Beckwith, Louis. "Here & There with the Wagon Boss." *South Dakota Stockgrower* 12, no. 6 (July 1958): 3.

Black, Henry Campbell. *Black's Law Dictionary,* 5th ed. St. Paul, Minn.: West Publishing Company, 1979.

Brophy, William A., and Sophie Alberle. *The Indian, America's Unfinished Business: Report of the Commission on the Rights, Liberties, and Responsibilities of the American Indian.* Norman: University of Oklahoma Press, 1966.

Burnette, Robert. *Tortured Americans.* Englewood Cliffs, N.J.: Prentice-Hall, 1979.

Burt, Larry. *Tribalism in Crisis: Federal Indian Policy, 1953–1961.* Albuquerque: University of New Mexico Press, 1982.

Cahn, Edgar S., and David W. Hearne, eds. *Our Brother's Keepers: The Indian in White America.* Washington, D.C.: New Community Press, 1969.

Cohen, Felix S., *Handbook of Federal Indian Law.* Albuquerque: University of New Mexico Press, 1942.

Congressional Quarterly: Almanac 83rd Congress 1st Session—1953. Vol. 9. Washington, D.C.: Congressional Quarterly News Features.

Congressional Quarterly: Almanac 83rd Congress 2nd Session—1954. Vol. 10. Washington, D.C.: Congressional Quarterly News Features.

Congressional Quarterly: Almanac 84th Congress 1st Session—1955. Vol. 11. Washington, D.C.: Congressional Quarterly News Features.

Congressional Quarterly: Almanac 84th Congress 2nd Session—1956. Vol. 12. Washington, D.C.: Congressional Quarterly News Features.

Congressional Quarterly: Almanac 85th Congress 1st Session—1957. Vol. 13. Washington, D.C.: Congressional Quarterly.

Congressional Quarterly: Almanac 85th Congress 2nd Session—1958. Vol. 14. Washington, D.C.: Congressional Quarterly.

Congressional Quarterly: Almanac 86th Congress 1st Session—1959. Vol. 15. Washington, D.C.: Congressional Quarterly.

Congressional Quarterly: Almanac 86th Congress 2nd Session—1960. Vol. 16. Washington, D.C.: Congressional Quarterly.

Congressional Quarterly: Almanac 87th Congress 1st Session—1961. Vol. 17. Washington, D.C.: Congressional Quarterly.

Congressional Quarterly. *Members of Congress since 1789.* Washington, D.C.: Congressional Quarterly, 1977.

Daniels, Walter M., ed. *American Indians.* The Reference Shelf Series, Vol. 29, No. 4. New York: The H. W. Wilson Company, 1957.

Davis, Laurence. "Criminal Jurisdiction over Indian Country in Arizona." *Arizona Law Review* no. 1 (Spring 1959): 62–101.

Deloria, Vine, Jr. *Custer Died for Your Sins: An Indian Manifesto.* New York: Avon Books, 1969.

———. "The Twentieth Century." In *Red Men and Hat Wearers: Viewpoints in Indian History.* Ed. Daniel Tyler. Boulder, Colo.: Pruett Publishing Company, 1976, 155–166.

Ducheneaux, Frank. "Frank Ducheneaux's Rebuttal to Matthews' Blast at Rehab Program." *South Dakota Stock Grower* (15 December 1956), Vol. 10, No. 11: 10–10A.

Faragher, John M. *Rereading Frederick Jackson Turner.* New York: Henry Holt and Company, 1994.

Farber, W. O., Philip A. Odeen, and Robert A. Tschetter. *Indians, Law Enforcement, and Local Government: A Study of the Impact on South Dakota Local Government with Special Reference to Law Enforcement.* Vermillion: University of South Dakota Government Research Bureau, 1957.

Fey, Harold E. "Our National Indian Policy." *The Christian Century,* 30 March 1955, 72 (13): 395–97.

Fixico, Donald. *Termination and Relocation: Federal Indian Policy, 1945–1960.* Albuquerque: University of New Mexico Press, 1986.

Getches, David H., and Charles F. Wilkinson. *Federal Indian Law, Cases, and Materials.* 2d ed. St. Paul, Minn: West Publishing Company, 1986.

Hauptman, Laurence M. *The Iroquois Struggle for Survival: World War II to Red Power.* Syracuse, N.Y.: Syracuse University Press, 1986.

Hoover, Herbert T. "The Sioux Agreement of 1889 and Its Aftermath." *South Dakota History* 19 (1989): 56–94.

Institute of Indian Studies. *Program and Proceedings of the Conference on Indian Affairs.* Vermillion: University of South Dakota, 1955.

———. "Law Enforcement Study Progresses." *News Report* 3 (1956): 2–3.

———. *Program and Proceedings, Third Annual Conference on Indian Affairs.* Vermillion: University of South Dakota, 1957.

———. *Program and Proceedings, Sixth Annual Conference on Indian Affairs.* Vermillion: University of South Dakota, 1960.

Karolevitz, Robert F. *Challenge: The South Dakota Story.* Sioux Falls, S. Dak.: Brevet Press, 1975.

Lawson, Michael L. "Reservoir and Reservation: The Oahe Dam and the Cheyenne River Sioux." *South Dakota Historical Collections* 37 (1974): 102–223.

———. *Dammed Indians: The Pick-Sloan Plan and the Missouri River Sioux, 1944–1980.* Norman: University of Oklahoma Press, 1982.

———. "The Fractionated Estate: The Problem of American Indian Heirship." *South Dakota History* 21 (1991): 1–42.

Lee, Bob, and Dick Williams. *Last Grass Frontier: The South Dakota Stock Grower Heritage*. Sturgis, S. Dak.: Black Hills Publishers, 1964.

Limerick, Patricia N. *The Legacy of Conquest: The Unbroken Past of the American Frontier*. New York: W. W. Norton, 1987.

Madigan, La Verne. *The American Indian Relocation Program*. New York: Association on American Indian Affairs, 1956.

Matthews, James J. "Attention Fellow Tax Payers." *South Dakota Stock Grower* 10 (November 1956): 14B.

Mooney, James. *The Ghost-Dance Religion and Wounded Knee*. New York: Dover Publications, 1973.

Ornstein, Norman, Thomas E. Mann, Michael J. Malbin, Allen Schick, and John F. Bibby. *Vital Statistics on Congress, 1984–1985 Edition*. Washington, D.C.: American Enterprise Institute for Public Policy Research, 1984.

Purcha, Francis P., ed. *Documents of United States Indian Policy*. Lincoln: University of Nebraska Press, 1975.

Reifel, Ben. "Future of South Dakota Indian." *Museum News* 15 (6): 1–6. W. H. Over Museum, University of South Dakota, Vermillion, June 1954, Box 168, EYB Papers.

Richards, Clinton G. "Federal Jurisdiction over Criminal Matters Involving Indians." *South Dakota Law Review* 2 (Spring 1957): 48–58.

Roberts, W. O. "The Vanishing Homeland." *Indian Affairs*, January 1957, 19:3–4, Box 252, EYB Papers.

Schell, Herbert S. *History of South Dakota*. 3d ed. Lincoln: University of Nebraska Press, 1961.

Schulte, Steven C. "Removing the Yoke of Government: E. Y. Berry and the Origins of Indian Termination Policy." *South Dakota History* 14 (1984): 48–67.

Schusky, Ernest L. "Political and Religious Systems in Dakota Culture." *The Modern Sioux: Social Systems and Reservation Culture*. Ed. Ethel Nurge. Lincoln: University of Nebraska Press, 1970.

South Dakota Bar Association. "Report of Committee on Criminal Law." *South Dakota Bar Journal* 25 (July 1956): 43.

———. "Report of the Twenty-fourth Annual Meeting of the State Bar of South Dakota." *South Dakota Bar Journal* 25 (October 1956): 37–39.

South Dakota Stockgrowers Association. "Resolutions Passed at the 62nd Annual Convention of the South Dakota Stock Growers Association." *South Dakota Stockgrower* 7, no. 4 (June 1953): 21–23.

———. "Stock Growers Get New Contracts on Indian Lands." *South Dakota Stockgrower* 7, no. 6 (August 1953): 14.

———. *South Dakota Stockgrower* 15 December 1956.

South Dakota Stockgrowers Association Resolution No. 1. 66th Annual Convention, 1957.

Taylor, Graham D. *The New Deal and American Indian Tribalism: The Administra-tion of the Indian Reorganization Act, 1934–45.* Lincoln: University of Nebraska Press, 1980.

Tyler, S. Lyman. *A History of Indian Policy.* Washington, D.C.: GPO, 1973.

University of Chicago, Department of Anthropology. "Federal Indian Legislation and Policies, 1956 Workshop on American Indian Affairs." Photocopy. 1956.

Van Every, Dale. *Disinherited: The Lost Birthright of the American Indian.* New York: William Morrow, 1966.

Washburn, Wilcomb E. *The Indian in America.* New York: Harper Colophon Books, 1975.

Watkins, Arthur V. "Termination of Federal Supervision: The Removal of Restric-tions over Indian Property and Person." *The Annals of the American Academy of Political and Social Science* 311 (1957): 47–55.

Webb, Walter Prescott. *The Great Plains.* New York: Grossett & Dunlap, 1931.

Zimmerman, William, Jr. "The Role of the Bureau of Indian Affairs." *The Annals of the American Academy of Political and Social Science* 311 (1957): 31–40.

Index

Acheson, Dean, 34, 35

Aid to Dependent Children, 89–90, 92, 160–62, 232n28, 249–50

allotments, 100–107, 139n58; alienation of, 93, 95; economy of scale, 100–101; fee patents for, 83–84, 119–20, 139n69; fractionation (heirship), 81–82, 84, 104–7, 109; size of, 100, 139n57; and "surplus" lands, 103. *See also* assimilation; Berry; fee patents; leasing

American citizenship, 13, 36, 139n69

Americans: as defined racially, 72–73; and profile of, 23, 25–27

Anderson, John. *See* leasing

assimilation: as condition for receipt of state services, 156–57; and degrees of, 72–74; and factors of, 39, 72–75; integration as, 20, 34–35, 52, 78; as solution to "Indian Problem," 34, 42. *See also* blood quantum

Atkins, J. D. C., 74, 136n5

Bakewell, R. C.: on adverse effects of damming on Dakota, 77–79, 136n13

Berry, E. Y.: as apologist for illegal leasing, 114–15; and appeal to Interior Secretary Lewis, 126; as Congressman, 41, 54, 67–68n69, 110–11, 140n74; and criticisms of TLE, 84–85; and duplicity regarding Dakota-Lakota consent, 178; introducing H.R. 1220, 89–92, 96, 138n53; as land

broker for whites, 113–20, 123–27; as pseudo civil-rights advocate, 110–13, 246; as SDSGA member, 147; and submarginal land bills, 209–12; on termination as great white experiment, 178, 199–200; and testimony on "land disposal," 111–12; and use of "Red Scare" to shape Native policy, 23–25; on Wheeler-Howard Act, 61n15; white backlash against, 210–12, 218. *See also* Interior Department

Black Peoples, 19–21, 24, 70n96, 79. *See also* civil rights

blood quantum: as Aryanism, 72–73, 107–9; and ethnicide, 20, 30. *See also* genocide

Brophy, William, 57

Bureau of Indian Affairs: and abolishment of agency offices, 18, 88; and approval on land sales, 81–84, 93–94, 99–100, 112–13; budget for, 58–59, 86; and church mission similar to, 75; congressional investigation of, 35, 40; and contempt for Native Peoples, 160, 225; as co-opting Native self-rule, 109–10; and cost reimbursement to S.D. counties, 182–83, 197–98, 222–23; and illegal kickbacks to S.D., 92–95; leasing rules and regulations of, 93–94, 99–101, 107, 113–14, 118–19; and LBSTC, 171; reduction of services of, 30–31, 58–59; and removal of OST land-use tax, 128–31; and sale of grazing privileges, 121–30; as

EDWARD CHARLES VALANDRA is Sicangu Lakota born
and raised on the Rosebud Reservation. He received his B.A.
from Minnesota State University at Mankato, Minnesota; his
M.A. from the University of Colorado-Boulder; and his Ph.D.
from SUNY Buffalo. He is an assistant professor of Native studies
at a university in California. His research focus is the national
revitalization of the Oceti Sakowin Oyate (People of the
Seven Fires).

The University of Illinois Press
is a founding member of the
Association of American University Presses.

Composed in 10.5/13 Minion
with Meta display
by Jim Proefrock
at the University of Illinois Press
Manufactured by Thomson-Shore, Inc.

University of Illinois Press
1325 South Oak Street
Champaign, IL 61820-6903
www.press.uillinois.edu